ARTIFICIAL INTELLIGENCE
AND HUMAN LEARNING

ARTIFICIAL INTELLIGENCE AND HUMAN LEARNING

Intelligent computer-aided instruction

Edited by
John Self

LONDON   NEW YORK

Chapman and Hall

First published in 1988 by
Chapman and Hall Ltd
11 New Fetter Lane, London EC4P 4EE
Published in the USA by
Chapman and Hall
29 West 35th Street, New York NY 10001

Printed in Great Britain by
J. W. Arrowsmith Ltd, Bristol

ISBN 0 412 16610 0 (hardback)
0 412 30130 X (paperback)

British Library Cataloguing in Publication Data

Artificial intelligence and human learning:
   intelligent computer-aided instruction.—
   (Chapman and Hall computing series).
   1. Computer-assisted instruction
   I. Self, John
   371.3'9445   LB1028.5

   ISBN 0-412-16610-0
   ISBN 0-412-30130-X Pbk

Library of Congress Cataloging in Publication Data

Artificial intelligence and human learning.

   Bibliography: p.
   Includes index.
   1. Artificial intelligence. 2. System design.
3. Computer-assisted instruction. I. Self, John.
Q335.A78719 1988   371.3'9445   87–11587

   ISBN 0-412-16610-0
   ISBN 0-412-30130-X (pbk.)

Contents

Contributors   **xi**

Preface   **xiv**

PART 1   THEORETICAL ISSUES

1   **Representing complex knowledge in an intelligent machine
         tutor**   **3**
        Beverly P. Woolf
        1.1   Introduction   3
        1.2   Knowledge of the domain   4
        1.3   Knowledge of teaching   14
        1.4   Evaluations   25
        1.5   Conclusions   26

2   **Of course ICAI is impossible ... worse though, it might be
         seditious**   **28**
        Jim Ridgway
        2.1   Introduction   29
        2.2   Problems for ICAI in mathematical education   30
        2.3   The needs of mathematical education   41
        2.4   Computers in education?   43
        2.5   Can ICAI be seditious?   45
        2.6   Suggestion: transparent ICAI systems   46

3   **The role of qualitative models in instruction**   **49**
        William J. Clancey
        3.1   What are qualitative models?   49
        3.2   Situation-specific models   50
        3.3   Simulation or executable models   55
        3.4   Representation requirements   56
        3.5   Use of models: the central role of diagnosis   60
        3.6   Student model assessments   64
        3.7   Conclusions   67

4   Methods and mental models in theories of cognitive skill   69
Stephen J. Payne
    4.1   Introduction   69
    4.2   Computational accounts of cognitive skill acquisition: skill
        as method   70
    4.3   Weaknesses in the skill-as-method theories   73
    4.4   Mental models   77
    4.5   Integrating methods and mental models   79

5   The requirements of conceptual modelling systems   88
Stefano A. Cerri
    5.1   Introduction   88
    5.2   Common mistakes in knowledge engineering   89
    5.3   Programming as translating   95
    5.4   Conceptual modelling systems   102
    5.5   About the architecture of conceptual modelling systems   103
    5.6   Conclusions   107

6   The appraisal of an ICAI system   109
Lindsey Ford
    6.1   Introduction   109
    6.2   Overview of system   110
    6.3   Appraisal of behaviour   114
    6.4   How well have the research aims been met?   119
    6.5   Conclusions   122

7   Methods for evaluating micro-theory systems   124
Tony Priest and Richard M. Young
    7.1   What is a micro-theory system?   124
    7.2   Micro-theory systems and ICAI   125
    7.3   Micro-theory systems and statistics   126
    7.4   Criteria for a desirable measure   127
    7.5   Measures for evaluating micro-theories   129
    7.6   Summary of the four methods   135
    7.7   Applications and conclusions   136

PART 2   ICAI TECHNIQUES

8   The role of the episodic memory in an intelligent tutoring system   141
Gerhard Weber, Gerd Waloszek and Karl Friedrich Wender
    8.1   Some constraints on intelligent tutoring   141
    8.2   Levels of programming knowledge   143
    8.3   Episodic memory and the role of generalization   144
    8.4   An example   146
    8.5   Failure-driven learning   153

9   **A resolution based method for discovering students'**
misconceptions   **156**
Ernesto Costa, Sylvie Duchénoy and Yves Kodratoff
    9.1   Introduction   156
    9.2   Working hypothesis   158
    9.3   An example   160
    9.4   Conclusion   164

10   **Guided discovery tutoring and bounded user modelling**   **165**
Mark Elsom-Cook
    10.1   Introduction   165
    10.2   What is the nature of 'guidance' in tutoring?   168
    10.3   How can appropriate guidance be offered?   171
    10.4   Conclusions   178

11   **The application of machine learning to intelligent tutoring**
systems   **179**
David Gilmore and John Self
    11.1   Introduction   179
    11.2   Student modelling methods   180
    11.3   Current uses of machine learning in tutoring systems   181
    11.4   Concept learning systems   186
    11.5   An alternative student model   191
    11.6   Conclusions   195

12   **Self-organized learning within an intelligent teaching system**   **197**
Rosemary R. Todd
    12.1   Introduction   197
    12.2   An intelligent teaching system   197
    12.3   Domain   199
    12.4   Self-organized learning   200
    12.5   ITSSOL: an idealized version   201
    12.6   ITSSOL: current version   205
    12.7   The research strategy: a preliminary study   208
    12.8   Summary   210

13   **Plan recognition and intelligent tutoring systems**   **212**
Mark R. Woodroffe
    13.1   Introduction   212
    13.2   Literature review   213
    13.3   A detailed description of FITS-2   216

14   **Understanding user behaviour in command-driven systems**   **226**
John Jones, Mark Millington and Peter Ross
    14.1   Introduction   226

14.2   Existing techniques for plan recognition   227
14.3   Why recognize plans and goals?   229
14.4   User modelling in command-driven systems   230
14.5   Conclusion   235

15   SCALD—towards an intelligent authoring system   236
Rod Nicolson
15.1   Introduction   236
15.2   The design for an IAS   237
15.3   The SCALD-1 prototype IAS   240
15.4   Current status and projected developments of the SCALD
       project   248
15.5   Comparison of the IAS cycle with the 'standard' program
       development cycle   251
15.6   Summary   253

PART 3   ICAI APPLICATIONS

16   Design choices for an intelligent arithmetic tutor   257
*Tim O'Shea, Rick Evertsz, Sara Hennessy, Ann Floyd, Mike Fox and
Mark Elsom-Cook*
16.1   Introduction   257
16.2   Background to project   258
16.3   Children's conceptions of arithmetic   259
16.4   Modelling the student   263
16.5   Representation techniques for modelling   265
16.6   Methodology   267
16.7   Diagnostic consultants   268
16.8   Mathematical microworlds   270
16.9   Supporting formal and informal arithmetic   272
16.10 Conclusions   274

17   A framework for the design of a writer's assistant   276
Mike Sharples and Claire O'Malley
17.1   Introduction   276
17.2   Writing skills   278
17.3   Assistance for the writer   281
17.4   Existing support and teaching systems   283
17.5   Framework for a writer's assistant   283
17.6   Conclusions   290

18   Modelling the students' errors in the ELECTRE tutor   291
Michel Caillot
18.1   Introduction   291

18.2 Outline of the ELECTRE system 292
18.3 Modelling students' knowledge 293
18.4 Conclusion 298

19 Interfaces that adapt to the user 300
Martin Cooper
19.1 Introduction 300
19.2 Self-adaptive user interfaces 301
19.3 An adaptive interface for electronic mail 303
19.4 Discussion 307
19.5 Conclusions and further work 308

20 Coaching in help systems 310
Joost Breuker
20.1 Introduction 310
20.2 A help system for UNIX-Mail 311
20.3 Functions of help systems and the IPS world 317
20.4 Teaching expertise: strategies and tactics 325

21 Question answering and explanation giving in on-line help systems 338
J. Roger Hartley and Michael Smith
21.1 Introduction: some requirements of an intelligent help system 338
21.2 Some issues in explanation giving 340
21.3 The classification of users' activities and questions 343
21.4 The interpretation of users' questions 346
21.5 Question answering 350
21.6 Concluding comments 358

22 A Pascal program checker 361
Mark Elsom-Cook and Benedict du Boulay
22.1 Introduction 361
22.2 Overall goals of the program checker 362
22.3 A stand-alone syntax error checker 363
22.4 Future development 373

23 Modelling programmers' intentions 374
W. Lewis Johnson
23.1 Introduction 374
23.2 An overview of PROUST's intention-based analysis 375
23.3 Empirical evaluation of PROUST 383
23.4 Current and future directions 386

24   Bridge: an intelligent tutor for thinking about programming   391
Jeffrey Bonar and Robert Cunningham
   24.1   Introduction   391
   24.2   Design issues for an intelligent programming tutor   392
   24.3   An overview of the Bridge system   394
   24.4   Using Bridge with students   408
   24.5   Future plans   408

References   410

Index   429

Contributors

JEFFREY BONAR Learning Research and Development Center, University of Pittsburgh, Pennsylvania, USA.

BENEDICT DU BOULAY Cognitive Studies Programme, University of Sussex, Brighton, UK.

JOOST BREUKER Department of Social Science Informatics, University of Amsterdam, The Netherlands.

MICHEL CAILLOT Laboratoire Interuniversitaire de Recherche sur L'Enseignement des Sciences Physiques et de La Technologie. University of Paris, Paris, France.

STEFANO A. CERRI Knowledge Engineering Research Unit, Mario Negri Institute for Pharmacological Research and Department of Information Science, University of Milan, Milan, Italy.

WILLIAM J. CLANCEY Knowledge Systems Laboratory, Stanford University, Palo Alto, California, USA.

MARTIN COOPER British Telecom Research Laboratories, Martlesham Heath, Ipswich, UK.

ERNESTO COSTA Department of Electrotechnics, University of Coimbra, Coimbra, Portugal.

ROBERT CUNNINGHAM Learning Research and Development Center, University of Pittsburgh, Pennsylvania, USA.

SYLVIE DUCHÉNOY Laboratoire de Recherche en Informatique, University of Paris-Sud, Paris, France.

MARK ELSOM-COOK Institute of Educational Technology, The Open University, Milton Keynes, UK.

RICK EVERTSZ Institute of Educational Technology, The Open University, Milton Keynes, UK.

ANN FLOYD Institute of Educational Technology, The Open University, Milton Keynes, UK.

LINDSEY FORD Department of Computer Science, University of Exeter, Exeter, UK.

MIKE FOX Institute of Educational Technology, The Open University, Milton Keynes, UK.

DAVID GILMORE Centre for Research on Computers and Learning, University of Lancaster, Lancaster, UK.

J. ROGER HARTLEY Computer Based Learning Unit, University of Leeds, Leeds, UK.

SARA HENNESSY Institute of Educational Technology, The Open University, Milton Keynes, UK.

W. LEWIS JOHNSON Information Sciences Institute, University of Southern California, Marina del Rey, California, USA.

JOHN JONES Department of Artificial Intelligence, University of Edinburgh, Edinburgh, UK.

YVES KODRATOFF Laboratoire de Recherche en Informatique, University of Paris-Sud, Paris, France.

MARK MILLINGTON Department of Artificial Intelligence, University of Edinburgh, Edinburgh, UK.

ROD NICOLSON Department of Psychology, University of Sheffield, Sheffield, UK.

CLAIRE O'MALLEY School of Social Sciences, University of Sussex, Brighton, UK.

TIM O'SHEA Institute of Educational Technology, The Open University, Milton Keynes, UK.

STEPHEN J. PAYNE Departments of Psychology and Computing, University of Lancaster, Lancaster, UK.

TONY PRIEST Department of Mathematics, Statistics and Computing, Oxford Polytechnic, Oxford, UK.

JIM RIDGWAY Department of Psychology, University of Lancaster, Lancaster, UK.

PETER ROSS Department of Artificial Intelligence, University of Edinburgh, Edinburgh, UK.

JOHN SELF Centre for Research on Computers and Learning, University of Lancaster, Lancaster, UK.

MIKE SHARPLES School of Social Sciences, University of Sussex, Brighton, UK.

MICHAEL J. SMITH Computer Based Learning Unit, University of Leeds, Leeds, UK.

ROSEMARY R. TODD Behavioural Science Division, Admiralty Research Establishment, Teddington, Middlesex, UK.

GERD WALOSZEK Institute of Psychology, University of Braunschweig, Braunschweig, West Germany.

GERHARD WEBER Institute of Psychology, University of Braunschweig, Braunschweig, West Germany.

KARL FRIEDRICH WENDER Institute of Psychology, University of Braunschweig, Braunschweig, West Germany.

MARK R. WOODROFFE Department of Computer Science, University of Essex, Colchester, UK.

BEVERLY P. WOOLF Department of Computer and Information Science, University of Massachusetts, USA.

RICHARD M. YOUNG Medical Research Council Applied Psychology Unit, Cambridge, UK.

Preface

Artificial Intelligence (AI) is now recognized as one of the major scientific endeavours of the twentieth century. In the last few years there has been an extraordinary growth in the practical application of AI to many fields: expert systems in industry, natural language understanding systems, robotics, and so on. This growth has been fuelled by unprecedented support from American, European and Japanese governments.

At the same time, the education industry has had problems: dwindling public and government backing, pressure to provide more vocational training, demands for measures of teacher performance, difficulty in obtaining skilled staff, and the pace of technological change. It seems inevitable, therefore, that the new science of AI will be brought to bear on the problems of education.

If the reader has not winced at the crassness of this argument – which is, in essence, the official reason for developing intelligent computer-aided instruction (ICAI) – then it is a measure of how distorted our perceptions of both AI and education have become. AI, the science of designing computers to do things which would be considered intelligent if done by people, has a very wide brief – the fact that AI can save an oil company millions of dollars by telling it where to drill does not necessarily imply that AI can similarly solve problems in other areas, such as education. And it is a rather uninspiring philosophy of education which sees it as just another industry, whose prime aim is to serve the rest of industry.

The chapters in this book give better reasons for considering ICAI interesting and important. The authors were asked not to write detailed technical reports of their latest research but to put their work in a wider context (so that readers may better understand the aims and achievements of ICAI), and also to discuss problems – encountered or foreseen, solved or unsolved – and to speculate on future developments (so that readers may better judge the longer term importance of ICAI).

The result is a collection of papers which gives a considerable insight into what motivates people to work in this increasingly vibrant field. On the whole, it is not the prospect of improving educational efficiency – it is the prospect that ICAI will be an area where they may refine their ideas about important issues which interest them regardless of ICAI. Issues such as: What is the nature of knowledge? How can an individual student be helped to learn? What precisely is 'learning'? What styles of teaching interactions are effective when? ICAI is important to education because it may help to develop answers to these general questions.

Like all new fields, ICAI is both derivative and innovative. On the one hand, ICAI researchers bring with them or adopt theories and methodologies from associated disciplines such as psychology and computer science. This interdisciplinarity is, as usual, a strength and a problem, and it is reflected in this book where we have different, sometimes conflicting, perspectives on the same issue.

On the other hand, ICAI is innovative in that, as mentioned above, it contributes ideas back to associated disciplines and also – as it must if it is to justify its own label – generates research questions of its own. Many of these questions are discussed in this book. But there is no need to delimit precisely the field of ICAI (indeed, some of the authors in this book would not consider themselves to be working in ICAI at all!). We can be content with a broad definition, for example that 'ICAI is concerned with developing computer systems which interact knowledgeably with learners'.

This book, then, is intended to give a general introduction to ICAI. It is hoped that all the chapters will be accessible to the non-specialist, at least sufficiently so to allow the issues and objectives to be appreciated. The book should therefore be of interest to a wide spectrum of readers, including

- Researchers in artificial intelligence, human–computer interaction, cognitive science and education.
- Computer scientists,
- Information technologists,
- Psychologists,
- Educationalists,
- Teachers, and
- Anyone else concerned with educational innovation.

INTRODUCTION: A BRIEF GUIDE TO THE CONTENTS

The 24 chapters have been grouped into three parts: papers in Part 1 are mainly concerned with theoretical issues common to all ICAI systems; those in Part 2 are mainly concerned with techniques appropriate for certain components of ICAI systems; and those in Part 3 are mainly concerned with the application of ICAI to particular subjects.

The first chapter, by Beverly Woolf, sets the scene by presenting the ICAI enthusiast's 'standard line' on the potential of ICAI. She describes some state-of-the-art ICAI systems and discusses the benefits they provide. But she also emphasizes the fact that fundamental research remains to be done, particularly in the area of knowledge representation. The field of AI has made progress recently by recognizing the central role of knowledge representation, and it is clearly particularly important for ICAI systems, which might alternatively be described as knowledge communication systems. Indeed, ICAI differs from CAI primarily in its focus on the representation of knowledge of the subject matter and of pedagogical knowledge.

Jim Ridgway, in Chapter 2, presents a sceptic's view of ICAI. Readers will, I am sure, be able to form their own judgements about the force of his strictures after reading the other chapters. The only point I would raise here is that his perspective is from school-based mathematical education. We must be careful to distinguish between 'the classroom' as a generic term for a place of learning and as a term for the physical arrangement in present schools and colleges. ICAI researchers have no commitment to the latter. Other learning environments are conceivable and maybe even preferable. At this moment, the European Economic Commission is considering proposals to develop by the year 2000 studios and workstations to permit European learners to learn what, when and how they wish. ICAI will be indispensable for the fulfillment of such a proposal. In general, however, ICAI researchers – regrettably, perhaps – are more interested in the computational expression of principles of learning and teaching than in the provision of systems for real use in present educational settings.

Perhaps the main distinctive contribution that ICAI makes is in the area of student modelling. Within computer science, ICAI was the first area to take seriously the notion that successful human–computer interaction requires that the computer have some understanding of the human. The development of 'user models' is now an active research topic throughout interactive system design. It is particularly important in ICAI because it is the one class of interactive system whose express purpose is to change the cognitive state of the user, and we therefore need a dynamic representation of the user's current state of knowledge in order to determine how it may be modified. Within psychology, the student modelling effort can be seen as part of a trend emphasizing the individualistic nature of cognition rather than general cognitive processes. And within education, student models help clarify how we might provide the individualized instruction advocated by some educational philosophers.

William Clancey reviews the role of qualitative models in Chapter 3. As in AI generally, ICAI prefers 'qualitative' models, in which objects, processes and the relations between them are described symbolically or structurally, to 'quantitative' models, which might use numeric or physical analogues. Although, as Clancey remarks, student modelling is, unlike most other parts of AI, 'unabashedly psychological', it has in practice been driven mainly by computational theories of knowledge representation. In Chapter 4, Stephen Payne attempts to redress the balance by relating student models to theories of cognitive skill acquisition and particularly to recent ideas about 'mental models', which share the emphasis on individualized theories.

In Chapter 5, the most technically demanding chapter in the book, Stefano Cerri picks up the knowledge representation theme raised by Beverly Woolf. He argues that all cooperative dialogue systems, including ICAI systems, would benefit from new computational paradigms for knowledge representation languages, demanding the resolution of certain philosophical and psychological questions concerning the nature of knowledge itself.

The last two chapters of Part 1 address different aspects of the question of how we evaluate ICAI systems. Evaluation may be attempted at a global level, that is, in terms of whether the complete system meets specified objectives – as discussed by Lindsey Ford in Chapter 6. Or it may be attempted at a 'local' level since often the ICAI system designer's real interest lies not in building a complete system but in developing a micro-theory serving as one component of such a system. As Tony Priest and Richard Young explain in Chapter 7, traditional methods are not satisfactory for evaluating the kinds of theories used to build student models. They propose two new methods and discuss their properties.

The chapters in Part 2 discuss particular techniques and ideas for components of ICAI systems. The first two chapters develop proposals for student models. Gerhard Weber, Gerd Waloszek and Karl Wender argue in Chapter 8 that knowledge is mainly case-based and hence that student models should be more episodic in nature. This, they believe, would better enable ICAI systems to provide individualized remindings and analogues to promote learning.

One of the functions of a student model is to help diagnose misconceptions – indeed, there is little point in maintaining a student model if the student learns as predicted or hoped. Two approaches to diagnosing misconceptions (discussed in other chapters) are to build extensive subject-dependent libraries of misconceptions ('bug libraries') and to use machine learning techniques to generate the misconceptions. In Chapter 9, Ernesto Costa, Sylvia Duchènoy and Yves Kodratoff describe another method, that of inferring a student's misconception using the formal technique of resolution from computational logic.

The next three chapters all combine an acceptance of the fact that accurate student modelling is a practical impossibility with a proposal that ICAI systems should adopt a less rigid tutorial style than is usual in order to foster more exploratory learning. In Chapter 10, Mark Elsom-Cook discusses the use of 'bounded user models', which essentially provide bounds for student models, to support a range of teaching styles. The maintenance of dynamic computer-based student models is necessarily a problem of machine learning, an area of AI research which its practitioners claim has progressed significantly in the last decade. However, David Gilmore and John Self conclude in Chapter 11 that machine learning techniques are not yet adequate for direct incorporation in intelligent tutoring systems but that they may be able to support a collaborative style of interaction. Rosemary Todd in Chapter 12 echoes the rejection of expert-system-based ICAI expressed in the preceding two chapters and elsewhere in the book – it being a standard misconception outside the field that ICAI systems are, by definition, implemented by enclosing an expert system (a program capable of high performance in some specialized domain of expertise) within a tutorial package. Her approach makes use of the principles of self-organized learning to support individualized learning.

An ICAI system should endeavour to interpret the student's inputs to the system not merely in terms of items of knowledge understood or not but as evidence about the student's goals, i.e. what he is trying to achieve. This, of course, is more important as we move from directive to open styles of interaction, as advocated by many authors in this book. The problem is closely related to a well-established body of AI research, that on planning and specifically on plan recognition. Chapter 13 by Mark Woodroffe and Chapter 14 by John Jones, Mark Millington and Peter Ross both address the problem of understanding a user's goal-directed behaviour when using a computer system, coincidentally the same system, the file commands of the UNIX operating system.

The last chapter of Part 2, by Rod Nicolson, applies AI techniques not to the implementation of ICAI systems but to the development of an authoring system to aid the implementation of (conventional) educational software.

The nine chapters of Part 3 are concerned mainly with applications of ICAI to particular subjects. One of the trends in ICAI in recent years has been to move away from subjects in traditional curricula towards intrinsically computer-based subjects. There are several reasons for this. Firstly, the implementation of any ICAI system demands considerable subject knowledge and it is more convenient for designers to have ready access to this knowledge, which tends to mean that it is knowledge of some aspect of computing. Secondly, designers of ICAI systems for standard school subjects have to argue their benefits over existing methods, an argument which is often of no direct interest – the argument scarcely arises with ICAI systems for computer-based subjects such as programming since there are no non-computer-based existing methods. Thirdly, there are few philosophical objections to the appropriateness of ICAI for computer-based subjects, it being seen as just part of a general desire to provide user-friendly, learnable software systems. In any case, the present somewhat incestuous emphasis in ICAI is perhaps a temporary matter, for much of what students need to learn will become increasingly computer-based and so susceptible to the ICAI approaches being developed.

The chapters of Part 3 fall into three groups. The first group applies ICAI to 'traditional' subjects, specifically, arithmetic, writing and basic physics. The three chapters share an emphasis on trying to elucidate the nature of conceptual understanding and misunderstanding within their respective domains, rather than 'merely' building a system to support subject learning. In Chapter 16, Tim O'Shea, Sara Hennessy, Rick Evertsz, Ann Floyd, Mike Fox and Mark Elsom-Cook describe a project to build an arithmetic tutor which replaces the focus on drill and practice with an attempt to provide tools to promote mathematical thinking. In Chapter 17 Mike Sharples and Claire O'Malley develop a framework for a computer-based writer's assistant. This chapter illustrates how the nature of skills may be radically altered by the provision of computational tools and how we need to re-think how those skills may be learned. Michel Caillot in Chapter 18 describes the design of a tutor for basic electricity, concentrating on the role of prototypical knowledge.

The next group of three chapters illustrates the use of ICAI techniques to make computer systems more learnable and usable. All are concerned with the design of interfaces for electronic mail systems, although the principles are, of course, intended to be more general. In Chapter 19 Martin Cooper describes the design of a self-adaptive interface, mainly from an MMI (man–machine interface) perspective. The next two chapters consider intelligent help systems, that is, systems which support the user while he is trying to perform some computer-based task. Joost Breuker, in Chapter 20, describes the implementation of teaching and coaching strategies initiated by the help system while monitoring and interpreting the performance of the user. In Chapter 21, Roger Hartley and Michael Smith describe the 'user-initiated' component of the same help system, that is, the part which provides appropriate explanations in response to user questions.

The design of systems to help students learn computer programming is the subject of the final group of chapters. Here, ICAI merges with more standard computer science, such as compiler design, software engineering and formal specifications of programs. Mark Elsom-Cook and Benedict du Boulay describe in Chapter 22 the use of chart-parsing techniques to check the syntax of Pascal programs, to provide more appropriate and more informative error messages for beginning programmers. Lewis Johnson's system (Chapter 23) is more concerned with interpreting syntactic and semantic errors in terms of the programmer's intentions, i.e. what the programmer is trying to achieve. This requires that the system have some means of describing 'intentions' and it is interesting to see that this project is merging with more formal approaches to defining program specifications. The final chapter, by Jeffrey Bonar and Robert Cunningham, is not concerned with an after-the-event analysis of complete programs but with supporting the novice programmer on-line through all stages of the programming process. They describe the use of modern workstations to help students define and manipulate intermediate representations such as programming plans.

The book ends with a cumulative bibliography for ease of reference. Please note that where the pronouns he or she occur in the text, referring for example to the student or the teacher, they should be taken to mean either sex.

ACKNOWLEDGEMENTS

On behalf of all the participants, the editor would like to thank the American Association for Artificial Intelligence and the UK's Science and Engineering Research Council for supporting the Workshop from which these chapters are derived. I am deeply grateful to the chapter authors for so enthusiastically providing readers with this informative introduction to the important field of ICAI.

John Self   *November 1986*
Lancaster

Part one

Theoretical issues

1

*Representing complex knowledge in an intelligent machine tutor**

BEVERLY P. WOOLF
University of Massachusetts, USA

In this chapter, we discuss and give example solutions to two knowledge engineering issues that remain central to the successful development of intelligent tutoring systems: 1. representing domain knowledge, e.g. concepts and processes of the domain, and 2. representing teaching knowledge, e.g. instructional and discourse strategies to teach domain knowledge. We also address issues related to up-scaling existent intelligent tutoring technology to practical levels to bring tutoring systems into the real world.

1.1 INTRODUCTION

We are on the verge of developing substantially more powerful tutoring systems that will reason about a student's knowledge, monitor his solutions, and custom-tailor their teaching strategies to his individual learning pattern. Such systems will simulate 'worlds' (e.g. the ocean, atmosphere, power plants, ecosystems, etc.) in a visually rich and informationally dense way not currently possible. Obviously, we are not yet capable of building these systems; formidable barriers, in the realms of both hardware and software development, stand between us and full realization of the potential. However, many of the remaining barriers are theoretical, rather than engineering; i.e. they depend on providing the computer with new and more complex knowledge.

The very fact that knowledge representation remains an issue for successful development of intelligent tutors underscores the distinction between intelligent teaching systems and computer-aided instruction, CAI. Intelligent teaching systems are designed to represent both the concepts to be taught and how a student might learn those concepts. Often an intelligent tutor is built so that the

*Reproduced with permission from *Computational Intelligence*, 3(1). © 1987 The National Research Council of Canada.

components of the teaching process itself are clearly differentiated, e.g. knowledge of the student (Johnson and Soloway, 1984; Miller, 1982) might be separated from knowledge of the domain (Stevens, Collins and Goldin, 1982; Brown and Bell, 1977) and both these types of knowledge separated from strategies about how and what to teach (Clancey, 1982; Woolf and McDonald, 1984a). Given this wealth of knowledge, often coded in the form of hundreds of 'if–then' rules, such systems can perform fine-grained reasoning about a student and his progress. Codification of this tacit knowledge and transmission of this knowledge to the computer is what enables the intelligent tutor to represent what the student knows and to provide guidance in a form such that the student remains in control of the interaction. Though dozens of major intelligent tutoring projects have been completed in the past decade (see Sleeman and Brown (1982)), few have left the laboratory, due in part to the complex knowledge that is required in each system.

In addition to the distinction between CAI and intelligent teaching systems, a second distinction between 'strong' and 'weak' teaching systems demonstrates the additional complexity required in building intelligent teaching systems. A strong teaching system is able to solve the same problem it presents to the student. In addition to recognizing errors, recording missing or extraneous components of an answer, and correcting errors, which a 'weak' system can do, the strong system solves the problem along with the student and assists him when he gets 'stuck' during a partial solution. To do this, a strong system needs to be an expert system in addition to being a teaching system.

1.2 KNOWLEDGE OF THE DOMAIN

Historically, the first knowledge issue addressed by researchers of intelligent tutors was knowledge of the domain (Brown and Bell, 1977; Clancey, 1982). As tutoring systems developed, the more powerful systems required more sophisticated knowledge of the domain. For example, lists of concepts and rules, such as found in textbooks, were insufficient for enabling a system to observe errors, to assist the student in recognizing misconceptions behind those errors, and to provide custom-tailored remedial action. Careful representation of domain knowledge for a tutoring system required at least an investigation into an expert's understanding of the laws of the domain, possibly divided into classifications such as concepts, procedural rules, and meta-rules by which the concepts were used, heuristics or rules of thumb to use the rules, and simulation rules to graphically implement the data and rules. This breakdown is not offered as a singular way to divide domain knowledge, but serves as an indication of the complexity of knowledge required to build an intelligent tutoring system.

To illustrate the complexity of domain knowledge in a strong intelligent tutor, we describe the Recovery Boiler Tutor, RBT, a tutor built for a kraft recovery

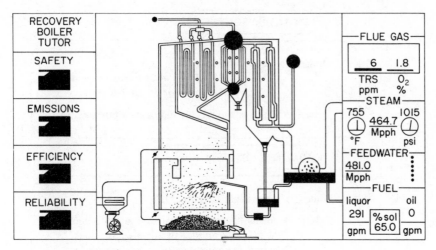

Fig. 1.1. Sectional view of the recovery boiler.

boiler, which is a type of boiler found in paper mills throughout the United States*.

RBT provides multiple explanations and tutoring facilities tempered to the individual user, a control room operator. The tutor is based on a mathematically accurate formulation of the boiler and provides an interactive simulation complete with help, hints, explanations and turoring[†]. A student can initiate any of 20 training situations, emergencies, or operating conditions, or he can ask that an emergency be chosen for him. He can also accidentally trigger an emergency as a result of his actions on the boiler. Once an emergency has been initiated, the student is encouraged to adjust meters and perform actions on the simulated boiler to solve the emergency.

The goal in building the system was to challenge the student operator to solve new problems while monitoring and commenting upon his actions. The system can recognize optimal, less than optimal, and clearly irrelevant actions. The operator continues his freewheeling or purposeful problem-solving behaviour

---

*RBT was built by J.H. Jansen Co., Inc., Steam and Power Engineers, Woodinville (Seattle), Washington and sponsored by The American Paper Institute, a non-profit trade institution for the pulp, paper, and paperboard industry in the United States, Energy Materials Department, 260 Madison Ave., New York, NY, 10016.

[†]RBT was developed on an IBM PC AT (512 kb RAM) with enhanced graphics and a 20 Mb hard disk. It uses a math co-processor, two display screens (one colour), and a two-key mouse. The simulation was implemented in Fortran and took 321 kb; the tutor was implemented in C and took 100 kb. Although we tried to implement the tutor in LISP, we found extensive interfacing and memory problems, including segment size restrictions (64 k), incompatibility with the existing Fortran simulator, and addressable RAM restrictions (640 k). To circumvent these problems the tutor was developed in C with many LISP features implemented in C, such as functional calls within the parameters of C functions. Meter readings and student interactions in the simulation were transferred between Fortran and C, through vectors passed between the two programs.

AN ALARM SOUNDS

Student: Check smelt spout cooling water.
           [*Student's action does not result
           in a change in the boiler.*]

Tutor: It looks as though the liquor isn't burning...

STUDENT REQUESTS HELP

Student: Help. What is going on?

Tutor: A partial blackout is occurring and this causes
         TRS, CO, SO2 and 02 to increase. Steam
         flow and steam temperature are dropping.

         I think part of the bed is not burning.

GRAIN OF TRUTH CORRECTION

Student: Rod the primary air ports.

Tutor: Your action is correct; however, at this time
         rodding alone is not effective...

Student: Raise the liquor temperature.

Tutor: Rodding the air port apparently was not enough
         to undo the blackout.
                              [*No improvement.
                              New alarm sounds*]

CONFIRMATION

Student: Increase the oil fuel supply.
                    [*Emergency is now reversed.*]

Tutor: That solved the problem alright.
         Good thinking.

Fig. 1.2. Dialogue between tutor and operator.

while the tutor offers help, hints, explanations, and tutoring advice when needed or requested. The operator is expected to observe the impact of his actions on the simulated boiler and to react before the tutor advises him about potential problems.

An example interaction* between the student and tutor is shown in Fig. 1.2. As the operator changes setpoint controllers and requests information about the boiler, the tutor selectively discusses the optimality of his actions (we show how below) and suggests how he might better focus his action or better utilize his data. An important feature to note about this dialogue is that at any point during the simulated emergency there are a large number of actions an operator might take and, as the problem worsens, an increasing number of actions that he *should* take to correct the operating conditions. Thus, an immediate and correct response might require only one action, such as rodding the primary air ports, but a delayed response causes the situation to worsen and requires the addition of auxiliary fuel.

The operator's interactions with the tutor are through a hierarchy of menus, two of which are shown in Fig. 1.3. Menu A allows an operator to select a physical activity to be performed on the boiler, such as checking for a tube leak or rodding the smelt spout. Menu B allows the operator to select a particular computer screen, such as the alarm board or control panel board.

While the simulation of the recovery boiler is running, the operator can view the boiler from many directions and can focus on several components, such as the fire bed in Fig. 1.4. The tutor provides assistance through visual clues, such as a darkened smelt bed, acoustic clues, ringing alarm buzzers, textual help, explanations, and dialogues, such as that illustrated in Fig. 1.2. The operator can request up to 30 process parameters on the complete panel board, Fig. 1.5, view an alarm board (not shown), change 20 setpoints, and ask menued questions such as 'What is the problem?', 'How do I get out of it?', 'What caused it?', and 'What can I do to prevent it?'[†]. The operator can request meter readings, physical and chemical reports, and dynamic trends of variables. All variables are updated in real time (every 1 or 2 seconds).

In addition to providing information about the explicit variables in the boiler, RBT provides reasoning tools designed to aid a student in reasoning about implicit processes in the boiler. One such tool is composite meters (left side of Figs 1.1, 1.4, 1.5 and 1.6), which records the state of the boiler using synthetic measures for *safety*, *emissions*, *efficiency*, and *reliability* of the boiler. The meter readings are calculated from complex mathematical formulae that would rarely, if ever, be

---

*The dialogue of Fig. 1.2 was not actually produced in natural language; student input was handled through menus (Fig. 1.3) and tutor output produced by cutting text from emergency-specific text files loaded when the emergency was invoked.
[†]These four questions are answered by cutting text from a file which was loaded with the specific emergency. These questions do not provide the basis of the tutor's knowledge representation, which will be discussed below.

```
┌─────────────────────────────────────────────┐
│           What Are You Going To Do            │
├───────────────────────────────────────────────┤
│     Determine source of dilution              │
│     Check instrumentation                     │
│     Check dissolving tank agitators           │
│     Rod smelt spout                           │
│     Use portable auxiliary burner             │
│     Remove liquor guns                        │
│     Put in liquor guns                        │
│     Clean liquor guns                         │
│     Rod primary air ports                     │
│     Rod secondary air ports                   │
│     Check smelt spout cooling water           │
│     Start standby feedwater pumps             │
│     Restore water flow to deaerator           │
│ (a) Quit                                      │
└───────────────────────────────────────────────┘
```

0:23:49

```
┌─────────────────────────────────────────────┐
│            What Do You Want To Do             │
├───────────────────────────────────────────────┤
│     Look at boiler                            │
│     Manually adjust controls                  │
│     Flip emergency switch                     │
│     See panelboard                            │
│     See alarm status                          │
│     Go do something                           │
│     See trends                                │
│     Examine report                            │
│     Help                                      │
│     Go to analysis & quit                     │
│     Change RBT's mode                         │
│ (b) Nothing                                   │
└───────────────────────────────────────────────┘
```

0:00:15

Fig. 1.3. Means to select tasks to be performed on the boiler.

used by an operator himself to evaluate the boiler. For instance, the safety meter is a composition of seven independent parameters, including steam pressure, steam flow, steam temperature, feedwater flow, drum water level, firing liquor solids, and combustibles in the flue gas. Meter readings allow a student to make inferences about the effect of his actions on the boiler using characteristics of the running boiler*.

---

*These meters are not presently available on existing pulp and paper mill control panels; however, if they prove effective as training aids, they could be incorporated into actual control panels.

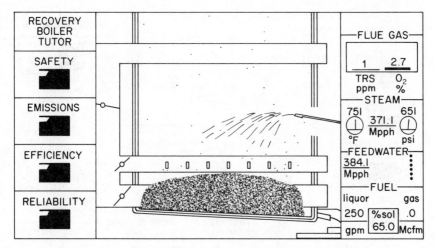

Fig. 1.4. Focused view of the fire bed.

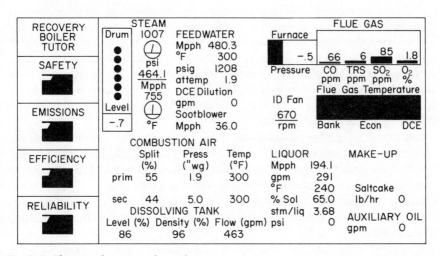

Fig. 1.5. The complete control panel.

Other reasoning tools include trend analyses, Fig. 1.6, and animated graphics, such as shown on boiler figures. Trend analyses show how essential process variables interact in real time by allowing an operator to select up to 10 variables, including liquor flow, oil flow, and air flow, etc., to plot each against the others and against time. Animated graphics provide realistic and dynamic drawings of the several components of the boiler, such as steam, fire, smoke, black liquor, and fuel.

Each student action, be it a setpoint adjustment or proposed solution, is

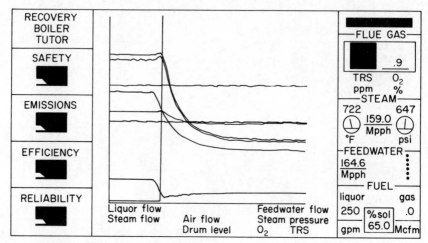

Fig. 1.6. Trends selected by the operator.

recorded in an accumulated response value, which reflects an operator's overall score and how successful, or unsuccessful, his actions have been and whether actions were performed in sequence with other relevant or irrelevant actions*.

In order to build such a tutor, we had to represent domain knowledge, including concepts, rules, and learning strategies specific to the domain. Such knowledge was specified in excruciating detail before the tutor was built. We describe this knowledge as broken into three classifications: conceptual, procedural and heuristic knowledge.

Conceptual knowledge includes the data, concepts, and relation between concepts in the domain. This knowledge has traditionally been the primary domain knowledge represented in a tutoring system. In many systems concepts are represented by a frame or other data structure that encodes default values within an explicit set of attributes for each concept. Such a data structure expresses information about both the attributes of a concept and the relationship between concepts.

Procedural knowledge includes the reasoning used by the system to solve problems in the domain. This knowledge has traditionally been included only in teaching systems that reason about procedural tasks, such as solving arithmetic problems (Brown and Burton, 1978) or simulating the operations of a steam engine (Forbus and Stevens, 1981). Such knowledge is typically missing from tutoring systems that use a simulation without a tutor for advising the student about his interaction with the simulation. STEAMER (Hollan, Hutchins and

---

*This accumulated value is not currently used by the tutor, but the notation might be used to sensitize the tutor's future responses to the student's record. For instance, if the operator has successfully solved a number of boiler emergencies, the accumulated value might be used to temper subsequent tutoring so that it is less intrusive. Similarly, if a student's past performance has been poor, the accumulated value could be used to activate more aggressive responses from the tutor.

Weitzman, 1984; Forbus and Stevens, 1981) is an exception in that it attempts to explain the qualitative processes behind a steam engine simulation.

Heuristic knowledge includes actions taken by an expert to make measurements or perform transformations in the domain. This knowledge has rarely been included in tutoring systems, but must be included if tutors are to monitor their students' problem-solving activities. Heuristic knowledge defines the operations performed to solve problems in the field and is part of an expert's experiential knowledge about how to realize answers. It differs from procedural knowledge in that it does not add content to the domain, nor does it present *concepts in the domain*; rather, it adds knowledge about *how to solve problems* and describes actions taken by the expert in using the conceptual and procedural knowledge.

Using heuristic knowledge, a tutor begins to help a student *learn how to learn*. A tutor with heuristic knowledge can show the student false paths taken and can begin to give reasons behind the particulars of rule-of-thumb knowledge used to solve problems. The tutor provides the student with a variety of examples from which he can explore a large space of problem-solving activities. The student's path through the available activities and strategies is traced; by elucidating these activities and monitoring the steps taken by the student, the tutor begins to define properties of the underlying cognitive process. We recognize that we cannot derive the properties of learning and problem solving simply by elucidating the steps taken to solve problems. Nevertheless, we are compiling data that, along with cognitive studies, will elucidate some of the processes behind a student's problem-solving behaviour.

Philosophers of science believe that heuristic knowledge, unlike conceptual and procedural knowledge, is best acquired through experience and working examples illustrating aspects of the phenomenon (Kuhn, 1970). Educators and cognitive scientists have observed that students benefit from numerous hours spent solving problems. Yet, there is nearly a total absence of information about which strategies and heuristics work, how a student learns from doing homework, or what precisely is being learned from doing homework (see Larkin (1982) for some innovative studies along this line).

The computer helps to explain the process of learning from examples by recording the student's behaviour when confronted by examples of increasing complexity and linked with cognitive similarities. For example, RBT provides tools with which a student can build his own example emergencies. It simulates the newly made examples to 'work' or 'fail' according to the laws of the science domain. The student's ability to use rules of science in the simulation will in part predict his ability to work outside the simulation and within a complex science domain.

Kuhn states:

A student cannot, it is said, solve problems at all unless he has first learned the theory and some rules for applying it. Scientific knowledge [it is said] is embedded in *theory and rules; problems* are supplied to gain facility in their application. I have tried to argue, however, that this localization of the cognitive content of science is wrong.

After the student has done many problems, he may gain only added facility by solving more. But at the start and for some time after, *doing problems is learning consequential things about nature*. In the absence of such examples, the laws and theories he has previously learned would have little empirical content (Kuhn, 1970; emphasis mine).

Kuhn (1970) points out that scientific breakthroughs often result from a scientist's need to solve unique problems for which no existent rule applies. Given anomalous data, a scientist will 'retrofit' existent formulas, consider alternative solution paths, and, if possible, create new procedures to explain the phenomenon. Such techniques of modifying existent rules should be taught to students. Kuhn suggests that learning to recognize, apply and reject operant (procedural) laws of nature is a prerequisite for 'doing' science.

RBT articulates the steps behind using detailed operant laws of nature, for recovery boiler failures, by explicitly defining the operations performed to solve emergencies. Simply elucidating these operational components and the rules that apply to their use is not sufficient for learning. For this reason, the tutor provides tools for reasoning about the complex process. These tools include graphs to demonstrate the relationship of process parameters over time, meters to measure emissions, efficiency, reliability, and safety, and interactive dialogues to tutor the operator about the on-going process.

Because it is involved with strategies for solving a problem, heuristic knowledge must also point to the requisite pre-knowledge that a student should know before he can solve the problem. Such pre-knowledge, and the way the machine investigates it, is the focus of the next two sections.

1.2.1   Multiple representations of domain knowledge

Multiple concepts and processes were represented in RBT, some procedurally, some declaratively, and some in both ways. For example, emergencies in the steam boiler were first represented as a set of mathematical formulae so that process parameters and meter values could be produced accurately in the simulation. These same emergencies were then encoded within the tutor's knowledge base as a frame-like data structure with slots for preconditions, optimal actions, and conditions for solution satisfaction so that the tutor could evaluate and comment upon the student's solution.

RBT can recognize and explain

- equipment and process flows,
- emergencies and operating problems as well as normal operating conditions,
- solutions to emergencies and operating problems,
- processes for implementing solutions, and
- tutoring strategies for assisting the student.

This knowledge was organized into four modules: *simulation, knowledge base, student model,* and *instructional strategies*. Development of the last three components was inspired by prior work in intelligent tutoring systems (Brown, Burton and deKleer, 1982; Anderson, Boyle and Yost, 1985; Sleeman, 1982; Slater, Petrossian and Shyam-Sunder, 1985; and Woolf and McDonald, 1984a, 1984b).

1.2.2 Simulation of equipment and process flow

The *simulation* uses a mathematical foundation to depict processes in a boiler through meter readings and four animated views of the boiler. It reacts to more than 35 process parameters and generates dynamically accurate reports of the thermal, chemical, and environmental performance of the boiler (not shown) upon request. An alarm board (not shown) represents 25 variables whose button will turn red and alarm sound when an abnormal condition exists for that parameter*. The simulation is interactive and inspectable in that it displays a 'real-time' model of its process, yet allows the student to 'stop' the process at any time to engage in activities needed to develop his mental models (Hollan *et al.*, 1984). The operators who tested RBT mentioned that they liked being able to stop the process to ask questions or explore boiler characteristics.

If a student working on a problem inadvertently triggers a second problem, the least serious problem will be placed on a stack and held in abeyance while the student is coached to solve the more serious problem. After the more serious problem is solved, the student is coached to solve the remaining one. Thus, the simulation provides facilities for handling multiple instantiations of emergencies.

One advantage of a formal representation of the process is the availability of a 'database' of possible worlds from which information based on typical or previous moves can be fed into the simulation at any time (Brown *et al.*, 1982) and a solution found. In this way, a student's hypothetical cases can be proposed, verified, and integrated into his mental model of the boiler.

1.2.3 Knowledge base of emergencies and operating conditions

The *knowledge base* contains preconditions, postconditions, and solutions for emergencies or operating conditions, described as *scenarios*. Scenarios are represented in frame-like text files containing preconditions, postconditions, and acceptable solutions for each scenario. For example, in LISP notation, a true blackout would be described as:

```
preconditions:
    (or  (< = blackout_factor 1)
         (< heat_input 5000))
postconditions:
    (or  (increasing O₂)
         (decreasing steamflow)
         (increasing TRS)
```

---

*Engineering details about the steam and chemical parameters in RBT and the boiler simulation capabilities can be found in Jansen *et al.* (1986).

```
            (increasing CO)
            (increasing SO₂))
     solution_satisfaction:
        (and   (= blackout_factor 1)
               (> heat_input 5200))
```

Scenarios in RBT have been teased apart to represent successively more serious problems. For instance, a smelt spout pluggage is represented as separate scenarios depending on whether the solution requires rodding the spout, applying a portable auxiliary burner, removing the liquor, or a combination of all three. Again, formalized knowledge of the domain made it easy to represent and evaluate graduated scenarios, as well as multiple operator actions.

The efficiency of the student's action is evaluated both through the type of action performed, such as *increasing O_2* or *increasing steamflow* for a true black-out, and the effect of that action on the boiler. Thus, if an inappropriate action nevertheless resulted in a safe boiler, the student would be told that his action worked, but that it was not optimal. For example, a partial furnace blackout requiring manual rodding of the air delivery system can be alleviated by shutting down the boiler. However, this is an expensive and unwarranted action and the student will be advised to use an alternative approach.

1.3   KNOWLEDGE OF TEACHING

The second theoretic issue to be addressed in building sophisticated tutoring systems is the represention of teaching knowledge. In addition to being an expert system that solves problems in the domain, the tutoring system must also *teach a student* how to solve those problems in the domain. Because teaching a topic is often more difficult than 'knowing' the same topic, a teaching system must be more complex than an expert system. The expert tutoring system will monitor a student's behaviour, advise him, respond sensitively to his answers, suggest new activities, and anticipate future actions based on inferences about his current activities.

Building such *teaching* knowledge is critical to development of the tutor. The machine should know how to *ask* the right questions and how to *focus* on the appropriate issue. The system should act as a partner, not as a disinterested, uncommitted, or uncooperative speaker. Effective communication with a student does *not* mean natural language processing (this has been achieved to some degree in some systems such as WHY (Stevens *et al.*, 1982), SOPHIE (Brown and Bell, 1977), and SCHOLAR (Carbonell, 1970)). Rather, effective communication requires looking beyond the words that are spoken and determining what the tutor and student *should* be communicating about. This problem becomes acute when the student organizes and talks about knowledge in a way that is different from the way the expert organizes and presents it.

Few systems have been effective in the way they communicate with the student. GUIDON (Clancey, 1982) is an exception that carries on a flexible dialogue with the student based on inferences made about his knowledge. It selects among alternative dialogues the one which is most appropriate based on inferences about the student's previous interactions and inferences about his current information. GUIDON can switch its discussion to any topic listed on an AND/OR graph, representing the rules of the expert system, and can respond to a student's hypothesis using a variety of techniques, one being 'entrapment', which forces the student to make a choice leading to incorrect conclusions, thereby revealing some aspect of his (mis)understanding.

In this section we describe our experience building teaching knowledge into two distinct systems, the Recovery Boiler Tutor and the Meno-tutor. The latter system extended our exploration of tutoring issues into the arena of discourse management and understanding. As a precursor to discussion of each tutor, we briefly describe the student model and the role discourse plays in prescribing teaching knowledge.

1.3.1   Knowledge of teaching in RBT

The student model is an essential component within the knowledge of teaching. It contains the system's knowledge of the student and must be represented in excruciating detail before the system is built and updated dynamically within the running system. The student model should not be a simple subset of domain knowledge; it should contain common errors and misconceptions specific to the domain as compiled by domain experts, teachers, and cognitive scientists.

In the Recovery Boiler Tutor, the *student model* records actions carried out by the student in solving the emergency or operating problem. It recognizes correct as well as incorrect actions and identifies each as relevant, relevant but not optimal, or irrelevant. In RBT, the tutor compares the student's actions with those specified by the knowledge base and uses a simplified differential model to recognize and comment about the difference between the two.

For instance, if a partial blackout has been simulated, the black liquor solids are less than 58%, and the operator adjusts the primary air pressure, the tutor might interrupt with a message such as:

'Primary air pressure is one factor that might contribute to blackout, but there is another more crucial factor – try again.'

or

'You have overlooked a major contributing factor to blackouts.'

Teaching knowledge in RBT contains the decision logic and rules to guide the tutor's intervention in the operator's actions. In designing the instructional strategy of the tutor, the intent was to 'subordinate teaching to learning' and to allow the student to experiment while developing his own criteria about boiler emergencies. Thus, the tutor guides the student, but does not provide a solution as long as the student's performance appears to be moving closer to a precise goal.

Represented as if–then rules based on a specific emergency and a specific student action, the instructional rules are designed to verify that the student has 'asked' the right questions and made the correct inferences about the saliency of his data. Special precautionary messages are added to the most specific tutor responses to alert an operator when a full-scale disaster is imminent. Responses are divided into three categories:

Redirect student: 'Have you considered the rate of increase of O_2?'
'If what you suggest is true, then how would you explain the low emissions reading?'
Synthesize data: 'Both O_2 and TRS have abnormal trends.'
'Did you notice the relation between steam flow and liquor flow?'
Confirm action: 'Yes, It looks like rodding the ports worked this time.'

The tutor selects from each category a response that addresses the operator's action, his presumed ability to solve the problem, and the need to encourage him to continue to generate hypotheses. Evidence from other problem-solving domains, such as medicine (Barrows and Tamblyn, 1980), suggests that students generate multiple (usually 3–5) hypotheses rapidly and make correct diagnoses with only two thirds of the available data*.

The RBT tutor was designed to be a partner and co-solver of problems with the operator, who is encouraged to recognize the effect (or lack of same) of his hypotheses and to experiment with multiple explanations of an emergency. No penalty is exacted for slow response or for long periods of trial-and-error problem-solving. This approach is distinct from that of Anderson, Boyle and Yost (1985) and Reiser, Anderson and Farrell (1985), whose geometry and LISP tutors immediately acknowledge incorrect student answers and provide hints. These authors argue that erroneous solution paths in geometry and LISP are often so ambiguous and delayed that they might not be recognized for a long time, if at all, and then the source of the original error might be forgotten. Therefore, immediate computer tutor feedback is needed to avoid fruitless effort.

However, the trainee in an industrial setting must learn to evaluate his own performance based on its effect on the industrial process. He should learn to trust the process itself to provide as much feedback as possible. In RBT we provided this feedback through animated simulations, trend analyses, and 'real-time' dynamically updated meters. The textual dialogue from the tutor provides added assurance that the operator has extracted as much information as possible from the data and it establishes a mechanism to redirect him if he has not (Burton and Brown, 1982; Goldstein, 1982).

---

*Medical students have been found to ask 60% of their questions while searching for new data and obtain 75% of their significant information within the first 10 minutes after a problem is stated (Barrows and Tamblyn, 1980).

1.3.2 Knowledge of teaching in Meno-tutor

Meno-tutor places more machine intelligence in service in the choice among tutoring strategies. It reasons about the *way* it communicates with the student and the *topics* that it chooses based upon a model of the student's goals, the domain complexity, and the current discourse history (Woolf and McDonald, 1984b; Woolf, 1984). Meno-tutor uses a student model, an annotated domain, and a representation of tutorial planning to custom-tailor its response to the student, both in content and form.

Meno-tutor discusses several domains, including causal reasoning in rainfall and programming loops in Pascal. In rainfall, we built a student model from cognitive science research about student misconceptions (Stevens *et al.*, 1982) and in the domain of Pascal we used groups of programming errors developed empirically (Bonar, 1982; Johnson and Soloway, 1985). Extensive testing and videotaped interviews of correct and incorrect programming strategies yielded high-level procedural plans that the authors suggest are used by experts to transform problem descriptions into programs.

A major thrust of Meno-tutor research has been to develop the control and data structures needed to plan responsive discourse, such as that observed in human tutoring. Meno-tutor (Woolf, 1984) is a 'generic' tutor, i.e. it is not committed by design to a single tutoring approach or tutoring domain. Rather, it provides a general framework within which tutoring rules can be defined and tested. Its knowledge of the two domains on which it has been defined is shallow.

We contrast our work with older tutoring and discourse systems (Brown and Bell, 1977; Burton and Brown, 1982; Mann, Moore and Levin, 1977; McKeown, 1980) that were 'retrieval-oriented'. While we have placed our emphasis on choosing among alternative responses that guide the learner based on what the tutor knows about him, other systems have placed emphasis on retrieving a correct answer. Such systems sought to produce a correct answer independent of the user's knowledge or current history (Finin, 1983; Wilensky, 1982). More recent interface and tutoring systems (Finin, 1983; Wilensky, 1982; Clancey, 1982) have begun to tailor their responses to the user and to discourse context.

As an example of discourses produced by the Meno-tutor, we present Fig. 1.7. Meno-tutor produced the actual text and high-level transitions in these discourses. Those discourses and twelve others were used to 'reverse-engineer' the tutor. That is, we analysed the common transitions and speech patterns used in these discourses and then defined the structures and knowledge necessary for a machine tutor to have a similar model of the student and to make the same transitions. For instance, in the first of the two discourses, the system recognized that the student made two wrong answers and it inferred that his knowledge was limited*. It then judged that the question-answer approach, which had been used

---

*It's not that those answers were simply 'wrong', rather that they reflect reasonable default assumptions about the weather in 'northern states'. An attempt to probe the student's default assumptions is made in the second discourse.

The First Human Discourse

Tutor: Do you know what the climate is like in Washington and Oregon?

Student: Is it cold?

Tutor: No, it is rather mild. Can you guess about the rainfall there?

Student: Normal, I guess.

Tutor: Well, the Japan current, which starts in south eastern Pacific, goes along the coast of Japan and across the North Pacific ending up off the coast of Washington and Oregon. How do you think that current effects the climate there?

Student: It's probably rainy.

Tutor: It is indeed very wet, there are rain forests in both Washington and Oregon. What does that tell you you about the temperature of the Japan current?

Student: It's warm.

The Second Human Discourse

Tutor: Do you think it rains much in Oregon?

Student: No.

Tutor: Why do you think it doesn't rain much in Oregon?

Student: Because the neighbouring states are dry.

Tutor: The neighbouring states are dry, but, you cannot generalize from that. In fact, it does rain a lot in Oregon. Can you guess what causes the rain there?

Student: Well, there are high mountains in the region and the states border the Pacific Ocean.

Tutor: Yes. The Pacific borders Oregon. How do you think it is involved in the heavy rainfall there?

Student: Ocean air rises and cools upon reaching the land.

Tutor: That is right.

Fig. 1.7. Two discourses produced by Meno-tutor.

until then, was ineffective and should be changed and that a new topic, the 'Japan Current', should be discussed because it is a dominant influence behind the region's climate. The system decided to supply the additional data in a descriptive, rather than an interrogative style, because the student seemed confused and might profit from the addition of supplemental data*.

The first discourse was generated by Meno-tutor in such a way that all the decisions, topics, and tutoring styles available to the system were explicit and modifiable by the authors. Modifying discourse decisions allowed us to generate additional discourses moving beyond the 'reverse-engineering' in this first discourse. The 'tutoring space' defined by our apparatus allowed us to vary the domain and the particulars of the rules. For example, the second discourse in Fig. 1.7 was based on the same domain as the first, but was done in an alternative tutoring style, brought about by modifying the 'meta-rules' that govern whether the tutor explores the student's frontier or probes the student's misconceptions about the current topic as soon as the first mistake is made.

Two meta-rules were modified to achieve this second discourse. The first moves the tutor to change its tutoring strategy. In the earlier discourse, this rule was used conservatively; the transition would have been made only after several topics were completely discussed and the tutor had some confidence in the student's knowledge or lack of knowledge. In this discourse, however, the rule was applied after a single incorrect answer, thus shifting the focus of the discourse abruptly at the beginning of the discourse.

The second modified rule causes the tutor to question the student about misconceptions. Typically, this rule is triggered after all topics are complete, either by the questions about them having been answered correctly or by the student having been corrected by the tutor. In the second discourse, however, the rule was modified to eliminate that requirement, with the effect that the rule was enabled after the student's first incorrect answer.

In addition to producing a variety of tutoring styles by changing the meta-rules, we explored the tutoring space by substituting a new domain knowledge base. We used the same teaching mechanism and used a knowledge base for elementary Pascal looping constructs[†]. We wanted to demonstrate the power of

---

*Meno tutor has been developed without a full-scale natural language understander or generator. The conceptual equivalent of a student's input is fed by hand to the tutor (i.e., what would have been the output of a natural language comprehension system) and the output is produced by standard incremental replacement techniques. We have not yet worked with MUMBLE, our surface language generator, because we haven't yet invested in building a large enough knowledge base to make the link-up useful. Our intent is to develop a complex knowledge base, probably in the domain of *Pascal*, to extend the surface language generator to deal with the domain, and to build a simple natural language parser to interface with the student.

[†]Meno-tutor was originally developed as part of a larger research effort directed at building an on-line run-time support system for novice Pascal users (Soloway *et al.*, 1981). As a part of this effort, a Bug Finder was developed that detected run-time semantic errors in novice Pascal programs and passed this information on to Meno-tutor. The Bug Finder could identify the type of error and the line numbers of related variables. It was used for three semesters on classes of several hundred students at the University of Massachusetts.

```
1     PROGRAM LESSON1 (INPUT, OUTPUT);
2     VAR
3        SUM, GRADES, STUDENTS:INTEGER;
4        MEDIAN:REAL;
5     BEGIN
6        SUM:= 0;
7        STUDENTS:= 0;
8        READ(GRADES);
9        WHILE GRADES > 0 DO
10          BEGIN
11          SUM:= SUM + GRADES;
12          STUDENTS:= STUDENTS + 1;
13          GRADES:= GRADES + 1;
                                    should be READ(GRADES);
14          END;
15          MEDIAN:= SUM/STUDENTS;
16          WRITELN
17            ('THE MEDIAN GRADE IS', MEDIAN:8:3)
18       END.
```

Fig. 1.8. A student Pascal program.

isolating reasoning about tutoring strategies from reasoning about the knowledge to be tutored. One reason for this was to see if the tutoring component could be interfaced with a different expert knowledge base and a different language generator and then be able to teach a new subject and even 'speak' in a new language. If our modularization was effective we could combine a Pascal knowledge base and, say, a Chinese language generator, with the tutoring component, and the resulting system could interrogate a student in Chinese and teach him about programming in Pascal. The difference in domain and language realization should force no changes in the tutoring component, though of course it might be quite inappropriate in China to use the same mix and structure of tutoring strategies as in the English language version of the system.

The program in Fig. 1.8 was actually submitted by a novice programmer and the discourse in Fig. 1.9 actually generated by the original Meno-tutor with changes to the expert knowledge base.

The changes required to produce each discourse are described in Woolf (1984). Though the number of discourses produced is still small, the fact that our architecture allowed us to produce varied but still quite reasonable discourses as we changed the particulars of just a few rules substantiates the overall effectiveness of our design.

Discourse produced using a Pascal database

Tutor: Do you know that GRADES, in line 9, is a control variable for the WHILE loop?

Student: Yes

Tutor: Does that mean that GRADES should be
a. Initiated before the loop?
b. Added into SUM within the loop?
c. Modified within the loop?
d. Both a. and c.

Student: C

Tutor: You seem to understand about the control variable of the WHILE loop. Now let's talk about some other command statements.
What do you think READ (GRADES) in line 8 does with the value of GRADES?
a. Reads all values of GRADES at one time.
b. Reads in a single value of GRADES.
c. Assigns several new input values to GRADES.

Student: A

Tutor: Then do you think that GRADES:= GRADES + 1 updates the next of those values?

Student: Yes

Tutor: There is your misconception.
Adding one to a variable is a common way to step through a range of values. But it cannot apply here because your READ instruction in line 8 retrieves only a single value. You should replace line 13 with a second call to READ (GRADES).

Fig. 1.9. Meno-tutor discussing errors from the program of Fig. 1.8.

1.3.3 The Discourse Management Network

The primary mechanism used by Meno-tutor to customize discourse to the individual student is the Discourse Management Network (DMN). Meno-tutor separates the production of tutorial discourse into two distinct components: the tutoring component which contains the DMN, and the surface language generator. The tutoring component makes decisions about what discourse transitions to make and what information to convey or query; the surface language generator takes conceptual specifications from the tutoring component

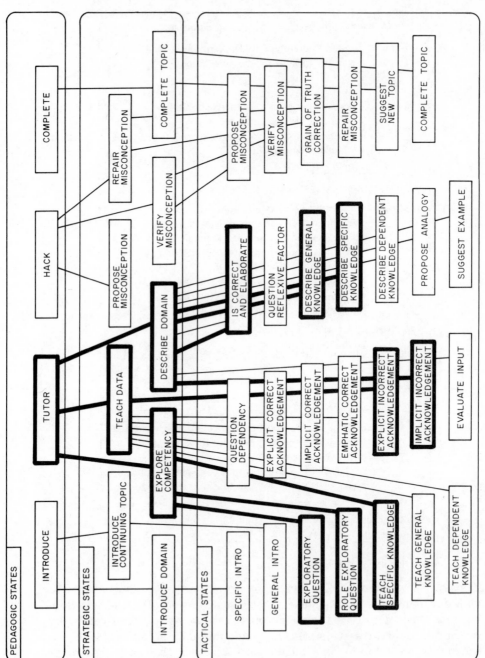

Fig. 1.10. DMN used by the tutoring component.

and produces the natural language output. These two components interface at the third level of the tutoring component as described below. The knowledge base for the tutor is a KL-ONE network annotated with pedagogical information about the relative importance of each topic in the domain.

The tutoring component is best described as a set of decision-units organized into three planning levels that successively refine the actions of the tutor (Fig. 1.10). We refer to the network that structures these decisions, defining the default and meta-level transitions between them, as a Discourse Management Network or DMN. The refinement at each level maintains the constraints dictated by the previous level and further elaborates the possibilities for the system's actions. At the highest level, the discourse is constrained to a specific tutoring approach that determines, for instance, how often the system will interrupt the student or how often it will probe him about misconceptions. At this level a choice is made between approaches which would diagnose the student's knowledge (*tutor*) or introduce a new topic (*introduce*). At the second level, the pedagogy is refined into a strategy, specifying the approach to be used. The choice here might be between exploring the student's competence by questioning him, or by describing the facts of the topic without any interaction. At the lowest level, a tactic is selected to implement the strategy. For instance, if the strategy involves questioning the student, the system can choose from half-a-dozen alternatives, e.g. it can question the student about a specific topic, the dependency between topics, or the role of a sub-topic. Again, after the student has given his answers, the system can choose from among eight ways to respond, e.g. it can correct the student, elaborate on his answer, or, alternatively, barely acknowledge his answer.

The tutoring component presently contains forty states, each organized as a LISP structure with slots for functions that are run when the state is evaluated. The slots define such things as the specifications of the text to be uttered, the next state to go to, or how to update the student and discourse model. The DMN is structured like an augmented transition network* (ATN); it is traversed by an iterative routine that stays within a predetermined space of paths from node to node.

The key point about this control structure is that its paths are not fixed; each default path can be preempted at any time by a 'meta-rule' that moves Meno-tutor onto a new path, which is ostensibly more in keeping with student history or discourse history. The action of the meta-rule corresponds functionally to the high-level transitions observed in human tutoring. Figure 1.11 represents the action of two meta-rules, one each at the strategic and tactical level. The ubiquity of the metar-rules – the fact that virtually any transition between tutoring states (nodes) may potentially be preempted – represents an important deviation from

---

*Augmented Transition Network (ATN) grammars are mechanisms for representing procedures. They have been used primarily for natural-language understanding, but in this case represent procedures for natural language generation. See Winston (1984, pp. 304–309) for a more technical discussion.

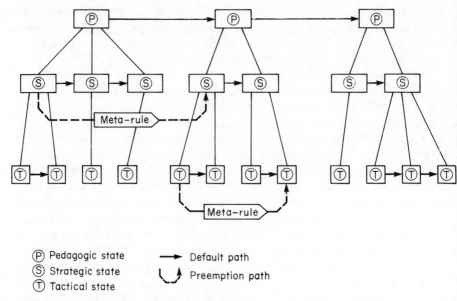

@ Pedagogic state   → Default path
Ⓢ Strategic state   Preemption path
Ⓣ Tactical state

Fig. 1.11. The action of the meta-rules.

the standard control mechanism of an ATN. Formally, the behaviour of Meno-tutor could be represented within the definition of an ATN; however, the need to include arcs for *every* meta-rule as part of the arc set of every state would miss the point of our design.

The system presently contains 20 meta-rules; most originate from more than one state and move the tutor to a single, new state. The pre-conditions of the meta-rules determine when it is time to move off the default path: they examine such data structures as the student model (e.g. Does the student know a given topic?), the discourse model (e.g. Have enough questions been asked on a given topic to assess whether the student knows it?), and the domain model (e.g. Do related topics exist?). Two meta-rules are described in an informal notation in Fig. 1.12.

1.3.4 Summary of teaching knowledge

This brief description of teaching strategies in RBT and discourse management in Meno-tutor has illustrated the kind of knowledge a tutoring system must have to make inferences about how to teach, independent of the content of the domain. The two systems provide a view of the tutoring space available to an intelligent system and demonstrate how, by changing tutoring topics and the particulars of the tutoring rules, we can plan and generate responsive tutoring discourse within distinct domains. The key point about discourse management is the need for

S1-EXPLORE – a strategic meta-rule

From: $teach-data
To: $explore-competency

Description: Moves the tutor to begin a series of shallow
                 questions about a variety of topics.

Activation: The present topic is complete and the tutor has little
                 confidence in its assessment of the student's knowledge.

Behaviour: Generates an expository shift from detailed
                 examination of a single topic to a shallow examination
                 of a variety of topics on the threshold of the student's
                 knowledge.

T6-A. IMPLICITLY – a tactical meta-rule

From: $explicit-incorrect-acknowledgement
To: $implicit-incorrect-acknowledgement

Description: Moves the tutor to make a brief acknowledgement
                 of an incorrect answer.

Activation: The wrong answer threshold has been reached
                 and the student seems confused.

Behaviour: Shifts the discourse from a explicit correction of
                 the student's answer to a response that recognizes but does
                 not dwell on the incorrect answer.

Fig. 1.12. Informal notation of meta-rules.

flexibility; the manager must receive its motivation, justification, and guidance from inferences made about the student's knowledge and the on-going discourse.

1.4 EVALUATIONS

Of the systems described in this chapter, only the RBT has left the laboratory. It has been well-received and is currently used in actual training in the control rooms of pulp and paper mills throughout the USA. Formal evaluation will be available soon. However, informal evaluation suggests that operators enjoy the simulation and handle it with extreme care. They behave as they might in actual control of the pulpmill panel, slowly changing parameters, adjusting meters through small intervals, and checking each action and examining several meter readings before moving on to the next action.

Both experienced and novice operators engage in lively use of the system after about a half-hour introduction. When several operators interact with the tutor, they sometimes trade 'war stories', advising each other about rarely seen situations. In this way, experienced operators frequently become partners with novice operators as they work together to simulate and solve unusual problems.

1.5 CONCLUSIONS

Several fundamental lessons about building intelligent tutors were learned from these two projects. The first and foremost was the need for 'in-house' expertise; in the case of RBT, the programmer, project manager, and director of the project were themselves chemical engineers. More than 30 years of theoretical and practical knowledge about boiler design and teaching were incorporated into the system. Development time for this project would have been much longer if these experts had not previously identified the chemical, physical and thermodynamic characteristics of the boiler and collected examples of successful teaching activities. This same need for expertise in the domain and in teaching the domain was evident in building Meno-tutor.

A second critical lesson was the need to clarify and implement the components of a teaching philosophy early in the intelligent tutor development process in order to ensure its full realization in the completed system. For example, in order to manifest a philosophy of subordinating teaching to learning, as realized in RBT, we had to build in the ability of the system to recognize partially correct as well as irrelevant actions (in the knowledge base), to custom-tailor the system's responses to each type of answer (in the instructional strategies), and to provide the ability to quietly monitor the operator while judiciously reasoning about when to interrupt him (in the student model). The need to limit authoritarian responses from the system and to restrict it to giving only as much help as absolutely needed meant that we could not build the expert system and at some later date tack on a tutor, but rather the tutor was developed as a component of the expert system. Even the tutor's ability to remain silent had to be carefully orchestrated. Indeed, the tutor's silence (inactivity) is in itself a recognition of the learner's role in the training process and provides an expression of our confidence in his progress.

A third and most surprising lesson learned from these projects was that tutoring systems can be designed for multiple students. For example, RBT was shown to be effective with groups of operators who work together and with the computer to solve problems. Novices and experienced operators, who might otherwise not be comparable in training and ability, can share their problem-solving knowledge, experience, and learning in a non-evaluative environment. As a group they are encouraged to move ahead in their exploration of unfamiliar scenarios.

Several issues remain unresolved in our continuing work to improve a computer tutor's ability to respond to the student. For example, we want the system to sort out those skills and concepts that a student has learned from those that he is still trying to learn, and to recognize which techniques have been effective in helping the student. Such knowledge might be built into the student model by way of inferences made about the student's knowledge, errors, and potential misconceptions to make progress along these lines.

In general, the knowledge that enables us to build intelligent tutors is not yet fully understood. Further research into each domain and tutoring knowledge is required to make further advances in this area. In this chapter we have suggested some ways that knowledge representations and control structures have been built to encode complete knowledge into tutoring systems. In addition, we suggest that sophisticated AI techniques, excruciating attention to detail, and intuitions about teaching and learning must continue to be researched and incorporated into tutors if we are to make progress in building more sophisticated machine tutors.

ACKNOWLEDGEMENTS

The author thanks Jeremy Metz, Bradford Leach, and the API Recovery Boiler Committee for their encouragement and support.

This work was supported in part by the Air Force Systems Command, Rome Air Development Center, Griffiss AFB, New York, 13441 and the Air Force Office of Scientific Research, Bolling AFB, DC 20332 under contract No. F30602-85-C-0008. This contract supports the Northeast Artificial Intelligence Consortium (NAIC).

2

Of course ICAI is impossible...
worse though, it might be
seditious

JIM RIDGWAY
University of Lancaster, England

This chapter will argue that current attempts at ICAI are seriously deficient in the pedagogical and epistemological assumptions implicitly made. Problems faced by ICAI in the domain of mathematical education are considered, to focus discussion. Contrasting examples are chosen: understanding the skills of subtraction; and fostering problem solving skills. DEBUGGY is criticized because it takes no account of pupil descriptions of process, and ignores idiosyncratic methods; it implicitly divorces algorithm from application; and, by diagnosing, takes over an intellectual task which may well be of value to pupils and teachers. Efforts to model the processes of pupils who attempt to solve more open problems are judged to be impossible in principle, for several reasons: the paucity of cues available to the program; problems of multiple representations by solvers, switches of representation, and changes in the operators used as the solver proceeds; and current naive views of the nature of expertise. Provision of help to the user is also judged to be problematic.

Current educational ambition seeks to de-emphasize the learning of technique, and to focus more on its application on open-ended problem solving, practical work, group work, and discussion. None of these is well suited to ICAI. which seems to be focused on individual tuition for technical mastery.

ICAI might be seditious too, if it acts to deskill teachers' jobs and pupils' tasks; if it directs attention away from human–human interaction; if it directs attention away from creative activities and the investigation of open problems, by focusing on technical mastery; if it presents a view of knowledge as the assembly of atoms of technique; and if it reinforces current societal views that, for every conceptual challenge (e.g. 'education') there is a quick technological fix.

The issues which ICAI attempts to tackle are important. How is knowledge represented? How should learning experiences be arranged? What misconceptions do learners have? and so on ... The chapter concludes that 'transparent'

ICAI systems should themselves be objects for study by pupils and teachers, rather than the educational activities that ICAI systems themselves might produce.

2.1 INTRODUCTION

All attempts to educate make assumptions about the nature of expertise and the nature of the learner, and also contain a set of epistemological assumptions. Sometimes these assumptions are explicit; more often they are implicit. In the domain of ICAI, researchers have offered a rich variety of accounts in each of these domains, and so no simple descriptions can be offered of the approaches taken within this energetic field. Nevertheless, there does appear to be a set of core assumptions which can be challenged.

In addition to the conceptual problems which ICAI faces, there are a range of pragmatic issues which few researchers have begun to tackle. These involve a consideration of current educational needs, the level of computer provision, teacher expertise, and issues concerning the processes of innovation in education.

As well as these conceptual and practical issues, ICAI might be associated with broader social attitudes to education, and indeed to the nature of humanity, which may prove to be seditious. Considered under this heading will be: ICAI as a panacea for the ills of education; and possible associations between ICAI and anthropomorphic views of computers. To leaven criticisms offered throughout the chapter, a suggestion will be made about an approach to ICAI which might side-step or defuse some of the criticisms raised earlier.

Disclaimer

Many of the comments made in this chapter will be critical of ICAI. It is appropriate to begin, therefore, by making some positive remarks. The purpose of the chapter is not to be dismissive of past achievements and future potentiality, but rather to help shape the direction in which research into ICAI might go.

Some of the virtues of ICAI are:

- It has obvious surface plausibility. Clearly the idea of injecting intelligent help into learning systems appears sensible; the development of systems which adapt to users' needs might plausibly be of benefit in education.
- AI/ICAI has a good track record in domains in which: money poses no problems for development, or for running costs; students are highly motivated; where domains are heavily factually based, and where these facts can be accreted in quantity.
- ICAI is great fun, exciting, poses a range of intellectual challenges for researchers, irrespective of the inherent educational utility of these challenges.
- ICAI/AI has had a great influence on both psychology and computer science and has encouraged researchers to talk to each other, to build models of processes, and to be explicit about such terms as 'knowledge representation',

'heuristics', and the like, in a way which was impossible before the advent of powerful computers.

Panegyrics on the benefits of ICAI and AI can be found in this volume and elsewhere (e.g. Boden, 1977). Here we will tackle the issue of the likely successes of ICAI both in principle, and in practice.

2.2 PROBLEMS FOR ICAI IN MATHEMATICAL EDUCATION

It is rather hard to describe the potential benefits and hazards associated with the development of ICAI across the whole framework of education. To limit the scope of the discussion and to provide concrete, illustrative examples, the discussion will be restricted to the problems which ICAI faces in the domain of mathematical education. Even within this domain, comments will be restricted to school-based education; the potential contribution of ICAI at a tertiary level will not be considered. The range of criticisms which can be levelled at ICAI approaches will be illustrated by considering two themes: the first concerns approaches to the modelling of user misconceptions in their use of algorithms, taking DEBUGGY as an example; the second involves the potential for ICAI techniques to support students who are engaged in open-ended problem solving. In the latter case there are no exemplars available for criticism, and indeed it will be argued that such exemplars are impossible in principle.

2.2.1 Problems with DEBUGGY

DEBUGGY (Brown and Burton, 1978) considers the errors which pupils make when they solve subtraction problems. One might assume that errors in subtraction arise simply from computational errors which occur at random. Closer analysis of the performance of individual pupils, however, reveals some systematicity in patterns of errors, which can lead one to draw inferences about specific errors which are implicit in the underlying subtraction algorithms. Errors can arise either from bugs within the algorithms, or from omissions. (Such error analyses are well known to the education fraternity, and can be traced back at least to the 1930s.)

The general insight that errors can arise from systematic misconceptions, and that these misconceptions can be diagnosed and remediated is a valuable one. If nothing else, this framework can encourage teachers to look hard at patterns of errors, and to devise methods for remediating their pupils' misconceptions, by the wide variety of means available to them. (Especially by finding realistic situations such as giving change, or counting sweets, which can be devised so that pupils themselves notice computational errors when their subtraction algorithms give rise to answers which clash with their experientially based expectations.)

DEBUGGY describes 110 primitive bugs which can be assembled into more complex bugs. It contains a lattice model of subtraction skill which is sub-divided

A	1225	B	1225	C	1225	D	1225
	876		876		876		8775
	349		226		1459		876
			123		349		9651
			349				349

Fig. 2.1. Four methods of subtraction.

into about 58 sub-skills. On the basis of the computer model of subtraction skills, pupil responses to subtraction problems can be fed into DEBUGGY, which can then provide a diagnosis of the pupil's current knowledge about subtraction processes. This can then be the basis for appropriate tutoring (as provided by DEBUGGY). Before we criticize this approach, it might be appropriate to try an example of understanding the processes involved in subtraction.

Figure 2.1 consists of four different methods for carrying out subtraction. Method A is commonly used; the other three methods are quite unusual. None of these methods contain any errors. Please try to explain how each method works, then say why the method works. You will find this a non-trivial task.

Now review your explanations of why the methods work.

You are likely to have deployed a variety of representations of the problem, including some algebraic methods and perhaps some diagrams which involve number lines.

What criticisms of DEBUGGY (and related approaches) are suggested by your experiences with this example?

- A variety of idiosyncratic methods and approaches can be taken to the task of solving subtraction problems. DEBUGGY has no access to the huge variety of individual methods which might conceivably be used.
- DEBUGGY has no means of access to pupil accounts of how they solve problems, and therefore cannot begin to learn about the possible range of such idiosyncratic methods.
- The knowledge involved in debugging algorithms which you – as a so-phisticated subtractor – have brought to bear, reveals the rich interconnec-tions between different domains in mathematics.
- When a range of pupil solutions to subtraction problems is considered, DEBUGGY fares no better than a human teacher. It seems reasonable to predict that DEBUGGY would fail completely to debug errors in the idiosyncratic methods presented in Fig. 2.1 (since teachers find it hard).
- One might reflect on the benefits of offering human teachers skills in debugging algorithms, rather than on devolving such tasks to a machine. Further one might argue that the pupils themselves should be the major agents in the debugging process, since they are the ones who have most to gain from it. The

notion of debugging as an intellectual task which might have great educational value is largely unexplored despite strong advocacy (e.g. Papert, 1980).

Divorcing algorithms from applications is a device of very doubtful pedagogical value. Subtraction should not be viewed as a self-contained topic which is separate from 'mathematical thinking'. It should be viewed as an integral part of mathematics and mathematical thinking, and teaching should focus on extending and strengthening links with other areas of mathematics. Many of the ways in which mathematics is currently taught have been strongly criticized (e.g. Cockcroft, 1982) because of their focus on technical success rather than understanding. DEBUGGY seems to reinforce such a view. Considerable problems are associated with divorcing algorithms from practice; most obviously, that algorithms can be quickly forgotten, but more importantly, that the contexts in which algorithms can usefully be deployed remain unlearned. Pupils find major problems in knowing when to deploy particular algorithms (e.g. *when* to multiply or divide or subtract) when faced with realistic situations. DEBUGGY is implicitly supporting this split between algorithms and application.

If our goals are to foster subtraction skills which are robust and useful to pupils we need to:

- encourage the exploration of idiosyncratic methods, rather than insist that pupils learn other people's algorithms;
- expose pupils to a wide variety of situations in which subtraction tasks are presented;
- offer pupils insight into the functioning of their own algorithms, and ask them to explain why they work and to identify faults for themselves;
- emphasize the role of estimation, since algorithms do sometimes go wrong because of simple (random?) errors. It is important that pupils have some sense of the likely size of the answer when they begin a computation, rather than simply possessing a carefully polished algorithm which occasionally produces disastrously wrong results.

2.2.2   Problems with open-ended problems

Problem solving is not an activity which is the exclusive property of mathematics; nevertheless, it is a topic which frequently emerges within the mathematical domain. For example, problem solving was chosen as the theme for the 1980s by the National Council of Teachers of Mathematics. There is a very large academic literature on the subject of problem solving to which AI researchers have made significant contributions. We will begin this discussion by sketching out a default model of problem solving to which many people subscribe. Some headings to be considered are shown in Fig. 2.2.

Knowledge base refers to a whole range of facts, skills, relationships, and

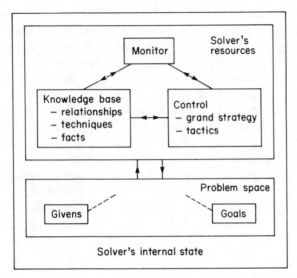

Fig. 2.2. Minimum requirements for a model of human problem solving.

techniques, which the solver brings to bear on a particular problem. This might be viewed as an intellectual tool-kit.

Control refers to the way in which these resources are deployed. Solvers have a range of ways of tackling novel problems both at the heuristic level (e.g. 'try simple cases', 'think of a related problem', 'work systematically', 'make a table') and at a more strategic level (e.g. 'choose different representations', 'plan out a solution path before you work on the details'). When dealing with a familiar problem users can recognize the problem type and can recall specific strategies, tactics, and resources in order to solve it. When faced with unfamiliar problems, solvers must take active control over their problem-solving processes and should be made aware of the need to think strategically and tactically about the way they tackle the problem and about the resources they will bring to bear on the problem.

Monitor: relatively recently attention has focused on the need for problem solvers to monitor their own performance. Concepts such as metacognition, reflection, and self-awareness all refer to the need for problem solvers to emerge from the solving process at regular intervals in order to assess their progress.

The problem space: as well as this rather static description of the skills which a solver has at his/her disposition which might be of help when solving problems, one can also describe the dynamic state of the solver during problem solving. Here we need recourse to a story about the problem space, which will include a description of the elements within the problem space, together with a description of the kind of operators that the solver chooses to use; some description of the problem goals as the solver judges them; and a story about the intellectual flow between elements within the problem space as mediated by the problem solver's resources, control system and monitoring system.

This sketch should not be viewed as a prescription for a particular architecture for problem solving. For current purposes, it makes little difference if *control* is described as being part of the *knowledge base*, or if *monitor* is subsumed under *control*, or if more explicit connections are made between the problem space, the world outside the solver, and the solver's knowledge base. The reader will probably have already noticed how much of this vocabulary has been derived from the AI literature; and how this model in its current descriptive state can be represented by a number of currently existing architectures.

This description appears quite familiar to members of the AI fraternity, so how can one justify the assertion that modelling this process in an individual is impossible in principle? Again, perhaps we should begin by an illustration of your own cognitive processes as you attempt to solve a straightforward but, hopefully, unfamiliar task. Please attempt the problem shown in Fig. 2.3. Don't throw any of your notes away: you will find it useful to reflect on them after you have solved the problem.

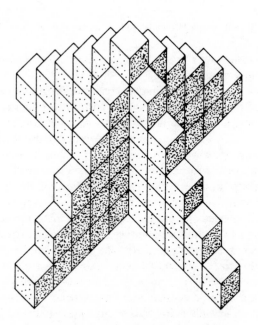

i. How many cubes are needed to build this tower?

ii. How many cubes are needed to build a tower like this, but 12 cubes high?

iii. Explain how you worked out your answer to part ii.

iv. How would you calculate the number of cubes needed for a tower *n* cubes high?

Fig. 2.3. Skeleton Tower.

What problems might emerge for ICAI systems that attempt to facilitate human problem solving?

(a) *Cues.* Understanding the processes that someone else goes through as they solve problems is hard for a human observer (even for observers who have set out to invent paper and pencil notations for just this purpose (e.g. Ridgway and Mansell, 1985)). One of the main problems which human observers face is that they are presented with a multiple parallel stream of cues about internal processes such as: diagrams; writing – odd notes, doodles; speech – often in fragmentary form; odd analogies and slang expressions; and a range of gestures such as pointing to different parts of the figure or gazing towards particular pieces of written work; social cues which yield evidence of understanding, ignorance, frustration, withdrawal, and the like. Each of these cues can have some relevance to the problem-solving process. None of them are accessible to the computer. If you review your work on Skeleton Tower you are likely to find a set of disconnected elements which relate to your early attempts to solve the problem. If you reflect on the process you went through during the solution of this problem you are likely to tell a rich story about cues you were able to make use of in the diagram, fragments of knowledge and half-remembered ideas that later proved to be relevant, and the like. The process of giving this range of cues to the computer is overwhelmingly difficult.

(b) *Representations.* Polya (1962) advocated that solvers should choose multiple representations when they begin to solve a problem. For Skeleton Tower, for example, one might choose a geometric representation, an algebraic one, or one might simply build up tables of numbers which correspond to towers of different sizes. It is also rather natural for humans to switch between these stages and states. This will prove to be rather problematic for computers to follow. Consider the different methods of internal representation which humans bring to bear. These include words, numbers, all sensory states; motor representations (indicated by gesturing such as hand-waving); varieties of imagery; spatial representations, and even algebra. While some translations between these states are possible, many such translations feel artificial and strange and fail to capture the essential quality of the representations. (For example, the efforts of writers to capture the essential qualities of music, art, or food and wine, in words can be a source of considerable mirth to readers.) From the view-point of user modelling, it is hard to see how a computer could keep track of multiple representations and the various degrees of transfer between each.

(c) *Changing representations.* Characteristics of solving unfamiliar problems are that one changes representations quickly; one changes the primitives which one chooses to work with; one changes the operators used as work progresses.

For example, in an early attempt to solve Skeleton Tower, one might well consider a block to be a fundamental unit. However, Fig. 2.4 illustrates a variety

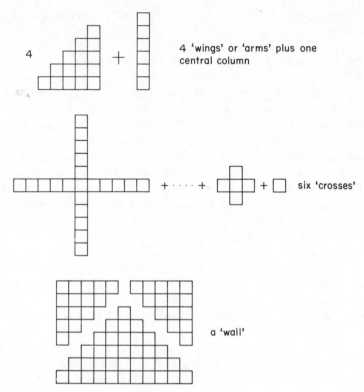

Fig. 2.4. Pupil methods.

of pupil solutions which involve the construction of a whole range of larger scale primitives and a range of different operators.

One pupil has pulled the tower apart and considered it to be four 'wings'; another has pulled off two 'wings', inverted them, and put them on the remaining structure to create a 'wall'; another views the Skeleton Tower as a set of crosses and so on.

So human problem solvers change representations qualitatively as they solve problems, and change the primitive elements within their problem space, as well as the operators quite dramatically. They also use idiosyncratic labelling systems, which depend on a lot of analogizing and forging relations with real-world knowledge. Examples are labels such as 'wings', 'wall' and 'cross'. All these changes are hard for humans to track, even given that humans have access to a large range of shared real-world knowledge (and in the case of trained observers, have access to knowledge of a large number of different solution attempts). I will conclude, therefore, that modelling on-going problem solving in real time is impossible for ICAI systems.

(d) *Machine–human interaction.* If the human solver is required to input details about problem-solving efforts, during solution, this activity of self-monitoring is quite likely to interfere with on-going problem-solving processes and is likely to have negative effects on the outcome of the problem-solving session. Questioning strategies might fail because students can know how to do things without being able to describe their knowledge.

Drawing inferences about control and monitoring processes from written or keyed responses is extremely difficult. In our work, we often adopt the device of setting pupils to work on problems in pairs. We have found this to offer a natural way of eliciting control and monitor remarks from pupils. Since pupils feel obliged to explain to each other why they are embarking on particular problem solving tracks, they experience pressures to explain idiosyncratic representations, and quite spontaneously generate monitoring remarks, such as 'I'm stuck!' and 'Why are we doing this?' A second major role, played by pairs, is that they naturally interrogate each other and demand explanations. It is hard to imagine machine dialogues which can be as responsive and helpful as a fellow pupil.

(e) *Problems with current attempts at user modelling.* "... at present there are not even any established techniques of user modelling, as such. All that exists is a collection of promising prototypes ..." (Ross *et al.*, 1986). User modelling is a major target of many efforts in ICAI. These efforts are usually based on the assumption that there exists a rather small set of naive models which can be readily diagnosed. We have already seen in the domain of subtraction that the range of naive models is in fact very large. As the domain gets increasingly complex, the range of possible naive models also increases dramatically. It seems highly likely that no exhaustive set of naive models will ever be produced in a complex domain. To be crudely pragmatic, is the effort to compile an exhaustive list of naive models itself worthwhile? Humans are rather good at understanding explanations which others propose; many teachers have sophisticated skills for unpicking interesting conglomerations of naive models, and misconceptions. In many cases, the pupils themselves have these skills.

At a more principled level, if we take the view that the machine is there to explore the user's naive model and to provide some diagnosis and subsequent remediation, then we are assigning an important learning task to the machine which could be performed by either a fellow pupil or by a teacher. From the learner's viewpoint this may be of no consequence. However, from the fellow pupil's or the teacher's viewpoint, it may have undesirable consequences in that they will thereby lose the opportunity to engage in a form of learning situation of considerable complexity and potential value. It seems a rather strange proposition that one should write computer programs which impoverish the potential for learning by teachers or by other pupils.

(f) *Domain specificity.* A well-known criticism of ICAI systems is that they focus on a particular narrow domain (e.g. chemical analysis, fault location in particular equipment, arithmetic, diagnosis of chest diseases ...). Knowledge is more than a repertoire of skills intended to perform some particular task. An intended outcome for education is that pupils will generalize their learning to a range of contexts. In order to make such generalizations, they must experience similar skills embedded in a variety of contexts. One educational device we employ is to involve pupils in activities which lead to the integration of mathematics and their everyday lives and experiences. So, many activities involve the use of objects such as counters, cups, cards, dominoes, beer mats and the like. Many of the mathematical activities involve them in shifting representations between written language, graphs, symbols, verbalizations, movement of objects, etc. Our overall approach might be said to be to attempt to enrich the semantic network of mathematical concepts by extensive elaboration, as well as the more obvious goals of introducing pupils to process and monitoring skills. Unless pupils elaborate their knowledge as they work they will be unable to generalize their learning experiences. The focus of ICAI on the performance of specific tasks (necessary because of the problems of representing semantically rich domains) can therefore be seen as a move toward a restricted educational environment, rather than towards an enriched one.

(g) *Helping students.* Choosing appropriate guidance for pupils who are experiencing difficulties can be problematic. We have developed modules for use in mathematics lessons which are intended to foster problem-solving skills in pupils aged 14–16 years (Ridgway *et al.*, 1984c; Shell Centre for Mathematical Education, 1984, 1986). Each module supports about four weeks of mathematics lessons, and consists of: photocopying masters for pupil worksheets: dumb CAI (suitable for use with groups, or the whole class, as well as with individuals); teacher support in the form of a video; and a teacher workbook which offers lesson plans, and explicit guidance to teachers about the kinds of help which are, and are not, appropriate for people who are learning to solve problems (as well as advice on marking schemes, and a full set of solutions to problems!). The modules recommend strongly that pupils be encouraged to struggle with problems. This might seem somewhat perverse. We argue, however, that since our major goal is to facilitate pupils' acquisition of control skills and self-monitoring, they must be placed in situations where they have the confidence to exercise these skills. One cannot exercise these skills if one deals exclusively with familiar problems or if someone else reduces the strategic load and the need to monitor one's performance by giving help ill-advisedly. Our helping hierarchy is shown in Fig. 2.5.

We offered this advice to teachers having seen several examples in class where the pupil was able to 'drive' the teacher to the position where the pupil's task was made trivially easy. 'Teacher driving' begins by asking for advice on how to tackle an unfamiliar problem. Here is an invented dialogue between an unsophisticated

When pupils learn to solve problems, they have to learn how to decide *what* to do and *when* to do it. If someone always tells them what to do, they *won't* learn these skills for themselves.

Aim to provide less and less guidance as you get further into the course.

Use freely any hints that make children think about the way they are tackling the problem:

'What have you tried?'
'Well, what do you think?'
'What are you trying to do?'
'Why are we doing this?'
'What will we do when we get this result?'

Use sparingly, particularly later on, hints about which strategies they should use:

'What have you found out so far?'
'Have you seen anything that is like this in any way?'
'How can we organize this?'
'Let's draw up a table of results'
'Can you see any pattern?'
'Have you tried some simple cases?'
'What examples should we choose?'
'How can we start?'
'Have you checked if that works?'

Avoid any hint referring to the particular problem:

'Do you recognize square numbers?'
'Explore it like this.'
'Why don't you try using 3 counters?'

Fig. 2.5. Checklist for the teacher.

teacher and a sophisticated child.

P: I don't know what to do, miss.
T: What have you tried so far?
P: Nothing really, miss; I don't know how to start.
T: Why don't you try a simple case?
P: How do you mean, miss?
T: Well, you could look at a much smaller tower.
P: How do you mean, miss?

T: Well, how many blocks would there be in a tower one cube high?
P: ...just one, miss?
T: And how many would there be in a tower two cubes high?
P: ..um..would there be six, miss?
T: So we can make up a table like this (draws) and count up the number of cubes in towers of different heights, then look for a pattern. You do that and I will come back and see you in a minute or two.

In this invented dialogue, the pupil faced with a difficult intellectual challenge, has successfully engineered the situation where the teacher has done all the strategic work and has left the pupil with a simple, clerical task of counting cubes and recording the results. It is easy to imagine how this dialogue will proceed when an appropriate number of cases has been built up and the task proceeds onto spotting patterns and looking for algebraic relationships. It is rather harder to imagine any educational benefit for the pupil.

It has been clear from our classroom observations that handling discourse with pupils, and the assessment of appropriate levels of help which students should be offered requires careful judgement. Certainly a whole range of social cues are available to the teacher; so is an extensive memory of past pupil behaviour in different circumstances as well as detailed knowledge of the pupil's learning history. None of these sources of information will be available to an ICAI system, and so the provision of help will be made on the basis of an impoverished set of information.

In educational terms this could well lead to pupils driving ICAI systems to present them with intellectually trivial tasks, rather than presenting pupils with the more challenging tasks which the ICAI designer had intended.

(h) *Individual work.* Since a major focus of ICAI involves the development of user models, the paradigm is usually for one pupil to interact with one machine. This has a number of disadvantages. In our work in problem solving, we have been keen to foster collaborative work for a number of reasons.

- Pupils are often called upon to explain to partners their reasons for choosing particular styles of attack.
- Pupils are more likely to engage in monitoring remarks.
- Trivial errors, e.g. in simple counting or elementary computation, are far fewer when pairs work together, and are detected far quicker. (In tasks such as finding algebraic descriptions of number patterns, the difficulty level rises dramatically if the number pattern contains some error.)

Is there scope for using ICAI to support group work? The task of monitoring the cognitive processes of two problem solvers, in conjunction with an attempt to monitor their corporate problem-solving space seems difficult, and compounds the problems of monitoring a single user's problem-solving processes. It will be argued later that a focus on one-to-one tutorial work goes against current movements which are setting out to foster more collaborative work in mathematics classrooms.

(i) *The expert problem solver.* A common misconception is that the novice deviates from the expert in some simple way. For example, the novices might be viewed as having too few routines, and needing to add more to their repertoire; or they might be viewed as having some misconceptions, bugs, or mal-rules. Both of these simplistic views are wrong. There are major differences between novices and experts which are not so readily remedied. Another common misconception is to talk about *the* way that an expert solves the problem. A major characteristic of experts is that they can solve the same problem in a variety of ways. Experts can also translate between representations and can relate and reconcile different approaches, and different modes of representation. Attempts to tutor pupils into *the* expert's methods are therefore fundamentally misguided. They also limit the kinds of educational activities which might be pursued.

2.3 THE NEEDS OF MATHEMATICAL EDUCATION

So far, oblique references have been made to educational goals in mathematics; perhaps these should be articulated more clearly so that the potential contribution of ICAI to mathematical education can be evaluated. A clear summary of these goals is provided by the Cockcroft Report (1982). Paragraph 243 states:

"mathematics teaching at all levels should include opportunities for
  exposition by the teacher;
  discussion between teacher and pupils and between pupils themselves;
  appropriate practical work;
  consolidation and practice of fundamental skills and routines;
  problem solving, including the application of mathematics to everyday situations;
  investigational work."

Where do current models of ICAI fit into the scheme of things? They certainly fit in rather well with the exposition – consolidation and practice aspects. However, surveys in schools (e.g. Her Majesty's Inspectors of Schools, 1979) reveal that these are predominant classroom activities anyway. The 'missing' activities of discussion, practical work, problem solving, and investigation, seem ill-suited to current ICAI approaches. Certainly dialogue strategies available on machines are extremely impoverished. It is hard to see how practical work can be facilitated, given current limitations on computer interfaces. Problem solving has been the subject of the earlier section where it was argued strongly that current conceptions of ICAI are quite unsuited to the fostering of problem solving. Investigational work probably poses even greater problems than does problem solving, since the thrust of an investigation is to take a simple mathematical seed and to explore its implications in some domain of the pupil's choice. It is clear that to monitor and facilitate investigational work one needs an extensive and elaborate knowledge base in the domain of mathematics and mathematical processes. The problems of representing extensive knowledge domains, including real-world knowledge, via computers, are well known, and at present can be judged impossible.

Paragraph 207 of the Cockcroft Report reads "the fundamental criterion at all stages must be the extent to which any piece of software offers opportunity to enhance and improve work in the classroom".

We have no evidence of any sort about the impact of ICAI techniques within the classroom. Given our reservations about the things that ICAI is likely to be good for, one might make the gloomy prediction that ICAI will focus on conservatism and a rather old-fashioned view of the nature of mathematical knowledge, and, if implemented, will become a barrier to innovation rather than an agent for the enhancement of mathematical curricula.

2.3.1   Missing activities

a. *Pupil explanations* both to fellow pupils and to the teacher are essential aspects of mathematical learning. In our work we encourage pupils to explain things clearly in words before they attempt to write down their explanations. It is not clear how this can be done using ICAI systems.

b. *Group work* has many advocates because of its role in eliciting control and metacognitive remarks; because of studies which show social facilitation (i.e. group performance which excels that of the best individual within the group); and because group work is an inherently valuable skill (i.e. the ability to work well in a group is in itself an educational objective, since such skills are likely to be useful outside the classroom). It is not clear how ICAI can facilitate group work.

c. *Reflection.* The general topic of metacognitive skill, self-description and self-evaluation is both fashionable and relevant to individual development. ICAI does not seem a terribly good vehicle for fostering reflection.

2.3.2   The new curriculum

Concerns over the nature of school mathematics and the ways in which it should be taught are the focus of a good deal of debate, internationally. In the UK, for example, debates are taking place about the nature of mathematics and the way it should be taught. The NCTM Conference on the Impact of Computing Technology on School Mathematics discussed the needs for the development of new curricula and new instructional methods. It was suggested that there should be a de-emphasis on mechanical and manipulative skills, and a corresponding increase in the emphasis and attention paid to the development of concepts, the establishment of relationships between mathematical structures, problem-solving and investigational skills. Again, we can view this as a move away from the kinds of intellectual activities which ICAI seems able to support.

More radical approaches to curricula have been brought about, somewhat paradoxically, by advances in AI. These are analogous to changes promised by ready pupil access to calculators. The calculator has caused a good deal of debate about the kinds of mathematics which it is appropriate to learn. Few people now would argue that pupils need high levels of technical proficiency in such tasks as long multiplication, long division and the calculation of square-roots by hand. Rather, emphasis has shifted towards mental arithmetic on small numbers, estimation skills about an approximate size of answers, a focus on the meaning of operations and knowledge about when to deploy particular operations, and, of course, skills in using calculators. The computer provides analogous challenges, since packages such as MUMATH can perform most of the technical mathematical tasks that pupils might need up to their first year at University. The mathematical community has begun to address the problem of deciding which aspects of mathematics should be taught and how they should be taught. If a machine can perform a task faster and more reliably than a student, and can also perform it for a wider range of cases, which of these skills should be taught and to what extent should students be required to master them?

Current educational goals are in a state of flux. As computers can take on more and more tasks hitherto the domain of expert humans, the definition of the range of tasks which humans should perform is changing. One can summarize this by saying that, as we try to meet current educational goals using ICAI we are actually shooting at a moving target. Worse than that, the movement of the target is controlled in some non-obvious way by the extent of our success to hit it.

2.4 COMPUTERS IN EDUCATION?

The role of computers in education could well be quite profound. Early explorations into language learning (e.g. LOGO, Prolog), the use of graphical packages, statistics packages, simulations, modelling packages, spreadsheets, word processors, and the like, have barely begun. (For a review of research frontiers for IT in Education, see Ridgway, 1986.) Our own studies have shown that the introduction of a computer programmed for use in whole class teaching can have dramatic effects on the social dynamics of the classroom, and can facilitate role shifts by the teacher which are notoriously difficult to achieve using other means (e.g. Fraser *et al.*, in press). Earlier criticisms about the challenges for stimulating problem-solving, investigational work, discussion and group work which ICAI seems unable to meet *can* be met by Dumb CAI and appropriate teaching (e.g. Ridgway *et al.*, 1984a).

The spirit of the times currently advocated by professional groups both in the USA and in the UK is towards a shift in teacher roles, away from an all-knowing expert, towards a facilitator of pupil learning. In this role, teachers will, we hope, foster collaborative learning, and act as models for problem-solving styles. From a student viewpoint, pupils will be expected to operate mathematically in more open environments, to acquire skills of discovery and skills for the acquisition of knowledge. The general concern in this brave new world is to integrate mathematical knowledge into general world knowledge, to be able to talk sensibly about mathematical processes and to know when and how to deploy one's skills. The major thrust of much current ICAI work adopts old frameworks which relate to the acquisition of formal algorithms.

2.4.1   Practical constraints

Despite the widespread belief that computers are readily available in schools, a number of recent surveys have shown rather low levels of machine provision, although these levels are rising steadily. For example, Becker (1984) conducted a survey of 1600 schools which used microcomputers in the US; he obtained replies from 1082 such schools. The survey was conducted in the period 1982–1983. This survey found that less than 20% of secondary school teachers had access to 8 or more micros at a time and that typically even with 8 computers "...students may spend as much as three-quarters of their time waiting for their turn at the computer".

In the UK Esterson (1985) reports a survey conducted in 1984 by BBC/MEP of UK secondary schools which reported that on average there were 10 microcomputers per school.

Given the dependence of ICAI on one pupil to one machine, there are considerable practical barriers to implementation. Of course this blanket assertion about the number of computers ignores the nature of the machines. These are almost invariably 8-bit machines with rather limited memory capacity, quite unsuited for running the large ICAI programs currently being developed.

2.4.2   Teacher resistance

Issues of reliability of hardware and software are often to the forefront of teachers' minds. Members of the computing fraternity have a certain tolerance for software foibles and even for the idiosyncracies of hardware. This tolerance does not necessarily extend to the teaching profession where the base-line for reliability is not another computer system that works even less well, but is a piece of chalk and a blackboard. Reliability of chalk is generally rather high; even when it fails, repair or replacement is rarely problematic.

All use of CAI in classrooms requires teacher training. We ask teachers to acquire new skills, both in handling machines and in reorganizing their classrooms. This can be associated with a range of practical problems, even when the application is rather straightforward dumb CAI (e.g. Ridgway et al., 1984b). If we are talking about the provision of ICAI these problems are likely to be amplified. At a higher level of concern, teachers may well have conceptual objections to ICAI that they do not have to CAI. Examples of such worries might be: If the program can do more maths than I can (for example, MUMATH) is it not a threat? If the computer can diagnose pupil errors better than I can, is it not a threat? One may well wonder whether teachers will be enthusiastic to use programs which appear to be more sophisticated in their mathematical knowledge (and of course in other domains) than they are.

If we reflect on surveys by Bialo and Erickson (1985) about the uses to which CAI is put, we can draw gloomier lessons than the most obvious ones that much software is of poor quality and that teachers are relatively untrained to choose or use it. Clearly, not all software is of poor quality. For example, there are commercially available packages such as spreadsheets and database management systems, which work robustly. Educational uses of such packages can readily be found (e.g. Catterall and Lewis, 1985). So the problem is not simply one of poor software but is more deeply ingrained in teacher views of the appropriate use of CAI in education. The strongest version of this argument is that the technology has been absorbed into the social values of the educational system. That is to say that rather than the technology offering ways of bringing about qualitative improvements in the educational process, and therefore being the focus of intense activity by the educational community, one might argue the converse: namely, that the computer is seen to be a potential threat which should be rendered impotent by trivializing its uses in class. If this fate befalls competent and robust dumb software, which has relatively modest educational goals, and offers rather little in the way of 'threat' to teachers, what fate is likely to befall ICAI, with its promise to be more sophisticated than the teacher in several areas where professional pride is at stake?

2.5   CAN ICAI BE SEDITIOUS?

• ICAI can be seditious if expertise is taken from the hands of teachers and placed in the hands of machines. Teachers need to learn how to teach and need to extend their knowledge of their subject specialism, in just the same way that academic researchers spend their lives learning more and more about their own particular subject specialisms. Removing major vehicles for teacher self-education (such as debugging skills and remediation) can be seditious.

• ICAI can be seditious if it acts to devalue communication between human beings, such as discussions between pupils, and discussions between pupils and teachers. It will be seditious if it draws attention away from the importance of group work, the importance of explanation, the importance of open-ended investigation, the importance of problem-solving activities, and the importance of reflecting on one's own mental processes.

• ICAI can be seditious if it increases a view that academic subjects should be viewed as consisting of atoms of technique which are divorced from applications and from each other.

• ICAI can be seditious if it is offered as a panacea for the ills of education. Of course no member of the ICAI community would make such bold claims, but who needs to? – they have already been made by others. For example:

"Consider for a moment a computer system that stores the knowledge, judgement, and intuition of the country's best educational diagnosticians. From this system, the information can be called up at any time to assist you, step-by-step in the assessment of your students ... These programs are called *expert systems."* (Hasselbring, 1984).

"It is a simple step to turn an expert system into an excellent educational simulation; and, by combining the knowledge of all top experts, it becomes a superior instructional device." (Foster, 1984).

• ICAI can be seditious if it supports the view that there is a quick technological fix for every conceptual problem. At present we live in a society which seems to believe that technological answers can be found to conceptual problems. In the domain of international relations we see Star Wars as being offered as a 'solution' to the problems of international diplomacy. Safe generation of nuclear power is simply a question of developing good technology, and so on.

• ICAI can be seditious if the links between artificial intelligence and cognitive psychology lead us to devalue aspects such as open-ended problem solving, creative writing, musical composition, just because they are hard to describe within existing intellectual paradigms.

• ICAI can be seditious if it is associated with anthropomorphism. Imbueing machines with 'intelligence' and discussions about what the machine might be 'thinking about' are associated with risks that we devalue biological intelligence, thinking, feeling, and the like. This is not a necessary consequence of the development of ICAI systems, as Boden (1977) has illustrated; nevertheless, we should be aware of the potential risks. If people are like computers and computers are machines like motor cars and motor cars get old and are scrapped when they cease to function efficiently, then ...

2.6 SUGGESTION: TRANSPARENT ICAI SYSTEMS

The overriding concern that has been expressed in this chapter is that the intelligence in ICAI is being used for the wrong purpose. There is little need for intelligent machines whose purpose is to tutor technique; rather, pupils and teachers need to be made more aware of epistemological issues, and to reflect on their own knowledge, and ways of acquiring knowledge. ICAI systems may well have a valuable role to play here.

ICAI systems usually possess, either explicitly or implicitly:

• A specification of the knowledge to be acquired (with some implicit epistemology);
• A set of teaching techniques (with some implicit theory of teaching);
• Rules to structure teaching sequences (with some implicit pedagogy);
• Descriptions of possible user states (with some implicit development theory);
• Beliefs about the current state of the user.

Users could be given access to some, or all, of this information. Of course, some information may be represented internally in ways which are quite opaque to the user, e.g. as tables of conditional probabilities, or as groups of production rules (and possible mal-rules). However, re-describing these states in ways intelligible to the user may have considerable advantages. In particular, if users are allowed to explore the knowledge domain in any way they choose (including being guided by the machine) then the teaching system might be able to offer differential support for users with different learning styles, such as Pask's (1976) wholists and serialists. Examining knowledge structures to be acquired before learning begins might offer benefits claimed by Ausubel (1968) for advance organizers. At a higher level of abstraction, one might expect some benefits to accrue simply by engaging in these metacognitive acts. Reflecting on the different ways in which knowledge can be represented, one's own preferred learning styles, devices to overcome misconceptions, and the like, is likely to have benefits outside the immediate learning environment, and will, we hope, transfer to other learning contexts. One might argue that these sorts of activities (exploring knowledge representations, teaching styles, user models, implicit philosophies) would be most beneficial to users who already possess a good deal of knowledge about the specific domain of interest. So transparent ICAI (TICAI) systems might have a useful role to play in fostering meta-cognitive skills, irrespective of their virtues as tutors within specific knowledge domains.

Making ICAI systems transparent to users is also likely to de-mystify their operation. Most systems have remarkably impoverished epistemologies and pedagogies, which users should be made aware of.

Offering the user a view from the machine about the user's state of knowledge may well have dramatic outcomes – either in terms of user outrage and rejection of the tutoring system, or perhaps as a stimulus for the user to update the machine model directly (either by demonstrations of competence in terms which the machine can recognize, or via statements of knowledge) or perhaps as a challenge to the user which increases motivation, then learning, dramatically.

How do TICAI systems relate to currently conceived ICAI systems? Surely, a competent ICAI system must precede the development of a transparent one? For most of the purposes here (notably ones concerned with fostering meta-cognition), TICAI systems need not function particularly well, since the user's task is to use the TICAI system to think about knowledge representation and acquisition – so impoverished systems will be quite adequate. For ICAI to work well, all the conceptual and practical problems described earlier need to be resolved. So the development effort needed for TICAI may well be less than that for functioning ICAI.

TICAI systems also have a role to play in teacher education. The ideas which underpin many ICAI programs – namely, that user models need to be under-stood, that one needs a clear story about the nature of the knowledge to be acquired, that a story about a logical sequence of knowledge acquisition should be developed, that misconceptions need to be explored, unravelled, diagnosed, and remediated, are all viewpoints which can cause teachers to reflect upon their own teaching practices. Their own analyses of conceptions and misconceptions might usefully be compared with those of the machine. Any device which causes one to reflect on one's current practices and actions is likely to be beneficial. While ICAI seems an extraordinarily expensive way of fostering teacher reflection, it may nevertheless prove to be an effective one. Offering TICAI systems may also help to diffuse teacher anxieties about the role of computers in education, when they see the rather impoverished set of constructs which are available to machines, compared to constructs which they possess, and which their pupils can readily be brought to possess.

3

The role of qualitative models in instruction*

WILLIAM J. CLANCEY
Stanford Knowledge Systems Laboratory, California, USA

This chapter broadly describes the kinds of models in an instructional program and introduces the following concepts: general model, situation-specific model, inference procedure, diagnosis, and bug. This framework is then applied to classify student modelling programs.

3.1 WHAT ARE QUALITATIVE MODELS?

It is easy to get bogged down in philosophical questions about the nature of models and theories. Terms like 'explain' and 'cause' have been the subject of much philosophical debate (e.g. Von Wright, 1971; Achinstein, 1983). In this review, I adopt some informal definitions and show how they are useful for describing what programs do.

A *model* is a representation, for some purpose, of some object or process (Webster, 1983; Goldstein and Goldstein, 1980). Scientists and engineers are familiar with the idea of numeric or *quantitative models*, such as Ohm's laws of electricity, economic models, mechanical engineering models of the stress behaviour of materials, predator–prey population correlations, and so on. Also, everyone is familiar with physical models, such as scale models of buildings used by an architect or plastic models of airplanes. *Qualitative models*, broadly put, are not numeric and not physical analogues; rather, they *describe* objects and processes in terms of spatial, temporal, and causal relations. Qualitative models may be written down in some notation (a *reasoning calculus* (de Kleer and Brown, 1984; Sowa, 1984)), believed by a person (a kind of *mental model*), or realized as a computer program (a kind of *computational model*).

Figure 3.1 classifies models according to *locus*, or where each exists. Student models, such as a model of how a student diagnoses a patient, may exist as

*Reproduced with permission from *Ann. Rev. Comp. Sci.*, **1**. © 1986 Annual Review Inc. The present chapter is a slightly modified subset of a comprehensive technical review of qualitative student models.

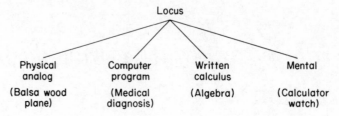

Fig. 3.1. Where models can exist.

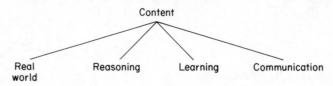

Fig. 3.2. Processes modelled separately in studying instruction.

computer programs. A student's model of the patient and how to do diagnosis is called a mental model; it exists in his mind. As a familiar example of a mental model, consider your understanding of what the buttons on a calculator watch do and your understanding of the procedure for setting the alarm (Young, 1983). This model is not written down, it is 'carried around in your head'.

A computer program may be either quantitative, involving precise numeric calculation, or qualitative, characterizing trends and causal relationships. We are concerned here with methods for representing qualitative models in computer programs. More specifically, we are interested in modelling *processes*, not static objects. Kinds of processes that are studied and formalized separately in order to construct instructional programs are shown in Fig. 3.2. These include processes in the world, reasoning, learning, and communication. While learning may be construed as a form of reasoning, it is usually treated separately.

3.2 SITUATION-SPECIFIC MODELS

A *situation-specific model* is a description of some situation in the world, generally an explanation of how a situation came about or a plan for action. For example, in medicine, a situation-specific model describes a patient's current state (e.g. fever, inflammation) and the disease processes that brought this state about (e.g. a particular infection). In general, the process of solving a specific problem can be described in terms of forming a *situation-specific* model (Fig. 3.3).

In this view of problem solving, a general model is related to the current situation by applying an *inference procedure*. The general model describes what is known about the world, for example, knowledge about stereotypic patients, diseases, and treatment plans. In some areas of AI, the term *domain model* refers to

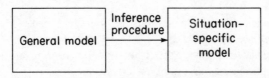

Fig. 3.3. Applying a general model to form a situation-specific model.

General model	Inference procedure	Program names	Reference
Math table	Subtraction procedure	BUGGY ACM	(Burton, 1982) (Langley *et al.*, 1984)
Geometry axioms	Rules of inference and proof procedure	GEOMETRY	(Anderson, Boyle and Yost, 1985)
Algebra axioms	Simplification procedure	PIXIE	(Sleeman, 1984a)
MACSYMA commands	Programming procedure	MACSYMA ADVISOR	(Genesereth, 1982)
Pascal programming language	Programming procedure	MENO PROUST	(Soloway *et al.*, 1981) (Johnson and Soloway. 1984b)
Electronic circuit theory and model of given circuit	Circuit diagnosis procedure	SOPHIE	(Brown *et al.*, 1982)
Game rules and rules of probability	Game playing strategy	WEST WUSOR	(Burton and Brown, 1982) (Goldstein, 1982)
Physics of pressure/temper-ature and meterological patterns	Qualitative causal reasoning	METEOROLOGY WHY	(Brown *et al.*, 1973 (Stevens and Collins, 1977)
Physiology, anatomy, disease processes	Medical diagnostic strategy	MEOMYCIN	(Clancey and Letsinger, 1984)

Fig. 3.4. General model and interface procedure for different problem domains.

the general model; sometimes it refers to the combined general model and inference procedure.

The inference procedure is a program that focuses and orders gathering of problem information and making assertions about the solution. For example, in medicine, the inference procedure is generally called a 'diagnostic strategy'; it is a procedure for gathering information about a patient and focusing on and testing disease hypotheses. Figure 3.4 gives common names for the general model and inference procedure in different domains*. The situation-specific model includes the specific problem information, transformed or reorganized in some way, depending on the nature of the task. For example, in diagnosis, the situation-specific model relates the symptoms to a description of processes that produced these symptoms. In medicine, this is called a patient-specific model (Patil, 1981) (Fig. 3.5). In geometry, the situation-specific model is the proof of the theorem, shown as a network (Anderson, Boyle and Yost, 1985) (Fig. 3.6). In programming, the situation-specific model is the constructed program, as well as unwritten descriptions of the underlying design, relating the code to the goals the program is supposed to satisfy. In subtraction, the situation-specific model is commonly written on paper, with borrowing between columns indicated by scratch marks, and the solution written below a horizontal line.

In a certain sense, the situation-specific model 'copies over' part of the general model, though the form varies across domains and tasks. For example, programming language constructs appear instantiated as particular statements in a program. In subtraction, the general fact that 5 minus 3 equals 2 appears in the situation-specific model for solving 452 minus 230. Similarly, geometry axioms and theorems appear in the proof. A medical diagnosis will mention general concepts and their relations, such as the link between infection and meningitis shown in Fig. 3.5.

A related, but different, idea is the *derivation trace* by which the problem was solved (VanLehn and Brown, 1980). This shows how the situation-specific model is modified over time, as particular inferences are made. For example, in algebra this is the familiar sequence of transformations of an equation in the course of solving for a particular variable. Similarly, a geometry proof, diagnostic explanation, or computer program can be written as a sequence of transformations.

Figure 3.7 shows three kinds of models integrated into an idealized instructional program: a. the model of problem solving to be taught (commonly called the *subject material*, now often called the target model, idealized model or expert model), b. the constructed model of the student's problem solving (student model), and c. the model of communication for interacting with a student to probe

*The term 'inference engine' (Davis, 1986) often refers to a simple rule interpreter, in which case the 'knowledge base' that it interprets is a program that combines the domain model and inference procedure. This is the relation between MYCIN's rules and rule interpreter. The trend is to identify the domain model with the knowledge base and to view the inference procedure as something much more complicated than a rule interpreter.

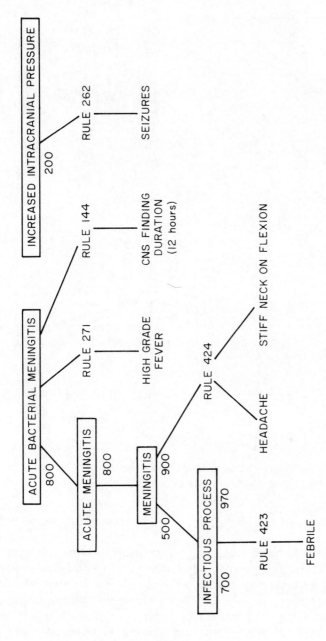

Fig. 3.5. Written notation for partial situation-specific model in medical diagnosis (from Clancey, 1986b).

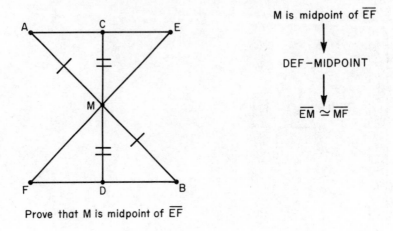

Prove that M is midpoint of $\overline{EF}$

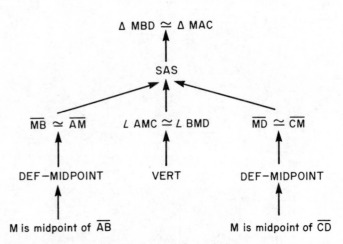

Fig. 3.6. Written notation for partial situation-specific model in geometry theorem proving (from Anderson, Boyle and Reiser, 1985).

his understanding and to explain or teach the target model (teaching or tutoring procedure).

Each of the models shown in Fig. 3.7 has a general and situation-specific form. For example, there is a general model of how to communicate (discourse processes) and a situation-specific model of the current dialogue. The general model describes what typically occurs during a teaching dialogue, how to detect these situations, what to do when they occur, what transitions are likely or advisable, and so on. Examples of communication processes are interrupting, assisting, orienting, explaining, evaluating, hypothesizing, probing, summarizing, and so on. In an interaction between student and teacher, both parties are using such a model to interpret and respond to each other's goals (Appelt, 1982).

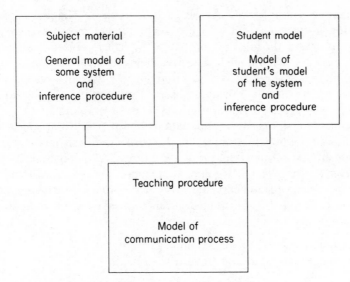

Fig. 3.7. Three kinds of model in an instructional program.

For example, a teacher must recognize when the student is confused about what to do (perhaps because he says so) and respond appropriately.

An inference procedure, a program, 'reads' the general communication model to produce a state description of the current dialogue: what has been discussed with the student, what the teacher and student are currently doing, what the student is trying to understand now, etc. Given this situation-specific model, the program will further interpret the general model to decide among alternative communication processes that achieve instructional goals.

Similarly, the general model to be taught is paired with a situation-specific description of the problem now being worked on, such as a partial diagnosis of an electronic circuit. The basic job of the inference procedure is to gain additional information and make connections from the general model that improve the situation-specific model, making it coherent, consistent, and specific enough for its purpose. The student model has the same components: a general model of the subject matter, an inference procedure, and a situation-specific model describing the problem being solved. (While a recursion of models can be imagined, including the participants' models of each other's models, this level of complexity is not considered in today's instructional programs.)

3.3   SIMULATION OR EXECUTABLE MODELS

In summary, problem solving, described at a high level, involves both a general model and some inference procedure. Together, they constitute a *simulation model of reasoning*. When the agent is a person, a simulation model of reasoning is often called a *cognitive model*. It is a simulation model because it can be used to simulate the reasoning process, to solve actual problems. That is, it doesn't just describe intelligence in a static way by traits or numeric measures of aptitude. It includes a program, the inference procedure, by which problems can be solved.

The inclusion of a simulation model of reasoning in an instructional program is of significant practical benefit. It means that the program can solve the problems that it gives to the student, providing a basis for interpreting his problem-solving behaviour, evaluating his partial solutions, and assisting him.

The student model is also a simulation model, paralleling the program's domain model and inference procedure. It doesn't just describe the probability that a student will do something or not, but describes the process over time by which he gathers problem information and makes assertions. If we think about the student as some phenomenon in the world that the instructional program is trying to understand, the student model bears the same relation to the student as the general model to be taught bears to the world:

general model : : real world system (e.g. the patient)
student model : : cognitive system (the student)

The primary characteristic of a simulation model is that it can be used to predict subsequent behaviour of the system being modelled. For example, a simulation of an electronic circuit can predict the internal states of its various components, as well as the behaviour of its output ports, such as voltage.

A simulation model of a student predicts what he will do next. More importantly, it can be used to work backwards from student behaviour to explain the basis of his behaviour, that is, to infer his general model and inference procedure. To highlight the contrast with a static description of the student's knowledge, interests, or preferences, a simulation student model is often called an *executable model*. The term is also used to describe simulation models of physical systems, such as an electronic circuit.

A *classification* model is an example of a qualitative model that is not a simulation model. For example, a classification model of diseases might only account for pain and other symptoms in a superficial way and might not explain in much detail how the symptoms occur. We can also use classification models to describe students and account for their reasoning. However, a simulation model allows us to construct an explanatory accounting that is *complete* on at least some level of detail and that relates behaviour to the many specific facts in the student's domain model. Inferring errors from a constructed simulation of reasoning is also more *efficient* than pre-enumerating them in a classification.

3.4 REPRESENTATION REQUIREMENTS

The clean separation between the general and the situation-specific model, and subsequent identification of the inference procedure, is an ideal that is not always explicit in computer programs. The advantages of separability and further constraints imposed by instruction are considered here.

3.4.1 The articulate expert

From early on, researchers realized that instructional programs cannot be constructed on top of arbitrary problem-solving programs (Self, 1974; Brown, Collins and Harris, 1977; Brown, 1977). Expressing knowledge in a simple, uniform language facilitates its multiple use for generating questions, evaluating partially correct responses, and responding to student questions. This is one advantage of the semantic network in SCHOLAR (Carbonell, 1970) and the rule base of MYCIN used in GUIDON (Clancey, 1979a). Moreover, if the network can be interpreted to solve problems, it can be used both to evaluate a student's problem solving and to provide assistance. Brown characterized this kind of problem-solving program, which could provide the basis for evaluation and explanation, as *an articulate expert*. Such a program has also been called a *glass-box expert* because its reasoning is inspectable by students or other programs (Goldstein and Papert, 1977). With further experience, we can be more precise today.

First, it must be clear from the encoding how problem information is being used to make situation-specific assertions, what the program's goals are, and how they relate to sub-goals. It is precisely these characteristics that can be made evident in a production rule language and that were used to good effect in GUIDON, WUSOR, and more recently in the LISP and GEOMETRY tutors. Compared to an arbitrary computer program, the data, conclusions, and goals of these programs are well indexed. Put in a simple way, variables have a consistent meaning, corresponding to entities in the world, and there are no implicit side-effects.

Second, it is advantageous for the domain-specific qualitative model (the general model) to be separated from the inference procedure. This enables an explanation program to articulate the problem-solving strategy and domain model separately, and provides the basis for reconstructing a student's domain model.

Third, after separating the domain model and inference procedure, for further explanation and student modelling capabilities, it is useful to represent a. why the domain model is believed, and b. what efficiency considerations, assumptions about data-gathering, memory, and problem situations lie behind the design of the inference procedure. Both questions focus on the *origin* of knowledge and reasoning and ask about support for beliefs and constraints that are satisfied by the inference procedure.

3.4.2 Beyond today's expert systems

Many readers of this review are familiar with the idea of an *expert system*, a computer program for reasoning about complex tasks such as system design, assembly, diagnosis and control (Hayes-Roth *et al.*, 1983). These programs use qualitative models for representing world knowledge and the inference procedure, with varying degrees of separation and generality of these components.

What requirements does teaching place on a model of problem solving, beyond that it must adequately solve problems? These requirements are reconsidered in the concluding section.

- Problem solving: Solve problems in multiple ways that allow syntactic variations in situation-specific models. Cope with, and to some degree explain, discrepant behaviour. The program cannot be an arbitrary model of intelligence; it must reflect human ways of thinking. Unlike other areas of AI, instructional research is unabashedly psychological.
- Explanation: Go beyond 'audit trail' statements of how the problem is solved. Articulate the general and specific model, why both are believed, and relate them to the student's models and underlying beliefs. Address the listener's expectations, persuade him to modify his model, and help him debug it. In particular, evaluate the student's explanations of how he solves a problem. Again, the research emphasizes that explanation is an act of teaching. Explanation is not just saying what you did when you solved a problem but also relating it to what the listener expected you to do and what he would have done himself.
- Learning: Explain a student's beliefs in terms of how he learned from experience ('developmental epistemology' (Piaget, 1971; Goldstein, 1982)) and predict what he is ready to learn next. Again, this is not arbitrary 'machine learning'; it must be psychological, a model of *how people learn*.

Summarizing broadly, instruction requires being able to *use models in multiple ways* – in solving problems, in explaining, and in learning from experience. Early research indicated that using knowledge in multiple ways is benefited by *meta-knowledge*: knowledge of the extent of what the program knows, its inference methods, representation, and reasons for failure (Davis *et al.*, 1982; Barr, 1979; Barr *et al.*, 1979; Schank, 1981; Kolodner, 1982; Kolodner and Simpson, 1984). This again motivates the separation of the general model and inference procedure. The instructional program must not only be able to say *what it did*, but ideally, should be able to reflect on the regularities in its behaviour, articulate them, reason about their validity, and determine what alternatives are possible.

A complicating factor is that human learning involves not just incorporating new facts but becoming more efficient and faster through practice (Anderson *et al.*, 1981; Laird *et al.*, 1984). Some researchers believe that experts lose meta-knowledge as they gain the ability to solve problems automatically, without conscious thought. In this respect, expert systems often reflect the expert's automatic way of thinking, without the articulation and abstraction (separation of model and inference procedure and attendant generality) useful for teaching. This makes it more difficult to construct instructional programs with the capabilities listed above.

Models of problem solving useful for teaching are thus inherently *empirical* (they must relate to what students do) and *open* (they must account for original, unexpected student behaviour). Recognizing and evaluating alternative models requires that knowledge be expressed at a high level of abstraction, as general theories, in sharp contrast with specially-engineered programs.

We start with the premise that students will have some means, perhaps incomplete, of solving problems. Forming a model of the student means learning about his general model and inference procedure. The variance in student behaviour from the ideal, and the extent to which a program can learn a model different from its own ideal model, crucially determine the extent to which the program can understand the student's behaviour and adapt its instruction to his approach. AI representations such as semantic networks and production rules generally offer the kind of indexing that enables a program to adapt to a student's order of inferences for solving a problem. For example, each relation between a symptom and diagnosis might be represented as a single production rule in the general model. Thus, regardless of the order in which the student gains information about the problem, the program can predict what he knows by applying the production rules.

However, to recognize a *different inference procedure* (the strategy that determines the order in which inferences are made) requires that the procedure be represented separately in what is called a *functional model*. While expert systems generally encode knowledge to fit the 'indexing' criteria, very few separate out the inference procedure or encode it so that it can be reasoned about by a modelling program. That is, most of today's expert systems could not be used as a representation of subject matter to provide the modelling assessments discussed in Section 3.6.

Of course, we might take an even broader view of the modelling problem. Insofar as we expect our students to perform and learn in ways that we cannot mimic on a computer today, the instructional program must have some way of articulating its limits and the assumptions upon which it is based, thus enabling students to relate its embedded theory to the larger world (Winograd and Flores, 1985; Suchman, 1985).

3.4.3 Qualitative reasoning

The representation of qualitative models is a burgeoning topic in artificial intelligence today (Bobrow, 1984); this review can only provide a very high-level introduction. The term *qualitative reasoning* is usually associated with simulation models. However, in this review, I adopt the view that most of AI is concerned with the representation of qualitative models. In stating this pattern, I am drawing different distinctions than appear in the literature of the 1970s.

• In the literature, a distinction is not generally drawn between the programming language, the inference process, and the general model. A paradigmatic example is describing MYCIN in terms of goals and chaining through rules (Davis, Buchanan and Shortliffe, 1977). This abstract description was very valuable for defining a new method of computer programming for implementing expert systems. However, in describing MYCIN as a model, we move up to the 'knowledge level' (Newell, 1982) and describe its diagnostic inference procedure and the classification of diseases embedded in the rules.

• The term 'qualitative model' has been restrictively applied to simulation models of processes based on a description of functional components (Bobrow, 1984). Other models of processes are given domain-specific names (such as 'nosology' in medicine) or are described only in terms of general constructs used to represent many different kinds of concepts (such as 'script' (Schank and Abelson, 1975) or 'state-transition network' (Brown *et al.*, 1973; Stevens *et al.*, 1982)). Classification and behavioural models of processes are not an inferior version of functional descriptions. They properly represent a certain form of knowledge that is common in domains such as medicine and everyday reasoning (Norman *et al.*, 1976). While this knowledge may not provide the same level of explanatory detail as a simulation model, it still *functions as a model* by enabling useful predictions and explanatory accounting. It is now generally believed that this is the form of expertise associated with quick, routine problem solving (e.g. see Feltovich *et al.*, 1984). Indeed, this is the kind of model described by Minsky in his frame theory (Minsky, 1975).

By separately identifying the model and the inference procedure in a knowledge base, it becomes clear that there are several kinds of qualitative models. It is convenient to call them all qualitative models because, first, they are all non-numeric, and, second, they are models describing situations in the world, so they can be recognized and acted upon.

3.5 USE OF MODELS: THE CENTRAL ROLE OF DIAGNOSIS

Diagnosis plays a special role in instructional programs. First, it is a common problem-solving task that we attempt to teach, e.g. debugging computer programs and diagnosing patients or circuits or equipment. More significantly, diagnosis plays a central role in teaching itself. An analogy can be drawn with the process of monitoring the behaviour of a physical system (such as an automobile engine), looking for discrepancies from an ideal specification, tracking discrepancies back to structural faults or misadjustments, and repairing by changing the device. In instruction, we monitor the behaviour of the student (a cognitive system), look for discrepancies from the ideal specification (target problem-solving model), track discrepancies back to faults in the student's presumed world model or inference procedure, and 'repair' the student by instruction. This process of causally tracking backwards from discrepant reasoning behaviour to hidden faults in a cognitive system is called *diagnostic modelling*.

Note that there are several levels of causal description: the discrepant behaviour, the system fault or malfunction (called a *bug*), and the explanation of how this bug came about. For example, in a computer program, we distinguish between: the incorrect output (what the program did wrong), the bug in the code (what statements are missing or incorrect), and the explanation for this bug (why the programmer did not use the correct code). In medicine, we distinguish between: a behavioural symptom such as a headache, the disease (or bug) in the body, and how this person happened to have this disease (e.g. why the immuno-response system failed to function to prevent the disease). In computer system diagnosis, we distinguish between: a system crash and the underlying cause of the problem (e.g. a queue that exceeded its resources caused by a stuck I/O controller) and the environmental problem (e.g. heat) or design flaw, etc., that brought about this situation. At each point we proceed from *system behaviour* to a mechanistic explanation of *how the system produced the behaviour* (bugs) to *causes outside the system* affecting system input or internal structure.

3.5.1 Bugs

Figure 3.8 summarizes the different levels of analysis involved in cognitive modelling, with an example from computer programming to make it concrete. The number of sources of error is somewhat surprising when it is laid out this way.

In general, a bug is some structural flaw (faulty part) manifested in faulty behaviour (a process). Thus, the term 'bug' is used to refer to the incorrect part of a constructed procedure (e.g. incorrect statement in a computer program). It also refers to an incorrect inference procedure (e.g. error in student's subtraction procedure) and, by extension, an error in the student's general model (e.g. believing that $9 - 4 = 6$). An incorrect general model is commonly called a 'misconception' (such as a misconception about the cause of a disease). Errors can be combined, because an incorrect computer program may involve a combination of a misconception about the operators of the computer language and an error in the inference procedure by which the student has pieced together these operators to accomplish some goal (i.e. how he writes a program).

Note that Fig. 3.8 expands the definition of an inference procedure given earlier. It shows that the inference procedure controls interaction with the outside world (e.g. to make observations or write things down). The inference procedure also applies general knowledge to the problem at hand. Parts of the general model applied to the current problem might be inferred, rather than explicitly stored. For example, a programmer might infer that an 'integer statement' should be placed at the start of a program because that is where 'declarations' are placed. Thus, specific facts are inferred from properties of classes. The figure also indicates that part of the general model may have been learned through processes such as analogy with other models (Matz, 1982; Gentner and Stevens, 1983). For example, knowledge about programming languages in general might be applied to form a model of a particular language (Johnson and Soloway, 1984b). Whether this occurs during problem solving or as part of the initial learning, and to what extent this background knowledge consists of unformalized 'raw experiences' (Winograd and Flores, 1985) are perhaps relevant considerations, but they have not played a part in student modelling research in AI.

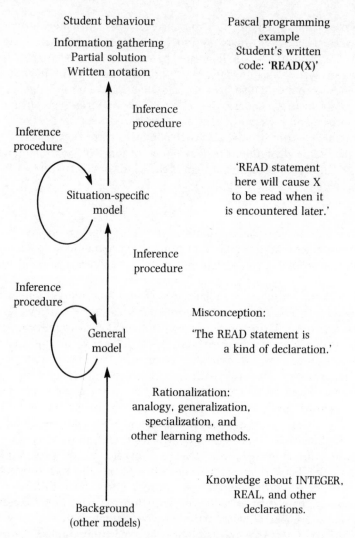

Fig. 3.8. Levels of analysis in cognitive modelling (example from Soloway *et al.*, 1982).

3.5.2   The origins of bugs

The instructional programs we are studying are particularly fascinating because of the researchers' attempts to understand the origins of bugs. This interest stems from several goals. First, if a program is constructed with a pre-enumerated set of bugs, not all students may fit the program's fixed models. A more capable program would attempt to *generate* a description of bugs from patterns in a particular student's behaviour and a model of how bugs come about, called a *generative theory of bugs.* Second, there may be too many possible bugs to practically pre-enumerate. For example, the possible misconceptions in medical reasoning are countless. A generative theory makes it possible to more efficiently engineer an adaptive program. Third, as part of the science of instruction, researchers want to understand the origin of bugs so they can more appropriately design instructional sequences, to possibly prevent bugs from forming or perhaps to catch them before they become ingrained.

The prevalent model, holding strong sway in the community, is that reasoning is not random, there is some causal explanation for every error. These explanations fall into three categories:

1. *Mis-learning.* The student's model of the world, his believed situation-specific information, or inference procedure is incorrect because of a learning error: a faulty textbook, an over-generalization, a false analogy, etc (Matz, 1982; Sleeman, 1984b).
2. *Construction.* The student's model and inference procedure did not allow complete solution of a problem. According to *repair theory*, weak problem-solving methods allow resolution of an impasse; the core deficiency is manifested by different constructed bugs, according to the context. Bugs may 'migrate' and not be explainable by the student (Brown and VanLehn, (1980).
3. *Slip.* The student knows better, he just didn't perform properly. Slips are caused by fatigue, emotional problems, conflict in memory, 'cognitive overload', reverting to a previous error, or even unarticulated wishes. (Freud, 1965; Norman, 1979; Matz, 1982).

Understanding the origin of bugs can be equated to articulating a 'deep structure' that accounts for implicit regularities in reasoning (Brown, Collins and Harris, 1977). Notice that models of physical systems have a deep structure, too. So this idea of detecting regularities and giving a causal accounting plays a role in both *first-order modelling* (e.g. medical diagnosis) and the *second-order modelling* of cognitive diagnosis, modelling problem-solving itself. This commonality is fortunate, for it provides us with even more examples to study: a better understanding of cognitive diagnosis models in instructional programs helps us to understand diagnostic models in expert systems and *vice versa.*

A cognitive diagnosis drives the instructional program's explanations and selection of new examples and problems. However, we do not understand the 'repair process' (Brown and VanLehn, 1980) that is going on in the student's mind (a mechanistic account of how a misconception or gap leads the student to revise his model). Consequently, it is unclear just how good a cognitive model must be for instruction to be effective. To some extent, the research of the past decade constitutes a scientific foundation that we will adopt in the future to construct pragmatic instructional programs, perhaps with less complex cognitive model-ling capabilities than our theories allow (Rouse and Morris, 1985; Wenger, 1986).

3.6 STUDENT MODEL ASSESSMENTS

The simplest kind of assessments classify the student in terms of behaviour, preferences, or background. Such a *stereotype user-model* (Rich, 1979b) is useful for 'priming' the modelling process when there is no prior experience on which to base expectations (Carr and Goldstein, 1977; Clancey, 1983b). Beyond this, what do existing programs learn about students as a result of watching them solve problems and evaluating their performance? What can these programs infer about a student? Recalling the distinction between a general (domain) model and a situation-specific model (Section 3.2) and the relation between the ideal model, bugs and underlying misconceptions (Section 3.5.1), a logical spectrum of interpretations can be laid out and illustrated by existing programs (summarized in Fig. 3.9).

1. Determine whether statements about the problem to be solved and the general model are correct.

	Assessment	Associated terms	Example programs
1.	Statements about general model	Quiz Question-answer	SCHOLAR
2.	Consistent situation-specific model	Hypothesis evaluation	SOPHIE
3.	General model and problem information used to form partial solution	Overlay or differential model	GUIDON WEST
4.	General model	Errors called misconceptions	WHY MACSYMA ADVISOR PROUST
5.	Inference procedure	Errors called mal-rules or bugs	BUGGY DEBUGGY PIXIE ACM
6.	Origin of inference procedure	Model of learning	SIERRA

Fig. 3.9. Assessments and associated terms for well-known modelling programs (numbers correspond to the discussion in Section 3.6).

a. Determine whether a student's statements about the problem are correct.
  - Example: In GUIDON, a student supports a medical diagnosis by listing facts about the current patient. The program indicates if the facts are correct before evaluating the hypothesis or its justification.
b. Determine whether a student's statements about the general model are correct.
  - Example: In SCHOLAR, a student is quizzed about geographic and demographic facts. The program indicates if his answers are correct by examining a semantic net.
  - Example: In WHY, a student is quizzed about the necessary and sufficient causes of heavy rainfall (e.g. 'Do you believe that every place with mountains has heavy rainfall?'). The program indicates if his model is correct.
  - Example: In GUIDON, when a student justifies a hypothesis by saying that a particular symptom is evidence for a particular disease, the program indicates whether this is part of the general model.

2. Determine whether a student's solution (situation-specific model) is consistent with the general model and the situation-specific information he has received.
  - Example: In SOPHIE, a student's hypothesis about a possible circuit fault is evaluated with respect to the measurements (voltage, etc.) he has taken. His hypothesis may not be the actual fault known to be present, but it may be consistent with the available information and the general model of how the circuit components interact. An error here could be caused by a faulty inference procedure (not taking available information into account) or by a faulty general model (interpreting information inappropriately).
  - Example: In GUIDON, a student's hypothesis about the possible presence of a disease is evaluated with respect to the symptoms he knows about. Treating the symptoms independently, the program determines if they are consistent with his disease hypothesis, even if this is not the diagnosis that could be deduced from further information.

3. Determine what knowledge (domain model and inference procedure) the student has used to form a partial solution (make a hypothesis). Generally reformulated as, What aspects of the program's general model are consistent with the student's partial solution?
  - Example: In WHY, a student's prediction about heavy rainfall occurring in a particular location (e.g. 'Southern California has heavy rainfall') is related to the general model. One can then determine whether the student has considered a necessary factor (presence of mountains), but believes that it is sufficient or whether he has omitted another necessary factor (e.g. presence of moisture-bearing air mass).
  - Example: In GUIDON, a student's diagnosis is related to the general model, producing a list of symptoms (or combinations of symptoms) that are consistent with the diagnosis.

- Example: In WEST, the program interprets a sequence of student moves in terms of the available operators, and determines which aspects of the general model (spinner combination operators) are consistent with the student's play. For example, the student may be avoiding certain operators (e.g. use of parentheses) whose use is consistent with the general model of winning the game, while his use of other operators (e.g. division) is consistent with the model of how the game should be played.

4. Determine which incorrect general model is consistent with the student's behaviour. This is often called a *student bug model*.
   - Example: In WHY, if the student incorrectly believes that heavy rainfall occurs in a particular place (making a false prediction), the program extracts a general rule of the form 'Known factor is a sufficient cause' (e.g. mountains are a sufficient cause of heavy rainfall). This general rule is then stated for the student to see if he believes it.
   - Example: In the MACSYMA Advisor, a student's sequence of Macsyma operators is related back to his goal to determine his beliefs about the prerequisites of these operators and what they produce as output. A consistent interpretation may involve positing a statement about an operator that is incorrect, a bug in the student's general model about Macsyma.

5. Determine what nonoptimal or incorrect inference procedure is consistent with the program's general model and the student's behaviour.
   - Example: In DEBUGGY, a student's subtraction solution is related to incorrect subprocedures (operators), such as an incorrect procedure for borrowing.
   - Example: In ODYSSEUS (Wilkins *et al.*, 1986), a student modelling program based on HERACLES (Clancey, 1985), the sequence of student requests for data is related to tasks for making a diagnosis; this allows detection of reordered and deleted conditional tasks in the ideal inference procedure.
   - Example: In WEST, a student uses mathematical operators to combine numbers on a spinner, thus determining how many spaces his player will advance on a game board. Assuming that the goal is to reach the final place on the board first, the program determines if the student's choice of operators is optimal, that is, consistent with the inference procedure dictated by the goal.

6. Determine what underlying misconceptions explain the student's incorrect general model or buggy inference procedure.
   - Example: In SIERRA (VanLehn, 1983b), *impasses* are generated from a subtraction procedure that is missing certain subprocedures. Inference procedure *bugs* are generated by weak problem-solving methods that *repair* the impasse, based on some assumptions about the correct *form* of a solution, such as putting a number in every column. Thus, imporper

behaviour is explained in terms of a missing part of the general model and a procedure for working around the gap.

- Example: In PROUST, programming errors (incorrect lines of code) are explained in terms of bugs in the general model (incorrect beliefs about what an operator (such as a READ statement) will do); these are in turn explained in terms of a mechanism, such as a false analogy (relating READ to an INTEGER declaration, and thus concluding that READ(x) is a general declaration about the variable x). Thus, improper behaviour is explained in terms of an incorrect general model and (informally, not by a simulation program) by a process for how this incorrect model may have been learned.

3.7 CONCLUSIONS

Surveying and evaluating a variety of existing instructional programs, I have stressed the following points in this review.

- AI programming methodology provides new means to model processes of physical systems, problem-solving procedures, how learning takes place, and methods and procedures for communication. In contrast with traditional CAI programs, these models are executable, so they can be used to solve the same problems presented to the student. They are also primarily qualitative and describe agents and processes by their causal, spatial, and temporal interaction. When subject matter is represented in this form, the internal model is called a 'glass-box' expert; it can both solve problems and be described in explanations by the teaching procedures.

- A general model can be separated from the inference procedure by which it is applied to specific problems. This is termed a *functional model*, in contrast with a *behavioural model*, which describes problem-solving behaviour in a situation-specific way. Functional models are represented in terms of hierarchical composition of functional operators and/or structural components. Behavioural models are expressed as links between system states in a causal-associational network.

- Both behavioural and functional models can be used to simulate physical and reasoning processes. However, a functional model characterizes purposes and goals abstracted from particular situations. For example, in a functional model of reasoning, these purposes are described in terms of general operators for manipulating a situation-specific model.

- A given functional model can be used in multiple ways. In an instructional program, this allows a single encoding of the general model to be interpreted for evaluating student performance, communicating with him, and modelling his learning behaviour. At the same time, this separation forces the problem-solving, communication, and learning models to be represented explicitly, in a well-structured way, enabling the formalized models to be properly communicated and shared in the scientific literature.

ACKNOWLEDGEMENTS

Research support has been provided in part by ONR Contract N00014-79C-0302 and the Josiah Macy Jr. Foundation (Grant B852005). Computational facilities have been provided by the SUMEX-AIM facility (NIH Grant RR00785).

4

Methods and mental models in theories of cognitive skill

STEPHEN J. PAYNE
University of Lancaster, England

This chapter critiques computational theories of cognitive skill acquisition according to the needs of student modelling. It is argued that current computational accounts which treat skill as a collection of problem-solving methods need to be elaborated with appropriate representations of conceptual knowledge. The idea of a mental model is advanced as a candidate construct to meet this need. Unfortunately, current knowledge of the nature and role of mental models is limited, and in particular their relationship with procedural skills is largely unexplored. The final section of the chapter addresses this problem, sketching a theoretical framework in which methods and mental models can be knitted together to account for the acquisition of cognitive skill. The framework is developed through consideration of an aspect of computer use, and then briefly applied to the very different domain of multi-column subtraction.

4.1 INTRODUCTION

It is now widely accepted that intelligent adaptive tutoring requires some dynamic representation of the current state of knowledge of the individual student. This individual student model must be generated from (or at least implicitly based upon) a theory of cognitive skill and its acquisition*: a theory which determines how knowledge in the target domain is represented, at various levels of expertise; and how it changes from one level to another, under what conditions.

---

*The term 'cognitive skill' is used in the psychological literature to denote skill in a loose confederation of complex domains, including physics, computer programming, mathematics and chess. The terminology is a little misleading: there is no intent to imply that all other skills are non-cognitive. Perhaps a more accurate if clumsy expression would be 'still-being-learned skills'. This usage suggests that 'lower-level' skills like word recognition or so called perceptual-motor skills may employ related cognitive constructs but are, in adults, at a much more developed stage than skills like computer programming ever reach. In any case, the extent to which theories of learning in one domain will apply to disparate domains is still an open question.

Of course, student modellers are not the only seekers after such a theory. For example, a direct counterpart to student modelling exists in the design of user interfaces to interactive systems, where it goes by the name of 'user modelling'. More broadly, a cognitive theory of learning is one of psychology's current holy grails, and 'machine learning' is a growing sub-discipline of artificial intelligence (Michalski, Carbonell and Mitchell, 1983).

As ever, there is no easy separation of pure from applied among these concerns. Questions raised by the problems of student – and user – modelling have forced theoretical developments in the psychology of cognitive skill, and in the development of techniques for machine learning. In this chapter I try to reflect this synergy by focusing on the theory of cognitive skill acquisition but keeping in mind the applied goals of student modelling.

I begin by overviewing current computational accounts of cognitive skill acquisition, feeding off some of the interplay between disciplines that has fostered progress in this area. I will argue that two central insights on the nature of cognitive skill acquisition – the development of pre-compiled *methods*, and the elaboration of explanatory *mental models* – are currently artificially fragmented into separate accounts of separate phenomena. The final section of the chapter offers a sketch of cognitive skill acquisition which attempts to weave the two strands together.

4.2 COMPUTATIONAL ACCOUNTS OF COGNITIVE SKILL ACQUISITION: SKILL AS METHOD

"What distinguishes cognitive skill from problem solving is the packaging of operator sequences into integrated methods." (Card, Moran and Newell, 1983, p 367.)

The most successful computational models of cognitive skill acquisition have viewed skill as the development of schematic *methods* for the accomplishment of tasks. These skill-as-method theories are a major contribution to the psychology of skill, and offer a strong basis for dynamic student modelling. The theories all share the following fundamental ideas:

- Procedural skills can be represented by production systems.
- Learning can be modelled by the transition from weak search to heuristic search, implemented in mechanisms which mutate general-purpose productions to specific productions which encode knowledge of the domain in their conditions and actions.
- The control of heuristic search can mimic expert planning strategies (methods) by referring to goals and subgoals in the conditions and actions of productions, and using a goal stack to provide hierarchical control flow.
- The methods, once learned, can be improved (made faster and more efficient) through various production-mutating mechanisms, thus modelling practice effects.

This is not the place for a full tutorial review of theories in this paradigm. I will limit my overview of skill-as-method accounts to brief elaborations of the central ideas listed above, referring on the way to some of the individual theories that exemplify the approach.

4.2.1 Production systems

The production system representations that Newell and Simon (1972) popular-ized as psychological tools remain the orthodox if not the universal represen-tation for procedural knowledge. The computational skill-learning theories of Larkin (1981), Anderson (1975, 1983), Langley (1983), Laird, Rosenbloom and Newell (1986), Neves (1978), Brown and VanLehn (1980) are among the many to use a version of production systems. Since the early designs, many refinements have been introduced, particularly in the pattern matching and conflict resolution strategies (compare Newell, 1973 with Anderson, 1983).

Production systems are convenient languages with which to model learning, because their modular structure (relatively independent productions) allows new code to be added to existing programs without complete rewriting. Early attempts to model learning added new productions by hand (e.g. Young, 1976).

4.2.2 From weak search to heuristic search

More recently, learning theories have been automated by specifying mechanisms that create new production rules from old, using a variety of transformation techniques (e.g. Larkin, 1981; Langley, 1983; Langley *et al.*, 1984; Anderson, 1982, 1983).

The fundamental approach of all these systems is the same. The initial production system solves problems in a domain by some combination of weak search methods, e.g. means–ends analysis, or depth-first search – that is, general problem-solving techniques which use little specific knowledge of the particular domain to direct the search for solutions. This starting production system is designed to model novice problem solving performance. As (or after) the novice production system solves problems in the domain, learning mechanisms (often themselves coded as productions) derive new productions that encode specific knowledge about the domain in their antecedent conditions.

The new productions take precedence in the solution of subsequent problems, allowing knowledge-based heuristics to control search. Expert performance is thus modelled by productions which encode methods for accomplishing tasks.

Consider Larkin's (1981) ABLE simulation of the transition from novice to expert solution of physics problems. The barely ABLE model solves problems by means–ends analysis. Every time it is able to use an operator (an equation) to successfully meet a sub-goal, it records the conditions which led to the success, together with the state-of-knowledge (particularly which variables have been assigned values) after the operator had been applied. This condition–knowledge pair is directly encoded as a new production, so that on subsequent problems the same condition can immediately lead to the derived knowledge. In this way, problem solving is transformed from a 'backward' strategy which first considers the goal and how it might be reached, to a 'forward' strategy which applies operators directly to the state initially described in the problem. Observations of physics students confirm the occurrence of this backward to forward strategy shift.

A related approach to learning is taken in the SAGE model of Langley (1983). SAGE begins, like ABLE, with a production system encoding of a weak method, in the case of SAGE the weak method is depth-first search, and the domain is a coin-sliding puzzle. SAGE stores the complete solution path produced by this version, so that on subsequent attempts at the puzzle, potential applications of a particular production can be checked to see if they lie on the solution path. When a production is offered that does not lie on the solution path, SAGE uses a discrimination process to specify conditions which distinguish the current context from those where that production has been used successfully. A new more conservative version of the original production, with the antecedents augmented by the discriminating conditions, is added to the production-set. Through this learning process, SAGE develops productions which enable it to solve similar puzzles without backtracking.

ABLE and SAGE both exhibit impressive learning behaviour in their limited domains. However, it is only through careful choice of problems, and, in the case of SAGE, careful design of the heuristic knowledge-based conditions that get added to the weak productions that the 'expert' versions of either program can avoid a great deal of backtracking. An important problem is finessed here. If production systems are going to learn in a meaningful sense, then the antecedent conditions must be sufficiently general to apply across a class of problems. But if they are too general, they will cause productions to apply inappropriately, necessitating backtracking. To successfully model cognitive skill in more complex domains it is necessary to find a way of organizing the flow of control that mirrors the problem decomposition strategies that human problem solvers routinely use.

4.2.3   Goal stacks

To meet these requirements, several researchers have suggested explicitly specifying goals and sub-goals as the conditions and actions of productions, and using a *goal stack* to direct the flow of control (e.g. Brown and VanLehn, 1980; Anderson, Farrell and Sauers, 1984; Card, Moran and Newell, 1983).

Goal stacks allow production systems to model the hierarchical planning which is typical of expert skilled performance. By dictating a control discipline in which only one sub-goal may be active, and in which pattern matching invariably depends on active sub-goals, a hierarchical structure can be imposed on the entire production system. This device represents a major shift from the early production system architectures, which are entirely 'flat', requiring all productions to be considered on each cycle of the interpreter. The models of

Langley and Larkin considered above are both completely flat in this respect.

An example of a cognitive skill theory that uses goal-driven production systems is Anderson's (1982, 1983) ACT* theory. Anderson combines his production system with a semantic network model of declarative memory to produce a highly elaborate and extremely general model of cognitive architecture, that captures many of the central notions of other skill-as-method theories.

Anderson's general learning mechanism ('knowledge compilation') works in a slightly different way from the models of Larkin and Langley described above. The initial novice productions retrieve methods for performing tasks that are already encoded declaratively in the semantic net. Learning takes place by copying specific information from the semantic net down to the productions, forming new goal-oriented productions which, unlike the general ones they supersede, do not have to make costly retrievals from declarative memory. A second mechanism composes sets of productions into a single production fulfilling the same function as the set. Anderson (1986) argues that these two mechanisms can emulate all the effects produced by separate generalization and discrimination mechanisms.

For our purposes, however, the relative merits of the separate skill-as-method theories are less important than their shared assumptions. Can they do the job demanded of a student model?

4.2.4 Skill-as-method theories as a basis for student models

Many of the attempts at computational student modelling have relied on the skill-as-method theories we have described. The LISP tutor of Anderson *et al.* (1986), derives from the ACT* theory, and the Automated Cognitive Modelling project of Langley, Ohlsson and Sage (1984), is a descendant of SAGE, to give just two examples. The theories meet several of the most important criteria for student models: they allow the expression of skill at various levels of expertise within the same representational framework, and they supply dynamics which allow novice representations to grow gradually into expert representations*. But I wish to suggest that the inadequacies of all the models arise from the weaknesses in their shared underlying theory.

4.3 WEAKNESSES IN THE SKILL-AS-METHOD THEORIES

I perceive three crucial shortcomings in the skill-as-method view: it neglects context effects, it neglects to model mistaken performance, and it neglects the role played by rich conceptual representations. No model can model everything, of course, and these oversights are not necessarily shortcomings according to the goals set by the theories' authors. They are shortcomings, I believe, for the more

---

*In fact the skill-as-method theories also provide explanations for the continued improvement in skills with practice (for example, see Newell and Rosenbloom, 1981). These mechanisms do not generally concern student modellers.

sweeping demands of student modelling. I will consider each weakness in turn before concentrating on ways of overcoming the third.

1. Theories have concentrated on specifying *mechanisms* of change at the expense of elucidating the *conditions* for change.

From a machine-learning perspective this concentration is inevitable, for deterministic mechanisms are the express goal and the better the learning the better the program, irrespective of psychological plausibility. Even from a psychological perspective the specification of mechanisms could be argued to provide a necessary first step – knowing how learning might occur is logically prior to wondering when it will occur in particular ways. However, the focus on mechanism has led theorists into a search for the psychological mechanism in cases where the better goal may be permissive theories embodying several alternative learning mechanisms for a single conceptual change.

In particular I believe that we should seek theories which elaborate conditions, or *cognitive contexts* in which particular mechanisms might be favoured. One might speculate, for example, that in the learning of artificial conceptual categories (to take a domain which has seen a great deal of what-is-the-mechanism research) generalization of schemas is a favoured learning mechanism in contexts which encourage guessing, but is less likely to occur when new items are directly prompted; such a speculation might be developed into a context-sensitive learning theory, which provides an analysis of the context-mechanism mapping function. Taking this perspective further, individual differences in learning might often best be explained in terms of the adoption of different strategies (one learner actively guesses but a second does not), which in turn engender different learning mechanisms.

To date, there has been very little concerted effort towards the development of context-sensitive learning theories. Psychological comparisons of instructional techniques are commonplace in educational psychology, but they typically try to identify the best learning overall, rather than to uncover qualitative differences between the learning engendered by each; and they seldom make contact with the learning mechanisms derived from computational approaches. Educational psychology has also seen a massive research effort on individual differences, but explanations have usually been sought in terms of relatively stable characteristics of the individual. Far less weight has been given to explaining between-subject variance on single learning tasks.

Anderson (1983) does question the conditions under which his production system mechanisms of generalization and specialization should be made to occur, but ceases investigation on realizing that good matches to the time patterns in performance data on repeated tasks can be obtained by making the mechanisms apply whenever possible. This tactic may be adequate for the data-prediction criteria Anderson has set himself, but it clearly fails as an approach to student modelling, where individual differences are the key. Although student models may be able to circumvent the problem in part, by selecting learning mechanisms *post hoc*, in response to students' particular behaviour, the design of instructional strategies based on a student model surely demands some predictive analysis of context/mechanism interactions, perhaps for individual students.

2. The lack of context sensitivity in skill-as-method learning theories is just one example of the generally over-determined nature of their descriptions of learning. A further critical symptom for the purposes of student modelling is that the focus is on accounts of appropriate skilled behaviour, not on mistaken, inappropriate behaviour.

An important distinction from theoretical psychology here is that between a mistake and a slip (Reason, 1979; Norman, 1981). A slip is defined as an action which deviates from the actor's intention. A mistake occurs when the intended action is carried out, but it was not the ideal one for meeting the actor's goals. Student models would do well to incorporate some version of this distinction, for the recognition of slips would mean they could be ignored by the tutorial strategy (which may otherwise be choosing lessons on algebra according to typing errors), whereas genuine mistakes clearly demand attention.

A more pressing problem though, than disambiguating slips from mistakes, is what to do about mistakes as a tutor. The student-modelling philosophy would suggest that an answer to this question depends on an account of the underlying causes of the mistake. Can skill-as-method theories offer such an account?

An early initiative on this front came from within the ICAI research domain, with Brown and Burton's (1978) work on *bugs*. They demonstrated that many of the errors occurring in procedural skills (for example, mistakes in children's subtraction exercises) could be generated by a relatively small number of buggy procedures. Buggy procedures are easy to represent in the vocabulary of skill-as-method theories. For instance, Young and O'Shea (1981) successfully modelled subtraction errors by making small perturbations to a production system model of subtraction (e.g. deleting rules). Similarly, the 'student model' in Anderson *et al.*'s (1986) LISP Tutor uses a library of bad productions to match against student errors.

This *mal-rule* approach has become the dominant attempt to understand students' mistakes. Beyond mere libraries of bugs, recent attempts have been made to model where the bugs come from. Just as skill-as-method theories moved from the hand-crafting of production system learning toward fully automated mechanisms, so mal-rule models have been pushed beyond hand-made catalogues toward generative models (Brown and VanLehn, 1980; VanLehn, 1983b; Sleeman, 1984a). This approach clearly shows promise for integrating accounts of mistakes with skill-as-method theories.

In my opinion, the mal-rule approach has intrinsic weaknesses, whether the mal-rules can be generated by a learning model or not. Mal-rules are defined behaviourally – mistaken behaviour that occurs regularly is understood to be symptomatic of a mal-rule. But it is not clear that all regularly-occurring mistakes have the same psychological status.

One possible underlying cause is that the student has encoded or generated a genuinely mistaken method – this is what I understand the claim of mal-rule models to be. A different possible cause of a regular error is that the student really 'hasn't a clue' how to answer certain questions, and so adopts a consistent *coping strategy* to produce some response. This coping strategy could, of course, be modelled by a mal-rule, but it seems to require very different instructional strategies. (Still a third possible distinct cause of bugs is a *matching bias*, such as those found in deductive reasoning tasks (Evans, 1982). Such a bias pre-disposes the problem solver towards answers based on certain surface features of the problem.)

A major problem with mal-rules, then, is that they may oversimplify the psychological status of regular mistakes; not all regular mistakes need be caused by buggy procedures. A second problem is a mirror image of the first: it is by no means clear that all problematic misconceptions will be manifest in regular mis-behaviours. To even begin to approach this second problem we need richer representations of skill than are afforded by skill-as-method theories. It is to this problem that we now turn.

3. Viewing skill as method denies the important role played by conceptual knowledge in the development of expertise. Whereas the first two weaknesses we have noted may be soluble within the framework of production system representations, this third weakness runs deeper, requiring a richer approach to knowledge representation.

Experts in a particular domain know more than can be easily represented as a collection of method-generating rules: they can cope with novel problems; their skill transfers to seemingly separate domains; they can reason and argue about the subject matter of their expertise. None of these abilities is addressed in the skill-as-method theories, because they concentrate on parsimonious explanations of performance effects on practised, familiar tasks.

To provide these explanations, skill-as-method theories rely on the incorporation of declarative knowledge into specific procedural representations, essentially by copying knowledge of the domain out of a declarative database and into the production system, where it can play a direct role in controlling search. It is therefore the implicit claim of skill-as-method theories that non-proceduralized conceptual information ceases to play a role in skill after the initial novice stage, and remains static as expertise develops. This seems unlikely, to say the least. My criticism here is not merely that there are other skills beside purely procedural ones (though clearly that is true, and important to ICAI designers). Rather, I am suggesting that even skills with a large procedural component rely on a great deal of conceptual knowledge, and that the content and structure of the conceptual knowledge may continue to develop with expertise, alongside the procedural methods. For example, consider high school mathematics, which has been the topic for some learning studies in the skill-as-method paradigm (Mayer *et al.*, 1984). In some parts of the curriculum it is possible to perform very well by memorizing a range of schematic methods, and by acquiring a sensitive pattern matching strategy to ascertain which question requires which standard method. Such knowledge will come unstuck, however, when faced with novel, or novel-looking, questions. Skill-as-method theories can model the performance of the high-school hack whose skill is restricted to standard tests, but they fail to model the more flexible competence of the student who has grasped the underlying mathematical principles.

The point I am trying to make here is of course not new, and is even captured in folk descriptions of skilled behaviour, where a distinction is often made between being able to perform a task by rote and *understanding* the conceptual structure of the task. The Gestalt psychologist Wertheimer (1945) discussed exactly this distinction, and studied it in the context of geometry theorem proving and other mathematical tasks. In modern day cognitive science, however, much of the work on conceptual representation of a problem has been confined to the solution of puzzles within a laboratory experiment, rather than considering the role that representation and representation changes play in cognitive skill and its development.

Recently, this situation has begun to change, and the study of conceptual representations in cognitive skills has again taken centre stage. However, this initiative remains completely decoupled from the skill-as-method learning theories, except in research on 'second generation' expert systems (Steels and van de Velde, 1985), where the concerns parallel those of this chapter quite closely.

To interrelate conceptual knowledge with procedural skills appears to demand more powerful constructions than mere networks of facts. A currently promising theme is the notion of a 'mental model': a cognitive representation of a particular content domain that can be 'run' to produce mental simulations supporting inferences and explanations.

4.4   MENTAL MODELS

Consider your high-street bank machine. When you first slide your card into the slot, there is a delay before the next instruction appears. What is going on during that delay? What would happen if you typed ahead, without waiting for the machine's prompt? To answer questions like these people construct, or consult, *mental models* of the bank machine. Consider a golfer on the green, crouched over the ball, aligning his putter. Very likely he is running through a *mental simulation* of the put, imagining the run of the ball on its way to the hole. He is 'running' his mental model of the situation – a model which contains some representation of the lie of the land, and of the physics of the ball's trajectory.

A mental model is a cognitive representation of some particular content domain. But how is this idea of a mental model different from any other enterprise in knowledge representation?

The choice of mental models as a fundamental construct for understanding skilled behaviour is, I believe, a commitment of two different kinds. The weaker is a commitment to particular questions and research strategies. The stronger commitment is only made by some researchers of 'mental models'. It is to a particular *mode* of representation; mental models allow certain sorts of inference to be made more readily than others. Work on mental models has not yet produced a paradigm theory of the sort described for skill acquisition, above. Nevertheless I believe that both theoretical commitments implied by the idea of a mental model are appropriate for student-modelling, and for understanding cognitive skill in general. I will try to explain why.

The first, weaker view of mental models is that they denote a relatively new research topic for psychology: what knowledge does an individual represent about a particular domain, and how does he or she use that knowledge to make inferences, solve problems, and so on? Mental models research shifts the emphasis onto specific content domains and postpones general architectural questions about the representation of knowledge in memory, or any search for content-free rules of thought.

This priority of 'what' over 'how' in understanding the computations of goal-oriented information processing systems is not a novel idea. It chimes with the writings of Marr (1982), and the approach to linguistics of Chomsky (1965). Mental models as a methodological orientation reflect these important insights.

In contrast with the work of Chomsky and Marr, and with almost all computational approaches to psychology, mental models shift the emphasis from universal properties of cognition to individuals' beliefs and theories. Universal truths about mental models are to be sought in the long term, but their specification is not the initial sub-goal for the endeavour. Again this ordering is a shift from the traditional psychological strategy.

Both these strategic commitments seem appropriate for student modelling, where the express purpose is to understand an individual's current knowledge in order to tailor instruction.

The stronger view of mental models dictates representational commitments as well as strategic ones; three independent representational commitments have been made in the literature.

a. Mental models are concrete, analogical representations – to be contrasted with abstract, propositional ones. So mental models are closer in kind to mental images than they are to verbal descriptions; they are more like signs than symbols. In particular, in the theory posited by Craik (1943) and elaborated enormously by Johnson-Laird (1983) mental models are crucially distinguished from other representations in that they share the *relation-structure* of the state-of-affairs they represent.

b. Mental models can be 'run' to produce *qualitative* inferences readily. Our golfer preparing to put is taking advantage of this facility. This constraint is of course more of a desideratum for the representational form of mental models than a solution. The best developed theories here are those from qualitative physics (e.g. Forbus, 1984; de Kleer and Brown, 1984). A psychological investigation of qualitative reasoning using mental models is presented by Williams, Hollan and Stevens (1983).

c. Mental models rely heavily on experiential knowledge (Rumelhart and Norman, 1983; Williams, Hollan and Stevens, 1983). For example, consider the questions about bank machines I posed above. Subjects asked these questions typically respond by citing analogies to other, more familiar situations: 'I expect you can type ahead through the pauses okay – you can on push-button telephones' (Payne, 1986a). As in this example, if mental models are to utilize knowledge gained through experience it will need to be stretched to fit the new situations. Mental models are often constructed through analogies and metaphors with the familiar situation.

I am aware that my attempt to define the notion of mental models is woolly. Mental models are far from being a general theory of cognition; they pose more questions than they answer. Nevertheless, the questions posed do seem important for the applied concerns of student-modelling. Beyond that, the very idea of mental models appears to be a promising way of ameliorating some of the problems with skill-as-method learning theories discussed above. At the same time, one way to develop our understanding of mental models is to analyse their role in procedural skills.

4.5 INTEGRATING METHODS AND MENTAL MODELS

In the final section I attempt to sketch some ideas which weave together mental models and skill-as-method theories. To make any progress, I have to sacrifice some of the glamour of either approach. The full richness of mental models and the inferences they support will not be considered – I will concentrate on one fundamental feature of models, the conceptual entities from which they are formed (Greeno, 1983). At the same time, the computational precision of skill-as-method production systems must be sacrificed (temporarily I hope) to allow some contact with mental models ideas.

4.5.1 Problem spaces and mental models

To move forward the first step I will take is backwards: to Newell and Simon's (1972) conception of a problem space. Newell (1981) develops the idea into the following all-encompassing conjecture:

> "The Problem Space Hypothesis
> The fundamental organisational unit of all human goal-oriented symbolic activity is the problem space." (Newell, 1981)

We should remind ourselves of just what is meant by a problem space. My reading is as follows: a problem space is a mental construct, consisting of a state space, which is the set of possible states of the world, together with operators which move from one state to another. The state space need not be an exhaustive listing of possible states; it can be represented generatively by some kind of grammar, or implicitly by specifying a single space together with the set of operators. A problem is defined by specifying a start state and a goal state (and perhaps some constraints on the path between one and the other). A problem solution is a sequence of operators which move from the start state to the goal state.

Under this formulation, problem spaces are concrete, non-abstracted representations of parts of the world*. Problem spaces and mental models are clearly very closely related. In particular, mental models provide problem spaces (and more besides). Problem spaces represent the minimal knowledge of a domain required to perform some particular goal-directed search; mental models often contain elaborations of this knowledge which provide a basis for inference. To illustrate with an analogy: a problem space is to a mental model what the contour lines are to a map (in the context of a search for the highest ground).

It is this very aspect of mental models – their provision of a problem space – which I wish to use to supply the conceptual level that is neglected in the skill-as-method theories[†]. But problem spaces are clearly redundant for those tasks which no longer require problem solving because some efficient method has been internalized. So why should they be elaborated with increasing expertise?

To answer this question I believe it is necessary to posit a more complex and layered view of problem spaces than is common in the puzzle-solving literature. This view grew out of research on the cognitive skill of using interactive devices. Using interactive devices may be thought of as a peculiar cognitive skill, and indeed it is more complex in many ways than some other skills. My strategy is based on the conjecture that the complexities of interactive devices force considerations on the analyst that may turn out to be useful in other domains.

I will introduce my ideas through an analysis of computer-based text-editing, and then apply them to a discussion of arithmetic subtraction.

The central idea is this: using a device to perform tasks requires the simultaneous maintenance of at least two distinct state spaces, a *goal space* and a *device space*.

The goal space represents possible states of the world and the device space represents possible configurations of the device. The device space, together with a set of operators, could be seen to define a classical problem space, but the learner's task is not to search this problem space but to go from one state to another in the goal space. This task must be achieved by applying operators in the device space. The device space must therefore be able to represent all the states in the goal space. The learner must also internalize a *semantic mapping* which defines this representation.

*In later work Newell appears to have sacrificed this feature of problem spaces to allow an analysis of abstract spaces themselves consisting of problems or problem solutions (e.g. Laird, Rosenbloom and Newell, 1986).
[†]The other aspects of mental models – their enablement of inferences – are clearly also important for a full understanding of cognitive skill. My goal in this chapter is limited to showing how mental models might be associated with the development of problem-solving methods.

4.5.2 Example: using a word processor copy-buffer

4.5.2.1 *Goal space, device space and semantic mapping*

For the user of a text editor, the goal space is the world of possible texts. A particular task may be to go from nothing at all (the empty text, if you like) to a full document; or it may be to transform an existing document by removing a paragraph or a word. All these tasks are structural: the skill of using a text editor is devoted to structural alterations to text, in contrast with the skill of authoring, for text editors do not generally cope with semantic constructs (although a few research tools are beginning to). The goal space can therefore be represented by some generative model of text structures.

Just as the goal space must model all the meaningful objects and possible states of the task domain, so the device space must model all the meaningful objects and states of the device. In a simple cut-and-paste display editor, text is represented as a string of characters – either text characters, spaces or return characters. Particular strings of characters can represent all the entities in the goal space, such as paragraphs, sentences, words and so on. It is important to note here that I am arguing that strings and characters are the conceptual primitives of the device space not because of the underlying representation of text in the machine, but because the available operators on the device space only distinguish these entities. A different text editor, which made available separate, distinct operations for deleting words, deleting sentences, moving the cursor to the end of a paragraph etc. would demand that words, sentences and paragraphs all be represented as primitives in the device space. This is true in general: the conceptual entities and the available operators of any mental model are interdependent. (This example hints at how for some machines the device space may be 'closer' to the goal space than for others, but the psychological nature of 'closeness' in this context is obscure – it provides a promising set of questions for research into the complexity of devices.)

As well as constructing the goal space and the device space, a user must construct a semantic mapping, which defines the representation of goal states in the device's terms. When the user wants to delete a word (a transformation in the goal space), he or she must use some sequence of operators in the device space. Cut-and-paste editors supply a 'delete string' operator, so knowing that a word is represented as a string allows the user to perform his task. This idea of a semantic mapping between goal space and device space derives from the work of Moran (1981, 1983), particularly his notion of external–internal task-mapping. The 'closeness' of a device space to a goal space must be defined by some metric over the semantic mapping (for example, the extent to which the mapping of objects is 'structurally redundant', see Fig. 4.1).

These three components of a user's model of a simple cut-and-paste text editor, goal space, device space and structure mapping are sketched in Fig. 4.1. The particular representation languages used are not meant to carry any theoretical

Goal space

    state = document
    document = paragraph*
    paragraph = sentence* horizontalspace
    sentence = [word punctuation? smallspace]* word stop
    word = letter*

Minimal device space

    state = string
    string = character*
    character = returnchar/spacechar/textchar

Semantic mapping

    document .... string
    paragraph .... string
    sentence .... string
    word .... string
    letter—textchar
    smallspace—spacechar
    horizontalspace—returnchar*
    punctuation—textchar

Fig. 4.1. The goal space, device space and semantic mapping for a simple cut and paste editor. The goal space represents the conceptual objects in the task domain, their interrelationship, and the generative space of possible states between which the user may wish to travel. The minimal device space must allow all the objects and possible states of the goal space to be represented, so that operators which are applied to the device will effect state changes in the goal space. The structure mapping determines the representation of the goal space by the device space.

Both the goal space and the device space are presented as simple rewrite grammars, in which ' = ' denotes the containment relation, '*' marks tokens that may be repeated one or more times, and'?' marks optional tokens. The semantic mapping shows the way in which every object in the goal space is represented in the device space. In this simple editor, when the low-level text objects – letters, spaces and punctuations – have been mapped onto their device space counterparts, the mapping of the higher level objects – word, sentence, paragraph, document – is completely determined by the structure of the two state spaces. For example, a *word* is a sequence of *letters*, each of which is represented in the device space by a *textchar*. A sequence of *textchars* in the device space is a *string*, so the representation of a *word* by a *string* is 'structurally redundant' (Payne, 1986b). Structurally redundant mappings are denoted in the figure by broken lines.

weight. The goal space and the device space are both kinds of mental model, as is the entire mental complex. A grammar does not capture the full richness of a dynamic mental model, but at least it displays the entities in the model, their structural relations, and the generative space of possible model states. A better description language will have to wait for a tested computational theory of mental models.

4.5.2.2   *Operational and figurative accounts*

The device space we have discussed so far can be termed the *minimal* device space for our editor. It allows complete representation of the goal space, but some of the operators available on the device may not apply to this minimal device space. Consider for example a command which marks a block of text (a string) for subsequent copying to other locations in the text. This operator does not affect the minimal device space, and consequently does not affect the goal space. How is the user to *make sense of* the mark-block operator?

There are two distinct possibilities. The first is to construct an *operational account*, whereby the primitive operator is given a syntactic role in a structurally complex operation which does affect the minimal device space. For example, the mark-block operator can be embedded as a necessary component of some 'copy text' operation, which has the structure: mark-block, move-cursor, put-block. Under this account mark-block achieves nothing on its own, it gains its semantics by playing a part in the copy-text operation. (The same applies to the 'put-block' operator.)

An alternative way of making the mark-block operator meaningful is by building a *figurative account*, which elaborates the device space into a more complex model that the primitive mark-block operator *does* affect. By conceptualizing a 'buffer' into which marked blocks of text are copied, and by extending the device space to incorporate the state of the buffer, the learner can give the mark-block operator an independent semantics.

There is a basic symmetry between operational and figurative accounts: an operational account embeds a primitive operator that does not apply to the existing device space into a method that does; a figurative account elaborates the device-space so that the primitive operator does apply to it.

Operational accounts provide the learner with new *methods*, and figurative accounts provide an elaborated *mental model* (the device space). Typically, of course, learners do not initially construct accounts, but adopt them. Either one, but not both, of the two accounts is directly promoted through instruction. For example, most machine manuals offer operational accounts of operators by packing instruction into 'how to do it' parcels. Learners must induce figurative accounts for themselves. Whether this is the best approach, or whether instead instructional materials should present figurative accounts of operators, leaving learners to induce operational accounts, is an empirical question – one with important implications for many ICAI systems.

Let us use our mark-block example to compare the advantages and disadvantages for the learner of constructing or assimilating operational versus figurative accounts.

When operational accounts are taught to learners, when new operators are only presented to the learner embedded in complex structured methods, the learner may not even recognize the constituent operators. To see this, imagine a text editor in which copying text was achieved by pointing a mouse to the beginning of the block, depressing the button, 'dragging' the mouse with the button still depressed to the end of the block, clicking the button, moving to a new location and clicking a second time. A learner who has been taught this method may not be aware of the autonomous operators which are embedded in the structure. If the learner parses the method at all, the final click–move–click sequence may seem a natural structural unit, but the more appropriate parse might group the depress–drag–release–click sequence (the mark-block operator), with the final click being the put-block operator. Only if the appropriate parse is constructed will the mark-block operator exist as an autonomous entity in the learner's model*.

A learner who only possesses an operational account of the mark-block operator will not be able to use it except in the context of the method into which it has been squeezed. This is obviously true for learners who have not even recognized the existence of an autonomous operator; it is also true in cases where the operator has been identified as a constituent, for it will still possess no independent semantics – it will still not independently affect the learner's device space. So to copy the same piece of text from one place to several others, the learner will apply the entire copy-text method repeatedly. This strategy will be successful, but obviously inefficient. Similar patterns are observed in real novice users of text processors.

The learner who adopts a figurative account (of both the mark-block and put-block operators) will initially have to problem solve in order to do any copying of text whatsoever. However, the problem is as easy to solve for multiple copies as it is for single ones, and the learner will be able to adopt the efficient multiple-copy method, only marking the to-be-copied block once. Furthermore, ordinary skill-as-method learning theories could explain how this problem-solution could in turn lead to a collection of specialized, efficient methods. The fact that a method can be constructed from a figurative account by problem solving gives figurative accounts an advantage of robustness – if a method is forgotten it can be

---

*This is a rather arcane design, for button clicks must be interpreted in a context-sensitive way – at the end of a marked block they confirm the completion of the marking operation, elsewhere they put the marked block. My purpose here is not to analyse the action requirements of the language and their complexity, but for a treatment of these issues see Payne and Green (1986).

In some designs the appropriate parse of a method will be afforded by the display, if the effects of the operator are perceptually distinct (the marked block may be highlighted, for example, as soon as the operator is completed). And in other interface designs, the appropriate parse may be made obvious by the command language, if the separate operators are effected by syntactically distinct actions, such as control keys.

reconstructed. Operational accounts do not share this robustness. The syntactic elements of an operational method have no independent meaning outside the context of the method and are easily forgotten unless practised often. Once forgotten, an operational version of a method cannot be reconstructed.

This analysis suggests that figurative accounts have advantages for the learner over operational accounts. I believe this to be true. The comparison allows us to frame the distinction between rote methods and understanding: a method is understood to the extent that all its component operators can be given figurative accounts.

4.5.2.3   *The need for learning theories*

Constructing figurative and operational accounts are qualitatively different ways of learning how to use a device. Although I have used the label 'account' to highlight the shared role of methods and mental models in 'making sense' of operators, I do not mean to imply that this is the only spur to the learning of structured methods, or to the elaboration of device spaces. Both these modes of learning can be expressed within the same descriptive framework of goal spaces and device spaces. The framework therefore at least manages to open the door of possibility for theories that overcome the weaknesses in the skill-as-method theories discussed above. An understanding of when and how the two modes of learning occur may provide the basis for a very general theory of cognitive skill that meets the requirements of student modelling.

Skill-as-method theories can account for the acquisition of operational accounts, and for the induction of methods from existing figurative accounts. What we do not currently have is a theory that can explain the construction of figurative accounts. (It seems clear that a major process in such constructions is analogy, but adequate theories of analogical learning are not forthcoming.) A still more important gap in our knowledge would be filled by a context-sensitive theory that explained why operational accounts are constructed by learners in some circumstances, whereas figurative ones are preferred in others.

4.5.3   Example: multi-column subtraction

I believe that the ideas introduced above have a wide application in cognitive skill. To support this position, I offer a brief analysis of a very disparate domain, multi-column subtraction. The flow of the analysis closely parallels the one above. Subtraction seems an appropriate example to tackle, not only because of its apparent dissimilarity to human–machine interaction, but because it has been a major focus for ICAI research (see O'Shea *et al.*, Chapter 16).

The goal space for subtraction is made up of the conceptual entities numbers and unknowns, and the function of arithmetic difference. A state in the goal space is an expression that one object is the difference of another two.

The *task* of subtraction is much more constrained and unitary than the range of tasks within text editing, so that only a single transformation of states in the goal space need be considered: from a start state in which the difference between two numbers is unknown to a goal state in which a third number is expressed as the difference of the two numbers. Note again that this transformation of states in the goal space cannot function as an *operator* because the problem solver has no way to effect it. Instead, the student's task, as always, is to apply operators in the device space to achieve the transformation of the goal space.

The device space is the space of numerals written on paper, in which operations such as subtracting one digit from a larger digit apply. The minimal device space must be able to represent all the numbers and expressions (states) in the goal space. We will discuss various versions of the device space below.

Let us consider a student whose ability only stretches to subtracting one digit from another. For this student, the goal space is constrained to numbers of 9 or less, and the device space consists of numerals 0–9, a single column in which one numeral is placed above the other, and the operation 'subtract bottom digit from top'. (For simplicity, I will assume that the student is never presented with problems demanding negative answers; teaching strategies conventionally ensure this constraint.)

So far so good. Now consider how the student must extend her skill to cope with multi-digit numbers. The goal space simply loses its constraint. The minimal device space will use the concept of a digit-string to represent large numbers. The previous operator, subtracting one digit from another, no longer applies to this device space, for it does not apply to digit strings, only to single digits, whereas the device space, in order to represent the goal space, must parse the written numerals on the page into rows.

The new operator that the learner must use is a simple refinement of the previous operator, namely: 'subtract digit in bottom row from digit in top, for a single column'. This operator does not apply to the minimal device space, so it must be given either an operational or a figurative account.

An operational account will embed the subtract-digit operator into a method for subtracting multi-digit numerals: 'arrange the digit strings on the page so that they line up in columns from the right and apply the subtract-digit operator to one column at a time, starting from the right'. This iterative method does affect the device space, for it results in a new digit string.

A figurative account must elaborate the device space so that a single subtract-digit operator will affect it. This can be achieved by representing multi-digit numbers not as *strings*, but as *arrays*, where digits are indexed from the right, and where the index of a digit is deemed meaningful.

An important feature of the operational account is that it requires a second meaningless operator, aligning the digit string, that is, it gives an operational account of this align-digit-string operator. Misalignment of columns is an observed bug in children's subtractions (Brown and VanLehn, 1980). This suggests that these children do construct operational accounts of multi-column subtraction, for under such an account, the alignment operation has no meaning, and if forgotten cannot be reconstructed other than through reinstruction. This seems to me to be a somewhat richer account of the source of difficulty than merely positing a mal-rule: 'WRITE/BOTTOM/LEFT/SMALLER' that produces incorrect alignments (Brown and VanLehn, 1980). Furthermore, if the difficulty does indeed arise from an operational account and the meaninglessness of columns then a child is quite likely to be random in her alignment behaviour, in which case the mal-rule analysis will miss the problem altogether.

The analysis so far has ignored the subtleties of borrowing, which accounts for the majority of buggy subtraction procedures in the literature. Space precludes me from pursuing the analysis. I hope it will be clear that the notions of operational and figurative accounting I have put forward can be extended readily to borrowing. An operational account will treat the borrowing operators as meaningless syntactic elements, whereas a figurative account will elaborate the device space to make the borrowing operators meaningful. In this case the figurative account must provide a device space which represents numbers not as mere arrays of digits but as meaningful arrays consisting of units, tens and hundreds.

Dienes blocks (see Resnick and Neches, 1984; O'Shea *et al.*, Chapter 16) are designed to help children construct a richer device space of this sort – different colours and shapes are used to denote units, tens and hundreds. The device-space/goal-space framework helps to show why Dienes blocks may have instructional benefits, and beyond this it encourages speculation about the ways in which the psychological idea underlying Dienes blocks may be extended to other domains. (Resnick and Neches' (1984) analysis of arithmetic learning with Dienes blocks contains some similar ideas to those presented here.)

By discriminating between the goal space and the device space, and showing how learning can proceed through either operational or figurative accounts of operators, I hope that I have provided a general framework in which the interrelationship of procedural methods and mental models can be analysed. Future developments of these ideas must address the learning mechanisms and strategies which allow figurative accounts to be developed in particular cognitive contexts.

ACKNOWLEDGEMENTS

The ideas in the final section of this paper developed in part during some very enjoyable discussions with Tom Moran. The chapter has been improved by the criticisms of my colleagues Mary Smyth, David Gilmore, Andrew Howes and John Self; it would probably have improved further had I taken all of their remarks to heart.

5

The requirements of conceptual modelling systems

STEFANO A. CERRI
*Mario Negri Institute for Pharmacological Research, Italy
and University of Milan, Italy*

In designing cooperative dialogues such as the ones supported by ICAI systems, by means of cooperative programming dialogues such as the ones supported by intelligent authoring systems, the real difficulty is the lack of methods and tools for representing the pragmatic aspects of these dialogues.

An analysis of common errors in simple knowledge engineering programming and the analogy between programming and translating are instrumental to a presentation of the requirements for conceptual modelling languages and systems, as we have called the ones that enhance the expressive power and the cognitive simplicity of knowledge representation languages and systems in order to include these pragmatic aspects, such as interpretation, user models, viewpoints and context-dependent meaning.

5.1 INTRODUCTION

Previously (Cerri, 1983) we have suggested an analogy between the activities of programming and translating. The goal of this chapter is threefold:

a. to argue that *knowledge transformation during programming can be viewed as a kind of translation;*
b. to show that *this viewpoint can clarify a number of important properties and limits* of existing knowledge representation languages and systems, and
c. to highlight on this basis the *requirements for the class of languages and systems* necessary to overcome these limits in future developments.

We will call languages and systems designed with this purpose conceptual modelling languages (CMLs) and systems (CMSs). As· CMLs and CMSs are planned 'for the potential user', they embody design principles that enhance their expressive power and their cognitive simplicity. As these are the main objectives of current research in knowledge representation, knowledge engineering environments and intelligent authoring systems, the impact should be relevant both for the advancement of fundamental artificial intelligence research and for its applications in education.

In Section 5.2 we present examples of common mistakes in knowledge engineering practice. In Section 5.3 we describe in more detail the analogy between programs and translations. Section 5.4 gives a first overview of the requirements of CMSs. Section 5.5 discusses recent developments that propose solutions to some of the problems which are a consequence of the requirements.

5.2 COMMON MISTAKES IN KNOWLEDGE ENGINEERING

Mistakes in a language are usually due to violations of rules defining the language. In general, classes of rules are defined as: syntactic, semantic and pragmatic.

While most work on debugging deals with violations of syntactic and semantic rules, *the real problems arise when a 'formally' correct program does not do what it is supposed to do, or does it inefficiently.*

Concerning violations of pragmatic criteria that make traditional programs *inefficient*, we have made some attempts to diagnose misconceptions for pragmatic errors in the use of loop structures in Ada (cf. the RADAR system: Cerri, Colombini, Grillo and Mallozzi, 1984). The analysis of misconceptions in RADAR was mainly concerned with the tentative discovery of causal relations between the incorrect conceptual structures of Ada novices and their previous experience in other programming languages.

One of the major contributors to discussion on the influence of cognition on programming proposes that cognitive principles be taken into account in the design of languages, not only in understanding the way programmers think (Soloway, 1984).

Our own hypothesis guiding the conception of RADAR was that programming skills in a known language may influence the way programmers learn and use a new programming language, in the same way as in natural languages. In regard to learning a foreign language, see the work on the analysis of mistakes due to the interference of two syntax models in translating from or into a second natural language (Schuster and Finin, 1985) and our own analysis of misconceptions occurring in translating 'complex' words and structures, due to the incorrect conceptualization of their meaning as denoted by the context (Cerri and Breuker, 1980; Cerri and Landini, 1985).

In the case of knowledge engineering, however, we usually prefer to consider efficiency issues less important than adequacy issues. If an inefficient program does not do what we mean it to do, we prefer to correct it before tackling its efficiency. However, while the 'meaning' of a traditional algorithm can often be specified – programming languages and software engineering studies are concerned with this – it is harder to provide detailed advance specifications of an AI program.

We give some simple examples here of violations of pragmatic criteria by a knowledge engineer (KE) trying to define the simplest knowledge base. The key to the examples is that, while the programs are 'formally' correct, they embody implicit knowledge that may result in explicit deductions which, while still formally correct, are unacceptable for the KE. The acceptability of the program's results is based on the interpretation by the KE or the user with respect to his/her 'world model'.

Interpretation models such as the ones studied by Wielinga and Breuker (1984)* seem very fruitful methods for knowledge acquisition, but do not yet address the specific issue of software tools, languages and environments for the representation and use of knowledge in a programming/question-answering dialogue. It may be useful to postpone any commitment to formalisms for representing knowledge, but there will come a moment when that commitment will be unavoidable. Whatever the first program embodying that knowledge looks like, a prototype or the final version, there will anyway be the need for powerful methods and tools of knowledge representation, aimed at preventing mistakes which may have been made by the KE.

The issues presented in this chapter are concerned exactly with that moment, i.e. when the KE transforms the results of his analysis of the domain expert's knowledge, however detailed and correct it may be, into pieces of code.

5.2.1 The pragmatics of programming: ambiguities in knowledge acquisition and knowledge use

Suppose the following knowledge has to be transformed into code by means of a knowledge representation language.

> Lions are animals.
> Lions are not extinct.
> Lions have 4 legs.
> Boris is a lion.
> Boris lives in Milan.

A suitable frame-based representation in KRS (Steels, 1984)[†] would be:

(Defconcept Lion
(An Animal
(Extinct False)
(Number-of-legs Number-4)))

---

*'The interpretation model functions as an interface between the raw verbal data and the implementation' and 'consists of a typology of basic elements and structuring relations for a certain class of domains' such as: objects, knowledge sources, models and strategies (Wielinga and Breuker, 1984).

[†]For a brief introduction to KRS see the Appendix to this chapter.

(Defconcept Boris
    (A Lion
        (Lives-in Milan)))

These KRS descriptions are logically consistent. If the user wants to ask: *Is Boris dead?* (s)he may consult the KE or there is a program transforming the question into an appropriate query to KRS. In both cases, the knowledge represented by the program does not deal with the 'being alive or dead' of Boris. Due to the closed world assumption, a question formulated as: *( )) State-of-life of Boris)* will receive the answer: ⟨ **False** ⟩ or perhaps ⟨ **I-don't-know** ⟩ – if the system reasons in an 'open' world – as there is no 'state-of-life' subject associated with 'Boris'.

One suggestion would be to attribute the same interpretation of the predicate 'State-of-life' to the existing predicate 'Extinct', and ask: *( )) Extinct of Boris)* which receives the answer: ⟨**False**⟩, i.e. No.

It is interesting to note that this interpretation would not be possible in English since individual animals cannot be referred to as 'extinct'. However, the term is acceptable in Italian (we say: *il caro estinto* when mentioning a person of the family who died; in English this might correspond to the attribute 'late'). However, one would not use *estinto* for a single dead animal. The different interpretation of the meaning of 'extinct' in English and of its Italian homophone *estinto* supports once more the conviction that the context – in this case English or Italian, but similar examples could be provided within the same natural language – and its associated assumptions, guide the interpretation even of single words to a much greater extent than might be expected.

Suppose now that we substitute *Boris lived in Milan from 1965 to 1982* for *Boris lives in Milan*.

(Defconcept Boris
    (a Lion
        (Lives-in (Location Milan)
                (Time-period (From Year-1965)
                        (To   Year-1982)))))

In this case, even if the Extinct predicate could be allowed in English – (Extinct True) as a synonym for Dead – Boris inherits (Extinct False) from Lion, while the new definition of Boris clearly has to be interpreted in the sense that Boris is dead, i.e. extinct. The question *( )) Extinct of Boris)* will get the incorrect answer ⟨**False**⟩ because there is no *explicit relation* between the (inheritable) value of Extinct and the *( )) To Time-period Lives-in of ? X)*.

According to Steels (1985), the mistake arises from the ambiguous definition of the concept Lion. While for instance the property (Type Animal) concerns the Lion as a class (in knowledge engineering sense), the property **(Extinct False)** concerns the Lion as a species (in the zoological sense) and the property **(Number-of-legs Number-4)** concerns the prototype of Lion. In fact, either Boris should never inherit the Extinct property, because (in its primary meaning) this is sound only for species and not for individuals, or there should be a representation of the relations between the two versions of the subject Extinct applied to Lion and Boris.

These are examples of a large class of common mistakes that are made in knowledge engineering. They are due to the incomplete specification of the relations supposed to be valid between terms of the representation in a 'natural' interpretation of the program. They frequently occur in the description of semantically complex domains of knowledge. Other properties of these mistakes and suggestions for avoiding them will be given in the following sections.

5.2.2   The pragmatics of programming: lack of glass-box visibility on inheritance mechanisms

The following example illustrates how a programmer may make a mistake in a very simple domain of knowledge, by incorrectly estimating the consequences of the control of inheritance used by the knowledge representation system.

```
(Defconcept Tower
   (Lower (a Block))
   (Upper (a Block)))
(Defconcept Cube-Tower
   (a Tower
        (Lower (a Cube))
        (Upper (a Cube))))
```

The question here is whether the description of Cube-Tower *and* the inheritance mechanism assumed to hold for this description do indeed convey the knowledge the programmer wanted to convey by his program (cf: Cerri, 1986a, for simple examples of a student's misconceptions which could be described by modelling his behaviour by means of correct facts and rules and an incorrect deduction mechanism).

Looking at the concept, it would appear that:

a. A Tower consists of a Lower and an Upper Block.
b. A Cube-Tower is a Tower, and therefore consists of a Lower and an Upper Block, but its Lower is a specialization of Block, i.e. a Cube, and so is its Upper.

The first question one may ask is whether the system – supposed to have strict inheritance mechanisms – checks whether the specialization Cube of Block has indeed been defined:

```
(Defconcept Cube
   (a Block))
```

In the case of a negative answer, the system should remind the programmer that he must make this specialization explicit.

If the referent of Lower of Cube-Tower is supposed not to have any relation with the referent of Lower of Tower, the system should have default reasoning and exception handling mechanisms, and the programmer must be aware of this in order to avoid misconceptions such as the one presented in this dialogue, where the 'redirection of inheritance' of KRS is the source of the programmer's problem:

ACQUISITION #1
```
(Defconcept Tower
   (Lower  (a Block
                (Supports-other-block True)))
      (Upper  (a Block
                (On-top-of-other-block True))))
(Defconcept Cube-Tower
   (a Tower
         (Lower   (a Cube))
         (Upper   (a Cube))))
(Defconcept Cube
   (a Block))
(Defconcept Block
   (Supports-other-block False) ;; default value
   (On-top-of-other-block False)) ;; default value
```

Question to the system
(⟩⟩ *On-top-of-other-block Upper of Cube-Tower)*

Answer from the system
⟨ **False** ⟩   ;; because (⟩⟩ Upper of Cube-Tower) is a Cube that inherits from Block, and not from the referent of Upper of Tower.

Answer (possibly) expected by the knowledge engineer
⟨ **True** ⟩   ;; because the KE may think that the referent of Upper of Cube-Tower inherits from its corresponding referent of Tower.

Solutions to the problem could be:
ACQUISITION #2
(duplication of the subject's value)

```
(Defconcept Tower
   (Lower  (a Block
                (Supports-other-block True)))
      (Upper  (a Block
                (On-top-of-other-block True))))
(Defconcept Cube-Tower
   (a Tower
         (Lower   (a Cube
                       (Supports-other-block True)))
            (Upper   (a Cube
                       (On-top-of-other-block True)))))
```

or
ACQUISITION #3
(subject's value independent on Element-type)

```
(Defconcept Tower
  (Element-type Block)
  (Lower   (a ( ) ) Element-type)
              (Supports-other-block True)))
   (Upper   (a ( ) ) Element-type)
              (On-top-of-other-block True))))
(Defconcept Cube-Tower
  (a Tower
     (Element-Type Cube)))
```

or
ACQUISITION #4
(inhibiting locally the redirection rule)

```
(Defconcept Tower
  (Lower   (a Block
              (Supports-other-block True)))
   (Upper   (a Block
              (On-top-of-other-block True))))
(Defconcept Cube-Tower
  (a Tower
     (Lower
         (a Cube
           (Supports-other-block
              ( ) ) Supports-other-block Lower Type))))
     (Upper
         (a Cube
           (On-top-of-other-block
              ( ) ) On-top-of-other-block Upper Type))))))
```

Finally, one may define meta-concepts (Maes, 1986b) that describe explicitly the inheritance behaviour of the system in specific cases (cf. Section 5.3).

The point here is not that one cannot design a program that behaves as it should, but instead that it is often conceptually hard to do so. For instance, as is apparent from the examples, the KRS rule, *As long as the concept-structure does not redefine the type, subjects will be inherited*, identifies a specific inheritance mechanism that may enable one to define structures with 'formally correct' behaviour, but such that the interpretation in the KE's world model is incorrect because his/her expectations *about aspects of the control* are different from those applied (implicitly) by the system.

Similar examples may be provided for other knowledge representation systems, such as KL-ONE, LOOPS, MRS, OMEGA,... (cf. Brachman, 1983; Clancey, 1983a) as well as for logic programming languages such as Prolog.

We agree with Brachman's view that the semantics of the system should be well defined, but this is not enough if the programmer's interpretation of the control behaviour of the knowledge representation system is not in agreement with it *at the moment he writes the code*! A really cooperative system should help the KE to prevent these misconceptions before they slip into the descriptions (s)he develops.

From the viewpoint of intelligent tutoring in AI programming, this observation focuses on the need for introducing user (programmer's) models into the programming environment for the prevention of mistakes more than for designing tutorial dialogues that assume these mistakes have already been made. This view has the clear advantage that one may prevent/correct *one misconception at a time*, instead of being confronted with the problem of separating multiple misconceptions causing a single mistake.

5.3   PROGRAMMING AS TRANSLATING

We will now examine in more detail the two classes of mistakes briefly presented above in the context of the analogy between programs and programming on the one hand, and translations and translating on the other.

The activity of programming can be viewed as a two-phase transformation: from a specification S to a conceptual representation R and from the representation R to the code C. The transformation $S \rightarrow R$ will be denoted by F; and $R \rightarrow C$ will be denoted by G. In Fig. 5.1 S is in natural language, C1 in KRS and C2 in MRS (Genesereth *et al.*, 1984).

In human programming activity, S may be partially explicit, often incomplete; R is in the programmer's mind and the only explicit, observable aspect of the transformation is the code C. There is a substantial difference between traditional

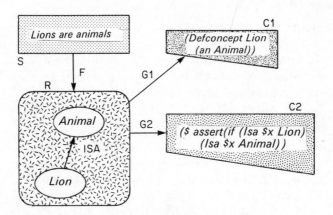

Fig. 5.1. Programming as a two-phase transformation.

software engineering (SE) and knowledge engineering. While there is a tradition in SE to define specifications S of programs as precisely and completely as possible, the methodology for building expert systems considers experimental programming, rapid prototyping and frequent tuning of partial programs (Genesereth, 1984) a requisite for success.

We will not argue here for or against this view. Hayward *et al.* (1984), for instance, claim that in order to make expert system development industrially viable one should define recipes for knowledge-based systems analogous to those for supporting the life cycle of traditional software. As the exploratory programming methodology was mainly based on the assumption that in many fields it is very hard or even impossible to provide explicit program specifications, the criterion for deciding the feasibility of the SE methodologies for knowledge engineering will probably be domain-dependent. In the domains where explicit and complete specifications of knowledge-based systems can be provided before the design and development phase, we will be able to consider S as an observable for these programs too.

Still, at least three components of the programming process are (and probably will long remain) poorly understood:

1. the *conceptual representation R*;
2. the *conceptualization function* F;
3. the *coding function G.*

Given S and C, and the rules of the languages of S and C, one can theoretically define an infinite number of two-phase transformations that transform S into C respecting these rules. However, only a few of these transformations are cognitively plausible. Most of the studies on debugging programs by means of inferring misconceptions from bugs try to use these cognitive constraints in order to find plausible criteria for debugging and remedying mistakes in programming.

Assuming that a two-phase transformation model can be accepted as a first approximation for the programming activity, the following holds:

1. Such a model fits with translation: F is the selection/construction of a conceptual meaning for a structure in the source language expression, on the basis of the context, and G is the selection/construction of a target language structure expressing the conceptual meaning (Cerri and Landini, 1985).
2. If program C is incorrect, the two-phase model makes explicit the intuitive notion that mistakes can be present in the outcome of the programming activity, even if coding (modelled by G) was correct.

Most studies on programming languages and, more recently, on knowledge representation languages have focused on the properties of the transformation G, i.e. from a (formal) representation of knowledge (e.g. an algorithm, or a strategy for problem solving such as the programmer or knowledge engineer might conceive them) to the code, while the transformation activity indicated by F has not received sufficient explicit attention.

Let us now examine the consequences of this – very general – model for analysis of the examples of common mistakes in knowledge based programs provided in the previous section.

Suppose we use KRS as a (first approximation of a) conceptual modelling language. KRS is suited for representing conceptual models because it is open-ended and reflexive. Therefore in KRS it is possible:

a. – *Open-ended* – to associate any meaning to any concept in terms of other concepts by specifying its referent (i.e. the extension), its definition (i.e. the intension) and its subjects (i.e. the properties and their associated values); and

b. – *Reflexive* – to define KRS definitions (dynamically), including its control, in terms of KRS itself (Maes, 1986a, b).

Therefore we will use KRS as a communication language more than as a target knowledge representation language.

5.3.1 The conceptualization function F: S → R

Instance to class

We now aim at the definition of F as a transformation of

S: Boris is a Lion

into a description that embodies our view of the conceptualization done by the KE. Suppose that the outcome R of this conceptualization is correctly represented, for instance, by the KRS concept definition:

R: (Defconcept Boris (a Lion))

including the default assumptions of the KRS interpreter (e.g. the uniqueness of the referent of a concept, the default inheritance method, etc.).

Notice that our aim is to model the *transformation* explicitly, i.e. how S (which is explicitly given) becomes its corresponding conceptual structure R by means of application of the function F, not just the outcome R of the transformation. We will use KRS to represent F and R.

In the transformation we wish to describe (or any other similar conceptualization), we should account for the following components:

a. Knowledge about the meaning of 'Boris is a Lion' in English, in the context of the problem description to which this sentence belongs.

b. Knowledge about the conceptual structures available to the programmer for embodying this meaning, specifically the types of inheritance notions and their associated constraints about the entities (i.g. the concept Boris, the concept Lion, etc.).

c. Knowledge about the transformation strategy.

We aim to associate a set of conceptual descriptions with each of these components. The output of the transformation we wish to model is not the code a programmer writes, but a representation of the result of his reasoning before any coding begins. Therefore this representation includes plans for checking consistencies, exploring different alternatives, etc. The knowledge about the programming (or knowledge representation) language chosen for the code is not considered at this point.

In order to model the specific behaviour of F

F(S: Boris is a Lion: *context*) → R:**(Defconcept Boris (a Lion))**

we assume the KE has answered several questions that influence the outcome R of the conceptualization such as, for instance (the list is not complete!):

a.   i. *Uniqueness of the concept identifiers*: Is 'Boris' a unique name? (or is there another Boris in the story that denotes, for instance, a character in a Russian novel?).
   ii. *Type of concepts*: Is 'Boris' a name of an instance-concept? Is 'Lion' a name of a class?
  iii. *Related knowledge that may need conceptualization*: What other properties of Boris, of Lion(s) and of the assertion 'Boris is a Lion' do I know? (for instance: it is a lie because it was said by someone I do not trust or, it is metaphorical because I know that Boris is a toy).
b. *Conceptual tools available*: On the hypothesis that I (the programmer) know default, strict and multiple inheritance mechanisms, what kind of mechanism is suitable for representing my knowledge? Why? What other examples of inheritance do I know? Can I use them in the current case?
c. *Planning the conceptualization*: On the hypothesis that I choose to conceptualize 'Boris is a Lion' using may default inheritance concept, does Boris indeed inherit all the properties of Lions that I know of? If not, I must explicitly conceptualize the exceptions. Is there any previous conceptualization plan in my conceptual-modelling knowledge base (my world model, i.e. what I consider relevant for representing the specifications for my KB system) that has to be considered now so as to avoid mistakes?

The transformation F produces a conceptual representation of a plan which – as a very first approximation – may look like the following:

F(Boris is a Lion: *context*) = **(Defconcept Boris (a Lion))**
```
    (Defconcept Assert-concept-instance-of-class
       ;;{the class of any conceptualization of this type}
    (a CMconcept
       ;;{the CM System is a set of these concepts}
    (Concept-to-be-defined
      (a CM-concept
          (Name   (a Symbol)))))
    (Concept-type-to-use
          (a CM-concept
```

```
                (Name   (a Symbol))))
(Preconditions-to-be-checked-in-CM-knowledge-base
        [predicate-list
        ((⟩⟩ Is-concept-name? Name Concept-type-to-use)
         (⟩⟩ Is-concept-name? Name Concept-to-be-defined)
         (...))])
(Consequences-to-be-checked-in-CM-knowledge-base
    [predicate-list ((⟩⟩...)...)])
(Definition
    (an Action
    {the procedural concept that first checks the preconditions, then
    makes the assertion in the CM-knowledge-base in the form as it
    should be, and last checks the consequences of the assertion})))))
(Defconcept F-(-Boris-is-a-Lion-;-context-)
    (an    Assert-concept-instance-of-class
        (Concept-to-be-defined
            (a CM-concept
                (Concept-name [Form Boris])
                (Concept-type Lion)))
        (Context
            ([here the information about the programmer's
            assumptions on Boris, Lions, etc.])))
```

It is at *this* moment that presuppositions, beliefs and general world knowledge should be represented, as part of the programmer's state, not when the programmer transforms his/her representation R into code.

For instance, if the assertion is made in the context of a novel where Boris is living in a forest then Boris should perhaps inherit the default value for the property defining where he lives, while if he is in a zoo, that value should refer to a cage, with its implications.

Our experience with ALICE (Cerri and Landini, 1985) has taught us that the analysis of errors in translating from or to a foreign language benefits greatly when the conceptualization is separated from the production of the code in the target language. Similarly, we claim that in the transformation of world knowledge into code, several pragmatic errors can be prevented by embodying in the knowledge engineering environment modules that assist the programmer in the conceptualization and coding phases.

Sub-class to class

The conceptualization of 'Lions are animals' may require explicit answers to the following questions:

a. Is 'Lion' a class? Is 'Animal' a class? Does each element of the first class also belong to the second? What else do I know about these classes within the specifications that I have for my program?

b. Am I aware of the possibility of constructing hierarchies of classes? Do I have any example in mind? Counter-example?
c. How can I use an example I know, changing the names of the concepts, for conceptualizing the new fact that 'Lions are Animals'? As I already know that Boris is a Lion, i.e. as I have conceptualized **(Defconcept Boris (a Lion))** is this compatible with this new fact?

Referent of a subject

The conceptualization of a property for an existing concept, 'Lions have 4 legs', may require even more attention:

a. The meaning of 'have' here refers to the body of Lions: it has 4 legs as a part. Are the meanings of the word 'legs' and of the modifier '4' well known? How?
b. Do I have in my CM knowledge base a concept for *body*, a concept for *part-of*, a concept for *leg*, a concept for *4*? Do I need them, or shall I define a concept (subject) *Number-of-legs* such that its referent is *Number-4* and this is asserted as a property of *Lions*? Is this a property of the class of *Lions*, or of a prototype of the class *Lion*?
c. As I already have the concept *Lion*, how do I add the subject *Number-of-legs* with its referent? Will my CM knowledge base need to answer questions such as: 'do Lions have legs'? In this case, let me remember that if a prototype of a class has a *Number-of-legs*, then it also has legs. However, is this generalizable to Number-of X?

Sometimes natural language is even more problematic. The representation of negation is known to be hard. Let us consider the assertion: 'Lions are not extinct'.

a. Is 'extinct' a class or a property? Does 'extinct' apply to the class of *Lions*, or to the race of *Lions*?
b. Will I better identify a set of views of my concept Lion that allow me to associate the *Extinct* subject to the race of *Lions*, the *number-of-legs* subject to the prototype-lion, and the *Type* subject to the class?
c. How can I transform the current conceptualization in order to include the recent observations?

5.3.2   The coding function G: R → C

Once the conceptualization has produced a representation R, which for our example of the Towers is given later explicitly in KRS – including part of the semantics of a specific inheritance mechanism – the programmer constructs a plan for coding this conceptualized knowledge by means of a programming language.

At this point the traditional mistake/misconception analysis can be applied. Application of the function G to R will be correct (irrespective of the correctness of R) if the programmer:

a. has knowledge about the target language Lc, i.e. the language for implementing the code;
b. has knowledge about how to transform R into Lc structures.

If the conceptualization contains concepts that cannot easily be implemented
in Lc, there is a higher probability of mistakes (Soloway, 1984). For instance, if
one is used to conceptualizing in terms of frames, slots, fillers and inheritance one
may have problems using rules for the code.

Suppose that R is the conceptual representation of the Tower, produced by a set
of applications of F to single chunks of knowledge, in a new form that requires the
association of special meta concepts*:

```
R:
    (Defconcept Tower
       (Lower (a Block
              (Supports-other-block True)))
       (Upper (a Block
              (On-top-of-other-block True))))
    (Defconcept Cube-tower
       (a Tower
          (Lower (a Cube
                 (Meta (a Special-meta))))
          (Upper (a Cube
                 (Meta (a Special-meta))))))
    (Defconcept Block
       (On-top-of-other-block False)
       (Supports-other-block False))
    (Defconcept Cube
       (a Block))
    (Defconcept Special-meta
       (a Meta-concept
          (Add-subject-action {default})
          (Make-instance-action {default})
          (Get-subject-action {default: no inheritance})
          (Inheritance-action
```

{when a subject – e.g. *On-top-of-other block* – is not explicit in the
concept – e.g. *(>>Upper of Cube-tower)* – the inheritance mechanism is
indicated by the Inheritance-action subject of the associated *Metaconcept*. If
this is a *Special-meta*, instead of looking into the hierarchy of the
concept – e.g. *Cube → Block* – search as if inheritance was not redirected})

This representation differs from the ones presented in Section 5.2 because it

---

*A meta concept may be associated to a concept as referent of the subject Meta, and the referent of a
meta concept is its associated concept (Maes, 1986b).

modifies the redirection of inheritance of (〉〉 **Referent Upper/Lower of Cube-tower)** by means of meta-concepts so that the question: *(〉〉 On-top-of-other-block Upper of Cube-Tower)* returns the *(〉〉 On-top-of-other-block Upper of Tower)*, i.e. 〈 **True** 〉, instead of *(〉〉 On-top-of-other-block Upper of Cube)*, i.e. *(〉〉 On-top-of-other-block Upper of Block)*, i.e. 〈**False**〉.

If this conceptualization is transformed into the code of Acquisition #1 (Section 5.2.2), i.e. assuming an incorrect default definition of the inheritance mechanism of KRS, then while the program is logically correct, an 'error' occurs. As the code presents two properties with possibly conflicting values: **On-top-of-other-block** and **Supports-other-block**, an 'intelligent' assistant in the environment may present the knowledge engineer alternative solutions such as described previously.

Unfortunately, if the knowledge base is large, a single mistake such as the one presented here may cause a series of errors which may come to light very seldom and in a form that makes it very hard to trace them with the current debugging aids. This is coherent with the fact that current debugging programs are not concerned with the soundness of the system, i.e. the acceptability of the interpretation of the system's outcomes with respect to the application.

5.4 CONCEPTUAL MODELLING SYSTEMS

Let us provide here a set of properties of conceptual modelling languages and systems, in order to come nearer to an informal definition. As such, it must be considered more as a set of suggestions for future work in this area than a set of recipes for deducing formalisms.

Conceptual modelling languages (CMLs) are to knowledge representation languages (KRLs) as KRLs are to programming languages (e.g. LISP and Prolog). The difference is certainly in the *cognitive simplicity* for modelling concepts (descriptions, procedures, icons) and perhaps in their *expressive power*. For instance, KRS has been used in the previous sections as a communication language, and may be used as an implementation language for CMLs, in the same way as LISP is used for knowledge representation languages and Prolog for languages for logic programming.

The components of CMLs are *linguistic* (e.g. descriptions, procedures, meta-concepts, viewpoints) and *analogical* (e.g. perceptual forms, such as images, icons, sound, or motor forms, such as the orientation of a robot's eye). CMLs aim at the integration of *several types of components* in order to describe more comprehensively the reasoning behaviour of systems consisting of several agents, including humans.

CMLs are designed for the *interpretation of messages and behaviour* in general, not just for its realization as usually conceived in current KRLs. The term 'interpretation' refers here to the capacity of these systems to assign to any agent's expressions a *pragmatic meaning* such as the one which can be associated, for instance, with a model of the user and not simply derived from the syntax and semantics of the single user's expression. Specifically, CMLs can express the properties of the transformation F, i.e. from a problem into its representation in a knowledge representation formalism.

The systems which embody architectures, descriptions and primitives of CMLs are called *conceptual modelling systems* (CMSs). These may be defined using KRLs or any other kind of formal language. Their specificity is not provided by the system's formalism, but by the explicit concern they incorporate about the dependence of the meaning of the code on the 'context', including the (general) world knowledge. In the case of programming, the world is the one that the programmer implicitly assumes to be valid when (s)he writes a piece of code. We do not claim that CMSs have a complete world knowledge but we do claim that whatever the world knowledge of these systems it is the best explicit representation we can provide, in order to interpret the code correctly as a function of its intended meaning.

The importance of conceptual modelling systems arises from three facts.

1. CMSs do embody an *interpretation component of the messages of their human users*. This is relevant in environments for designing software as well as in applications including any kind of man–machine interaction. In fact, there is no conceptual difference between system software (in the environment) and application software.

2. CMSs do embody an *interpretation component of the messages of any other message source*. Their primitives can express explicitly the aspects of mutual knowledge typical of *agents in a society of communicating but autonomous entities*, i.e. problem solvers with private memory (cf. Cerri, Landini and Leoncini, 1986; Benoit, Caseau and Pherivong, 1986). These agents' behaviour is typically strongly influenced by their models of the other agents, and this knowledge is supposed to be incomplete and possibly incorrect. Therefore – from a higher viewpoint – each agent may seem to behave incorrectly, though the collective behaviour of the society may converge to a common goal. 'Non-human-actors' may have a well-defined knowledge, while for human actors this is never true, i.e. whatever your model of their knowledge, it is always incomplete, so that computations require the retraction of assumptions which are incorrect in the agent's interpretation.

3. It is to be hoped that the *separation of concerns* about models of transformations from a real 'world description' into its representation, and from the representation to the code, as well as the explicit distinction between interpretation and computation, will help clarify issues of the current debate between the 'power/logic-based' and the 'knowledge/concept-based' approach to the construction of the intelligent machines of the future.

5.5 ABOUT THE ARCHITECTURE OF CONCEPTUAL MODELLING SYSTEMS

5.5.1 Multiple viewpoints in the environment

A central notion in computing is that of 'environment', i.e. the binding between the name of an entity (e.g. a variable) and its denoted value (as in LISP). Clearly, we do not refer here to the meaning of environment as a set of tools available for the programmer. Even this basic term is ambiguous in computer science!

In KRS environmental binding is embodied by the association between a concept and its referent, i.e. the extension of the concept. KRS is peculiar compared to other knowledge representation languages, because it enables one to define not only the referent of a concept, but also its definition, i.e. the intension of the concept, so that, when the referent of a concept is unknown, it can be found by evaluating the referent of the definition of the concept. However, as in any other programming language (including LISP) the uniqueness constraint holds, i.e. each concept may have only one referent (each subject may have only one filler).

We have shown (Cerri, 1986b) that there are situations that suggest a different architecture, including the traditional one but extending it to deal with multiple viewpoints. According to these observations, we argued that the constraint of uniqueness of the environmental bindings may be challenged by the more general notion of 'relevance' of a binding name/value or concept/referent *in a specific viewpoint*, defined by the context. Therefore computations are seen more as looking for the relevant item(s) within a viewpoint than evaluating a concept, a variable or a function.

5.5.2 Ambiguity

This brings the notion of ambiguity into focus. Computations are strategies for resolving ambiguities by looking at the most plausible context compatible with the available information.

In linguistics, a word is called ambiguous when it may have more than one meaning, according to the context. In knowledge representation we can associate the meaning of a concept with its referent. The concept (> >**Location of John**) may have as referent (**a Town**) or (**a Countryside**) according to considerations that have to be made when (> > **Location of John**) is required. If from the context *no single referent can be decided*, both possibilities should be left open for proceeding in the computation.

This way of describing concepts is more powerful, because it allows one to give several meanings to the same concept, provided one is also able to specify what meaning should be used, and when. In case of lack of some meaning (incomplete information) in a viewpoint, the system does not crash but asks for one. In the case of more than one meaning, the system tries to find out which ones could be part of the viewpoint. If several are available, then the system uses them all, providing for multiple computation.

This architecture is compatible with the existing ones, because if a viewpoint is not specified, the default is assumed. At the same time, it is also more friendly, because it does not assume at any time that one remembers what has already been defined in the system.

If you redefine a concept in the same way as one already defined, the new definition has no effect. If you add some more specifications, it defines a new viewpoint which is a specification of the viewpoint of the previously defined concept. If you define a new concept with properties incompatible with the existing ones, it defines a new viewpoint related to the previous one by the incompatibility relation.

Viewpoints are also concepts. They are used for guiding the system's computational behaviour. They make much use of the library of (meta) definitions of system's primitives, such as 'pre-condition' or 'conceptual inversion' (Cerri and Landini, 1985). However, viewpoints should be considered separate from meta concepts. A system such as the one in Maes (1986a) may have several layers of meta concepts, but it requires each concept to have a single referent.

For instance, if you ask:

(⟩⟩ On-top-of-other-block Upper of Cube-Tower)

the system should answer:

⟨False⟩;; **active context**
   when   (⟩⟩ **Inheritance-action Meta Upper of**
               Cube-Tower) → *Default-inheritance*
⟨True⟩ ;; **alternative context**
   when   (⟩⟩ **Inheritance-action Meta Upper of**
               Cube-Tower) → *Special-inheritance*

5.5.3   Consequences of multiple viewpoints

Models of agents communicating in natural language

The notion of ambiguity and ambiguity resolution draws on the ELISA/ALICE work (Cerri and Breuker, 1980; Cerri and Landini, 1985). It suggests that CMSs with multiple viewpoint reasoning will be good for modelling agents communicating in natural language.

Redundancy

Necessarily, in ambiguous systems one has to introduce redundancy. A nontrivial, artificial reasoning system has to have access to redundant information. For instance, knowledge reformulation provides, at least in part, for alternative views of the same knowledge, and therefore for redundancy. But knowledge reformulation is the essence of many discoveries! Further, knowledge reformulation helps in accessing knowledge efficiently. Knowledge reformulation strategies may be the main outcome of studies on learning, which is in turn fundamental for expert systems.

Negative computations

Another effect of defining viewpoint-dependent referents of concepts is that a computation may try first to eliminate the viewpoints that are incompatible with its goal, producing a sort of 'negative' behaviour. This can be important in domains where we are more certain of what our concepts do not mean than of what they do mean.

5.5.4   Context calculus

Conceptual modelling languages are not simply a set of higher level primitives for modelling partially defined meanings and behaviour using the same computational scheme as most traditional knowledge representation languages do. The CML computational scheme includes traditional ones, but extends them in the direction needed for fulfilment of the specific requirements of CMLs. We have called this extension of computational schemes a *context calculus* (Cerri, 1986b).

In a context calculus we have *components* and an *evaluation strategy*. The components are *concepts, subjects, referents* and *viewpoints*. Concepts, subjects and referents behave as the corresponding KRS components in a single active viewpoint.

Viewpoints (in a CML) are like KRS concepts as well, but their meaning (called *context*) is to bind existing concepts (and subjects) to existing referents. While concepts are supposed to exist independently on any viewpoint, the binding is activated by the viewpoint whenever this is needed for a computation.

A request to provide the value of a concept in a CML is transformed into the request to find (or define) one or more context(s) such that the concept has a value in the context(s).

In the example on programming, the request: What is the value of the concept 'write a piece of code that embodies the knowledge: Lions are animals?' is transformed into the request to find a set of contexts that can be organized coherently into one or more viewpoints, providing one or more referents to that concept. This may be modelled as a search for the (several possible) representations R resulting from the application of F to the contexts corresponding to the programmer's world models, followed by searching for each of the Rs, the (several possible) codes that result from the application of G to the contexts corresponding to the programmer's view of the target language.

Context calculus thus appears to be another name for viewpoint-based reasoning. In a certain sense, this may be true, but we believe that the explicit focus on the dependency of conceptual values on the context has advantages. First, it helps thinking in relative terms. Nothing is true or false, but may be either (or perhaps neither) according to a computational context.

Second, the heart of the computation is not to find a value of a concept but to find (and eventually construct) possible worlds where such a concept has a value, providing a dynamic and constructive view of computations.

Third, it provides for a natural metaphor for the representation of human cognitive activities, such as assumptions, remembering, forgetting etc. If concepts exist independently of their actual association with referents, one can define remembering – for instance – as the activation of the viewpoint binding concepts and referents, and so on.

Fourth, the traditional notion of environment as a function from identifiers to locations (or from names to values) is replaced by the notion of context which may also access names from values (and identifiers from locations). Beyond the conceptual simplicity of this metaphor, there is an architectural counterpart in content-addressable memories and in machines with programmable connections.

5.6 CONCLUSIONS

In this speculative chapter we have tried to address some of the most debated issues in knowledge representation research. We have done this mainly because of our conviction that, in order to make significant advances in cooperative systems (such as man–machine systems) in general, and in intelligent tutoring systems in particular, new computational paradigms (languages, architectures, formalisms) are needed. These should improve the expressive power and the cognitive simplicity of current knowledge representation languages, not simply their efficiency. They have been called conceptual modelling languages and systems.

The main limitation of current languages is the lack of an interpretation component. Systems which are 'internally' consistent and complete do not ensure that their solutions to problems are adequate, because the link with reality is left totally to the human, who may have access to incomplete or inconsistent or viewpoint-dependent knowledge.

In order to be concrete, we have worked out a few examples of simple – perhaps over-simple – knowledge-engineering problems. Using the analogy of programming as translating, we were able to separate the conceptualization and the coding activities. The analysis brought many unsolved issues into focus. While we are aware that the literature makes many other contributions to some of these issues, we have tried, as far as possible, to follow our own lines of reasoning.

These considerations have led us to propose a set of requirements for conceptual modelling systems. In order to solve the problems associated with these requirements, we have proposed investigating an alternative computational architecture – called context calculus – based on the notions of ambiguity, redundancy and viewpoint.

ACKNOWLEDGEMENTS

Part of this research was supported by a grant of the Commission of the European Communities, project COST 13, No. 9: An Intelligent Computer Aided Instructional System for Teaching Artificial Intelligence Programming.

The examples of errors in knowledge engineering were taken from papers by Luc Steels and Patty Maes on KRS. I am grateful to them and to Mauro Leoncini for having critically read previous versions of this paper.

APPENDIX: A SHORT INTRODUCTION TO KRS

KRS is a knowledge representation language based on one single primitive: the concept. A concept in KRS is similar to a frame; it may have subjects (comparable to the slots) and these relate the concept to other concepts.

Each concept has a referent, which is the value of the concept (its extension); the evaluation of the concept yields its referent. The referent of a concept is one of its subjects.

A concept may have a definition; the evaluation of the definition of a concept yields its referent. The definition of a concept is a subject denoting its intension.

Each concept has a subject Type; concepts inherit property values from their associated types. The Type subject may be abbreviated by 'a' or 'an'.

One of the subjects of each KRS concept may be the Meta subject; its value denotes a concept that describes how to define, modify and use the associated concept.

KRS is an object-oriented knowledge representation language. Whenever KRS concepts receive a message, they respond by activating the associated method. The method associated with a message is the concept which is the value of the subject that has the same name as the message.

Concepts are defined in KRS by the **Defconcept** primitive. The meaning of Defconcept is given by the definition of a (new) concept. Another KRS primitive is ⟩⟩: its meaning is given by the evaluation of a concept.

In KRS one can use LISP structures (atoms, lists, functions, ...) as values of special concepts called *data concepts*. Data concepts are denoted by square brackets '[' ']'. For instance:

Defconcept Number_5
   (a Number
       (Definition [Form (+ 2 3)])))

is interpreted as the definition of a concept Number_5, of type Number, with Referent given by the evaluation of the Definition subject of Number_5, i.e.: the evaluation of the LISP form (+ 2 3), i.e. 5.

   (⟩⟩Type of Number_5)

is interpreted as the value of the Type subject of Number_5, i.e. the concept Number.

A description of KRS primitives and conventions can be found in Steels (1985). For reflection in KRS see Maes (1986a). In Maes (1986b) there is also a first account of the semantics of the system.

6

The appraisal of an ICAI system

LINDSEY FORD
University of Exeter, England

An overview of Tutor, an experimental intelligent computer-aided instruction system, is provided. The system is appraised in two ways. First, how its behaviour measures against a set of desirable behavioural properties and, secondly, how well it meets its research objectives. It is concluded that several important behavioural properties are lacking in Tutor but that its research objects have been largely met.

6.1 INTRODUCTION

How can experimental intelligent computer-aided instruction (ICAI) software be appraised such that interested researchers are made aware of its research value in the context of their own work? A report giving sufficient information for others to reconstruct or obtain the software should be provided as a matter of course, but this needs to be supported by a more general account if the reader is going to be able to relate it to his or her own work meaningfully. The intention of this chapter is not to provide a report to facilitate reconstruction of the system that is to be discussed as this has already been done (Ford, Rivers and Tang, 1986) but rather to appraise it in a more general sense in the hope that researchers will be encouraged to adopt or refine the appraisal method as well as learn more about the particular system.

Ultimately all ICAI work that survives the experimental phase will need to satisfy stringent requirements of students and evaluators such as speed of response, cost, and so on, but prior to that we need to answer more fundamental questions concerning a system's ability to, in general terms, foster learning. Much ICAI work to date has focused on particular aspects of an overall system such as the problems associated with student modelling and subject representation, and while there is a need to report such work in fine detail it should not be absolved from being appraised in a wider context. For example, an account of the accuracy of a student modelling program should also address such issues as whether the model is suitable as a basis for tailoring explanations and selecting appropriate tasks, particularly as other researchers may wish to use such a model in these ways.

These concerns are reflected in the appraisal method used here. It has been motivated by a subject-independent set of questions suggested by Self (1985b) to determine how well an ICAI system lives up to its prefix of 'intelligent'. The questions ask about behavioural properties of a system in a fairly general way, for example, 'Does the system intervene if the user appears to be having difficulty?', but in providing an answer the reporter can be quite specific about the extent to which it does (by providing examples) and it does not (by giving counter-examples). The account can relate a system's behavioural properties to its architecture by stating how the system does it or why it is unable to. By appraising a system in this domain-independent way effective communication of ICAI research results may well be enhanced. The appraisal is provided in Section 6.3.

Apart from attempting to provide an ICAI system with some useful behavioural properties our research programme addressed other issues. These are reported in standard fashion in Section 6.4.

6.2   OVERVIEW OF SYSTEM

Tutor is an experimental ICAI system developed in Prolog. It aims to provide individualized tuition in a prescriptive manner through exposition, task present-ation, and remedial feedback, although some learner control is catered for. Our approach was tempered by a desire to have a clear separation of subject dependent and independent parts of the system so that at some future date we could explore the possibility of Tutor teaching a variety of different but essentially rule governed subjects such as legislation, emergency procedures, and the Highway Code (an official book of guidance for road users in the UK). These subjects are often well defined and lend themselves to being represented as rule-based programs. This is important to Tutor since it utilizes a rule-based representation of the subject expertise in order to impart knowledge of the subject. In this respect Tutor follows the line of research that resulted in systems such as SOPHIE (Brown, Burton and deKleer, 1982) and GUIDON (Clancey, 1982). By having a subject's competence knowledge represented in this way Tutor can, for a given task, 'execute' the set of rules and, on the basis of a comparison of its solution to a student's, provide a critique. It also clarifies the goal of training which is to impart all of the rules to the student. (In this chapter, although we discuss how situation-action rules are taught, Tutor is not restricted to only teaching rules or rules of this type. It can also teach declarative knowledge, concepts (definitional rules), and procedures.)

Situation-action rules such as those to be found in the Highway Code frequently relate to a single action within the context of an on-going situation or procedure. Informally these are represented in Tutor's subject rule base as follows:

IF   Sequence = ⟨name of sequence⟩

AND   NOT performed (⟨name of generic action⟩)
AND   pre-conditions for this action are true
AND   prerequisite actions in the sequence have been performed
THEN   Action = ⟨name of action⟩
AND   assert ((performed (⟨name of generic action⟩))).

The third step in the procedure for turning right is:

IF   Sequence = turning right
AND   you have not taken up position
AND   there are no space markings for turning right
        there is an opposing vehicle wanting to turn
        offside-to-offside passing is practical
        nearside-to-nearside passing is not indicated by other driver
AND   you have checked your mirror
        you have given a right turn signal
THEN take up position for offside-to-offside passing
AND   assert you have taken up position.

If a student is given a task requiring as a response the action following THEN in the rule above, but he provides an incorrect response, Tutor would compare the preconditions and prerequisites of the rule invoked by the student's response with the correct rule and use the differences as the basis for its critique. For example, if a student selects nearside-to-nearside passing then Tutor would indicate that since offside-to-offside passing is practical and the driver of the opposing vehicle has not indicated nearside-to-nearside passing the student should have selected offside-to-offside passing.

Tutor provides individualized tuition by adapting its pattern of behaviour to suit a particular student. This it does only in a rudimentary way and only with respect to what the system believes the student knows of the subject being taught. (It does not attempt to model other characteristics of a student such as his learning style and motivation.) Tutor recognizes just three states of knowledge a student may have of a rule he is learning: has not been taught a rule (it is assumed he does not know it); has mastered a rule (is aware of it and can use it appropriately); has been taught but not mastered a rule. One of these three states is assigned to each rule and this information constitutes the student model. This type of model falls into the category described as 'overlay' (Goldstein, 1982) i.e. the student model maps onto or overlays the rules being taught. An interpretation of the model suggests which rules require tuition or further tuition and it is on this basis that adaptivity occurs. The model is not used to predict student performance (and thus put Tutor in a position to determine which of perhaps several rules could have been invoked by a student's task response) or to analyse a student's difficulties in terms other than his rule learning (for example, by focusing on consistent misuse of pre-conditions and prerequisites) although there is no reason why this should not be attempted.

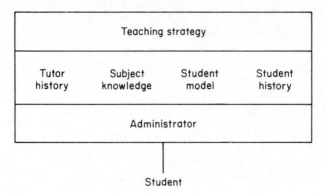

Fig. 6.1. The Tutor architecture.

Figure 6.1 serves to give an idea of how Tutor works. The administrator and teaching strategy are rule-based components (but with no semantic connections to the subject rule base) while the middle layer represents the data they use. Each is activated in a single cycle of interaction.

The subject knowledge comprises an explicit syllabus, a rule base of the subject, a library of tasks, and supporting textual strings. The syllabus is a tree structure of arbitrary depth where nodes represent topics, sub-topics, and individual subject rules at the lowest level, and arcs represent decomposition. Thus a node 'turning procedures' might have 'turning right' and 'turning left' as decompositions, each of which would be further decomposed to nodes representing single steps of the procedure. A list of tasks is associated with each leaf (subject rule). Textual strings are associated with tasks for presentation purposes, subject rules for expository purposes, and pre-conditions and prerequisites within subject rules for critique information.

The history databases are chronological lists of activities by the student and Tutor. For example, a Tutor history entry may indicate that a particular task had been presented to the student, and the student history his response to it.

Imagine that a student has been presented with a task to perform and has provided a solution. The administrator records the student's response in the student history database and then presents the task for the expert system (the subject rule base and its interpreter) to perform. A comparison of the two solutions – student and expert – enables the student model to be updated appropriately by the administrator. A correct solution results in credit assignment to the activated rule(s); debit assignments are made to the correct as well as the (student) activated rules in the case of an incorrect solution. Control then passes to the teaching strategy component.

A variety of decisions can be taken by the teaching strategy. As suggested by Fig. 6.1 the decision is based on the state of the student model, Tutor's knowledge of the subject (in terms of what tasks and topics are available to it) and what specific actions have been taken by Tutor and the student in the past (Tutor may not, for example, wish to re-present a recently given task). Other factors recorded in the histories influence the decision such as the type of training being given and who has the initiative (student or Tutor). For a wrong solution, the teaching strategy may decide to invite the student to try again. In this situation the administrator updates the Tutor history database (to indicate that the student should repeat the same task) and outputs a message to that effect to the student. A correct solution may result in the teaching strategy giving perhaps another but more difficult task associated with the same sub-topic (if the student model indicates the student has yet to gain mastery of it).

In any event the decision is communicated to the administator which performs an update of this information to the Tutor history database and then outputs a natural language sentence of it to the student. A new dialogue cycle is thus initiated.

At each point in the dialogue with a student, Tutor enables the student to take the initiative in a number of ways. He may select any topic from the syllabus and/or one of four types of training:

- novice
- skilled
- self-test
- examination.

If the student does not completely specify what he wants, the teaching strategy uses its four sources of knowledge to determine how best the specification should be completed.

Novice training consists of exposition followed by tasks and, where appropriate, remedial feedback. Skilled training assumes that the student has already received novice training either from Tutor or some alternative source, and provides tasks and remedial information. The self-test mode of training, which provides a range of tasks across the syllabus, is useful to the student using the system for the first time since it enables him (and Tutor) to assess the level of training required during subsequent use of the system. Tutor can set formal examinations, the results of which are made available to a human course administrator.

Other options available to the student include: WHY (or what is the justification for what you have just told me); I DON'T KNOW (I can't solve the task I have been presented with); ANSWER (give me your solution to the current task); CONTEXT (remind me what we're doing i.e. repeat the task or exposition); and HELP (indicate the options available to me and explain them).

Two prototypes were developed for Tutor. The first, the TL-Tutor prototype, was concerned with teaching the driving actions that are appropriate when a car is in the vicinity of traffic lights (Davies, Dickens and Ford, 1985). The 'traffic lights' domain was an artificial construction consisting of five well-defined variables: distance from the lights (far/near/at), state of the road (wet/dry), traffic condition (e.g. traffic ahead), colour setting of the lights (e.g. red and amber), and driving action (e.g. slow down). A restricted natural language interface was an important feature of this prototype since it allowed considerable freedom on the part of the student and, importantly, enforced recall for solutions to problems rather than recognition (which occurs for multiple-choice questions). The interface enabled a student to:

- Ask for a solution to a problem and its justification,
- Provide a solution to a problem in his own words,
- Define a new hypothetical problem for Tutor to solve,
  Ask for a solution to a problem refined in some way by a student, i.e. what if?
  Provide a conditional answer to a problem, i.e. if the problem X is refined to X′ my solution is Y,
- Ask a question about the problem (and not only about the well-defined variables but others too, e.g. am I going fast?).

The second prototype, HC-Tutor, drew but did not evolve from TL-Tutor, and was developed to explore the difficulties associated with a more realistic subject. Its aim was to teach a subset of the rules contained in the Highway Code. We did not attempt to provide a natural language interface for this prototype and this resulted inevitably in a loss of freedom on the part of the student; all but the first of the input types shown above were to be denied him.

6.3   APPRAISAL OF BEHAVIOUR

Self's set of questions concerning the behaviour of an ICAI system were derived from an informal set of 'motherhood' axioms that should apply in any teaching situation, computer-based or otherwise:

- The teacher should know something about the subject;
- The teacher should know something about the student;
- The student should be 'actively engaged' and not simply told;
- Learning is likely to be handicapped if the teacher and student have difficulty communicating with one another.

The fifteen questions fall into four categories relating to the above axioms:

- Subject knowledge,
- Student knowledge,
- Student control,
- Mode of communication.

Our appraisal is concerned with whether Tutor can behave in the way suggested by the questions.

6.3.1   Subject knowledge

Q.1   *Can the system answer arbitrary questions from the user about the subject?*

HC-Tutor's menu-based approach did not allow any questions from the student about the subject *per se*. This is not entirely due to the lack of a natural language interface since an underlying grammar reflecting the semantics of the domain could, in principle, have been constructed to allow such questions to be expressed through selection of semantic menu options. The student was, of course, allowed to ask for an answer and its justification to a set problem.

TL-Tutor with its natural language interface could answer various questions about the subject. The only limit to such questioning was the expressiveness of the semantic grammar used and the extent to which we were prepared to devote time to encoding information about the subject in a suitable form for query. It must be appreciated that this information is additional to the subject rule base since it is not needed to check a student's answer. Some examples of questions being asked, and the ability of TL-Tutor to answer them are shown below.

Tutor: what colour is next after red and amber?
Student: what comes after amber?
Tutor: the colour is green.
          ⋮

Tutor: you are far from the lights
          the lights are red
          there is traffic ahead
          what should you do?
Student: am I going fast?
Tutor: yes.
Student: I would slow down then.
Tutor: thats right.
          ⋮

Student: how fast am I going?
Tutor: I dont know.

The student's final question is parsed by the grammar but the administrator is unable to deal with it because the database of facts does not contain actual speed information.

Q.2   *Can the system give an explanation of a problem solution (including one of a problem posed by the user)?*

It was only in TL-Tutor that a student was allowed to suggest a problem. The difficulty of providing such a facility in HC-Tutor concerned the move away from a competent natural language interface. Without a natural language interface the student is denied a suitable medium to express the problem he wants to tackle. Other ways of allowing a student this freedom of expression are possible, for example through the use of menus, but the number of variables and values needed to uniquely specify a problem is high, and would necessitate sophisticated windowing and menu control techniques. We did not pursue this as a possible solution. For all problems set by HC-Tutor the system is able to give an explanation of a problem solution, e.g.

Tutor: you are approaching a roundabout from which you will take the
first exit,
do you need to use your indicator before reaching the roundabout?
Student: answer.
Tutor: you need to indicate left.
Student: why?
Tutor: to let other traffic know your intention.

In TL-Tutor, however, the student was allowed to suggest a problem by setting
scene variables and then asking what Tutor would recommend under those
circumstances and why.

Student: the lights are amber and the road is wet.
what should I do?
Tutor: you should continue.
Student: why?
Tutor: because with a wet road you would not be able to stop safely.

Tutor is able to achieve this because it enables scene variables to be established
through the interface as well as internally. Once a problem is defined, TL-Tutor's
expert system can provide the answer no matter where the problem originated.
Justifications for actions are associated with the activated subject rule.

Q.3   *Can the system give alternative explanations, using perhaps analogy?*

Alternative explanations could not be provided by TL-Tutor or HC-Tutor.
This stems from the fact that only one view of the subject has been
represented – namely, the subject rule base, and that there are no explicit links
between rules or rule components. By mapping a semantic net onto the rule base
it might be possible to use the supporting textual information for one rule to
explain another. For example, suppose two rules have similar prerequisites and
pre-conditions, then an explanation of one rule can be couched in terms of the
difference between its answer action and the answer action of the other rule, and
the critical differences of their prerequisites and pre-conditions.

Q.4   *Can it answer hypothetical questions, that is, questions not about the present
situation but about some imagined situation relating to it?*

Ideally a student should be allowed to conjecture ideas and explore them. This can
be facilitated by enabling a student to modify or specify a task and then allow him
to pose questions to the embedded expert system about the scenario he has
initiated. We were able to provide such a facility for TL-Tutor but not for HC-Tutor
with its limited interface. The 'what if?' facility of TL-Tutor enabled a student to
change scene variables for a presented scene, e.g.

Student: what if the lights are green and the road is dry?
Tutor: you should continue.

Questions such as the student's above could only refer to the well-defined scene variables and not supplementary variables such as speed, which are not recognized within the subject rule base.

Tutor's subject knowledge is therefore very limited, only Q.2 having been addressed by HC-Tutor (and then only for problems posed by Tutor). TL-Tutor, with its smaller domain and natural language interface, is a little better, with some capability for all questions except Q.3.

6.3.2   Student knowledge

Q.5   *Could the system give a report on the student's level of understanding?*

The student is assessed and graded by Tutor (as novice or master) for each topic in the syllabus and his particular strengths and weaknesses at a subject rule level are pinpointed. A profile of any named student, which provides the above information, can be generated by Tutor on request.

Q.6   *Are the system's explanations tailored to the user?*

For explanations to be understood, they should be pitched at the right level for a student and use only those concepts which the system has some evidence that he understands. Tutor does not tailor explanations for a particular user in the way envisaged by the question and explored by Sleeman (1984c).

Q.7   *Does the system provide informative feedback?*

This relates to the ability of a system to detect the need for informative feedback and to provide it if there is some evidence of misunderstanding. This Tutor achieves with some success, for example after presenting a series of tasks for a particular topic it will review those subject rules which the student model indicates the student shows a weakness on, but since it is assumed that a student's conceptual framework maps onto the one of the expert system it may make wrong assumptions about which particular misconceptions a student may have. TL-Tutor and HC-Tutor assume that a student's misconceptions are simply based on relationships between rule preconditions and prerequisites, and actions for the rule in question.

Q.8   *Are the problems presented by the system adapted to the user's needs?*

Tutor sets problems by selecting an appropriate task from a library of them. Task selection is based on the state of the student model (which indicates the strengths and weaknesses of a student in terms of the concepts he knows and does not know, and hence suggests tasks to probe particular weaknesses) and the history files (which inform the teaching strategy which tasks have already been undertaken by the student and thereby prevent repeated presentation of the same task).

6.3.3   Student control

Q.9   *Does the system actively engage the user?*

This question is difficult to answer decisively since some students may feel Tutor achieves it and others not. Tutor attempts to engage the student by selecting tasks that seem appropriate to the moment and indicating to some degree what it is doing and why, but in overall terms it is frustrated by its inability to sustain a lengthy dialogue.

Q.10   *Can the user initiate some new area of investigation?*

The student is able to exercise a reasonable amount of control over the level of the system. He can ask for:

- A self-test,
- An exam,
- Novice training,
- Skilled training,

and he can select any topic from the syllabus. He is not able, however, to ask directly for:

a. Harder/easier tasks
b. Higher/lower level exposition.

Indirectly he can achieve a. by selecting novice or skilled training as appropriate. Also, tasks are arranged in the library so that within either novice or skilled training easier tasks are presented for a concept when a student fails a more difficult one. Three levels of exposition were provided in TL-Tutor to meet b. but such a facility was not felt to be appropriate for the Highway Code which is couched in simple language that appeals to commonsense.

Q.11   *Does the system monitor such proposed changes, and comment upon them if they seem to be unwise?*

Although a student can range over the syllabus he is debarred from selecting topics which he has previously mastered. Tutor does not explain this to the student.

Q.12   *Does the system intervene if the user appears to be having difficulty?*

If a student has difficulty with tasks Tutor will provide easier tasks for the same topic and will eventually run out of them if the student does not succeed at some stage. In this situation Tutor provides some remedial exposition in the hope that the student will grasp the point. Again Tutor is frustrated through its inability to conduct a dialogue at arbitrary stages of its instruction – exposition is only provided at prescribed places, e.g. after the student has attempted and failed each task for a topic.

6.3.4   Mode of communication

Q.13   *Can the user express his inputs to the system in whatever way is most natural?*

SOPHIE provides an example of the sort of interface envisaged for Tutor. It has a restricted natural language capability based on the use of a semantic grammar. With SOPHIE there are but a handful of semantic categories to deal with and this perhaps explains the success of the interface. The Highway Code, on the other hand, has a vast number of semantic categories and it quickly became evident that it would require not only a very large lexicon but also a grammar of some size and complexity to deal with it. TL-Tutor, which deals with a small domain having only a few semantic categories, has a natural language interface comparable to SOPHIE's but HC-Tutor restricts the student to single-word and short-phrase inputs.

Q.14   *Does the system help if the user's input is not understandable by the system?*

HC-Tutor is not helpful if a student's inputs are not understandable but it makes up for this limitation by making clear to a student what inputs are legitimate and allowing some tolerance for mis-spelling and the use of synonyms and redundant words. HC-Tutor utilizes a semantic grammar but with a severely restricted lexicon. TL-Tutor is somewhat more capable. However, if a student's input is not parsable it does not indicate where the parse fails and thus help the student reformulate his input.

Q.15   *Are the system's outputs natural?*

All of Tutor's outputs are produced from pre-stored texts and templates. After some experience with the system this becomes quite evident to the student and we must admit that its outputs lack the naturalness suggested by the question.

6.4   HOW WELL HAVE THE RESEARCH AIMS BEEN MET?

A motivation of this project was to answer the question: 'Given that it is expensive to develop a knowledge base, could a knowledge base serve in a training system as well as in its more traditional role as a consultant?' To answer this satisfactorily we need to consider more detailed questions that are concerned with the original motivation for constructing the knowledge base:

a. Can a knowledge base constructed for operational purposes be used effectively, as it stands, within a tutoring framework, and if not could it be supplemented with support information (e.g. rule justifications) to do so?

b. Can a knowledge base constructed for instructional purposes be used, unaltered, for operational functions e.g. in a consultative mode?

c. Can a knowledge base be constructed with instructional and operational possibilities in mind and be used effectively for both?

Our research programme investigated b. to some extent; Clancey had previously investigated a.; but c. has not yet been addressed by the research community as far as we are aware.

In answer to a. Clancey was to find (Clancey, 1983a) that: i. a knowledge base does need support information if it is to be imparted effectively, ii. the knowledge base requires structure (and should not be a flat system of rules like MYCIN) if explanations are not to be limited to discussing individual rules, and iii. the rules themselves must be ordered with instruction in mind since the sequence of pursuing goals is important to a student (if not MYCIN).

In answer to question b., it can be stated that the Highway Code knowledge base was constructed solely for instructional purposes. Its success in that role is not easily judged: the critical comments that have been made in the previous section are not solely attributable to it – we can, for example, envisage a better ICAI system using the same knowledge base but with an improved framework. The HC knowledge base has not been used for operational purposes but it does demonstrate some performance characteristics that are associated with expert systems. It can be used to solve problems (which require situation-action information for their solution, unlike MYCIN which utilizes sub-goals-hypothesis rules) and it can provide simple explanations of its reasoning procedure. There is, then, some suggestive evidence that a knowledge base could serve in the two capacities mentioned but clearly, for the claim to be strengthened, much more evidence than has been provided is needed.

Although the research community has yet to undertake a concerted effort to examine question c. we are able to make some tentative comments based on our own experience about some differences between how a knowledge base is processed in the operational and the instructional situations. In the former case there is a need for one inference engine which, given a problem specification, determines a solution. This is the conventional use of an inference engine in the operational situation and it has a role in the instructional situation too. But, if the same knowledge base is to serve both operational and instructional purposes there seems to be a need for two additional inference engines to meet the specific needs of instruction. The conventional situation is shown in Fig. 6.2.

Problem P is presented to the inference engine and it determines a solution S to it. In Tutor the specification of a simple problem (e.g. one that involves a single

problem P ⟶ inference engine 1 ⟶ solution S

Fig. 6.2. Determining a solution.

step of a procedure) is expressed in terms of the variables (and their values) that are found on the left-hand sides of rules in the knowledge base, i.e. sequence name, unperformed actions, pre-conditions, and prerequisite actions. The solution to a simple problem of this sort is the action part of the right-hand side of the rule for which the left-hand side is satisfied by the problem specification. Since the left-hand sides of rules uniquely identify situations only one rule can be satisfied. Tutor uses this inference engine when a student does not attempt to solve a particular problem but instead asks for its solution, and Tutor uses it when the student does provide a solution in order to check its own derived solution against the student's. If the two solutions are different then a second inference engine is used.

Figure 6.3 shows how the second inference engine is used.

solution S' ⟶ inference engine 2 ⟶ problem P'

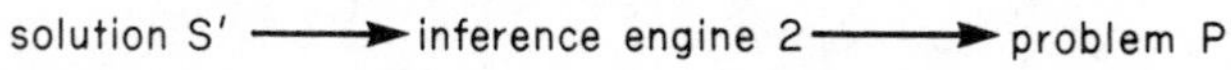

Fig. 6.3. Determining the problem solved.

It takes as input the student's incorrect solution S' and determines the problem P' that it solves. Clearly some solutions, e.g. check mirror, can be applied to many problem situations – turning left, turning right, and overtaking, for example. However, given a solution S', Tutor's search space of problems is constrained to those with the same sequence name as the one set to the student. Sequences are defined in terms of solution sets; thus there are no duplicate solutions in a sequence, and hence only one problem for a particular solution.

Tutor now has at its disposal two problem specifications – one for the set problem (P) and the other derived from the student's solution (P'). A third inference engine, shown in Fig. 6.4, uses the two specifications as inputs to determine a critique based on the differences between the two specifications.

problem P

\+   ⟶ inference engine 3 ⟶ critique

problem P'

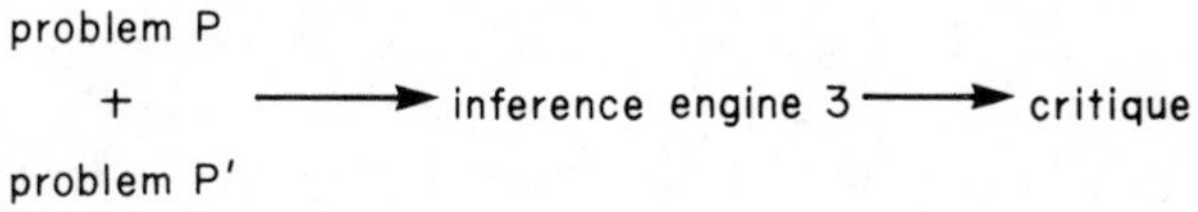

Fig. 6.4. Determining a critique.

In this case the inference engine is only applied to the two rules in the knowledge base associated with problems P and P', and it will make deductions about what should form the critique based on the differences between their left-hand sides. If, for example, the rule for P' has a pre-condition that is not a pre-condition for the rule associated with P then the critique would mention that the pre-condition has wrongly been assumed to be true.

It seems evident that the three types of access to a knowledge base that have been described are needed for instruction. That we have found it possible to provide a knowledge base formalism that allows these different types of access (which of course includes the type of access needed for operational purposes) encourages the belief that one knowledge base could serve in both instructional and operational roles.

A second stated research objective was to provide a general ICAI framework capable of instructing on a variety of subjects. Two questions which this raises are: 'what is the range of subject?' and 'how easily could a new one be slotted into the framework?'.

Although Tutor was designed with rule-based subjects in mind and so that the expertise in such subjects should be represented in a rule formalism, Tutor is not actually constrained by either condition, although it must be admitted that we have no results to support this claim. However, it seems evident that given a clean interface between expert system component and the rest of the system there is no reason why the expertise should not be represented as frames, semantic networks, or any other representation scheme. This allows, then, the possibility for Tutor to teach subjects which are not formalized as rules or cannot easily be represented in a rule formalism.

'Plugging in' a new subject domain is made possible by Tutor having a clear separation of its domain-dependent and independent parts. This aim has been met perhaps more convincingly than any other. Tutor's control mechanism is entirely independent of the subject to be taught as are its administrator and teaching strategy components. This is made possible by virtue of the way data are recorded in the student history, Tutor history, and student model. It is only the identifiers of data that are referenced by the two components and not their information content. Also, as we have mentioned, the subject knowledge base has a clean interface that enables us to consider knowledge and syllabus structures different to those presently implemented. It is fair to say that the cost of this generality has resulted in some loss of benefit in terms of richness of interaction with a student.

Finally, we wish to mention a third research objective – namely, that the software resulting from our endeavours should be able to be used as the basis for further research and development. The develop–test–review–throwaway sequence evident in much AI research is largely counter-productive and unnecessary. It encourages an undisciplined approach to software development that inevitably reduces the possibility of the originator or others refining his ideas through the developed software since it may lack the necessary structure and modularity that are needed, as well as being incomprehensible. In hindsight it seems evident that the utility of TL-Tutor would have been enhanced if we had paid greater attention to the relationship of behavioural properties (such as Self has suggested) and the elements of software architecture needed to support them. With the HC series we were wiser and we believe it has resulted in a robust and modular architecture that will serve for further research.

6.5 CONCLUSIONS

The Tutor system was developed for experimental purposes and our appraisal of it in terms of how well it stands up to a list of desirable behavioural properties suggests that more research and development of it is required. There are two fundamental weaknesses in Tutor. First, it needs a much richer description of the subject it is teaching, with a variety of views of the subject – some at a deeper level of understanding than provided by the surface rules of the Highway Code – if Tutor is to provide instruction for subjects of any complexity. Secondly, students (and Tutor) will suffer restricted patterns of behaviour unless an adequate interface component allowing a natural channel of communication is made available.

Our research objectives were largely met, however. We have gone some way to demonstrating that a knowledge base can in principle be used for both instructional and operational purposes provided it is developed with both purposes in mind. We have provided a general ICAI framework which we believe could be used to teach a variety of subjects – not necessarily rule-based. However, we are concerned on two accounts. Tutor has not been used to teach subjects of any complexity and we are uncertain of the impact this may have for our findings thus far. Also, it is not clear what the cost of having a general system is in terms of reducing the effectiveness of instruction. Finally, we have provided a framework that we believe to be robust and capable of evolving with our ideas.

ACKNOWLEDGEMENTS

The Ministry of Defence is gratefully acknowledged for its financial support for this research.

A number of people have contributed to Tutor in a variety of ways. The team at Logica has included Nigel Davies, Simon Dickens, Rod Rivers and Helen Tang. Steve Bevan, Dave Lowry and Philip Wetherall from the Royal Signals and Radar Establishment have provided much needed technical assistance and guidance. We have also benefited from consultations with Bran Boguraev, Rod Johnson, Tim O'Shea and John Self.

7

Methods for evaluating micro-theory systems

TONY PRIEST AND RICHARD M. YOUNG
Oxford Polytechnic, England
MRC Applied Psychology Unit, Cambridge, England

Cognitive scientists sometimes build computational models of human behaviour, in which different behaviour is explained by constructing different versions of the model. Traditional statistical methods cannot be used to evaluate such models. This chapter looks at two existing methods for evaluating such models, and proposes two new ones. The properties of the four methods are compared against a checklist of desirable criteria that such a method should ideally be able to satisfy. The use of psychologically based models of a student's knowledge are an important part of many ICAI programs, and progress in this field depends on being able to evaluate student models objectively.

7.1 WHAT IS A MICRO-THEORY SYSTEM?

Newell and Simon (1972) attempted to model human problem solvers in various domains by constructing computer programs that produced output comparable to the human subjects when placed in the same situations. The different programs were referred to by Newell and Simon as *micro-theories*. Such systems have been developed to model many human activities, such as logical inference, chess, the solution of cryptarithm puzzles (Newell and Simon, 1972), the solution of algebraic equations (Sleeman, 1984a), and the subtraction of integers (Young and O'Shea, 1981).

In this chapter we shall adopt the following terminology and assumptions:

- A *micro-theory system* is a set of related micro-theories intended to simulate the behaviour of a target population over some set of data points.
- A *micro-theory* is a computational model intended to simulate the behaviour of a subset of the target population.
- The set of data points over which the theory is held constant is termed the *span of consistency*. Typically, a micro-theory system will consist of a number of related micro-theories, each simulating a single subject. The span of consistency will in such a case be the set of behaviours of that one subject.

• Each micro-theory consists of the union of a *core procedure* and none or more variant procedures. Thus the core procedure will appear in every micro-theory of the micro-theory system. One may think of the set of variant procedures used in the different micro-theories as a 'kit of parts', used to build up particular models, or micro-theories.

The definition of what constitutes a variant procedure is necessarily implementation-dependent, but the system architecture must allow for the construction of programs which can be represented as sets, rather than lists, of procedures.

Clearly, these definitions do not suffice to describe every possible psychological model, but they do encompass a large number of such models. In particular, production rule systems and mal-rule-type models can be formalized in this way.

It needs to be emphasized here that the data points consist of human responses to external situations, and that the procedures of a micro-theory have access to the situation descriptions, but not to the human responses. For example, if one were considering the skill of long division, the situations presented to the human subjects would be long division problems, the natural span of consistency would be the set of questions answered by a single subject, and the responses would be the subject's answers; or possibly the answers together with their intermediate working. In such a case, the procedures used by the micro-theories are allowed access to the questions in order to produce their output, but are not able to access the student's behaviour.

Although the analysis given in this paper is rather more general, the micro-theories of greatest interest to ICAI will probably consist of cases such as the above where the situations are questions and the responses are the student's answers.

How variant procedures are selected to construct micro-theories is implementation-dependent. In existing micro-theory systems, the selection is usually done by hand after inspection of the data. There is no reason in principle, however, why this phase should not be automated. The use of a micro-theory as a student model in an intelligent computer tutor would only be possible if this process were carried out automatically.

7.2 MICRO-THEORY SYSTEMS AND ICAI

Micro-theory systems are of considerable importance to ICAI. Authors such as Clancey (Chapter 3) have suggested that accurate student models are essential for the construction of effective tutorial systems; and it is clear that the existence of an accurate student model depends on the validation of a psychological model of the domain under consideration.

Many of the skills relevant to ICAI can be represented by micro-theory systems. Thus, for example, the subtraction model developed by Young and O'Shea (1981), represents its knowledge as a set of production rules. The set of productions present in all the models is equivalent to the core procedure as defined in this paper, while other productions correspond to what are here termed *variant procedures.* Thus any method for evaluating micro-theory systems will apply to this one.

Another example of a micro-theory system directly relevant to ICAI is the LMS system of Sleeman (1984a), which models the solution of linear algebraic equations. LMS is more sophisticated than many systems in that it is capable of automatically identifying the relevant incorrect rules, or *mal-rules*, used by students; and therefore of constructing micro-theories automatically. In the production system architecture used by Sleeman, unlike that used by Young and O'Shea, the ordering of productions is significant. Therefore the variant procedures mentioned in this paper correspond not simply to mal-rules, but to ordered pairs of the form ⟨mal-rule, position⟩, where the second argument of the structure is the position of the mal-rule in the list of productions. Thus ⟨rule21, 13⟩ needs to be considered as a different variant procedure to ⟨rule21, 14⟩. This is a necessary qualification, because the same production can produce different results, depending on where it is placed.

Now suppose that we are interested in a particular skill, and that we construct a micro-theory system to model human performance in it; how can we evaluate this system . . . or is it impossible to do so?

7.3   MICRO-THEORY SYSTEMS AND STATISTICS

Traditional statistical tests cannot be applied to the evaluation of micro-theory systems for two reasons.

a. The particular micro-theories that are constructed are produced after the data has been collected, and are constructed in the light of that data. These micro-theories are built from procedures that pre-date the collection of the data, but the selection of procedures to form each micro-theory is data-dependent.

b. Traditional statistical methods of analysis involve calculating the probability that the results could have been obtained by chance. One may think of the methods of statistics as being addressed to the question: 'How do I know these results didn't come about by chance?'. Where the behaviour generated by a micro-theory is not a point on a one-dimensional scale, but a complex data structure, such as an equation or a chess move, the probability that this behaviour could have been obtained by chance is negligible. This renders much of the traditional statistical apparatus irrelevant.

Since micro-theories are constructed after examination of the data, it is not at all surprising or impressive when they are able to reproduce the behaviour they are designed to model, provided that they are allowed to make use of an unlimited number of variant procedures. If variant procedures corresponding to every conceivable behaviour are allowed, it would be strange indeed if the micro-theory system could not yield a good fit to the data. The term usually used to describe such a theory is 'trivial'.

In general, one would expect there to be a trade-off between parsimony of structure and goodness of fit when constructing a micro-theory system. At the opposite extreme, one can imagine extremely parsimonious micro-theory systems which use very few variant procedures, but whose goodness of fit to the data is negligible. Such micro-theory systems may also be regarded as trivial, though for a different reason.

The question of importance in evaluating micro-theory systems is therefore not 'Could the results have been obtained by chance?', but 'Are the results obtained trivially?'. Any micro-theory system when compared to an alternative, must demonstrate that it obtains its results in a way that is less trivial than its rival. Thus the evaluation of micro-theory systems depends on the existence of a method for measuring or demonstrating their non-triviality. There are two complementary approaches to this problem.

a. One option is to define an explicit measure which rates a micro-theory system for its parsimony in accounting for a variety of data. The development of such a method forms the theme of the rest of this chapter.

b. A second option is to constrain the model so that it maintains the same structure over some defined set of data points, here termed the *span of consistency*. The selection of a span of consistency greater than a single data point in itself prevents the construction of trivial models with one variant procedure corresponding to every data point. Therefore the larger the span of consistency, the greater the penalty for inconsistency. For many applications, the natural span of consistency is the output of a single subject.

7.4   CRITERIA FOR A DESIRABLE MEASURE

There are two ways in which a micro-theory system may be unsatisfactory and trivial: it may have negligible fit to the data, or it may use an excessive number of variant procedures in order to achieve its results. A satisfactory evaluation measure will therefore have to penalise both extremes, and thus it is necessary to take both goodness of fit and parsimony of structure into account.

As far as goodness of fit goes, it is necessary to compare the output of the student with that of the relevant micro-theory acting in the same situation. The simplest comparison is to classify each data point as a 'hit', or a 'miss' (where the micro-theory produces different output). This type of scoring has been adopted in the examples in this chapter, but there is nothing in the definition of a micro-theory to prevent the use of (domain-specific) partial matching scores in place of an integral count of hits. It will, however, be assumed that the matching score for each data point lies between zero and one.

There is here an issue as to the grain size at which one wishes to evaluate a given micro-theory system. One could look at the parsimony of the system in terms of the number of micro-theories needed to account for the hits achieved, or one could look at the number of variant procedures needed to construct the micro-theories, or one could look at the internal structure of the variant procedures themselves.

Considering the parsimony of the system in terms of the number of micro-theories used is initially attractive, but it leads to some conceptual problems. For, in a sense, the number of micro-theories that one would want a system to use is precisely the number of different types of behaviour shown by the human subjects, no less. The real explanatory power of a theory lies not in describing many subjects in the same way, but in accounting for a wide variety of behaviour by a small set of structural variations in the theory.

This would focus attention less on the number of micro-theories, and more on the number of variant procedures from which they are constructed. From this point of view, what one would be looking for would be a theory capable of producing many behaviours (micro-theories) from a limited range of basic variant procedures. Such an approach takes place at a finer level of grain size than a count of micro-theories, and yields a correspondingly deeper level of evaluation.

An analysis of variant procedures does not, however, take account of differences of size and structure of different variant procedures. Without placing further constraints on the nature of possible variant procedures, it would seem impossible to deal with an evaluation at any finer level of detail. But adding constraints on the structure of procedures reduces the generality, and hence the usefulness, of the evaluation method.

In the remainder of this chapter we shall consider two evaluative measures which treat a micro-theory system as a whole, one which analyses it in terms of its constituent micro-theories, and one which analyses it at the level of variant procedures.

An ideal measure for the evaluation of micro-theory systems would need to satisfy the following criteria:

1. *The numerical value criterion.* The measure should consist of a single number falling in a predetermined range of values. This ensures that different micro-theories tested against the same data can be ordered with respect to the measure.
2. *The accuracy criterion.* The measure should increase every time the model fits the data (scores a hit).
3. *The inaccuracy criterion.* The measure should decrease every time the model does not fit the observed data (scores a miss).
4. *The parsimony criterion.* The measure should decrease for every additional variant procedure added to the system to account for the data.
5. *The prediction criterion.* The value of the measure obtained from a data sample should provide an unbiased estimate of the value to be obtained from a larger sample.
6. *The assumption criterion.* The measure should not involve the introduction of assumptions about the distribution of hits outside the area covered by the data sample. For example, it should not assume that the relationship between the number of micro-theories or variant procedures used and the number of hits obtained conforms to any particular analytic function.

7.5   MEASURES FOR EVALUATING MICRO-THEORIES

This paper considers four methods which can be used for the evaluation of micro-theory systems. Two have been used already, and two are proposed here for the first time. They are:

a. The percentage of hits,
b. The error fit measure,
c. The micro-theory evaluation quotient,
d. The cumulative hit curve.

7.5.1   The percentage of hits

The *percentage of hits* is defined as:

$$\frac{\text{Number of hits} \times 100}{\text{Number of data points}}$$

This is the most simple-minded of the measures described here, and is applicable to types of theory other than micro-theory systems.

It satisfies the criteria of numeric value, accuracy, inaccuracy, prediction, and assumption; but not that of parsimony. This has the unfortunate result that theories of unlimited complexity are not discriminated against. Given such freedom, it would be surprising if even fundamentally inadequate models could not be 'tweaked' into yielding encouraging results. For a criticism of the inadequacy of this measure when used in isolation, see Ohlsson (1982).

7.5.2   The error fit measure

The *error fit measure* (Young and O'Shea, 1981) is defined as:

$$\frac{\text{Number of hits} - \text{number of false errors}}{\text{Number of data points}}$$

This was used to evaluate a model of children's subtraction (Young and O'Shea, 1981), focusing on erroneous solutions rather than correct solutions. The set of data points therefore consisted of the erroneous solutions, together with any solutions predicted to be erroneous by the model chosen.

The concept of a 'false error', depends on the span of consistency of the model. Where the model is optimized over a span of consistency larger than a single data point, the possibility arises that the model predicts an error which the subject does not actually make. This is defined as a 'false error'. Young and O'Shea used this measure to decide whether to add new micro-theories to particular models. If the use of a micro-theory did not improve their measure, it was not introduced.

This measure is obviously more sensitive to the presence of false errors than the 'percentage correct' measure, but it is not directly affected by the degree of parsimony of the model. It satisfies the criteria of numeric value, accuracy, inaccuracy, prediction and assumption; but not that of parsimony.

The defence of a micro-theory system evaluated by this measure against the charge of triviality depends on its use in conjunction with a sensible span of consistency. Since a given micro-theory has to stand comparison with the data over all points in its span of consistency, it is extremely difficult to envisage a trivial theory showing up well with this measure when used in conjunction with a significant span of consistency. However, there is no explicit calculus relating the measure, its span of consistency, and any conclusion regarding the degree of triviality of the hypothesis.

7.5.3   The micro-theory evaluation quotient

The micro-theory evaluation quotient, or μ-quotient, is defined as:

$$\mu = \frac{\text{Number of hits} - \text{number of variant procedures}}{\text{Number of data points}}$$

Assuming that no variant procedure is introduced unless it yields at least one hit, this defines a measure whose value lies in the range $0 <= \mu < 1$. The value may be exactly zero, but can only approach unity asymptotically at best. This measure satisfies the criteria of numeric value, accuracy, inaccuracy, parsimony, and assumption; but not that of prediction. Note that in the extreme case where a micro-theory system requires as many variant procedures as there are data points, the value of μ is zero.

The first two methods considered above do not involve consideration of variant procedures. This one does, and if it is to be used in practice, it is necessary to have some guarantee that a degenerate micro-theory system has not been created in which the core procedure accounts for the entire variability of the data, and no added variant procedures are required. Three alternative conditions are proposed, any one of which would be sufficient to preclude this state of affairs. It is therefore a requirement of the method that at least one of the following conditions should apply before the micro-theory evaluation quotient is used.

1. Every subject should be placed in the same set of situations (e.g. asked the same set of questions). Since the core procedure necessarily produces the same responses in the same situations, this prevents a degenerate micro-theory system containing only a single core procedure from accounting for any variation in response between subjects.

2. The core procedure should consist of the procedures for correct problem solution, and each variant procedure should correspond to a mal-rule. This would be an appropriate condition to apply to a micro-theory system designed to explain errors in a skill which could be done correctly in only one way.

3. The core procedure should be such that every branch within it is executed for every situation it is presented with. This would prevent having a core procedure that behaved in different ways in different situations.

Item	Micro-Theory	Score
1	None	Miss
2	C + V1	Hit
3	C + V1 + V2	Hit
4	C + V3	Hit
5	C + V1	Miss
6	C + V1	Hit
7	C + V1 + V2	Hit
8	C + V3	Hit
9	None	Miss
10	C + V3	Hit

Fig. 7.1. A table of results.

The criterion not satisfied by the μ-quotient is the one that requires that the value of the measure found from a small data sample should provide an unbiased estimate of its value over a larger sample of data items. In fact, as one considers smaller and smaller subsets of a given set of data items, the μ-quotient decreases to zero. To see how this happens, consider the imaginary table of results shown (Fig. 7.1). Here, 'C' stands for the core procedure, and $\langle Vi \rangle$ for the variant procedures.

The μ-quotient can be calculated for the first item alone, for the first two items, the first three items, and so on. These values are given in Fig. 7.2 and clearly demonstrate how using a small data set results in a low value for the μ-quotient.

No of items in data set	μ-quotient
1	0
2	0
3	0
4	0
5	0
6	0.167
7	0.287
8	0.375
9	0.375
10	0.4

Fig. 7.2. Values for the μ-quotient.

One thing that becomes explicit when a μ-quotient is used is the possible degree of benefit of introducing a new micro-theory. For example, if it were possible to match the subject's output for item 5 by introducing a single new variant procedure, this would not affect the value of the μ-quotient. There would therefore be no incentive to introduce a new procedure in such circumstances.

7.5.4 The cumulative hit curve

This approach involves tabulating the frequency of particular micro-theories: that is, the number of hits each has accounted for. Micro-theories can then be ranked by frequency of hits, and cumulative frequencies calculated. These are expressed as percentages of the total number of data points, and so this value will only reach 100% if all the data points have been classed as 'hits'. For the fictitious example given above, this yields the following results:

Micro-theory	Rank	Frequency of hits	Percentage cumulative hits
C + V3	1	3	30
C + V1 + V2	2	2	50
C + V1	3	2	70

Figure 7.3 shows a curve rising monotonically with negative acceleration. From the graph may be read the number of micro-theories needed to achieve any given percentage of hits, up to the maximum value plotted on the graph.

In this example, we think of micro-theories being successively added to the

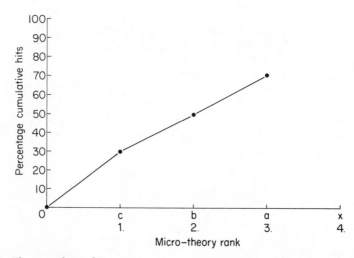

Fig. 7.3. The cumulative hit curve.

system, and we look at the effect that this has on the percentage of data points accounted for. This is why micro-theories 'C + V1 + V2', and 'C + V1', are given ranks of 2 and 3, and not ranked at 2.5 each.

From the graph we can also obtain upper and lower limits to its rightward extension, if we allow ourselves to introduce the assumption that the micro-theories with the highest frequency are identified first. Thus any newly-constructed micro-theory can be expected to have a rank lower than any existing micro-theory, and will have a frequency equal to or less than the lowest micro-theory frequency measured so far.

The minimum possible frequency for a new micro-theory under these assumptions is one (since no micro-theory is introduced unless it results in at least one hit); and the maximum possible value is equal to the frequency of the previous entry in the table.

So in the example given, the possible percentage cumulative frequency values for a possible new micro-theory range from 80 to 90, as shown in Fig. 7.4.

The cumulative hit curve is not a single numeric measure like the other measures considered earlier, but it can still be looked at in the light of some of the criteria for an evaluative measure.

1. *The numeric value criterion.* The curve can be used to derive numeric values for the number of micro-theories needed to achieve $X\%$ of hits, for any arbitrarily chosen value of X. For instance, the number of micro-theories needed to account for 50% of the data points can be read off the curve.

2. and 3. *The accuracy and inaccuracy criteria.* These criteria are satisfied by the numeric values derived from the curve.

4. *The parsimony criterion.* The criterion of parsimony does not relate directly to the curve as such. This is possibly its weakest point as an analytic tool.

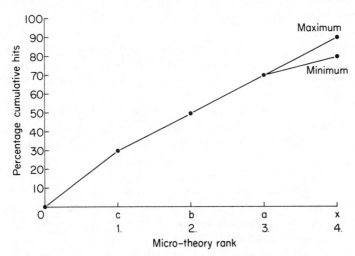

Fig. 7.4. Possible extensions to the cumulative hit curve.

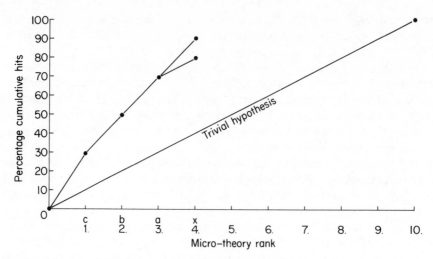

Fig. 7.5. The cumulative hit curve compared with a trivial hypothesis.

However, one may infer something about the economy of the underlying model from the shape of the curve.

A micro-theory system which is trivial because it is unable to account for the data will be represented by a line along the horizontal axis, because the cumulative percentage frequency is always zero. A micro-theory system which is trivial because it involves the construction of a different micro-theory to account for every data point will result in a cumulative hit curve which is a straight line through the origin and the point $(N, 100)$, where N is the number of data points. Of course, such a micro-theory system may be ruled out in a particular case by the requirements of the span of consistency. For the example data considered above, this gives a curve as shown in Fig. 7.5.

The more economically the micro-theory system being evaluated can account for the data, the faster will its cumulative hit curve rise to a value near its maximum before levelling off. This can be clearly seen in the diagram, and gives a characteristic shape rising swiftly to a 'knee' point, flattening off beyond.

5. *The prediction criterion.* This does hold, in contra-distinction to the μ-quotient, which is not an unbiased estimator of larger samples. Of course, the accuracy with which results obtained from small samples reflect those obtainable from large samples is subject to random error; but there are no systematic distortions introduced by the definition of the artefact.

6. *The assumption criterion.* As presented above, the cumulative hit curve involves no assumptions about the data. If this requirement is relaxed, the fitting of an analytic function to the known data points permits an indefinite extension of the curve to the right, from which values otherwise unobtainable may be derived, as shown in Fig. 7.6. This can be used as a pragmatic tool to estimate how many more micro-theories would be needed to account for any arbitrary proportion of

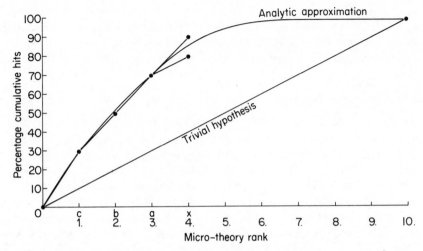

Fig. 7.6. Analytic approximation to the cumulative hit curve.

the data. In the case of the curve shown in Fig. 7.6, it would not appear useful to spend time trying to construct more than seven micro-theories, if that.

The difficulty with such a relaxation of this criterion is that there is no reason in principle to expect the curve to be of one analytic form rather than another. This renders such a process of limited use in evaluating micro-theory systems that have already been developed.

7.6   SUMMARY OF THE FOUR METHODS

7.6.1   Percentage correct

This is easy to calculate, but doesn't address the problem at the heart of micro-theory evaluation: 'How do we know that this score has not been obtained trivially?'

7.6.2   Error fit measure

This measure is specifically adapted to evaluate micro-theory systems designed to model the production of errors. When used over a large enough span of consistency, it penalizes micro-theories which predict false errors, but it does not deal with the issue of structural parsimony in an explicit and predictable way.

7.6.3   Micro-theory evaluation quotient

The μ-quotient deals with the triviality question explicitly. All micro-theory systems will give μ-quotients falling in the range $0 < = \mu < 1$, and values near zero are indicative of extremely trivial systems.

Unfortunately, the μ-quotient of one sample cannot be used as an estimate of the μ-quotient of a larger sample, although it can give a lower bound to it. Nor does this measure distinguish between a very economical theory applied to a few data points, and a less economical theory applied to many.

7.6.4   Cumulative hit curve

The cumulative hit curve provides a representation which can be taken in at a glance, and from which numeric data may readily be derived. It yields an unbiased estimate of the behaviour of the micro-theory system with a larger data sample.

It has no explicit way of representing triviality, but such a property in a micro-theory system can be seen reflected in the shape of the curve. The relationship between the shape of the curve and the degree of economy of the corresponding theory also allows competing micro-theory systems to be compared in this respect.

7.7   APPLICATIONS AND CONCLUSIONS

Some method of micro-theory evaluation is urgently required, not least for the development of psychologically accurate models of human problem solving which are needed in the next generation of computer-based tutors. Overlay models, production systems, and mal-rule-based student models are all examples of micro-theory systems; and a method applicable to micro-theory systems in general could be used with all of these formalisms.

We have outlined two existing methods and two new methods for looking at this problem. The μ-quotient consists of a single number which gives a direct measure of the explanatory economy of a micro-theory system. The cumulative hit curve gives a more complex, but easily comprehensible view that does not make the degree of explanatory economy explicit, but gives a pragmatic indication of whether it is worth developing further micro-theories for a given domain.

Neither of these approaches has been related to traditional forms of statistical analysis, nor does either measure deal with behaviour at any finer level of detail than that of counting complex data structures as (possibly partial) 'hits' or 'misses'. Nor do any of the methods described here have anything to say about which situations should be selected to elicit behaviour from experimental subjects. It may be possible to load the scales in favour of a theory by presenting subjects with situations for which the theory performs well – ignoring situations for which it performs badly. Such 'data loading' is clearly contrary to the spirit of scientific enquiry (i.e. it's naughty), but this issue is not dealt with by any of the measures described here. Nor, of course, is this problem addressed in any general way by the methods of conventional statistics. It would seem to the authors that this is a matter which can only be dealt with adequately in a domain-specific, or even an implementation-specific, way. Data loading is therefore not considered any further here.

Thus although the μ-quotient and the cumulative hit curve deal with some of the methodological issues in this area, there are others still waiting to be tackled, and the need for solutions to these problems can only increase with time.

ACKNOWLEDGEMENTS

The authors wish to acknowledge the helpful and constructive criticism they have received from Donald Broadbent, Ben duBoulay, Thomas Green, George Kiss, Roger Lindsay, Rod Nicolson and Steve Payne. Any remaining flaws or errors in this paper are entirely the authors' responsibility.

Part two

ICAI techniques

8

The role of episodic memory in a intelligent tutoring system

GERHARD WEBER, GERD WALOSZEK AND
KARL FRIEDRICH WENDER
Technische Universität Braunschweig, West Germany

Intelligent tutorial systems usually include a component which simulates the current knowledge of a learner. Learner models differ with respect to whether they explicitly model the individual learning history or not. So far, this has been done in a rudimentary fashion only. We plan to incorporate into our computer-based tutor for the programming language LISP psychologically more plausible assumptions about knowledge acquisition, integration and application. According to Schank and his co-workers, knowledge is considered to be non-formal, mainly case-based, and may be generalized on demand. These ideas will be put into an individualized learner model which is basically episodic in nature. This contrasts with more static models e.g. differential learner models. Such an episodic learner model enables the tutorial system to offer remindings and analogies to the learner which are based on his or her own learning history. By an example it is explained how the structure of an episodic learner model might look and how generalization might reflect the subject's learning process.

8.1 SOME CONSTRAINTS ON INTELLIGENT TUTORING

Learning a programming language is one area in which intelligent computer-aided instruction (ICAI) is used most appropriately. Compared to other domains where someone learns to work with the computer it is reasonable that the computer itself guides and assists the interaction with the learner. Our contribution to research in ICAI is to build a computer-based intelligent tutoring system (ITS) for the programming language LISP which possesses certain properties. This LISP-tutor is intended to teach programming novices without prior experiences in other programming languages, e.g. students in psychology, but also students who have already learned other programming languages and programming techniques, e.g. students in computer science.

One may ask why it is interesting to build yet another tutor, since there already exists a well-functioning one. However, one can also ask this question if someone does yet another experiment on short-term memory or list learning. Our main goal is not merely to develop another tutor, but to model the processes of knowledge acquisition and to diagnose these processes. As Anderson (1984) has pointed out, building an ITS is a valuable research tool for the study of mental processes that are involved in learning. Thus, from a psychological point of view, modelling the learner and exploring tutorial strategies are the most interesting psychological aspects in building computer-based tutorial systems. As an example, the LISP-Tutor GREATERP (Anderson and Reiser, 1985) is psychologically based on Anderson's ACT* theory (Anderson, 1983) and may be viewed as a test of the ACT* theory.

Intelligent tutoring systems usually include a component which attempts to reflect the current knowledge of the learner. These learner models differ with respect to whether they explicitly model the individual learning history or not. So far, this has been done in a rather rudimentary fashion only. In some cases, the model concludes from the successful work on specific problems that the learner has reached a certain level of knowledge. Such a 'canonical' learner model is individually modified only during the actual work on problems within a learning session. This is done on the basis of rules which identify bugs and correct solutions, e.g. GREATERP (Anderson and Reiser, 1985). In other cases, the model summarizes whether concepts in question are already learned and how successfully they were applied, e.g. WEST-game (Burton and Brown, 1982).

Our computer-based tutor for the programming language LISP is intended to differ in several aspects from current systems. While these systems rely heavily on AI techniques, we plan to incorporate more psychologically plausible assumptions about knowledge acquisition, integration and application. These ideas will be put into an individualized learner model which is mainly episodic in nature, in contrast to more static ones like difference learner models. What we mean by an 'episodic model' is described in Section 8.3.

Our position is influenced on the one hand by our own experiences in teaching LISP and on the other hand by criticisms of AI concerning formal approaches to the representation of human knowledge, by the novice–expert paradigm, and by work on natural language understanding. In the following these positions will be outlined.

Human knowledge is considered by us to be non-formal. Though some syntactic programming knowledge may be formalizable, the more abstract algorithmic and planning knowledge may not be. Moreover, it is questionable whether even formal knowledge is formally represented in humans at all. So, restricting ourselves to formalizable domains seems psychologically not very interesting.

Expert knowledge is often considered as a collection of formal rules. This is contrasted with the view that expert knowledge consists mainly of a vast collection of examples which allow generalization and planning behaviour. Moreover, experts are often unable to specify the rules that guide their behaviour. This leads to the view that those rules are either inaccessible or 'abstractions of the behaviour' but not explicitly represented. It seems plausible that experts are able to 'reconstruct' such rules on demand. But this might be a special generalization process – the rules need not correspond directly to certain memory structures.

Knowledge is dynamic. New knowledge is interpreted in terms of prior knowledge. Knowledge that fits into the existing body of knowledge may be generalized if certain aspects are in common. Knowledge that does not fit may lead to specialization of existing cases.

Knowledge may be used to generate expectations and hypotheses. Differences between expectations and behaviour may lead to revisions of knowledge, in the learner model, or to appropriate tutoring behaviour (e.g. reminding). Building hypotheses may guide the tutoring process itself.

From our own experience in teaching LISP we conclude that students use remindings of their solutions of previous problems. These remindings are drawn from concrete LISP learning episodes which are analogous to the problem under consideration. Corresponding results are stated by Anderson's group (Anderson, Farrell and Sauers, 1984; McKendree, Reiser and Anderson, 1984). While these authors report that such remindings occur mainly in the first hours of LISP learning, we assume that remindings occur during all phases of learning, even when the programmers have reached expert level. However, these remindings need not rely on single concrete episodes since advanced problems may differ in too many aspects. Instead, they rely on generalizations from related episodes which may be similar to rules in other types of representations (e.g. production systems). In a later section a framework will be outlined describing how learning to program may be modelled in terms of an episodic long-term memory.

To summarize, knowledge is considered to be non-formal and mainly case-based, and may be generalized on demand. This notion may be captured in a dynamic episodic memory which is used to collect, integrate, and apply this knowledge.

8.2 LEVELS OF PROGRAMMING KNOWLEDGE

Over six months we have systematically documented our experiences with teaching LISP. Our main goals were to:

- Find out which bugs are produced by beginners in learning LISP,
- Determine on which levels those errors occur, and
- Discover which strategies human tutors use in teaching LISP.

We investigated LISP-learning in two different situations.

First, the participants of a LISP course were observed during their interactions with the LISP interpreter while working on exercises. The input by the learner as well as the output of the interpreter were continually recorded into a file. Half of the participants were students of psychology, the other half were students in computer science. There were novices without any knowledge about computers and programming as well as students with some background in other programming languages.

Second, we observed learning situations of single LISP learners with individual human tutors. Here again, all interactions with the LISP interpreter were recorded. Additionally, we tape-recorded the verbal interaction between the learner and the tutor.

As one result of these experiences in teaching LISP, we conclude that programming knowledge comprises three different levels:

- The implementational or syntactic level, which in our case consists mainly of syntactic and semantic knowledge of LISP;
- The algorithmic level consisting of the actual steps of computations, which may be expressed in some kind of natural language, but may be influenced by the programming language used;
- The planning level, comprising the intentions of the programmer, often given as input/output specifications.

The assumption of three levels is more differentiated than distinctions reported in the literature about programming–learning. There we find the distinction between the 'depth-first' programming style which corresponds to the implementational level and the 'breadth-first' programming style which is mainly based on the planning level. A programmer is able to switch between these levels. In contrast, novices tend to prefer the implementational level, whereas experts tend to prefer the more abstract levels. A tutor has to reflect this change in a two-fold manner. First, as an educational tool it should facilitate the change from a novice's representation to an expert's representation. Second, as a psychological model, it should reflect this representational change in its learner model. We think that an episodic learner model serves both purposes equally well.

From our own experiences we conclude that the algorithmic level plays a dominant role in learning to program, especially in later lessons when problems depend more on algorithmic knowledge (e.g. iteration, recursion) and when LISP is the learner's first programming language. So, the tutor has to assist the learner in acquiring the needed algorithmic knowledge. One example of a computer-based tutor which supports the learner in the first natural-language-based planning phase, where in the first case much algorithmic knowledge is needed and less syntactic and semantic knowledge of the special programming language necessary, is the Pascal-tutor Bridge (Bonar and Cunningham, Chapter 24).

8.3 EPISODIC MEMORY AND THE ROLE OF GENERALIZATION

There are only a few ideas in current literature on how to organize an episodic memory effectively. We follow the studies of Schank and his co-workers on natural language understanding (Schank, 1982; Kolodner, 1983; Lebowitz, 1983). Though there are large differences between programming languages and natural languages, some parallels give some insight into knowledge integration and use. Of course, programming languages do not provide dialogues. Instead, programming is a kind of one-way communication: the programmer wants the computer to do something (of course, he gets some sort of response, either error messages, successful or unsuccessful runs). On the other hand, and more important, programming and natural languages convey far more than a literal sense of words or sentences. In programming languages, these are the algorithms and plans of the programmer. The difficulty of finding errors is comparable to that of interpreting natural texts, especially if there are no constraints available (context, task). Hence, predicting the programmer's intentions and plans is one of the most difficult tasks of a diagnostic system in an ITS.

Knowledge may be encoded in different ways, but none of them has been proven to be psychologically valid so far. Instead, it has been shown that most of them are formally equivalent in some way or another. So it seems to be a matter of personal taste, which representation is chosen. In knowledge-rich domains scripts and frames have become popular – as has object-oriented programming, the corresponding AI technique. This idea, though, is not free from problems and has undergone considerable changes in the past. The use of scripts varies from static knowledge structures to dynamic structures that are constructed during processing. As many other AI techniques, scripts or frames have problems with contradictions and with the creation of new categories. Up to now, categories are solely pre-determined by the programmer. Since we intend to build our user model as a learning system, this status is not sufficient – even in restricted domains like programming.

Many ideas for our research project are drawn from the work of Schank (1982) on natural language understanding. In this section, we want to address some of the differences between his approach and our ideas. These differences mainly originate from the different domains the theories focus upon. Schank's main interests lie in memory processes and structures. He focuses on internal processes that build and change memory structures, without any concern about external actions by the understander. This is quite different from problem solving as involved in learning to program which requires a person to exhibit certain external behaviour. Schank's efforts resulted in programs that take texts as input and create memory structures from these texts. The involved internal processes of generalization and specialization can be called 'automatic', because they occur whenever a situation calls for them. For example, in Lebowitz's program IPP (Lebowitz, 1983) generalization takes place whenever two episodes can be integrated into a more general structure.

In our case the situation is quite different because the memory structures are built partly during reading of text-books or instructions and partly during programming experience (learning by doing). The written material may suggest some sort of general knowledge structure, e.g. frames, for iteration or recursion. But it is not evident whether the learner's memory structures already reflect this knowledge. This can only be inferred on the basis of observed problem-solving behaviour. Often, especially in the beginning, the learner refers to the text material to refresh his or her knowledge. Therefore, it should take quite a number of learning episodes to establish such knowledge structures in memory. On the other hand, with written material at hand learners are able to generalize already in early learning stages. For example, they are able to use general problem solving strategies in order to generalize. These generalizations are often based on analogies.

The difference to Schank's approach lies in the manner in which memory structures are established and modified. In the beginning, external 'memories' are used (or needed) until the structure is sufficiently established. The generalization process is not automatic, at least not all parts of it, but is rather based on active, attentional problem solving. The same holds for processes of specialization and discrimination. Failures are actively processed. These attentional processes give rise to memory processes which may lead to revisions in the memory structure. It should be noted that Anderson (1983) assumed automatic generalization and discrimination processes in his ACT* theory, but has revised this assumption for discrimination processes (Lewis and Anderson, 1985).

Our approach has another important implication for the episodic learner model: not only differences from prototypes (prototypical memory structures) should be recorded in the episodic learner model, but the actual problem-solving episodes, too. They may serve as important cues for indexing the relevant knowledge. That is, they may contain problem features as well. Of course, this 'episodic' knowledge may lose its effectiveness, when many similar problems have been worked on. But sometimes even some irrelevant, exterior features of such episodes may persist and remain effective retrieval cues. Obviously, an ITS will have problems with recognizing many of these features at all (e.g. working on one particular terminal at a specific time of the day).

What we want to stress in this section is that the actual problem-solving behaviour plays an important role in the creation and modification of the domain knowledge. Reading examples in text-books is not sufficient for effective revisions and improvements of the knowledge base as it should be, if one follows Schank.

8.4   AN EXAMPLE

Our main goals for the development of the episodic user model are to:

- Capture the process of learning by integration of new knowledge, and
- Capture the generalization processes that accompany learning and lead to expert behaviour.

These ideas shall be illustrated by an example. It is based on our experience in tutoring a student while she was learning numeric iteration in the fifth lesson. She had only very little prior programming knowledge. This example will show how the representation of learning episodes in an episodic memory might look. There is no empirical evidence that information is represented exactly in this manner or in another way.

The concept of iteration was introduced in our LISP course via the traditional *prog*-scheme and was illustrated by the problem to compute all positive integers up to an arbitrary integer n:

sum $(n) = 1 + 2 + \ldots + n$

The corresponding LISP code was:

```
(DEFUN SUM (N)
   (PROG   (I RES)
           (SETQ I N)
           (SETQ RES 0)
       LOOP
           (COND ((ZEROP I) (RETURN RES)))
           (SETQ RES (PLUS RES I))
           (SETQ I (SUB1 I))
           (GO LOOP)))
```

Additionally, the definition of the function *SUM* was explained by the notion of a general *PROG*-scheme for numeric iteration:

```
(PROG   ⟨list-of-loc-vars⟩
        ⟨initialisation-of-loc-vars⟩
     ⟨looptag⟩
        (COND (⟨test on end-of-iteration⟩
                  ⟨return⟩))
        ⟨prog-body⟩
        ⟨update-of-loc-vars⟩
        (GO ⟨looptag⟩)))
```

We start from the assumption that the learner uses the *PROG*-scheme as a frame for storing information in an episodic memory. This seems plausible because the single parts of the function definition were associated with the corresponding parts of the *PROG*-scheme in the text of the lesson. Therefore, the representation of this learning episode might look as shown in Fig. 8.1.

In this figure, one can see how the special episode ⟨1⟩ is represented in an episodic memory. Only those parts are recorded which differ from the super-ordinate structure, in this case the *PROG*-scheme, or are special instances in that template. The super-ordinate structure is sometimes called a *memory organization package* (MOP) (Schank, 1982).

The first exercise asked the learner to define an iterative function which computes a to the power of n for integer values of a and positive integer values of n:

power $(a \ n) = a^n = a \times a \times \cdots \times a$ (n times)

A typical novice's strategy was to go step by step along the analogous example of the function-definition *sum* (n). This was done without further reflections about a general iteration-scheme. The strategy was additionally supported by the fact

```
*prog*                              episode ⟨1⟩
                                    is-a *prog*
(PROG
    ⟨list-of-loc-vars⟩              (I RES)
    ⟨init-of-loc-vars⟩              (SETQ I N)
                                    (SETQ RES 0)
    ⟨looptag⟩                       LOOP
(COND (
    ⟨test-on-end-of-iter⟩           (ZEROP I)
    ⟨return⟩                        (RETURN RES)
))
    ⟨prog-body⟩
    ⟨update-of-loc-vars⟩            (SETQ RES (PLUS RES I))
                                    (SETQ I (SUB1 I))
(GO
    ⟨looptag⟩                       LOOP
) ))
```

Fig. 8.1. Episodic memory after the first episode. Representation of episode ⟨1⟩: *sum (n)*.

that the LISP code was typed in sequentially on the LISP top level or into the editor.

A solution for the function *power (a n)* of a novice was as follows:

```
(DEFUN POWER (A N)
    (PROG   (I RES)
            (SETQ I N)
            (SETQ RES 0)                 ⟨---buggy
        LOOP
            (COND ((ZEROP I) (RETURN RES)))
            (SETQ RES (TIMES RES A))
            (SETQ I (SUB1 I))
            (GO LOOP) ))
```

The bug we observe in this example stems from an inappropriate analogy to the example in the text. The learner did not realize that in the case of the addition operation the result variable must be initialized with *sum (0) = 0* whereas in the case of a multiplication operation the result variable must be initialized with *power (a 0) = 1*. The learner was corrected by the human tutor by saying that in the case of an addition (e.g. in *sum (n)*) the result variable must be initialized with zero whereas in the case of a multiplication (e.g. in *power (a n)*) it must be initialized with one.

This bug could have been avoided if *sum (n)* and *power (a n)* were initially

```
*prog*                        episode ⟨1⟩              episode ⟨2⟩
                              is-a *prog*             is-a *prog*
(PROG
   ⟨list-of-loc-vars⟩         (I RES)                 (I RES)
   ⟨init-of-loc-vars⟩         (SETQ I N)              (SETQ I N)
                              (SETQ RES 0)            (SETQ RES 1)
                                     add                     mult
   ⟨looptag⟩                  LOOP                    LOOP
COND (
   ⟨test-on-end-of-iter⟩ (ZEROP I)                    (ZEROP I)
   ⟨return⟩                   (RETURN RES)            (RETURN RES)
))
   ⟨prog-body⟩
   ⟨update-of-loc-vars⟩ (SETQ RES (PLUS RES I))       (SETQ RES (TIMES RES A))
                        (SETQ I (SUB1 I))             (SETQ I (SUB1 I))
(GO
   ⟨looptag⟩                  LOOP                    LOOP
) ))
```

Fig. 8.2. Episodic memory after the second episode. Representation of episodes ⟨1⟩: *sum (n)* and ⟨2⟩: *power (a n)*.

presented in terms of a recursive definition, e.g.:

sum $(0) = 0$
sum $(n) = n + $ sum $(n - 1)$ for $n > 0$

and

power $(a\ 0) = 1$
power $(a\ n) = a * $ power $(a\ n - 1)$ for $n > 0$

After the correct solution of the problem the representation in episodic memory could be as shown in Fig. 8.2.

As can be seen in Fig. 8.2, the representation of the two episodes appear to be quite similar. According to generalization processes in the IPP (integrated partial parser) (Lebowitz, 1983), we assume a generalization process on the episodic representation whenever there are such similarities. The matching parts of the episodes are merged into one new super-structure and only the deviations from this structure are recorded together with a tag to the episodes. This is illustrated in Fig. 8.3.

After this generalization the episodic representation has become much more economic. Most of the episodic information can be inferred from the general PROG-scheme and from the generalized numeric *prog*-scheme *prog-1*. Only the information which differs from episode to episode is represented explicitly.

On the basis of this episodic representation it should be easy, even for the

prog	*prog-1*	episodes ⟨1⟩, ⟨2⟩
	is-a *prog*	is-a *prog-1*
(PROG		
⟨list-of-loc-vars⟩	(I RES)	
⟨init-of-loc-vars⟩	(SETQ I	
	⟨start-value⟩	N
	)	
	(SETQ RES	
	⟨start-value⟩	0 if add -- ⟨1⟩
	)	1 if mult -- ⟨2⟩
⟨looptag⟩	LOOP	
(COND (		
⟨test-on-end-of-iter⟩	(ZEROP I)	
⟨return⟩	(RETURN RES)	
))		
⟨prog-body⟩		
⟨update-of-loc-vars⟩	(SETQ RES	
	⟨update-form⟩	(PLUS RES I) -- ⟨1⟩
	)	(TIMES RES A) -- ⟨2⟩
	(SETQ I (SUB1 I))	
(GO		
⟨looptag⟩	LOOP	
)))		

Fig. 8.3. Episodic memory after generalization on the first two episodes. Representation of episodes ⟨1⟩: *sum (n)* and ⟨2⟩: *power (a n)*.

beginner, to define an iterative function to compute the factorial of *n* (*n*!). Let us skip the LISP code for the factorial function. After successfully resolving the factorial problem the episodic representation might look as shown in Fig. 8.4.

But what happens if the learner has to solve a problem which does not fit into the already represented rudimentary iteration scheme? The next more complex problem the subject had to solve in our LISP lesson was to define an iterative function to compute the sum of all integers from *m* to *n* with *m* less than or equal to *n*.

$$\text{sumall } (m\ n) = m + (m + 1) + \cdots + n$$

In this case the previously generalized *prog-1*-scheme does not fit completely.

Now, there exist numerous solutions for this task. For example, one could try to preserve the *prog-1*-scheme as far as possible, or, one could build up a new, more general iteration-scheme with the *prog-1*-scheme as a special case. In any case, a lot of revising, reorganizing, building of new concepts, etc. has to be done.

If the learner wants to maintain the already learned *prog-1*-scheme, she must transform this new problem into such a form that it becomes a special case of the

prog	*prog-1*	episodes ⟨1⟩, ⟨2⟩, ⟨3⟩
	is-a *prog*	is-a *prog*
(PROG		
⟨list-of-loc-vars⟩	(I RES)	
⟨init-of-loc-vars⟩	(SETQ I	
	⟨start-value⟩	N
	)	
	(SETQ RES	
	⟨start-value⟩	0 if add -- ⟨1⟩
	)	1 if mult -- ⟨2⟩, ⟨3⟩
⟨looptag⟩	LOOP	
(COND (		
⟨test-on-end-of-iter⟩	(ZEROP I)	
⟨return⟩	(RETURN RES)	
))		
⟨prog-body⟩		
⟨update-of-loc-vars⟩	(SETQ RES	
	⟨update-form⟩	(PLUS RES I) -- ⟨1⟩
	)	(TIMES RES A) -- ⟨2⟩
		(TIMES RES I) -- ⟨3⟩
	(SETQ I (SUB1 I))	
(GO		
⟨looptag⟩	LOOP	
)))		

Fig. 8.4. Episodic memory after the third episode. Representation of episodes ⟨1⟩: *sum (n)*; ⟨2⟩: *power (a n)*, and ⟨3⟩: *factorial (n)*.

prog-1-scheme. The following definition of *sumall* will do this:

```
(DEFUN SUMALL (M N)
   (PROG   (I RES)
           (SETQ I (DIFFERENCE N M))
           (SETQ RES 0)
      LOOP
           (COND ((ZEROP I) (RETURN (PLUS RES M))))
           (SETQ RES (PLUS RES I M))
           (SETQ I (SUB1 I))
           (GO LOOP)))
```

This function-definition may be implemented in the previously existing representation in the episodic memory as shown in Fig. 8.5.

Not one single subject from a total of 25 solved the *sumall* problem in this manner. Novices without knowledge in mathematics did not realize the implicit *lower bound 0* or were not able to transform this special lower bound *0* to a more

	prog	*prog-1* is-a *prog*	*prog-11* is-a *prog-1* episodes ⟨1⟩, ⟨2⟩, ⟨3⟩	episode ⟨4⟩ is-a *prog-1*
	(PROG			
⟨list-of-loc-vars⟩		(I RES)		
⟨init-of-loc-vars⟩		(SETQ I	N	(DIFFERENCE N M)
		⟨start-value⟩		
⟨start-value⟩		)		
		(SETQ RES		
		⟨start-value⟩		
		) 0 if add-- ⟨1⟩, ⟨4⟩ 1 if mult-- ⟨2⟩, ⟨3⟩		
⟨looptag⟩		LOOP		
	(COND (			
⟨test-on-end-of-iter⟩		(ZEROP I)		
⟨return⟩		(RETURN ⟨result⟩))	RES	(PLUS RES M)
	))			
⟨prog-body⟩				
⟨update-of-loc-vars⟩		(SETQ RES		
		⟨update-form⟩	(PLUS RES I) -- ⟨1⟩ (TIMES RES A) -- ⟨2⟩ (TIMES RES I) -- ⟨3⟩	(PLUS RES I M)
		)		
		(SETQ I (SUB1 I))		
⟨looptag⟩		LOOP		
	(GO			
⟨looptag⟩				
	)))			

Fig. 8.5. Episodic memory after reorganization caused by the fourth episode. Representation of episodes ⟨1⟩:*sum* (n), ⟨2⟩:*power* (a n), ⟨3⟩:*factorial* (n), and ⟨S⟩:*sumall* (m n)

general lower bound *m*. Learners who possessed a more abstract iteration-scheme defined the following *sumall* function:

```
(DEFUN SUMALL (M N)
  (PROG   (I RES)
          (SETQ I M)
          (SETQ RES 0)
    LOOP
          (COND ((GREATERP I N) (RETURN RES)))
          (SETQ RES (PLUS RES I))
          (SETQ I (ADD1 I))
          (GO LOOP)))
```

The LISP code for this *sumall* definition is accompanied by a complex reorganization of the structure in episodic memory. For example, a more general iteration-scheme, **prog-2**, may be created. It entails the new explicit concepts of a *lower* and an *upper* bound for the iteration process and a distinction whether the iteration goes from the upper to the lower bound or the other way. The old **prog-1**-scheme is now a sub-structure of the more general **prog-2**-scheme. Episodes ⟨1⟩ to ⟨3⟩ are subsumed under the **prog-1**-scheme whereas episode ⟨4⟩ is directly connected to the **prog-2**-scheme. Fig. 8.6 shows the resulting structure of the episodic memory.

For a novice programmer who has no previous knowledge of a general iteration algorithm this situation will lead to some confusion and will result in errors or even incomplete definitions. Errors must be corrected piece by piece. The error messages of the LISP interpreter have to be analysed and interpreted, and, if there is a tutor, he has to explain errors and to offer hints.

This example stresses the importance of *algorithmic knowledge* when learning a programming language. The novice does not possess the necessary algorithmic knowledge and has to reach this level of programming knowledge before he is able to create the concrete LISP code. Without any help from the text of the lesson or from a tutor the programmer may fail to solve the problem. However, this failure does not stem from inappropriate knowledge in the programming language nor from missing techniques to design a LISP function but from missing knowledge about relevant algorithms. On the other hand, programmers who have acquired this algorithmic knowledge in connection with other programming languages do not have any problem in solving this task, if there are no problems on a lower implementational level. This is what we observed in our LISP course. All students who had prior knowledge and experiences in other programming languages solved this simple problem without any difficulties.

8.5 FAILURE-DRIVEN LEARNING

As pointed out in the last section, the second prominent process working on the structure of episodic knowledge besides the principle of generalization on the basis

	prog-2 is-a *prog*		*prog-1* is-a *prog-2* episodes ⟨1⟩, ⟨2⟩, ⟨3⟩	episode-⟨4⟩ is-a *prog-2*
prog				
(PROG				
⟨list-of-loc-vars⟩	(I RES)			
⟨init-of-loc-vars⟩	(SETQ I	⟨start-value⟩)	⟨upper bound⟩ N	⟨lower bound⟩ M
	(SETQ RES	⟨start-value⟩)	0 if add -- ⟨1⟩ 1 if mult -- ⟨2⟩, ⟨3⟩	0
⟨looptag⟩	LOOP			
(COND (				
⟨test-on-end-of-iter⟩			(ZEROP I)	(GREATERP I ⟨upper bound⟩) N
⟨return⟩	(RETURN RES)			
))				
⟨prog-body⟩				
⟨update-of-loc-vars⟩	(SETQ RES	⟨update-form⟩)	(PLUS RES I) -- ⟨1⟩ (TIMES RES A) -- ⟨2⟩ (TIMES RES I) -- ⟨3⟩	(PLUS RES I)
	(SETQ I	⟨update-form⟩)	(SUB1 I)	(ADD1 I)
(GO	LOOP			
⟨looptag⟩				
)))				

Fig. 8.6. Episodic memory after the fourth episode. Representation of episodes ⟨1⟩:*sum* (*n*), ⟨2⟩:*power* (*a n*), ⟨3⟩:*factorial* (*n*), and ⟨4⟩:*sumall* (*m n*).

of similarity is the principle of *failure-driven learning*. Erroneous or missing strategies, buggy concepts, and faulty generalizations result in failures which guide the reorganization or completely new arrangement of structures in episodic memory.

The appropriate integration of new knowledge and the organization of new structures is not the most important aspect in modelling the learner according to a dynamic episodic memory. Much more important, an episodic memory can record which erroneous attempts the learner made to solve a problem, which hints were given, how the correct solution was found, and so on. An ITS should be able to find within the individual learning history which will be represented in the individual episodic learner model, any episode that is analogous to the problem under consideration. These analogies from the learner's own learning history, called remindings, should be offered by the ITS if the learner does not find the next step in the solution of the problem or if he makes the same error as in the analogous episode. Such a tutorial strategy was repeatedly observed in learning situations with human tutors in our own tutorials or by Anderson's ITS-group (McKendree *et al.*, 1984).

So far, it has not been clear how the principle of 'failure-driven learning' may be adequately implemented in an episodic learner model. Some suggestions (Riesbeck, 1981; Kolodner 1983) to mark erroneous structures, episodes and processes may also be helpful in the case of an its. Their markings contain explanations and reasons why the error happened, and lead to the correct solution, if there is one.

At this point in time it is too early to make specific suggestions for solutions to these problems of the representation of incorrect solutions and dead ends. But we think that modelling the learner in terms of a dynamic episodic memory would be an important step towards individualization in the research on ITS.

ACKNOWLEDGEMENT

This project is supported by the Deutsche Forschungsgemeinschaft under Grant We 498/12.

solution based method for discovering students' misconceptions

ERNESTO COSTA, SYLVIE DUCHENOY AND YVES KODRATOFF
Universidade de Coimbra, Portugal and Université de Paris-Sud, France

A good computer tutor is one which clearly understands the student (the concepts he/she knows, the strategies he/she uses and the misconceptions he or she has), adapting itself to the student's capabilities. As a consequence the main part of an ICAI system is the student model module containing a 'picture' of the learner. In this chapter, we describe how to infer students' beliefs by using resolution. Resolution is used not only to suggest hypotheses but also the prove them, contrasting with some machine-learning methods which construct inductively a theory from examples.

9.1 INTRODUCTION

9.1.1 Traditional approach

Computers have been involved in education for a long time (O'Shea and Self, 1983). One of the first proposals was a consequence of the behaviourist theory of stimulus-response: learning is not independent of the stimulus received by the student and so teaching is conceived as the organization of a stimulus in order to induce in the student a desirable behaviour (Skinner, 1968). The most primitive systems are programmed learning-like, students being exposed to the same fixed sequence of teaching material independently of their performance. More sophisticated systems try to avoid this linearity by introducing some branch capabilities. They are obliged to anticipate all possible answers of the student to choose the alternative appropriate to that answer. These systems used author languages as an aid in the preparation of the teaching units.

One can criticize this approach from different points of view. The more important of them are 1. the absence of individualization (everyone receives the same sequence of units) and 2. the fact that students are considered to be passive elements of the learning process (they just answers questions put by the system).

9.1.2   Artificial intelligence approach

In contrast to this approach of 'learning by being told' another methodology based on Piaget's theory of learning was proposed. It states that the role of a student acting as a learner is to develop general problem-solving skills and this can be achieved through programming (Papert, 1980). The language LOGO was developed to attain that goal, by using graphic facilities. Important concepts like sequencing, branching and recursion are learned as primitive problem-solving tools. We are at the opposite side of the theories of learning spectrum, which can be characterized as 'learning by doing'. The advocates of this approach claim that this is the way to achieve individualization.

We can argue against that: 1. using the computer only as a passive tool is too poor: computers are not used to guide students in solving their problems; 2. it is not clear at all that programming will increase general problem-solving skills. Even if it is so this is not enough: learning a particular topic requires some specific knowledge which cannot be attained through programming.

To overcome the drawbacks of these approaches artificial intelligence proposes a new paradigm for learning which we may define as *learning through interaction:* learning is a task involving an intelligent being interacting with his or her environment. The environment may take several forms. In particular, it can be the physical world and we call it *learning through experimentation*: it can be another intelligent being and that is *learning through communication*. In this chapter we will be mostly interested in learning through communication. The AI community traditionally views the learner as the computer itself, the problem being thus the transfer of expertise or knowledge from a human to the computer (Michalski, Carbonell and Mitchell, 1983); for educational purposes we are interested in the reverse situation, that is, in building systems which enable the controlled transfer of knowledge from an expert computer to a human learner.

In order to be effective these intelligent computer-aided instruction systems (ICAI systems for short), besides being truly interactive (both the student and the computer may take the initiative at any moment), must have certain characteristics, in particular (Barr and Feigenbaum, 1982; Costa, 1986; O'Shea and Self, 1983; Sleeman and Brown, 1982):

a. Friendliness: it must be possible to communicate using natural language, graphics, sound, etc.;
b. Intelligence: to emulate a human tutor. This depends on knowledge about i. The domain being taught, ii. The student (what he knows, his misconceptions) and iii. Teaching strategies.

The majority of existing ICAI systems are constructed around a (previously existing) expert system (Clancey, 1982). As Self (1985a) points out, this leads to putting the emphasis on conducting the learner to the level of expertise of the system. Nevertheless, the main goal of teaching is not to transform each learner into an expert (an impossible task!). Rather, a good computer tutor is the one which clearly understands the students, adapting itself to the students' capabilities (the concepts they know, the strategies they use and the misconceptions they have). As a consequence the main part of an ICAI system is the student model module containing a 'picture' of the learner.

As learning is a complex task a student model may be characterized by several aspects. In this chapter, we are only interested in studying a student's misconceptions. We present a deductive method for discovering the sources of misconceptions based on the resolution principle (Robinson, 1965).

Other approaches have been proposed to the problem of discovering misconceptions (see Gilmore and Self, Chapter 11). They are mainly based on the existence of a set of *mal-rules* defining a set of possible incorrect student's behaviour. The student's model is dynamically constructed by matching his or her answer against the set of these mal-rules. These methods have been applied to domains which can be modelled as procedural skills (like algebra or geometry) and are meant to give an explanation of *how* a certain wrong behaviour was produced. Our method, on the contrary, can be applied to domains other than well-structured ones detecting misconceptions which also involve concepts. Furthermore, in our framework we try to answer the deeper question of understanding *why* a student has a particular misconception. These points will be made clear later in the chapter.

9.2 WORKING HYPOTHESIS

9.2.1 Meaning, context and understanding

As we said, we are interested in studying the problems which arise during a learning process by communicative interaction involving a human learner and a teaching machine. Our thesis is that the reasons for failure in the communicative process may be, in some cases, ascribed to the student's misunderstanding of the meaning of the sentence (or text) produced by the teacher. A single sentence like 'Tomorrow I will go to your home' may be perceived in different ways by someone depending on the context. It may be purely informative (I will visit you), it may be a menace and so on. So, meaning is linked to a person and a context. Misunderstanding may thus be caused by teacher and learner working with different contexts.

In order to determine the student's misconceptions an ICAI system must establish not only the context where the lesson takes place, but also the related contexts which possibly may explain the reasons for a wrong answer. For instance, Fig. 9.1 shows two related taxonomies which may provide different interpretations of sentences.

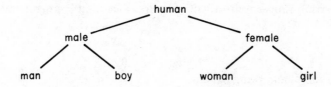

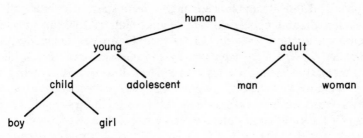

Fig. 9.1. Two related taxonomies.

9.2.2 Student model

In our system, a student is represented by two boxes: one is called *semantic memory* and contains all his previous knowledge (in principle); the other is called *working memory* and incorporates the student's immediate understanding of the facts. These boxes are connected: the current understanding of the facts is validated by the semantic memory and, conversely, what has been learned (in the working memory) is transferred to the semantic memory.

9.2.3 Knowledge representation

Knowledge is represented by mean of taxonomies (like the ones above) and axioms (either facts or rules) all expressed as Horn clauses (Kodratoff, 1985). For instance,

Domain: Natural science

1. Object(x) :−Living(x).	% living and not living
2. Object(x) :−Not_living(x).	% 'things' are objects
3. Eat(x, y) :−Living(x), Likes(x, y).	% x eats y if x is
	% living and likes y
4. Living(cat).	% a cat is a living thing
5. Living(person).	% so is a person
6. Not_living(bridge).	% but not a bridge

is a (partial) simple context, with 1. and 2. defining the taxonomy

$$\text{Object}$$
$$\diagup \qquad \diagdown$$
$$\text{Living} \quad \text{Not\_living}$$

and all the others being axioms.

9.2.4   The method

Before giving a detailed example of our method let us start with a brief outline of it.

We assume that after being exposed to some material the student is asked to give some explanation for a fact. The student's answer indirectly gives his interpretation for the facts expressed by the question, and this is his initial working memory. The task of the system will be to infer completely what is in the student's semantic and working memory, fixing the context used by the student. From the context we deduce a reason for the answer. The system has the correct meaning for the question (its 'ideal' working memory) as well as other pieces of knowledge related to the facts of the lesson (its 'ideal' semantic memory).

To fill the student's semantic and working memory we pick one assertion from the answer, say A, and try to validate it by resolving its negation against the system's semantic and working memory. This is the standard technique for proving theorems by resolution in computational logic. Details of the technique are given in Chang and Lee (1973).

If we can infer the empty clause, A is validated and the clauses used in the resolution are assumed to be in the student's semantic memory. We try the other assertions.

Suppose we cannot derive the empty clause and that R is the remainder of the resolution. This means that the system doesn't have a rule expressing under what conditions R is true (in logic terms, a Horn clause like $R :- Q$ is missing). The system asks an *oracle* (whose nature will be discussed later) why R is true or false. Let us call Q the answer. This implies that $R :- Q$ is a theorem and that the fact $Q :-$ is assumed by the student (in order to be possible to derive the empty clause). That information may be used to discover the context in the semantic memory of the system (if it exists) where the theorem is valid.

9.3   AN EXAMPLE

Suppose that our domain is history, more precisely French 17th century history. The 'teacher' is trying to have from the learner an explanation for the fact that 'Louis XIV used to wear wigs'.

First of all the sentence must be interpreted in the system's ideal working memory. For instance,

Wig (A, LOUIS XIV)
Wear (LOUIS XIV, A)

ct1:
AX1:
    $\forall x$ Man(x) & Noble(x) & Live(x, 17th century) $\Rightarrow \exists y$ Wig(y, x)

ct2:
AX2:
    $\forall x$ People(x) & Disguise(x) $\Rightarrow \exists y$ Wig(y, x)
AX3:
    $\forall x$ People(x) & Disguise(x) $\Rightarrow$ Have–Fun(x)

ct3:
AX4:
    $\forall x$ Woman(x) & Bald(x) $\Rightarrow \exists y$ Wig(y, x)

Fig. 9.2. Three possible contexts expressed in first order logic.

A $\in$ ornament (LOUIS XIV)
Live (LOUIS XIV, 17th CENTURY)

The predicates and functions mean that:

- the main characters are LOUIS XIV and an object A, which is a Wig belonging to LOUIS XIV;
- the main action is Wear;
- a secondary action is the fact that LOUIS XIV lived during the 17th century;
- and A is a kind of ornament that belongs to LOUIS XIV.

The use of the function *ornament* will be justified later.

Now let us suppose that one of the pupils gives the following interpretation: 'Indeed Louis XIV always wanted to have fun'. His working memory will thus be:

Have-fun(LOUIS XIV)

To discover the reason for the misunderstanding the system must have in its ideal semantic memory some information defining several possible contexts. Using first order logic axioms we may have the situation shown in Fig. 9.2.

These axioms must be transformed into Horn clauses defining the ideal semantic memory. During this process we are obliged to introduce Skolem functions, which of course, must refer to the data type of their variables (see Chang and Lee (1973) for details). We have already used one of them in our interpretation of the teacher sentence, namely ornament. The set of clauses is:

$\alpha 1$: Wig(ornament $(x), x$) $: -$ Man(x), Noble(x),
                              Live$(x,$ 17th century).
$\alpha 2$: Wig(gadget $(x), x$) $: -$ People(x), Disguise(x).
$\alpha 3$: Have-fun(x) $: -$ People(x), Disguise(x).

α4: Wig (aesthetic_prothesis (x), x) : — Woman (x), Bald (x).

Note the role of the Skolem functions, defining the possible interpretations for the fact of using a wig.

The ideal semantic memory also includes some more obvious general axioms and instantiated facts like

α5: People (x) : — Man (x).
α6: Man (LOUIS XIV) :–.
α7: Noble (LOUIS XIV) :–.

This set of clauses (or a subset) may belong to the student's semantic memory. Our method, while explaining the student's belief, will make some of those clauses appear as belonging actually to him.

Let us now try to understand the student assertion Have-fun (LOUIS XIV) by inferring how it is a student axiom.

We use the resolution principle to derive the empty clause from the ideal semantic and working memory together with the goal:

: — Have-fun (LOUIS XIV).

Using the axiom AX3 of the context ct2 (the only applicable axiom in the example) and general axioms and facts we have:

Have-fun(x) :– People(x), Disguise(x)
          | ___:– Have-fun(LOUIS XIV)
:– People(LOUIS XIV), Disguise(LOUIS XIV)
          | People(y) :– Man(y)
:– Man(LOUIS XIV), Disguise(LOUIS XIV)
          | Man(LOUIS XIV) :–
:– Disguise(LOUIS XIV)

with $\{x, y \leftarrow \text{LOUIS XIV}\}$.

Since no other axiom can be used to derive the empty clause, the system ask the oracle why – considering the lesson – he thinks that 'Louis XIV disguised himself'. Suppose the answer is 'Because he wore his wig'. As we said in in Section 9.2.4, this answer implies that

Disguise(LOUIS XIV) :–
    Wear(LOUIS XIV, A), Wig(A, LOUIS XIV)

is a theorem and, thus, that the facts

Wear(LOUIS XIV, A) :–
Wig(A, LOUIS XIV) :–

are assumed by the student. Using resolution again, the system will be able to deduce the empty clause:

:– Disguise(LOUIS XIV)

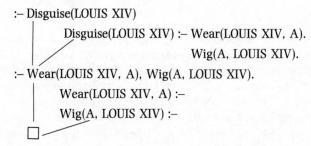

Disguise(LOUIS XIV) :– Wear(LOUIS XIV, A).

Wig(A, LOUIS XIV).

:– Wear(LOUIS XIV, A), Wig(A, LOUIS XIV).

Wear(LOUIS XIV, A) :–

Wig(A, LOUIS XIV) :–

This result enables the system to connect Disguise and Wig, and defines a context – ct2 – in which the student is, probably, reasoning. The system may try to 'discover' more links by resolving, for instance, Wig with other clauses in that context. Using AX2:

$\text{Wig(gadget}(x), x) :– \text{People}(x), \text{Disguise}(x)$

—————————————— :– Wig(y, x)

:– People(x), Disguise(x)

—————————————— People(LOUIS XIV) :–

:– Disguise(LOUIS XIV)

with $\{x \leftarrow \text{LOUIS XIV}, y \leftarrow \text{gadget (LOUIS XIV)}\}$ and $A \in$ gadget (LOUIS XIV).

We find the same remainder as before. In order to obtain the empty clause the system needs again to use the previous inferred student's belief. This means that the student strongly believes that the theorem is true. More important, this gives us a reason why this belief is so strong: he thinks that the wig of Louis XIV is a gadget!

Having found a context, the ct2, we may explore this in several ways. In particular, the system may try to prove other beliefs belonging to ct2 or may try to conduct the student to ct1, which is the correct context. Note that in this context wig has the correct interpretation of being an ornament. In fact, using AX1:

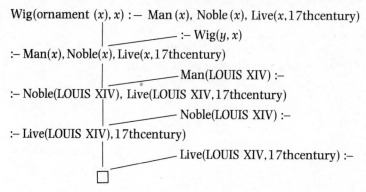

$\text{Wig(ornament }(x), x) :– \text{Man }(x), \text{Noble }(x), \text{Live}(x, 17\text{thcentury})$

—————————— :– Wig(y, x)

:– Man(x), Noble(x), Live$(x, 17\text{thcentury})$

—————————— Man(LOUIS XIV) :–

:– Noble(LOUIS XIV), Live(LOUIS XIV, 17thcentury)

—————————— Noble(LOUIS XIV) :–

:– Live(LOUIS XIV), 17thcentury)

—————————— Live(LOUIS XIV, 17thcentury) :–

and $\{x \leftarrow \text{LOUIS XIV}, y \leftarrow \text{ornament (LOUIS XIV)}\}$. As we also had the interpretation $y \leftarrow A$, we also can say that $A \in$ ornament (LOUIS XIV).

9.4   CONCLUSION

We have described how to infer students' beliefs by using resolution. Resolution is used not only to suggest hypotheses but also to prove them, contrasting with machine learning methods which construct inductively a theory from examples. Nevertheless, it shares with machine-learning techniques its dependence on the existence of an *ideal* interpretation possessed by the system. The explanation of a pupil's misconception is based on the existence of an *oracle* used as an assistant which appeared as external to both the system and the user. Actually, this is not mandatory, and the student himself can be the oracle, explaining, when asked by the system, some aspects of his world. This is a more real learning situation.

We use contexts to represent knowledge, each context giving an interpretation of the different problems which can arise within a teaching unit. For simplicity, we have assumed that contexts are independent of each other and complete. In practice, however, this is not the case. Contexts may share some information (for instance axioms $\alpha5$, $\alpha6$ and $\alpha7$ in our example). They form a hierarchy: common knowledge could be placed in a separate context at a higher level. Moreover, contexts are, in general, incomplete, because it is impossible to anticipate all possible interpretations a student can give to a problem (for instance, in our example, we can think of another context relating wigs with judges).

Our method is not restricted by these problems. In particular, regarding the problem of completeness, if the system doesn't have an explanation for a misconception in its semantic memory (in a context), it can, by asking the student, dynamically construct a new context, thus (self-) improving its knowledge about possible causes of wrong answers.

Although the ideas developed in this chapter may not cope with all types of misconceptions, we think they will be a fruitful basis for a general diagnosis technique to be included in the student module of an ICAI system.

ACKNOWLEDGEMENTS

The authors would like to thank John Self for many detailed comments, which helped us to improve this work.

This research was partially supported by the grant of EEC to the COST-13 project 'Machine Learning and Knowledge Acquisition'.

10

Guided discovery tutoring and bounded user modelling

MARK ELSOM-COOK
The Open University, England

The chapter discusses a range of teaching styles possible for ICAI and suggests that they may usefully be thought of as points within a framework of guided discovery teaching methods. The use of bounded user modelling within a guided discovery framework is introduced, and an application of the technique in a LISP teaching system is described. Extensions to the system to support more flexibility of teaching styles in conjunction with this user-modelling method are outlined.

10.1 INTRODUCTION

When we think of teaching, the first thought tends to be of an individual standing in front of a group of students holding forth on a particular topic. While acknowledging the existence of other approaches to teaching, practical considerations prevent us from affording them a central role in our current view of possible educational interactions. In particular, since our educational system has become oriented towards group teaching, we forget about the range of educational techniques which are possible in a one-to-one interaction between pupil and teacher. Socratic tutoring, free discovery learning, guided discovery learning, chalk and talk methods and programmed learning techniques are all examples of well-defined educational styles which can be (and have been) used in a one-to-one teaching situation.

One of the advantages of computer-based approaches to education is the possibility of providing a one-to-one correspondence between pupils and machines, facilitating individualization in learning. If we wish an ICAI system to offer a valuable educational experience on an individualized basis, we must require it to adapt the teaching style which it chooses to the needs of the pupil and the domain. There is a need for the system to reason about the style of tutoring which it performs, and to continually reassess the appropriateness of that style to the situation it is currently in.

A key dimension along which to categorize these teaching styles is the degree of constraint which is imposed upon the pupil. The range of actions which the pupil can perform is constrained by the environment in which she is operating. There are also constraints imposed by the tutor upon the pupil. It is the latter constraints being considered here. Such constraints may take a variety of forms, and the nature of the constraints imposed is determined by the style of tutoring which is adopted.

A free discovery interaction does not impose any of these constraints on the pupil. Any intervention by the teacher, however, is interfering with the course which the pupil would have followed, and hence is imposing an external constraint on the pupil (even advice which is ignored affects the pupil). It is therefore important, as part of the decision to take any teaching action, to be aware of the constraint being imposed upon the pupil and to be prepared to justify that constraint. This justification is likely to be in terms of the difference between the educational value of the course of action which the pupil was expected to follow and the course which she actually follows due to the intervention.

Although a real teacher will vary her teaching style as mentioned above, no existing ICAI systems are capable of this behaviour. Each system embodies a single teaching style, which is commonly a formalization of the intuitions of the designer about teaching, rather than being derived from any firm educational grounding. The style which is chosen is normally highly constrained, with the system controlling the interaction strongly. This approach is adopted for practical reasons, to avoid dealing with some problems which are currently very difficult to handle. A primary reason is that it simplifies problems of communication with the pupil by allowing the tutoring system to maintain strong expectations about the possible range of student input.

Many systems claim to use some form of 'Socratic dialogue' – a question and answer sequence directed towards uncovering the underlying misconceptions of the pupil. Although these systems have the surface form of such a dialogue, it is by no means always the case that the dialogue is truly Socratic. To structure such a dialogue for the benefit of the pupil requires Socrates (Broudy, 1969) or an equivalent intelligence in the machine! Instead, most systems achieve a surface form which looks like such a dialogue without the underlying reasoning, and hence without the structuring which gives the dialogue its 'Socratic' value (though that does not imply that such dialogues have no educational value).

Figure 10.1 is intended to be suggestive of the location of some existing systems

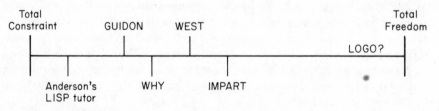

Fig. 10.1. Constraint in teaching style.

on a dimension of constraint imposed upon the·pupil: one end of the scale corresponds to totally 'free' learning, while the other represents a strictly controlled style. Clearly, there is a range of forms of constraint, and the systems should really be organized in a space of constraint, rather than along a single dimension. The approximate ordering afforded by this illustration serves to give an overall feel for the range of tutoring systems, however.

For example, Anderson's LISP tutor (Anderson and Reiser, 1985) is based on a very specific model of how LISP should be learnt. The tutor tracks the actions of the pupil, and as soon as the pupil deviates from this 'correct' learning path the tutor interrupts and moves her back onto that path. At the free extreme we find computers being used as free learning LOGO environments in the manner advocated by Papert (1980) (though this is not necessarily how LOGO is actually used).

Clancey's system GUIDON (Clancey, 1979b) is based around an expert system problem solver in the domain of medical diagnosis. The tutor generates a problem solution with this expert system, and assists the student in solving the same problem. Some experimentation which is not directly on the solution path is permitted, but the system immediately uses such experiments to initiate a dialogue which will bring the student back onto the 'correct' solution path.

The WHY system (Stevens, Collins and Goldin, 1982) permits the user more scope for directing the interaction. It initiates discussions on topics, and by default controls the interaction. If the pupil fails to respond directly to a question by the system, but chooses to introduce a related topic instead, WHY will permit the diversion, but remember the topic it was working on and return to it when the opportunity arises.

WEST (Burton and Brown, 1982) acts as a 'coach'. It observes the student carrying out a task, and tries to develop a model of the pupil's ability to perform that task. The system sometimes offers advice to the pupil, but it does not necessarily correct the pupil every time it realizes that she has made an error.

IMPART (Elsom-Cook, 1985a) is a coaching system which provides guidance for pupils during the early stages of learning to program in LISP. It observes a pupil interacting with a LISP system, and provides advice about the semantics of the language only when it believes that the pupil has made an incorrect inference about the behaviour of a primitive LISP function.

Optimally, we would like a tutoring system to be able to move backwards and forwards along this scale, using a variety of teaching styles which provide different levels and forms of constraint on the activities of the pupil. I wish to suggest that the whole range of tutoring styles may be thought of within the framework of guided discovery learning – offering differing degrees and forms of guidance involves choosing (and justifying) a point on this continuum of constraint which is appropriate to the current needs of the pupil and identifying teaching actions which provide the appropriate constraints. The sort of partially-directed tutoring (which has been called 'coaching' (Burton and Brown, 1982)) normally associated with guided discovery methods deals with a single point (or a small range) in this continuum of constraints. If we accept this redefinition of guided discovery, then moving between teaching styles corresponds to making a decision about the amount and form of guidance to provide.

The remainder of this chapter will explore these issues in more depth by discussing the nature of guidance in tutoring and possible ways of providing such guidance (with particular reference to building models of the pupil). It concludes with a summary of the way in which such a model is used in a guided discovery LISP tutoring system, IMPART (Elsom-Cook, 1985a) and some suggestions for ways to achieve this flexibility of teaching style.

10.2   WHAT IS THE NATURE OF 'GUIDANCE' IN TUTORING?

R.S. Peters explains the essential idea behind guided discovery learning in the following manner:

> "The cardinal function of the teacher, in the early stages, is to get the pupil on the inside of the form of thought or awarness with which he is concerned. At a later stage, when the pupil has built into his mind both the concepts and mode of exploration involved, the difference between teacher and taught is obviously only one of degree. For both are participating in the shared experience of exploring a common world. The teacher is simply more familiar with its contours and more skilled in finding and cutting pathways. The good teacher is a guide who helps others to dispense with his services." (Peters, 1966)

It is clearly not the case that pupil and teacher are always jointly exploring a domain as equals. Interactions which appear to be very similar on the surface may differ greatly when we explore the models which the participants in the interaction possess. Consider the following simple exchange:

A: 'Can we talk about i/o now?'
B: 'Sure, let's look at the 'write' predicate.'

It may be the case that the tutor (B) has assessed the current knowledge state of the pupil with respect to the prerequisites and concepts associated with the domain, has decided that this area (i/o) is an appropriate one for further exploration, and has selected the 'write' predicate as a suitable topic for introducing the domain because it is not far beyond the current state of knowledge of the pupil. On the other hand, B may simply have no clear idea about what to do next, and may have responded to the suggestion of looking at i/o by mentioning the only thing she knew about that domain.

Some child-centred approaches to education have run into difficulty by making the assumption that pupil and teacher are fellow explorers, with no significant difference between them. The educational approach of Rousseau (1762), on the other hand, while retaining the basic idea of joint exploration/guidance, represents the opposite extreme in that it invariably assumes that the teacher has 'the correct version' of what is to be learnt, and constantly restructures the learning experience of the pupil in order to guide her to that model (which corresponds to enforcing a goal of the teacher on the pupil). Such an approach is clearly still child-centred in that the focus is firmly on adapting the educational experience to the individual (since the teacher's goals are determined by the state of the pupil), but it acknowledges an 'ultimate authority' vested in the tutor on the grounds of her greater knowledge of the domain. It is not the case that there will always be a 'correct version' of the thing which the pupil is learning, or that, even if such a correct form exists, the teacher will know it. As the pupil becomes more proficient in the domain the authority of the tutor will diminish, and it is important that this should be reflected in the interaction. Our tutor must, therefore, be able to act appropriately both as guide and as fellow explorer with the pupil.

A guided discovery approach to learning a new domain, then, will take the pupil along the continuum of constraint from a heavily structured, tutor-directed interaction to one in which the tutor plays no role. How this transition occurs depends upon specific details of the pupil, domain and teacher. To explore this further it is necessary to be more explicit about what guided discovery learning methods mean. In particular, what is the permissible range of guidance methods which the system should embrace, and how can it decide about making a transition from one method to another?

At the free extreme of the scale, the tutor will be completely invisible, leaving the student to explore the task being taught. Clearly, the tutor is still present, and must be observing the actions of the pupil in order to decide whether changing to an approach with more intervention is necessary. At the other extreme, the tutor controls the interaction completely, but should be eliciting information from the pupil which is used to adjust the interaction to match the abilities of the pupil. Using these styles as the end points for our teaching methods explicitly excludes 'free' learning at one end of the scale, and rote learning methods/pure presentation methods etc. at the other end. These can reasonably be excluded on the grounds that they are not teaching interactions. The former because no teacher is present, and the latter because no account is taken of the presence of the pupil; though this is not to deny that they may be valid educational experiences.

Within this framework we can regard the teaching interaction as a negotiation between two agents, one of which (the tutor) brings domain-specific knowledge and teaching techniques to the interaction, while the other (the pupil) brings various pre-existing cognitive structures and preferred learning methods (Fig. 10.2). If we are considering a situation in which the pupil wants to learn, and the teacher wants to teach, then these agents have the joint goal of imparting the domain-specific knowledge which resides in the teacher's head to the pupil. This requires changing that knowledge from the form in which it is useful to the teacher (i.e. as applied expertise in the domain) into a form suitable for communicating, transferring that knowledge to the pupil, and ensuring that the knowledge is fully integrated with the existing cognitive structures of that pupil. Any inconsistencies between the pre-existing knowledge of the pupil and the new information must be resolved. It must also be ensured that the knowledge is

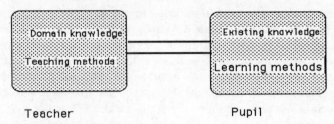

Fig. 10.2. Teaching interaction.

integrated in such a way that it can be applied appropriately, rather than simply being 'inert' information (Whitehead, 1932). This task of integration is often more important and difficult than the task of transfer. In achieving the form of interaction discussed above, the teacher restructures the domain expertise using knowledge about the teaching process, the learning processes of the pupil, the current state of the pupil and, optionally, some domain-specific expertise about the common difficulties of students in this domain. Few of these forms of knowledge are represented in existing tutoring systems. It should be clear from this discussion that an expert system approach to ICAI is inappropriate. Knowledge is encoded in such systems in order to be used, rather than in order to be imparted to others (Clancey and Letsinger, 1984) and achieving an appropriate restructuring for tutoring (which is dependent on the particular pupil being taught) requires a deeper representation of the domain than that which expert systems technology can provide.

As described above, guided discovery teaching requires the system to constantly reassess the appropriateness of the teaching activities which it is performing, monitoring the success (and possible future choices) of the pupil, and (either by direct or indirect methods) ensuring that the pupil follows paths corresponding to a fruitful educational experience (avoiding blind alleys etc.).

In achieving this, I wish to suggest that the teacher has four major forms of goal which must be satisfied by the guidance being given: presenting new material, finding out about the current state of knowledge of the pupil, maintaining an appropriate form for the teaching interaction itself, and maintaining/developing the motivation of the student.

These goals can be expanded into more detailed goal structures which are dependent on the current state (and history) of the tutoring interaction (and the pupil). The tutoring task then becomes one of (partially) satisfying multiple goals simultaneously. One utterance may provide input to many of these goals. This task is closely related to the sort of models of goal-directed dialogue which have been developed recently (e.g. Perrault, 1980; Appelt, 1982) and it seems natural to regard the tutoring interaction as being a special application of more general dialogue mechanisms.

Miller (1982) offers a flavour of the issues which we need to explore in deciding on appropriate guidance by presenting the following set of questions:

1. What constitutes a good hint?
2. Should the computer spontaneously interrupt the student to provide remedial advice?
3. How often should the tutor intervene?
4. How much should it say?
5. When should it say it?
6. How should it say it?

Most of these questions are associated with the goal of presenting material appropriately. This reflects the fact that tutoring systems have tended to focus on this particular aspect of the tutoring problem.

10.3   HOW CAN APPROPRIATE GUIDANCE BE OFFERED?

Providing appropriate guidance for a pupil is difficult. There are many unresolved educational issues in this area, of which the most important is probably that of control in the interaction. Who controls the interaction has been a topic of discussion in education theory for many years, but since the move away from one-to-one education it has become less central. ICAI systems bring this issue to the foreground once again. Under what circumstances is it justifiable for the tutor (human or computer) to take control of the interaction and direct the pupil – possibly in directions contrary to those which the pupil wishes to pursue. In terms of the two agent model described above, this becomes an issue of resolving goal conflict between the agents. The teacher cannot control the interaction without gaining the cooperation of the pupil in achieving that goal – either by providing a justification for following a particular goal in terms the pupil can understand (which Whitehead (1932) claims is a basic prerequisite of any educational decision) or by appealing to some higher level goal in the interaction (e.g. 'You said you wanted to learn this, so trust me for half an hour and you will!').

Of central importance to the provision of this negotiated tutoring interaction is an understanding of the problems which confront the pupil at a particular time. Offering appropriate information in forms comprehensible to the pupil at the right times, generating suitable problems, providing useful feedback on progress, maintaining motivation etc. all require some model of the current state of knowledge (and emotion!) of the pupil. ICAI work has focused on building models of the pupil to permit selection of appropriate teaching material, but another important aspect of the user model has often been neglected. I wish to suggest that deciding what to teach next must be based *not* primarily on what the teacher perceives as the logical structure of the domain, but on the options which the pupil perceives to be within her capabilities at a particular time. This involves maintaining some model of the reasoning processes which the pupil uses to acquire knowledge. These processes include inductive reasoning, analogical reasoning, problem solving, theory testing etc. There will be both domain-independent and domain-dependent learning skills involved.

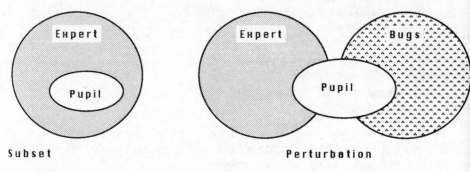

Subset   Perturbation

Fig. 10.3. Expert-based modelling methods.

10.3.1 Providing and using models of the learning process

Most existing ICAI systems build models of the pupil as variants of an 'expert proficiency' in the domain. There is assumed to be some expert competence which can be broken down into a set of skills so small that the pupil either has them or doesn't. The task of the tutor is then to fill the student with these skills like filling a bucket with knowledge. This can be described as 'subset modelling' (Fig. 10.3) (often known as 'overlay modelling'). The alternative expert-based approach is to include a second bucket ('bugs') containing tiny sub-skills which the expert doesn't have, which produce incorrect behaviour, but which have been observed to exist in pupils learning about the domain. The tutor must now pour in sub-skills from the first bucket while removing any sub-skills which the pupil has acquired from the second bucket. This may be described as 'perturbation modelling' (Fig. 10.3). These approaches both imply a very simplistic model of the learning process (not far removed from rote learning), which takes no account of the rich range of learning styles and capabilities for which there is psychological evidence.

If we move away from the common expert-based modelling methods then we should replace them with an approach in which the model is constructed in terms familiar to the learner, with reference to the range of reasoning processes mentioned above. I wish to propose that an appropriate framework for this activity is that of bounded user-modelling (see Fig. 10.4). In this type of model, the understanding of the state of the pupil exists as a set of upper and lower bounds on the possible states of the learner. The tutor will not necessarily know 'exactly' what state the pupil is in. Such 'exact' knowledge is not generally possible (certainly human teachers do not use it), and much teaching can be done using approximations to the state of the pupil.

The bounds on the model are generated by applying a model of the reasoning activities which the student uses when confronted with some event in the world. Obviously the model of reasoning processes in the system will not match that of the student perfectly, and avoiding major errors involves the system in a cycle of

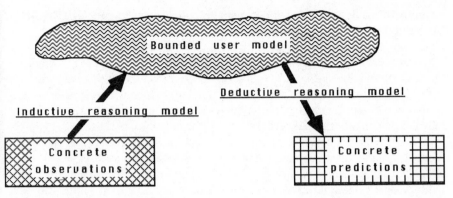

Fig. 10.4. Bounded user modelling.

generating bounds from concrete observations which the pupil could make, then testing them by generating some concrete predictions from those bounds and comparing them with what actually happens (an example is given below). The student's reasoning processes are themselves changing over the course of time (though not with the frequency of the domain model) and should themselves be the subject of user-modelling activities (these changes reflect the student learning about learning in this domain). It may be the case that there are more levels of change (learning to learn about learning etc.), but since each level is considerably more stable than the last, we will not consider these higher levels any further.

The use of upper and lower bounds in the bounded user model is related to Mitchell's version space (a way of formally representing the range of permissible descriptions of an event in terms of a greatest and least member of the set of descriptions) (Mitchell, 1981) but is different in several respects. In Mitchell's approach, a focusing algorithm is used which generates the most general and most specific descriptions of an event. Subsequent events are used to focus on the correct concept being learnt, by making the general description more specific and the specific description more general. These two descriptions will converge as more events are observed. In IMPART, there may be a number of things to be learnt from each event, and consequently each event may generate a completely new upper and lower bound. There is not a one-to-one mapping between events and concepts to be acquired. In effect the system is maintaining a set of version spaces. This approach has the advantage of permitting the use of multiple partial models of the learning process, and allows the representation of inconsistent beliefs held by the pupil (though these advantages are not explored in the implementation discussed below). The price paid for this approach is the loss of the partial ordering of descriptions on which Mitchell's focusing algorithm relies. This results in an increase in the complexity of the algorithm which must be used to obtain descriptions of events, and a greater range of possible models to examine. How IMPART deals with this problem is further discussed below.

Moving towards learner-based modelling methods was also a motivation behind the development of the genetic graph (Goldstein, 1982). This data structure represents a domain by linking the domain knowledge with arcs describing the form of learning which must take place in order to move from one piece of knowledge to another. As originally described this approach involved making these links static and explicit (in effect embodying a theory about one possible way to learn the domain). An individual student is represented as a subset of the genetic graph. In many ways such an approach is like the expert-based modelling methods described above – the difference being that the pupil is now being compared with one particular expert learner instead of one particular domain expert. It does not provide any scope for extension such that individual differences in learning style, or developmental changes in the pupil (other than with respect to domain knowledge) can be handled. The original version was intended for modelling acquisition of procedural rules, and though Goldstein has subsequently discussed extensions to this approach to support multiple representations, declarative knowledge, planning etc, this work has not been pursued.

As has been observed, creating and maintaining a bounded user model relies on having some model of the reasoning processes which the pupil is applying in order to organize the environment. This dependence on models of inductive and deductive reasoning processes appears to cause a problem for this approach. At present, there are no suitably complete and formal models of these processes available. Psychological theories in this area are normally incomplete, rarely formalized and (except in special cases) can only be shown to have very restricted applicability.

If the task which we are attempting to perform with our tutor is a pure learning task, as would be the case at the 'joint exploration' end of the path of development discussed earlier, then this shortage of theories severely restricts the usefulness of the tutor. The tutor cannot guide the pupil in a manner that avoids dead-ends and unproductive courses of study, because the tutor cannot assess such problems, and will get drawn into the same traps as the pupil. The tutor cannot serve usefully as a co-explorer because this shortage of theories will render it less effective than the pupil, and may result in it leading the pupil away from an appropriate course of exploration due to its lack of knowledge. For earlier parts of the tutoring process, however, the problem is not so serious because the tutoring system can be provided with some description of what it is that the pupil is expected to learn. Since the tutoring system has such knowledge, it has some 'target' against which to compare the hypotheses generated by the model(s) of the learning process, and some way to prevent those hypotheses becoming too far divorced from useful models of the domain. In consequence, less reliance is placed on the completeness or consistency of the learning models which are used. This approach places IMPART much closer to Rousseau in terms of the approaches it can support than more naive pupil-centred approaches.

The availability of a benchmark model describing what the pupil is expected to learn facilitates the use of multiple partial models of the learning process rather than requiring a single correct model, because any discrepancy between the predictions of different learning models can be resolved by reference to this model. This avoids the 'joint exploration' problem of permitting tutor and pupil to wander hand in hand up blind alleys and become hopelessly stuck. There seems to be no clear evidence for the existence of a single learning mechanism in any case, so permitting the tutor to 'mix and match' among multiple learning models is likely to permit a closer approach to an accurate model of the pupil.

The best formalized models of learning which currently exist are those derived from the machine-learning literature. These models are currently quite simple, applicable only to special domains, and (generally) have no particular claim to relate to human learning. Any attempt to use these systems directly to model a learner would fail for these reasons, but used at one remove to create possible bounds for the model of the internal state of the student, such machine learning approaches are useful. The following section discusses the way in which such techniques are applied in an existing experimental tutoring system.

10.3.2 Machine learning in IMPART

IMPART (Elsom-Cook, 1984) is a tutoring system which applies guided discovery methods in the domain of programming. It teaches the student about the syntax and semantics of LISP through experiments with a LISP interpreter. It assumes that the student initially knows nothing about the language, and applies the bounded user modelling technique described above to develop a model of the pupil which contributes to decisions about the actions which the tutor should take. This bounded user model is one of the primary inputs to a goal-directed dialogue system which structures the educational interaction (for a sample interaction see Elsom-Cook (1985a)). The system only supports the early stages of learning LISP, and has not been used with real pupils. It does not achieve the wide variation of teaching style that was discussed earlier, but supports a small range of guidance methods.

The learning model which is used is a simple inductive learning algorithm based upon standard machine-learning methods (Michalski, 1983). No attempt to change the learning mechanisms over time is made.

IMPART is provided in advance with a set of descriptors that can be used to describe the possible attributes of an event in LISP, and a set of descriptions of the actual behaviour of each LISP function couched in terms of those descriptors. When an event occurs (such as the evaluation of a LISP expression), the tutor uses the descriptors to produce a description of the observable behaviour corresponding to that event. This is the lower bound on the student model.

Having established this description of the surface form of the event, the system then does a depth-restricted exhaustive search through a set of inductive inference and transformation rules in order to derive the most general description of the event which is consistent with the learning model which it uses. IMPART embodies a subset of the algorithm mentioned above in a set of seven inference rules which can be applied at any time. It also includes a set of transformation rules which may be regarded as corresponding to domain-specific learning methods and heuristics for making sense of the world. They consist of suggestions for discovering relationships between things (for example, if some *s*-expression whose origin is unclear appears, then evaluate all the available atoms to see if it the value of one of them). The details of these rules can be found in Elsom-Cook (1985c).

These two descriptions (surface and general) are actually a maximally-specific conjunctive description and maximally-general conjunctive description of the event, and can be regarded as lower and upper bounds on what the student would infer from this example. Regarding these bounds in this way is obviously an assumption about the nature of the learning processes which the pupil is using; it is quite possible to imagine a range of idiosyncratic inferences which the student could make and which do not fit into this model, but IMPART does not approach such issues.

The pair of bounds which are generated are compared with bounds generated by other events. If the new bounds are more specific versions of older ones, then the older ones are removed. If they are more general then the newer ones are removed. Since the partial ordering of the version space has been lost, not all bounds can be assigned to one of these categories, and in this case IMPART simply leaves the bounds in the model. This is one area where the system requires much further work.

Of course, the inferences made by this system are normally more general than those which the pupil makes, and are often wrong (since induction is not truth-preserving). The problem of making the correct inductive inferences and narrowing the bounds is difficult, and IMPART uses two mechanisms to avoid dealing with the full learning problem.

Firstly, the inference process is constrained in two ways; by limiting the depth of inference (i.e. number of rules which can be applied), and by using a number of domain-specific heuristics (which can be taught to the pupil) that restrict the search space by making use of knowledge about the likely range of descriptions of LISP events.

The second mechanism is the deductive reasoning model shown in Fig. 10.4. This is a simple forward-chaining deductive mechanism which is applied to the descriptions in the bounded user model to generate a range of predictions about the behaviour of other expressions. As the model changes, the predictions change. These predictions are used to generate problems for the pupil to solve, together with predicted answers whose origin can be traced back to a specific part of a specific description in the model. If the pupil solves the problem, the solution can be compared with the predictions and used to update the model. A sample of problem generation appears in Elsom-Cook (1985b).

To illustrate this approach, consider the model which would be generated from a very simple LISP event, assuming no previous LISP experience of the pupil:

```
EVENT: (QUOTE IRENE)
        IRENE
Lower bound:
  quote(irene)
        [type(quote(irene),sexpr),
        type(irene,atom),
        out(value,irene)]
Upper bound:
  quote(ARG1)
        [type(quote(ARG1),sexpr),
        type(ARG1,sexpr),
        out(value,ARG1)]
```

In this case, the lower bound is purely a description of the surface form of the event (i.e. things that are directly observable). The information about types of objects, and about function/argument distinction which are used in this description are things which would be flagged as being necessary to teach directly to a naive pupil. The upper bound is (coincidentally) a correct description of the behaviour of QUOTE. Between these descriptions lie many possible errorful descriptions such as QUOTE being a function with one argument which always returns the value IRENE, or which can only be applied to atoms. If the system were to ask the student what behaviour the event (QUOTE (EAT FROGS)) would cause, the following predictions would be made:

Lower bound prediction: Dunno,nothing,error
Upper bound prediction: (EAT FROGS)

Examples of intermediate cases (which are not actually generated, but which can be derived from the bounds if the pupil makes a prediction other than those given above) are:

Returns value irene: IRENE
Applies to atoms: That's not an atom, error

The learning model in IMPART is extremely naive and simplistic, even by the standards of machine-learning theories let alone from the psychological viewpoint. However, it does produce useful behaviour and is a major factor contributing to the smoothness of interactions with the system. Further development of this approach should include supporting multiple models, permitting modelling of the learning processes of the student, and enriching the deductive reasoning processes used by the tutor.

10.3.3 Bounded user modelling and flexibility of teaching style

The central idea behind bounded user modelling is that it is not possible to create a completely accurate model of what is inside the pupil's head, and that any attempt to do so cannot succeed. Human teachers do not appear to build models of this type, but they *do* build models. These models provide approximations to the student's knowledge.

An approximation to the knowledge of the student provides a sound basis for teaching, since one particular teaching act is often applicable to a range of states within the pupil, and it is only necessary to ensure that the pupil is in one of those states in order to know that the teaching act is appropriate. There is a close link between the level of detail of the model and the amount of control which can be exercised in teaching style. Only very accurate models are adequate for highly directive teaching styles, but guidance can be given with less detailed knowledge.

Because the uncertainty about the knowledge of the pupil is explicitly represented in the bounded user model, it provides a limit for the range of teaching styles which can be applied at a particular moment. Highly directed styles cannot be used if the knowledge about the pupil in that area is very vague, for example. IMPART only had one teaching style, comprising about six separate teaching actions, and so made little use of this facility. I wish to suggest that a wider variety of teaching actions, each associated with information about the level of detail needed in the model, would provide the basis for a mechanism of selecting between a range of teaching activities as was discussed earlier. IMPART did not contribute to such a mechanism, but this is an area in which further research is being conducted.

10.4 CONCLUSIONS

In summary, I wish to suggest that tutoring styles should be thought of as existing as points along a continuum of guided discovery teaching styles. Tutoring systems should aim to cover a range of adjacent styles on that continuum, and be prepared to switch between them. It is important that guided discovery learning systems possess domain-specific knowledge which can be used to ensure that the pupil does not move too far away from fruitful models of the domain. The user modelling in these systems should relate to models of the learning process, and should operate by imposing fuzzy bounds on the knowledge of the pupil rather than attempting to build an exact model. Given the current state of machine learning techniques, some simple versions of such an approach can be implemented, but a richer range of formal models of learning is ultimately required.

11

The application of machine learning to intelligent tutoring systems

DAVID GILMORE AND JOHN SELF
University of Lancaster, England

This chapter considers the problem of maintaining dynamic student models using techniques based on machine learning,. After surveying existing methods for constructing student models and previous applications of machine learning to intelligent tutoring, we suggest an alternative role for a student model, as a psychologically credible description of a collaborative partner.

11.1 INTRODUCTION

The concept of a student model is central to research in intelligent computer-aided instruction, even though the term has acquired a variety of meanings. 'Student model' can be used to refer to an ideal model, which represents the knowledge to be acquired by the student. Such a model may include a library of common errors, in which case it is a typical, rather than an ideal model. Alternatively, the term 'student model' can be used to refer to a description of the current user, representing the knowledge (right or wrong) which she has acquired. A major problem for the development of tutoring systems is obtaining these changing models of students. One possibility is to use machine-learning techniques to develop and maintain individual models of students. *Machine learning* is an area of artificial intelligence research concerned with developing computational theories of learning processes and building machines which learn. In this chapter we intend to examine the potential of machine learning for building student models.

We will begin with a coverage of existing methods for constructing student models, before concentrating on three tutoring systems which have used machine-learning techniques. All three apply only to topics which can be modelled as procedural skills (e.g. algebra, geometry, programming), ignoring the conceptual elements of these subjects. But machine-learning research has, in general, been most successful in relation to concept learning, and so we continue the discussion by looking at the potential of machine learning techniques for modelling concept learning. We conclude the chapter with a suggestion for an alternative view of student models and a brief description of some exploratory work in this direction.

11.2   STUDENT MODELLING METHODS

There are three basic methods by which a student model (related to an individual student) can be constructed:

1. With specially prepared task-model pairings;
2. By mapping behaviour to a predefined set of bugs;
3. By inferring the model from observed behaviour.

11.2.1   Task–model pairings

In the Leeds Modelling System (Sleeman and Smith, 1981; Sleeman, 1984a), which models students' performance solving algebraic equations, the student is presented with a specific task set of problems designed to distinguish between the application of a correct rule of algebra and a *mal-rule*. A mal-rule is, obviously, any rule which incorrectly transforms the equation and is usually a simple perturbation of some correct rule. The student models are pre-determined and contain a collection of rules and mal-rules. Although LMS was not used as part of a tutoring system, its use in classroom settings to diagnose student models was an important step.

The main weakness in this approach is the rapid growth in the number of mal-rules needed to explain the children's behaviour, and the resultant growth in the number of student models which had to be considered. It became clear that there were limits to any attempt to collect a catalogue of all mal-rules, which led to the development of a system which could generate mal-rules as it went along. This is described in more detail in Section 11.3.1 below.

11.2.2   Bug catalogues

The BUGGY/DEBUGGY systems (Brown and Burton, 1978; Burton, 1982) used a library of mal-rules ('bugs') to diagnose errors in children's subtraction. The DEBUGGY system could take a child's answer to any question – unlike LMS which required particular task-sets – and try to match it by applying each of its rules to the original problem, and the rule set which generated the child's answer was the student model. The system would try to model the student using only one mal-rule, but if necessary would try combinations of two, three or four mal-rules.

The problems here are similar to those for LMS. First there is the need to collect and specify all the mal-rules. In fact, DEBUGGY was very nearly complete for subtraction errors, but the collection process took many years, and subtraction is a very limited domain. The development of this research tried to explain why mal-rules arose, with a generative theory, which would then remove the need for the time-consuming protocol analyses. This theory – repair theory (Brown and VanLehn, 1980) – although plausible was not a great success, generating only a relatively small number of bugs. In order to improve the generative approach to bug catalogues the focus of this research has shifted to a closer examination of the learning process (e.g. VanLehn, 1983a).

11.2.3   Inferring models

The two methods already described depend heavily upon catalogues of mal-rules, which have, at present, been collected through an extensive protocol analysis of the domain. The main hope for powerful ICAI systems is that from a smaller amount of initial knowledge they will be able to infer a student model from the student's response.

In such a system a library of mal-rules is not strictly necessary, though it might be faster and it could be built up from the inferred mal-rules. This approach to student modelling is where machine learning could be most useful to ICAI systems, since the inference of the student model requires progress from a small amount of correct knowledge and an observation, to a collection of correct and incorrect qualifications of this knowledge.

Thus the application of machine learning to student modelling and ICAI seems like an inevitable step, if the process is to be relieved of the costly domain analyses.

11.3   CURRENT USES OF MACHINE LEARNING IN TUTORING SYSTEMS

11.3.1   PIXIE – an algebra tutor

PIXIE (Sleeman, 1983a) is the name for the development of the Leeds Modelling System. PIXIE can generate new mal-rules to explain behaviour which cannot be described by existing mal-rules.

PIXIE contains the mal-rules which are already known (including those in LMS), but it also contains heuristics which enable it to work backwards from an answer towards the question, filling in the missing gap with a mal-rule. Figure 11.1 shows an example of how this works, along with some example heuristics. It should be emphasized that the student has only supplied the answer and not the intermediate steps – these are inferred by PIXIE. The heuristics used will, of course, generate a large search tree, any branch of which may lead to a point where a mal-rule could bridge the gap to the original question. Sleeman (1983) does not indicate how PIXIE is able to decide which gap is 'smallest', i.e. which of the many possible mal-rules to actually use. There seems to be an assumption that only one branch will produce a plausible mal-rule.

This problem could be avoided by giving further test problems to disambiguate

a. An example pair of heuristics from PIXIE. 'Target' means the target equation (i.e. the original problem), and 'eqn' means the current equation.

HEURSUM1

if   lhs(eqn) $\langle\rangle$ lhs(target)
AND rhs(eqn) $\langle\rangle$ rhs(target)
AND rhs(eqn) $= i$

then   replace $(i, [i-n] + [n])$.

HEURSUM2

if   lhs(eqn) $\langle\rangle$ lhs(target)
AND rhs(eqn) $=$ rhs(target)
AND contains (lhs, i)

then   replace $(i, [i-n] + [n])$.

b. An example of using these heuristics to infer the mal-rule '$MX \Rightarrow M + X$'.

Target $= 3X + 5 = 6$ Answer given: $X = -2$

HEURSUM1 $\Rightarrow X = (-2 - n) + n$

Instantiate n to rhs(target) $\Rightarrow X = -8 + 6$

Apply rule NTORHS $\Rightarrow X + 8 = 6$

HEURSUM2 $\Rightarrow X + (8 - n) + n = 6$

Instantiate n to lhs(target) $\Rightarrow X + 3 + 5 = 6$

Mal-rule inference $X + 3 \Leftarrow 3X$ (ie. $MX \Rightarrow M + X$)

Fig. 11.1. Inferring mal-rules from observed behaviour (adapted from Sleeman, 1983).

the mal-rules, but there still remains the serious difficulty that this approach can only generate one mal-rule per problem. In other words, there is an unavoidable assumption that only one mal-rule is to blame for the child's error. The system

"attempts to see whether the pupil's answer can be explained by the application of *one* such perturbation." (Sleeman, 1983; p. 221).

An important feature of PIXIE is the representation of algebra knowledge as a collection of rules, with no explanation of how mal-rules are generated, nor how they may be removed. This system does not contain any representation of the conceptual knowledge required in algebra (e.g. the nature of variables, the purpose of the task, etc. etc.), which may be the root cause of a number of mal-rules.

Sleeman (1984b) has written about a mechanism, called mis-generalization, by which mal-rules could be generated, but this is not contained within the PIXIE system. He compares his approach with repair theory (Brown and VanLehn, 1980) and with the work of Young and O'Shea (1981). However, it is not at all clear what sort of evidence would be needed to empirically distinguish these approaches and, therefore, their explanations of bug generation are difficult to compare.

PIXIE is an interesting system which can generate mal-rules from a student's responses. Unfortunately, the heuristics used appear to be domain-dependent (see Fig. 11.1), which means that a lengthy domain analysis may not have been avoided, since instead of looking for mal-rules in the domain, it will now be necessary to discover the likely set of heuristics.

11.3.2 Automated cognitive modelling (ACM)

ACM (Langley, Ohlsson and Sage, 1984) is not strictly a tutorial system, since it only generates the student models. Unlike PIXIE which has used new machine-learning techniques, ACM uses conventional techniques to generate a model from an already defined problem space and from a student's answer.

The system has a production rule representation of skill and uses this representation in the context of search through a problem space. Initially ACM contains only the primitive operators for the chosen domain, along with some potentially important distinguishing properties of the domain (e.g. for subtraction, 'greater than', 'above (spatially)', 'is zero' etc.). Having obtained the student's response to a problem the system performs breadth-first search through the problem space, until the answer is obtained. This supplies a 'solution' path, which (it is hoped) describes the operations performed by the student. If there should be two solution paths then the shorter of the two is taken (breadth-first searching ensures this), and if there are two of equal length then carefully designed test problems are used to distinguish them (though the details of this have not been calculated).

Given this 'solution' path through the problem space it is possible to apply standard inductive-learning techniques (Quinlan, 1986) to distinguish those contexts where the operators were applied successfully (i.e. lying on the solution path) and those where they were not successful (i.e. lying one step removed from the solution path). Using the properties already supplied, ACM constructs a discrimination network, which provides a model of the constraints placed by the student on each of the operators. Figure 11.2 shows the final student model for a child who, when subtracting, never borrows, but simply subtracts the smaller number from the larger.

The success of the discrimination network in modelling the student depends heavily upon the dimensions supplied initially (i.e. 'greater than' etc.). For the current system these have been supplied intuitively, but for practical purposes this may be inadequate, since their psychological validity is crucial. However, since they are domain-dependent successful ACM systems may still require a costly domain analysis.

FIND-DIFFERENCE

> if   processing column 1
> AND number 1 is in column 1 and row 1
> AND number 2 is in column 1 and row 2
> AND number 1 is greater than number 2*
>
> then   find the difference between number 1 and number 2
> AND write this as the result for column 1.

SHIFT-COLUMN

> if   processing column 1
> AND have result for column 1
> AND column 2 is to left of column 1
>
> then   process column 2.

*This is the extra condition which has been added by the learning component of ACM.

Fig. 11.2. A student model for 'smaller from larger' bug (from Langley, Ohlsson and Sage, 1984).

Unfortunately, there are a number of other limitations with ACM. First, not only do the dimensions of discrimination have to be supplied, so do the operators. However, this can be turned into a strength, because the ability to describe the operators at any level of detail enables student errors to be described at a variety of levels. Langley *et al.* argue that the operators should be supplied at the highest level of description which describes the student's errors. Thus, a system could contain a hierarchical description of the operators and the problem space would be searched with the highest level first, moving down only when the student's answer cannot be found in the problem space. This could also avoid the problem of finding too many solution paths to the same answer.

A further problem is that the problem space must be small enough for this search procedure to be feasible and therefore ACM is only suitable for tightly defined subject domains, with only a few operators. Also it offers no explanation of where errors come from, nor how they can best be corrected.

11.3.3   Advanced Computer Tutoring Project

The ACTP group at Carnegie-Mellon University, led by John Anderson, has developed tutors for geometry and for LISP programming, based on Anderson's computational theory of learning, ACT* (Anderson, 1983; Anderson, Boyle and Reiser, 1985). Although this is a theory of human learning its computational representation and use of production rules qualifies it as machine learning too.

Unlike the two systems already described these tutors are based on the learning theory but they do not use it to generate a dynamic, individual student model. Instead the theory generates an ideal student model, though just how this is achieved is not clear. The theory also explains the errors observed in protocols, which are then included in a library of errors. It is against these that any student's performance is compared.

A further feature is that the learning theory generates principles which underpin the design of the tutoring process (Anderson, Boyle, Farrell and Reiser, 1986). These principles include the following:

1. Represent the student as a production set;
2. Communicate the goal structure underlying the problem solving;
3. Provide instruction in the problem-solving context;
4. Provide immediate feedback on errors.

None of these principles is derived solely from the ACT* theory, but the theory does explain their importance. The tutors aim is to progress the student towards the ideal model, using specially prepared modules for correcting any errors which are detected.

There are other important features in these tutors, which contribute towards the satisfaction of these principles. For example the geometry tutor includes a graphical representation of the growing solution (a 'proof graph'), which not only eases the student's memory load, but also communicates the goal structure of the problem. In the LISP tutor there are many points of menu selection, which avoid problems of language comprehension by the tutor (which must know what algorithm is being coded). The items on the menu are generated dynamically from the student model and from the library of errors.

The main weakness of these tutors is that there is no explanation of where bugs arise, nor any ability to cope with novel errors. Also, there is no representation of the student's conceptual knowledge of programming or geometry. Although these tutors are less interesting to us, since they do not generate dynamic student models, it must be acknowledged that they are working tutors, which are currently being evaluated.

To summarize, the ACTP tutors use a computational theory of learning to create an ideal model to guide the tutoring process. Since the ACT* theory is limited to procedural skills, so are these tutors, which contain no representation of conceptual knowledge.

11.3.4 Summary of existing systems

The systems described above are the three main systems which have blended tutoring systems with machine learning research. All these three systems apply only to procedural skills, using production rules to represent knowledge. None of them includes a representation of conceptual knowledge of the domain.

It could be argued that conceptual knowledge of a domain is only an artefact of a particular configuration of production rules. But even if this were true, the absence of any explicit representation makes it difficult to diagnose or correct errors in this knowledge. It seems likely that while some mal-rules may cause deeper misconceptions, so it is likely that misconceptions can give rise to mal-rules.

The rest of this chapter will investigate the area where machine learning has been more successful, namely concept learning, and it will consider the potential of concept learning systems to contribute to the development of student models.

11.4   CONCEPT LEARNING SYSTEMS

In contrast to the skills of equation solving or programming, the learning we are interested in here is the learning of concepts. The example which we will use in the rest of this chapter is from chemistry, where there are a number of concepts within the periodic table (e.g. metal, semi-metal, rare earth metal, etc.) examples of which have characteristic values for certain features. Although concept learning can be construed as learning a classification procedure, it is clear that none of the techniques described above would work. For example, neither ACM nor PIXIE could cope with a situation where the only possible response was 'yes' or 'no'. We must look for non-procedural representations of concepts.

This problem has been tackled by machine learning, though usually in well-constrained domains. The purpose of this section is to look at these techniques to see whether they could be used for modelling a student learning about chemical concepts. There are three types of system which we will look at and they can be distinguished both by the methods used and the resulting representation.

11.4.1   Decision trees

Decision trees are classification procedures in which each node specifies a particular feature of the object under consideration and the node's branches represent the possible values of that feature. To classify an object the branches are traversed from the root node downwards according to the values of the object on each of the features encountered. At each node is a feature to be tested and at the end of each branch will be a response (classify as positive, negative or unknown). ACM, described above, produces decision trees to describe when it is appropriate to apply each particular operator.

Quinlan (1986) describes a family of inductive-learning systems which produce decision trees, all derived from CLS (Hunt, Marin and Stone, 1966), an early attempt at cognitive modelling. CLS was supplied with examples of a concept specified as a collection of values on a predetermined set of features. In order to produce a decision tree the examples are examined and a feature is chosen to be the root node. This partitions the examples into two sets, described by a smaller collection of features. If all the examples are positive or all of them are negative, then that response is included in the tree. However if the examples are

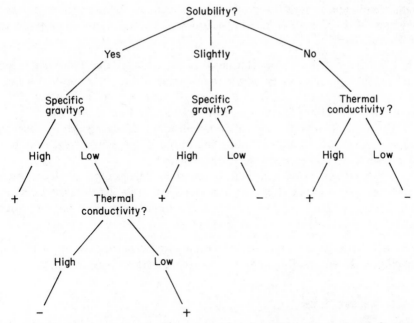

Fig. 11.3. A decision tree for classifying examples of some imaginary chemical concept.

still a mixture then a decision tree is built for them, recursively. Eventually, since the number of features decreases by one each time, a classification must be included as the leaf.

Of course, there are a large number of trees which could be built for any set of examples, depending upon which feature is chosen for testing at each node. However, most of these trees will be unnecessarily complex, testing irrelevant features first. Ideally, the tree should test the most important feature first, followed by the next most important, etc. An example of an imaginary chemical concept and a decision tree which can be derived from the examples are shown in Fig. 11.3.

Much of the development of inductive-learning systems has concerned itself with this problem of making the decision trees efficient. For example, ID3 (Quinlan, 1983) used a complex, information-based measure which enabled it to assess the most informative test at any stage. ACM used a simpler measure, which examined the proportion of positive and negative examples at each leaf of the tree. The tree which best separated the positive and negative examples was then developed. Such a measure provided a fast learning system, but one that was limited to features with binary values.

The power of inductive-learning systems cannot be denied, especially since developments which allowed the inclusion of features which had integer values. Anecdotal evidence (see Quinlan, 1986) suggests that some industrial companies have saved a very large amount of money through the use of expert systems based on these techniques. Nevertheless, our concern here is whether these techniques are applicable to ICAI, in particular to student modelling. Three main problems can be described.

1. For these systems to work efficiently (or maybe at all) they require access to all the examples of the concept at the same time, in order to determine the most discriminating feature. This is an unacceptable constraint on student modelling, where the student will observe and learn from individual examples.

2. The result of the system depends upon the metric used to determine the most discriminating feature, and for modelling purposes we would need to impose constraints for psychologically acceptable metrics.

3. Although some concepts may be mentally represented as classification procedures, it is unlikely that such a representation would be appropriate for guiding a tutoring system, partly because the student model would not be in a form which fostered easy communication between student and tutor.

Thus it seems that inductive techniques are inappropriate for a student modelling task, though they may have a role in systems such as ACM.

11.4.2 Relation trees

Relation trees express concepts as a collection of values on particular features; for example, colour (red) and shape (square). The learning techniques (reviewed by Bundy, Silver and Plummer, 1985) vary, but in general they begin with a collection of . candidate descriptions for the target concepts and refine this collection on the basis of the presented positive and negative examples. The main techniques are candidate elimination and focusing, though they only differ in their representation of the collection of candidate concepts. For this reason this discussion will describe focusing.

The important component of these techniques is the description space, which describes all the possible concepts. For each feature there is a set of possible values, which have a particular structure, and this can be represented as a tree. Figure 11.4 shows an example of such a tree, for the feature colour. Each leaf represents a value which may be observed in some example of the concept, and the nodes represent the relations between these values. Thus, in Fig. 11.4 the values red and green can both be described as coloured, whilst black, grey and

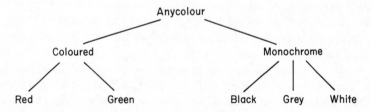

Fig. 11.4. A relation tree for five values of the feature 'colour'.

white are monochrome. Coloured and monochrome can only be described together as any colour, which is the root node of the tree.

The result of these learning techniques is a specification of one node from each tree, which describes the concept. Focusing achieves this by generalizing from positive examples and discriminating from negative examples. The system maintains a maximally specific and a maximally general description of the target concept. Positive examples allow generalization of the specific description; for example, on presentation of a green, positive example, a specific description 'red' would generalize to 'coloured'. Negative examples enable discrimination of the general description; for example, a green, negative example would lead to a general description 'coloured' being discriminated to 'red'. The algorithm terminates when the two descriptions coincide – they are not allowed to overlap.

Given a description space which contains many features the process of discrimination may generate many possibilities for the maximally general description. Solutions to this problem include the use of 'near misses' only, which means that the discrimination process can only produce one possibility. 'Near misses' are defined as negative examples which differ from positive examples on only one feature. Another solution is to store all possibilities and wait for further examples to exclude them.

Another problem, which has been tackled by Wielemaker and Bundy (1985), is the dependence of the technique on the supplied structure of the description space. Their solution, however, involves the storage of the already presented examples which raises similar problems to those discussed above for the inductive techniques.

In contrast to the inductive approaches, focusing has not been widely applied, but its ability to learn incrementally makes it seem more plausible for the task of student modelling, since it removes the need to remember every presented example. Also, Bruner, Goodnow and Austin (1956) describe a version of focusing (without the discrimination process) and provide some evidence for it as a psychological process. But there are problems with the algorithm, which make it less suitable for the student modelling situation.

1. The use of 'near misses' only is unacceptable, since the student will need to observe many different examples, positive and negative. This raises the memory overload problem of having many possibilities generated by the discrimination process.

2. The algorithm as described above is only capable of learning conjunctive concepts, which could be a considerable limitation.

3. The provision of the description space limits the learning which can occur. There is no way of knowing the student's 'psychological description space'. The ability to construct the space from the observed examples is important, but Wielemaker and Bundy's method seems to depend on memory for all examples.

4. Without a discrimination component, Bruner, Goodnow and Austin's algorithm learns nothing from negative examples, which seems psychologically unacceptable.

11.4.3 Schemata

Both the above techniques suffer from their impoverished representation of concepts and examples. In psychology the classical view of concepts as a collection of values on certain features has been superseded by notions of prototypes and exemplars (Medin and Smith, 1984). This change has been paralleled in machine learning by attempts to represent concepts more richly; for example using schemata, which are more flexible than tree representations and less dependent on a predetermined set of features.

One technique which uses schemata to represent concepts is explanation-based learning, in which learning occurs as explanations are generated of why some example is an example of the concept. Such a system (see Mitchell, Keller and Kedar-Cabelli, 1986, for a review) must have prior knowledge of the domain and the sort of concept which is being learnt, in order to generate the explanations. Proponents of such systems emphasize the fact that they can learn from a single example of a concept, but they fail to indicate how the knowledge of the domain and concept were obtained (possibly through previous, implicit examples?).

A typical system is that described by DeJong (1986), known as 'explanatory schema acquisition'. This system is given a short story which embodies some unknown concept, and it attempts to explain how the actions in the story achieve the goals of the main actor (also supplied to the system). The goal of the main actor is described as some known concept, which is then adjusted to explain the action. These adjustments can occur through four mechanisms.

1. 'Schema composition' occurs when the story contains two known schemata and the actions can be explained by a particular connection between the two. A new concept can be learnt which composes the two schemata in the right way.

2. 'Secondary effect evaluation' is when the desired outcome arises through the secondary effect of some schema contained within the story. Thus a new concept is created which has this effect as its primary effect.

3. 'Schema alteration' occurs when a known schema does not work for some reason and this reason has to be incorporated into a new concept. Generalization may also occur, preventing the new concept from occurring only in the context in which it was learnt.

4. 'Volitionalization' creates new concepts with agents from concepts which previously had no main agent. For example, *traffic accident* is suggested by Dejong as a concept with no agent, though following a story in which a car's brakes were deliberately tampered with this concept would have to be 'volitionalized' to create a new concept which included this new possibility.

For example, a story about a kidnapping might be given to a system which knows the concepts of *bargain* and *steal* and which knows that the actor's goal is to acquire wealth. Schema composition is the mechanism invoked here since the story will include elements of both *steal* (the abduction) and *bargain* (the ransom negotiations). Thus, the achievement of the actor's goal can be explained by using *steal* to satisfy the preconditions of *bargain*. Thus, according to DeJong's system, a new concept is acquired in which Person *A* requires money, Person *B* has money and values Person *C*, and so *A* can achieve the goal by kidnapping *C* and collecting a ransom from *B*. This new concept can then be used for further learning.

For the purposes of a student modelling task these types of system have the advantage of appearing to have psychological validity, but as Dejong admits

> "The author's intuition is that real-world adult human learning is largely explanation driven, but no psychological experiments have yet been performed to test this hypothesis." (DeJong, 1986; p. 572)

But there are other problems too. First, it is not clear whether the four mechanisms described above are a complete set. They appear to be arbitrary and not derived from any theory. There is no indication how to decide which mechanism to use when there is conflict.

Second, and more problematic, there is no specification of the prior knowledge included within the systems. For example, what would be the effect on the kidnapping example of making small changes to the bargain or steal schemata. Also, that example included the fact that the object stolen in a kidnapping is a person, but there is no indication of how this conclusion was drawn. An equally adequate explanation of the story would have Person *A* stealing any object which Person *B* values. This extra deduction must arise from some prior knowledge which is unspecified.

Explanation-based learning is currently a popular area within machine learning and there are some interesting possibilities ahead, if the details become more clearly defined. Although present systems seem to be inappropriate for the problem of student modelling, this may not be true of future explanation-based systems.

11.4.4   Summary of concept learning systems

None of the above systems is immediately appealing as a psychological model. They have some significant weaknesses, of which two prevail. One is that the representation of concepts is frequently impoverished (for example, the tree descriptions) and the other is that the prior knowledge involved is often poorly specified. Unfortunately it also seems to be the case that the richer the concept representation, the poorer the specification of prior knowledge. Thus it seems unlikely that any of these systems could be used to construct psychologically valid student models. It is necessary to look for alternative approaches.

11.5   AN ALTERNATIVE STUDENT MODEL

Some alternatives lies within the standard ICAI framework: for example, conducting more research on the construction of richer student models, or on the conceptual models used during learning (see Payne, Chapter 4). However, the alternative we wish to sketch here involves a reconstruction of the notion of a student model.

In the introduction we described two types of student model; a model of the ideal student and a model of the particular student using the system. However, a third option is to model some student, not necessarily this particular one, receiving the same information. Expressed another way, this student model would function as a collaborative partner, able to offer advice and suggestions about the material and the learning process. In this context the psychological validity of the student model becomes less important, since the model is used to generate interactions, not determine the tutorial strategy. For these purposes the model need only be 'psychologically credible', by which we mean that the student must consider the model's learning performance to be possible for her to emulate. For example, a learning system which required large memory resources would not be psychologically credible, but focusing could be, since Bruner, Goodnow and Austin (1956) observed its use in psychological experiments.

Of the three systems described above, focusing seems to offer the greatest potential for this radical approach and it is this which we have attempted to implement. The work described below is only at a very early stage and should not be interpreted as a working system.

11.5.1   A collaborative learning system for concepts

First of all, we must clarify the envisaged (admittedly contrived) learning situation. Imagine that a student has access to a database containing details of the properties (e.g. boiling point, thermal conductivity, etc.) of the chemical elements (e.g. antimony, arsenic, etc.) which have been assigned to one of three classes (metal, semi-metal, non-metal), and that she decides to explore the database in an attempt to discover why these assignments have been made. Imagine also that we aim to design a system able to collaborate in this investigation, the system itself not knowing the rules (if any) by which sets of properties are mapped onto classes.

The various components of such a system, shown in Fig. 11.5, might be as follows.

1. *Prior domain knowledge.* If we adopt the focusing algorithm then this has to include the descriptions of the relation trees, i.e. the structure of the properties. (No doubt learners bring much other 'world knowledge' to bear but this is ignored in machine learning and so it will be here.)

2. *Concept knowledge.* This is the description of the system's current understanding of the concepts to be learned, expressed as bounds within the relation trees. It is hoped that this description bears some comparison with the learner's current understanding of the concepts.

3. *Program's learning strategies.* This is a set of rules to determine, on the basis of the current concept knowledge, what would be a useful piece of inform-

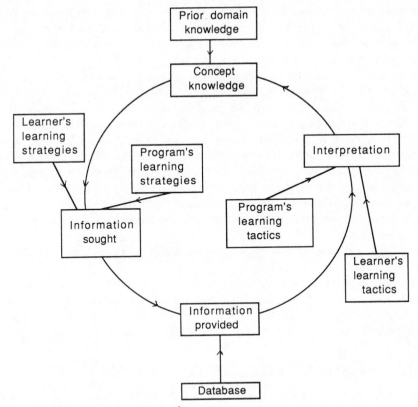

Fig. 11.5. The concept learning cycle.

ation to seek. This is not part of the focusing algorithm *per se*, since focusing is concerned with the passive interpretation of data given to it, but an adaptation whereby the system deliberately asks for examples which would enable it to adjust the bounds. For example, if the system suspected that all metals are shiny it could ask for an example of a metal which is not shiny.

4. *Learner's learning strategies.* This, of course, is not directly accessible to the system, but it might be modelled as a variation of the program's learning strategies. The relationship between these two components is considered further below.

5. *Information sought.* After some discussion between program and learner, some agreement is reached as to what information to seek. The nature of a successful such discussion needs to be determined. Obviously, we would like the system to have a rather more subtle style than the extremes of an intrusive backseat driver and a dumb passenger. Pending the experimental study of successful human–human and human–computer collaboration, we can at least implement an advisory style, whereby the system is able to answer 'What would you do next?' and 'Why?' questions.

6. *Information provided.* This is just the answer to the query. The queries may be arbitrarily complex, e.g. 'Which metals heavier than lead melt below 0 °C?'.

7. *Database.* This is a conventional database giving the values for various properties for each element.

8. *Program's learning tactics.* This is the program's learning algorithm, taking the new information and the current understanding of the concepts to form a revised understanding. It is a variant (called MULTI) of the focusing algorithm, modified to overcome some of the limitations discussed above (MULTI is described in detail in Gilmore, 1986). In particular, the problem with 'far misses' is overcome by regarding negative examples as examples of some other concept (as they are in this case and indeed most often in practice) and then generalizing over them, leaving discrimination for what Holte (1985) calls the performance system, i.e. the part which classifies unlabelled examples. This enables the system to learn more than one concept simultaneously, as we require, and to learn some disjunctive concepts.

9. *Learner's learning tactics.* Again, this is modelled as a variation of the above, and will be discussed further below.

10. *Interpretation.* Again, we have some collaborative discussion between the system and the learner on what is to be learned from the new information, with similar issues about the nature of such a discussion. The outcome of such a discussion is a revised description of the concept knowledge.

11.5.2   The role of the 'student model'

The program's learning skills (i.e. components 3 and 8) are expressed as a rule-based set of heuristics, such as 'If you've an example from two classes and they have very different values for some attribute, see if this is a distinguishing attribute', and a rule-based version of the MULTI algorithm itself. The intention is that components 3 and 8 have sufficient psychological credibility that the learner can appreciate the advice and comments offered. These comments could range from the very specific – 'Ask about the solubility of sulphur' or 'It seems that all metals are insoluble in water' – through the general – 'See if semi-metals have extreme values for any attribute' – to the subject-independent – 'Concentrate on just one attribute first'.

However, since components 3 and 8 are not psychologically valid, as discussed above, then, if used alone, the program's description of the concepts being learned will become progressively out-of-step with the learner's understanding, and so the advice and comment would become increasingly irrelevant. (In fact, it would be no use if components 3 and 8 *were* perfect psychological models because, by definition, the system would not be able to offer any comment beyond what the learner has determined by herself.) It is one of the functions of the collaborative discussions to enable the system to gather some evidence so that it can maintain a realistic description of the concepts to be learned, as understood by the learner, so that comments are to the point.

If the system is to make comments about learning skills (as well as about the concepts being learned) then we may hope that, through the interaction, the learner's skills will improve. For the system's comments on learning skills to be appropriate we need to maintain a dynamic model of the learner's learning skills. This model (components 4 and 9) will, initially, be expressed as an overlay model (see Clancey, Chapter 3) on components 3 and 8, i.e. we will assume that the learner has some subset of the program's learning skills. If, for example, the learner seeks a piece of information which the program itself would have sought on the basis of some particular heuristic then the system may hypothesize that that heuristic should be included in component 4. The differences between components 3 and 8 and between components 4 and 9 form the basis for 'tutorial' type comments about learning skills. Clearly, the issues that arise at this 'learning level' are similar to those that arise at the 'knowledge level' in more conventional tutors concerned with subject matter.

This approach, then, is in accord with the general trend in ICAI to de-emphasize the role of transmitting certified knowledge to students – indeed, it takes it to the absurd extreme of dispensing entirely with knowledge of the subject to be learned! In reality, of course, the system's knowledge resides in the learning components.

11.5.3 Some open questions

The above comments on a machine learning based computer collaborator are only provisional. Many open questions remain to be answered, by experimentation and implementation, among them

- Can focusing (or any other concept learning algorithm) be adapted to be sufficiently psychologically credible?
- Can we adequately represent the effect of real world knowledge outside the specific subject domain?
- Will students be at ease with a collaborative computer, or do they prefer a 'servant' or 'guru' mode?
- What precisely is a 'collaboration'?
- Can students verbalize meta-level skills such as learning strategies, and does it help them to do so?

11.6 CONCLUSIONS

The student-modelling effort is intimately related to machine learning. To maintain a description of a student's changing knowledge, a tutoring system must be able to learn from the evidence provided by the student's activities. But, of course, for student modelling we must seek a stronger psychological basis than is common in machine-learning work, which is more often motivated by performance criteria.

No existing machine-learning techniques seem adequate to maintain dynamic student models. Instead we have proposed an alternative role for both machine learning and student modelling, namely that we use machine learning to maintain a model of a potential collaborator. For this role, the machine-learning techniques need to have psychological credibility, not fidelity. Our aim is not to suggest that a collaboration is necessarily more effective than a tutorial but to force us to take seriously the notion that 'learning abilities are required not only from the student but from the tutor as well' (Michalski, 1986).

ACKNOWLEDGEMENT

This research is being carried out under the Science and Engineering Research Council's grant D/16079.

12

Self-organized learning within an intelligent teaching system*

ROSEMARY R. TODD
Admiralty Research Establishment, England

A particular problem arises in training when it is impossible or inappropriate to make reference to an authoritative expert in the task. It is suggested that in some respects submarine command tactics present a training problem of this kind. This chapter describes the structure and evolution of an intelligent teaching system designed to address this problem, using the war game HUNKS to simulate the command task environment. The work makes use of the well-developed theoretical principles of self-organized learning and its associated research strategy in the progressive implementation of ITSSOL, an intelligent teaching system for self-organized learning.

12.1 INTRODUCTION

Ideally computer-based instruction should combine the flexibility of a gifted personal tutor with the consistency of a machine. The gifted teacher brings qualities of perceptiveness and responsiveness to the tutorial interaction which make it possible for instruction to be tailored to the personal and changing needs of the learner. This is a major aim of intelligent teaching systems (Sleeman and Brown, 1982), which are being developed at the Admiralty Research Establishment Behavioural Science Division. This chapter reports research on the application of the theory and methodology of self-organized learning (Thomas and Harri-Augstein, 1985) to the development of an intelligent teaching system. The domain, submarine command tactics, is simulated in a war game HUNKS, an abbreviation of HUNter Killer Simulation.

12.2 AN INTELLIGENT TEACHING SYSTEM

The skeleton framework of the intelligent teaching system (ITS) is shown in Fig. 12.1 (Sheppard, 1981). The learner is able to engage in HUNKS play via the

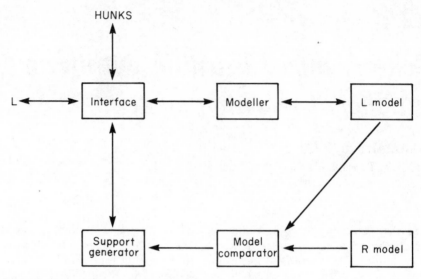

Fig. 12.1. An intelligent teaching system.

interface; this interface also serves for the communication of instructional guidance and support from the *support generator* to the learner. The system is able to make its support intelligible to the learner, by virtue of its knowledge of him/her as a HUNKS player. This knowledge is acquired by the *modeller* by direct interrogation of the learner during game play through the interface, which is simultaneously observed by the modeller. The interrogation results in the construction of a *model* of the learner as a HUNKS player. The system also includes a *referent model* with which the *learner model* may be compared in the *model comparator*. This referent model may represent an expert player of HUNKS. If this *expert* has an authoritative status within the instructional programme, it can provide a goal for the instruction. In this case, the learner's skill as a HUNKS player is evaluated against the *expert model*, and the support generator operates to reduce or eliminate the difference between the learner model and the expert model. It is worth noting that the domain expertise, represented in the expert model, is functionally distinct from the instructional expertise, supplied by the support generator.

An ITS may be seen as a development from current computer-based instruction systems. Many CBI systems incorporate automatic assessment of the learner's level of knowledge or skill; this feature provides the system with some perceptiveness of the learner's needs. However, assessment is usually a very much abbreviated sampling of the learner's knowledge or skill, based on a few summary measures of performance or a test score assumed to be representative of his capability in the domain (or sub-domain). A CBI system may also show some degree of responsiveness to the individual by selecting for him an appropriate pathway through the instructional material, but this is usually restricted to a simple branching lesson structure. Alternative pathways represent its capacity for response variation, and together with self-pacing are the chief means by which the system accommodates individual needs. In contrast, the capability of an ITS to construct an elaborated model of the learner as game player provides it with a perceptiveness of the learner's current state which is not normally achieved in CBI. The comparison with an expert model enables the system to locate precisely the lacunae in the learner model and thus to identify the current personal needs of the learner. The learner model also provides for support to be couched in terms which the learner is known to understand. The capacity of an ITS to respond appropriately to the learner's needs depends on the degree of elaboration of the support generator. In these ways an ITS is able to adapt to the individual learner to a degree not achieved by most CBI systems.

This description of an ITS framework allows many interpretations. Different styles of teaching may be associated with dissimilar instructional goals and dissimilar methods. These will be reflected in differing contents for the support generator, possibly also in special purpose modellers, and in distinct mechanisms for the control of the instructional process. In part, the choice between alternative realizations of an ITS may depend on the nature of the task to be learned. The view of HUNKS play adopted here has led to the choice of self-organized learning as a compatible approach to be realized within an ITS.

12.3   DOMAIN

The game of HUNKS, in spite of its formal simplicity, elegantly captures many of the features of the submarine command decision-making environment. Previous work at ARE (Todd, 1982) has shown that submarine tactics require, among others, skills which are inventive and adaptive. Given almost any tactical problem, no two submariners are likely to agree on its solution; to some extent, it is a question of individual style. Tactics need to be inventive, to cope with the unexpected event or one which has never been encountered before. Finally, the domain is an evolving one: changes in sensors, weaponry or vessel capabilities on either side can present new tactical problems or offer new solutions. In these aspects, the domain of submarine command decision making does not lend itself to training based on an expert model. Tactics which replicate those of an expert would lead to stereotyped behaviour, ultimately predictable to an opponent, and lacking in adaptability. For the present-day context, training based on an expert model is undesirable; for tactics of the future, the relevant expert does not exist. Training which does not rely on an authoritative 'expert' version of task competence presents a challenging problem for the training designer, in particular within CBI.

The whole relationship between the learner, the domain and the instructor changes when there is no domain expert to call upon and refer to. A new basis for defining a training objective has to be found, together with alternative criteria for assessing the learner's progress and determining his needs. If the expert-based training environment is regarded as one in which the learner, via the instructor, interrogates the expert about the domain, and is informed by him under the direction of the instructor, the expert-less training environment by contrast appears as one in which there is no known answer to the learner's questions. The learner's position resembles that of a researcher.

12.4 SELF-ORGANIZED LEARNING

An approach to learning which is particularly well suited to this problem is self-organized learning. The theory and methodology were originated and developed over twenty years by L. Thomas and S. Harri-Augstein (e.g., 1983a) at the Centre for the Study of Human Learning (CSHL), Brunel University, and have been shown to be applicable to many skill areas or domains. Because their approach is strongly centred on the individual learner, and does not rely on an authoritative domain expert, it appeared to offer an attractive solution to the problem of HUNKS learning within an ITS. The collaboration between CSHL and ARE has been directed towards the implementation of their theory and its associated methodology within an ITS.

A basic premise in self-organized learning theory is that most people fail to realize their potential as learners, because their experiences of education and training environments have required them simply to submit to being taught. As a result, they have never learned how to learn. When students engage in self-organized learning rather than dependent learning, studies have repeatedly shown (e.g. Thomas and Harri-Augstein, 1976) that learning is accelerated and the resulting achievement is much superior.

The self-organized learner acts as a researcher or 'personal scientist' within the domain (Thomas and Harri-Augstein, 1983a; Kelly, 1955). His or her learning is conducted as a personal exploration of the domain; an investigation of the cause and effect relationships that hold within it, by carefully planned probes and detailed appraisal of the results. He takes the same deliberately questioning approach to his own learning processes, regarding them as equally open to experimentation. Three attributes in particular distinguish the self-organized from the dependent learner.

- The self-organized learner is self-aware: he is conscious of his own experience and behaviour in the domain and in learning, and understands his own processes. This is in contrast to the dependent learner who relies on the *teacher* to monitor such aspects of the learner's activities as are relevant in the teacher's view.

- The self-organized learner is self-directing: he is able to function purposefully towards goals he has defined himself. The dependent learner, on the other hand, responds passively under the teacher's definition of purposes.

- The self-organized learner is self-critical: he can construct his own evaluative criteria and assess his achievement and progress himself. He can observe the behaviour of others within his own evaluation scheme, and make productive use of comparisons with himself. He differs here from the dependent learner, who is reliant on the teacher's assessment against criteria which are often covert.

These different roles or perspectives within the individual are in communication and can act on each other; the learner can sustain a dialogue with himself.

The purpose of the self-organized learning methodology is to enable the learner to become self-organized. Most learners are initially unable to generate and maintain these communicating perspectives, and the dialogue needs to be articulated and supported through a *learning manager* (Thomas and Harri-Augstein, 1983b). A substantial body of techniques has been developed by Thomas and Harri-Augstein to provide this conversational support, and to encourage a learner to become self-organized. His new learning skills are gained and practised within a particular domain, so that he is simultaneously engaged in learning the domain and in learning how to learn. The aim of the current work is a machine implementation of these techniques for the HUNKS domain, i.e. to produce a computerized 'manager'. The next section outlines these techniques, with their theoretical foundations, in an *idealized version of an intelligent teaching system for self-organized learning* (ITSSOL).

The learning environment for promoting self-organized learning is a radical departure from conventional CBI and also from other interpretations of an ITS. In particular, the role of the *instructor* in CBI is completely reformulated in the *learning manager* in self-organized learning. While the instructor acts to impart the expert's knowledge to the learner, and assesses his progress against the expert, the learning manager acts to enhance the effectiveness of the learner's exploratory interactions with the domain, and to promote his autonomy as a learner. The learning manager has no need of a domain expert as referent. There is a second important difference. In most teaching systems, learning is conterminous with teaching, and is discontinued when instructional support is withdrawn. In an ITS designed to promote self-organized learning, the learner becomes progressively more able to direct and control his own learning, and the support provided by the learning manager becomes no longer needed. The function of the learning manager is designed to be obsolescent, and is gradually withdrawn as the learner becomes able to take over its function himself, and to continue learning autonomously.

12.5 ITSSOL: AN IDEALIZED VERSION

The idealized system towards which we are working is an integration of certain components of an ITS being developed at ARE with techniques developed over many years at CSHL and more recently in collaboration with ARE (Thomas and Harri-Augstein, 1983b).

Figure 12.2 shows the idealized system in a representation parallel to the ITS framework of Fig. 12.1. The single modeller in the ITS skeleton is replaced by multiple modellers in Fig. 12.2. The use of multiple models is an integral part of self-organized learning theory; they enable the learner to explore different facets of his experience and behaviour, to observe himself from different perspectives, and they encourage him to generate multiple internal representations of his

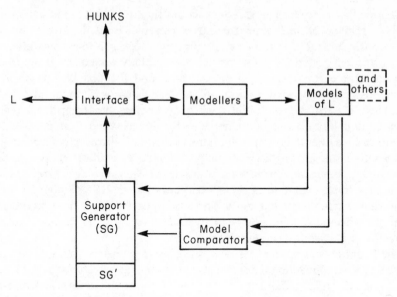

Fig. 12.2. ITSSOL: idealized version.

experience and behaviour. The intention is not to restrict the learner in his construction of internal models, but to promote the possibility of alternatives through the parallel and comparative use of those provided. In comparison with Fig. 12.1, the idealized version shows the reduced emphasis on machine comparison of models, and the flexible rather than mandatory use of referent models, which reflect the underlying theoretical principles. These referent models no longer have the status of an authoritative expert. They include models of co-learners, non-authoritative experts and possibly earlier versions of the learner himself, and are available for the learner's use, to encourage flexibility and to enhance his development as a critical observer.

Most of the operations of the learning manager are represented within the support generator, which can act to provide guidance and support which is sensitive to the individual learner. His needs are known to the support generator from the learner models. Other aspects of the learning manager's function are represented elsewhere in the system, in the modellers themselves. The sequence of an elicitation procedure in a modeller, for example, exerts a directive influence on the responding learner. This kind of guidance is not adaptive to the individual but is invariant across learners. The interventions of the learning manager can be more or less heavily directive. An activity which imposes a fixed sequence on the learner corresponds to a high degree of directiveness, whereas an activity which offers the learner many or repeated choices is much less strongly directive.

Since the system works to promote self-organized learning, the functions of the learning manager are gradually taken over by the learner himself. This includes the control exercised by the support generator, SG. The withdrawal of this control probably also depends indirectly on the contents or use of the various models, and is mediated by a secondary control function, SG′.

Figure 12.3 is an expansion of the modelling component in Fig. 12.2, the idealized version of ITSSOL. It shows the modellers in two groups: one concerned with modelling the learner's activity in the domain, his task; the second concerned with the modelling of learning itself.

The three task modellers capture different aspects of the learner's experience and behaviour in the HUNKS game, and serve different purposes. The modeller based on PTR (*personalized task representation*) is being constructed at ARE. The PTR modeller (Gregory, 1979, 1981) captures the learner's HUNKS play, and its causal and teleological bases through direct interrogation of the learner. The resultant model of the learner is intended to be operable, i.e. when sufficiently complete, it can substitute for the learner and play as he would himself. Similarly it is open to interrogation by means of the PTR questions, and will respond as the learner would. Models of other players are available for inspection and use as

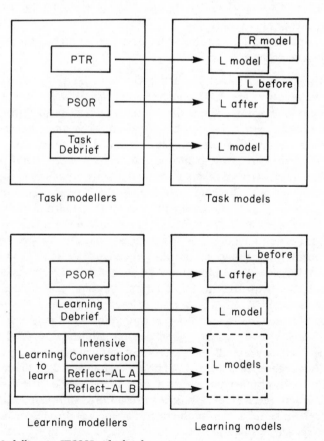

Fig. 12.3. Modelling in ITSSOL: idealized version.

machine players by the learner. Since they have been constructed by the PTR modeller, they can also describe and explain their own play in response to PTR questions, although naturally their accounts will be in the terms of their originators. It is our expectation that PTR modelling will have the effect of focusing the learner's attention on the rational basis of his play as structured by the PTR questions. The principal value of PTR modelling within the system, however, is in terms of its product, the PTR model, which can be deployed by the learner or by the support generator in various ways to promote learning.

The function of the second modeller is in complete contrast to this. The PSOR modeller provides the learner with the facility to formulate and execute contracts relating to the task. A contract is both a plan for the next episode of HUNKS activity and a commitment which the learner makes with himself. Its fixed components (abbreviated as P, S, O and R) are:

- Purpose: the learner defines his own intentions,
- Strategy: the learner specifies the means by which he will achieve his purpose,
- Outcome: the learner generates criteria by which he will assess the quality of the outcome of his strategy,
- Review: a retrospective appraisal of his purpose-definition, choice of strategy, and outcome criteria.

When the learner is provisionally satisfied with his purpose, strategy, and outcome, he executes his PSOR contract. His ensuing activity will frequently engage him in HUNKS play. Finally, the learner reviews his performance in the light of his contract, and re-examines his contract. Occasions where the contract has not been successfully executed are regarded as particularly significant learning opportunities: they confront the learner with inconsistencies or inadequacies in his internal model of the task. The comparison between before- and after-task versions of his contract is used by the support generator to identify the direction of development, and by the learner in the formulation of the next contract. Like the PSOR contract itself, the comparison is a means to an end; its purpose is to encourage the learner to think positively and constructively. In the course of learning, a sequence of contracts will have different foci, different scopes and differing time scales. Unlike the PTR modeller, PSOR modelling is more closely concerned with the process of formulating and executing the contract than with the contents of the contract. The elicitation and execution of the 'model' are themselves aspects of the learning manager's support.

The *task debrief* is an activity which is normally interpolated between the learner's HUNKS play and his contract review. It is a modeller in the sense that it leads the learner to represent aspects of his performance in a particular structure. As with PSOR, its primary purpose is to engage the learner in a process rather than to extract a product. He is asked to recall his game play episode, and to reconstruct it and analyse it with the help of a replay of the episode. The exercise helps the learner to integrate his remembered experience with the objective record of his behaviour, which allows him to test and develop his perceptions and expectations within the game of HUNKS against observed event sequences. These activities enhance the learner's awareness of himself as a HUNKS player, and enable him to be a more effective 'personal scientist' in the domain. The debrief stimulates the learner to reorganize his experience, which in turn generates content for his subsequent contract review.

Both PSOR and the debrief procedure can be applied to the modelling of learning as well as to the modelling of the task. The structure of the activity remains exactly the same; the only difference is in the content. At early stages, learners frequently find it difficult to think and speak about their learning; they lack awareness of themselves as learners. The support of the learning manager encourages this transition, and enables the learner to act as 'personal scientist' with respect to his own learning. A further group of activities, the *learning-to-learn* procedures, serve both to widen the learner's perspective and to sharpen his focus on his own learning. The idealized version of ITSSOL includes three such procedures among the learning modellers. The *intensive conversation* can be regarded as a remedial activity for the learner whose PSOR contracts fail because they are poorly formulated. It leads him into a detailed examination of each of the contract components, so that he becomes better able to produce well-differentiated and significant contents for his PSOR contracts. Because the intensive conversation increases the learner's capability to use PSOR contracts productively, it increases his ability to learn. The *reflect-and-learn* procedures shift the learner's attention to a broader perspective on his own learning, by directing him to survey either a group of his contracts (Reflect-AL B) or his experiences of games learning in general (Reflect-AL A). These learning-to-learn procedures incorporate *repertory grid* techniques, based on Kelly's Personal Construct Theory (Kelly, 1955). Repertory grid methodology provides a way of eliciting and structuring verbal data and has many applications in exploring an individual's values, attitudes, perceptions and experiences. The resultant grid may be used simply as information for the investigator, or it may be disclosed to the individual and also used, as it is in ITSSOL, to prompt the individual to recognize in a novel way aspects of his attitudes and experience. In such cases, the repertory grid may itself be an instrument of change in the individual.

12.6   ITSSOL: CURRENT VERSION

The current version of the system (developed by Thomas and Harri-Augstein at CSHL) is implemented on an Apple II microcomputer in Applesoft Basic. The components which are already available as software are shown in Fig. 12.4. The HUNKS game is also implemented on an Apple, together with a computer player which can provide an opponent for the learner in game play.

The system comprises a suite of programs which explain themselves to the learner, offer him choices of activity, and lead him through the elicitation procedures of model building. The learner can choose to be addressed as a 'novice', when he will receive full explanatory annotations to the procedures, or

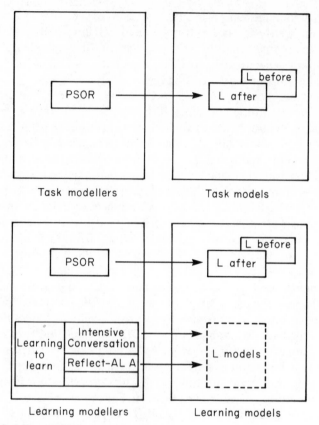

Fig. 12.4. Modelling ITSSOL: current version.

as an 'expert', when the explanations are withheld. The learner is free to traverse the elicitation and associated procedures in almost any order he chooses, although some routes are suggested as more sensible than others. The dialogue conducted via the VDU and the keyboard is augmented by hard copy print-outs of the learner's models which may be accompanied by non-evaluative comments which draw the learner's attention to omissions in the model or suggestions for the learner to reflect on. The system cannot comment on the meaning of any of the contents of the learner models, because it has no language understanding mechanism.

There are essentially three activities available to the learner, corresponding to the three modellers in Fig. 12.4: PSOR contracts, the intensive conversation, and Reflect-AL A, concerned with the learner's experience of games. PSOR contracts may address either the HUNKS task itself or HUNKS learning; the system provides no constraints on the contents of the learner's contracts.

The PSOR modeller leads the learner through the elicitation of his contract, prompting him always to formulate his contract with the utmost care and to revise its contents, repeatedly if necessary. This emphasis reflects the importance attached to the process of contract-making as one which itself induces change in the learner. Together with the definition of the contract topic, its purpose, strategy, outcome and outcome criteria, the learner is asked to specify the resources he will need or draw upon to execute his contract. An expansion of the contract follows, although here as elsewhere the learner can opt out of the suggested sequence. The learner is asked to specify both a superordinate context and a set of subordinate elements for each of the components of his contract, so that he is constructing a three-level hierarchy. Again he has the opportunity to revise his contract. When he is at least provisionally satisfied, he attempts to execute it in game play. The suggested sequel to game play is the contract review procedure, in which the learner reconstructs all the components of his contract and his resource list in the light of his experience in game play. A comparison of his before- and after-task versions of a contract is provided as a print-out, and the learner invited to reflect on the differences.

Each of the three modelling activities conducted in the current version of the system is self-contained, and can operate in the absence of a human learning manager. However the system does not include a support generator which can steer the learner between activities, and this function has to be performed in person at present. Figure 12.5 shows the current version represented as an ITS parallel to Fig. 12.1. The three modellers can be supplemented by a pencil-and-paper version of the debrief, which is most appropriately used after HUNKS play and before contract review. The pencil-and-paper version of a procedure can be

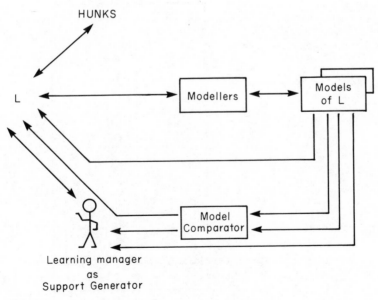

Fig. 12.5. Current version as an ITS.

seen as an intermediate stage in the implementation of a procedure which initially exists only in the head of the skilled learning manager. This process of externalizing and articulating the art of the learning manager is the first step towards a machine implementation, and is served by a research strategy based on empirical study.

12.7 THE RESEARCH STRATEGY: A PRELIMINARY STUDY

The development of the current version of an ITS based on self-organized learning towards the idealized version is expected to be an incremental process. At each stage, further aspects of the learning manager's function will be incorporated within the system. Each intermediate version will be tested in operation, and the empirical trials will serve in the identification of the next series of additions and modification to the system.

Figure 12.6 illustrates this strategy (Thomas, 1976). It shows a learner in interaction with an intermediate version of the system. The human learning manager acts as a critical observer to this interaction, in order to identify shortcomings in the system. He also acts as a participant in the interaction, supplementing and structuring the self-organized learning support provided to the learner. In this role, he or she is observed by a *researcher*, who analyses the interventions of the learning manager. This analysis is continued subsequently, with the learning manager contributing his experience and retrospectively sharing in the researcher's role. The result of this analysis is a specification for the

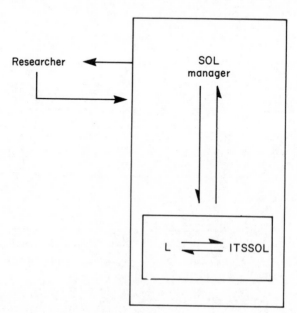

Fig. 12.6. The ITSSOL research strategy.

changes and extensions to the system which will produce a closer approximation to the idealized version. Once this specification has been implemented, the new version is itself the subject of empirical trials in a repetition of the development cycle.

The current version of the system, shown in Figs 12.4 and 12.5, has been the subject of empirical study in line with this strategy. The benefits of the study were expected to be:

1. Feedback for the researchers on the usability and comprehensibility of the current system, at the level of the lucidity of explanation provided by the system, the transparency of its structure, the suitability of input and print-out facilities, and the style of the dialogue the system conducts with the learner.

2. Articulation of the manager's role. The management of the learning conversation is a highly skilled activity, and difficult for its practitioners to articulate, depending as it does on tacit knowledge and sensitive response to the learner's needs. Video records of trial sessions were able to show exactly what interventions the manager made, to steer the learner towards productive use of the system, to supplement its existing procedures and to introduce techniques as yet not present in the system.

An empirical study of the current system was conducted at CSHL with four Brunel University undergraduates participating as learners, each for four half-day periods. Part of the first period was used to familiarize the learner with the rules of the HUNKS game, and to introduce him or her to the system in the experimental context. The learner was provided with a game rules book, and engaged in preliminary HUNKS game play before the learning sessions began. A researcher supplied further explanation of the game rules where necessary.

After this preliminary orientation, the learning sessions began. The learner worked with the system and with the HUNKS game, under the supervision of the learning manager. The learner was free to ask any necessary questions of the learning manager, to consult the rules book and to ask for further clarification of the rules where needed. The learning manager observed the learner's interaction with the system, and intervened to guide the learner and to supplement his learning activities with pencil-and-paper procedures and with direct personal interaction. Each session was observed by a researcher and also video-recorded. At the end of the session, the learner's comments on his experience with the system and the learning manager's perception of the session were recorded. Subsequently, the video, the learner models stored by the system and the perceptions of the three participants were analysed by the learning manager and the researcher, both at this point assuming the researcher role. The recorded games played by the learner and the products of the pencil-and-paper exercises were also included in the analyses.

A comprehensive exploration of the issues of interest would require a much more extended study than was conducted here. However, there were several promising early indicators:

1. Evidence was found that subjects do learn HUNKS with the current system. Without any guidance on how to play, other than the very elementary rules of the game, they quickly started to invent game skills. In particular, their play and their accounts of their play showed that they were developing a better appreciation of the game situation, more awareness of the opponent, more differentiated goal-setting and new tactics.

2. Evidence was found that improvements to the dialogue were necessary. The existing components of ITSSOL need to be totally self-explanatory and unambiguous for the learner to be able to respond appropriately, and instances where the learning manager intervened to clarify what the learner was being asked to do showed where improvements were required.

3. The discovery was made that the learner needs much more flexibility in his use of the game. If he is to be encouraged to act as a 'personal scientist' and experiment with game play, he needs to be able to manipulate the variables. Possible future inclusions would include facilities to:

- engage in part-games, to explore a single aspect of game play in isolation,
- slow the game down, when a particularly thought-provoking situation arose,
- run replays backwards, to explore the events which led up to a particular situation,
- stop a game replay and try out alternative tactical solutions.

4. The last and most interesting class of discoveries concerned the additional activities by which the learning manager supplemented ITSSOL. One of the most frequent types of intervention by the learning manager is designed to encourage the learner to detect and explore relationships – relationships between game events, between games, and between the learner's plans and their outcomes. Part of this activity can now be proceduralized and incorporated into an enhanced version of ITSSOL. Further, one of the modellers in the idealized version, the debrief procedure, is now amenable to formulation and inclusion in the next ITSSOL. Finally, the improved system would include models of other learners, to be used as demonstrations under the control of the learning manager.

This preliminary study serves to illustrate the rich potential for learning research offered by the current version of ITSSOL. A more comprehensive study would draw on a larger group of learners, and would focus particularly on the longitudinal aspects of learning which have not been explored here. The required extensions and modifications to the current system which are identified by these empirical trials can then serve in a progressive implementation of the learning manager functions and a closer approximation to the idealized version of ITSSOL.

12.8 SUMMARY

A particular problem arises in training when it is impossible or inappropriate to make reference to an authoritative expert in the task. It is suggested that in some respects submarine command tactics present a training problem of this kind.

This chapter describes the structure and evolution of an intelligent teaching system designed to address this problem, using the war game HUNKS to simulate the command task environment. The work makes use of the well-developed theoretical principles of self-organized learning and its associated research strategy in the progressive implementation of ITSSOL. This approach appears particularly well suited to individual training, in tasks which are primarily cognitive in content, and as a possible solution to the problem of training in the absence of an expert, ITSSOL potentially offers a valuable contribution to the development of advanced CBI systems.

ACKNOWLEDGEMENT

The author wishes to acknowledge the collaboration with L.F. Thomas and E.S. Harri-Augstein under ARE/APU Contract no. 2066/034.

13

Plan recognition and intelligent tutoring systems

MARK R. WOODROFFE
University of Essex, England

The optimal design of intelligent tutoring systems varies according to the structure of the subject domain. In many domains the student is required to achieve some goal by executing a number of explicit steps. For example, the student may be required to modify the UNIX file hierarchy. It is in such domains that the student will typically execute a plan which, in order to provide the appropriate guidance, the tutoring system needs to recognize. This chapter will briefly review some of the existing plan recognition systems. It will then describe in detail a plan recognition program called FITS-2 which the author has written to form the basis of an intelligent tutoring system (ITS) shell. FITS-2 predicts the student's plan by combining pre-defined plan knowledge with knowledge of the student. This hypothesized plan is then used to interpret the student's input.

13.1 INTRODUCTION

Planning is a frequently used human skill which results in the generation of plans which, according to the knowledge of the planner, will achieve a particular goal or goals when executed. The execution of such plans usually requires the execution of a sequence of actions. An example of plan generation, taken from Wilensky (1983), is where a man at work is phoned by his wife, and asked to buy some milk. The man then generates a plan which combines driving home and stopping at a shop to buy some milk.

A skill closely related to plan generation is plan recognition. This is the process of observing another person's actions and inferring the plan which he is executing and the goal he is hoping to achieve. For example, if a person is observed holding some keys by the front door of a house, it is possible to infer his goal as being to open the door. This will require a plan which includes placing the key in the lock and turning it.

There exists a body of artificial intelligence (AI) literature which combines ideas from the areas of planning and intelligent tutoring systems (ITS). This chapter will start by describing and comparing some of the more important systems within this literature. It will then describe in some detail an existing plan recognition system, written by the author, called FITS-2.

13.2 LITERATURE REVIEW

This literature survey will describe some of the relevant projects, attempting to highlight their strengths and weaknesses. This background information will help justify some of the more important design decisions made in FITS-2.

13.2.1 The Computer-Based Consultant

Many of the planning-based tutoring systems centre upon an *expert-based paradigm*. This means that the tutoring system has the knowledge of an expert and the student's behaviour is compared with this. An early example of this approach is found in the Computer-Based Consultant (Sacerdoti, 1977). NOAH, the plan generator at the heart of the Consultant, generates a procedural network, and monitors the student's progress through it.

The procedural network is a hierarchy of increasingly abstract actions, each of which represents a possible student action or action sequence. Each action contains a slot called the expansion which specifies the actions in the next lower level which make up the higher level action. The actions in the expansion are *partially ordered*. This means that they can be executed in any order, except where essential action orderings are specified.

NOAH generates the procedural network layer by layer starting with the action at the top of the hierarchy. In the example of assembling an air compressor, given in Sacerdoti (1977), the top action is 'try to achieve: assembled air compressor'. The depth to which the network is generated is controlled by the level of understanding of the student. At one extreme, if the student has no knowledge it would be necessary to generate the whole hierarchy down to the level where the actions correspond to physical actions made by the student, such as 'turn the screw'. Alternatively, if the student is able to assemble the air compressor unassisted, then none of the network would be generated.

One of the advantages of the Consultant's approach to tutoring is that the student is given advice at an appropriate level of complexity. However there is no student modelling and the task which the student is tackling needs to be explicitly specified.

13.2.2 POISE

In most domains, if a number of student actions are observed the student could be executing any one of a number of plans. In this situation the planning program usually needs to make a choice between the possible plans.

The POISE system (Carver, Lesser and McCue, 1984) contains a plan library which represents all the typical student plans in a hierarchy of increasing abstraction. This library is similar to the procedural network in NOAH, but it is pre-generated. The library enables the system to monitor the student's inputs, matching them against the leaf nodes of the hierarchy as they are entered. This causes plans to be activated at a number of levels of abstraction. These plans act as interpretations of the student's input sequence and help restrict the search space for subsequent inputs.

In POISE, the choice of parent action within the hierarchy is controlled by a number of heuristics. The assumptions that result from the application of these heuristics are stored explicitly. These assumptions are maintained and updated by a reason maintenance system, as further evidence for or against the choice of plan becomes available. If incorrect or conflicting assumptions are detected, resulting from the input sequence not matching the chosen plan, dependency directed backtracking occurs, locating and altering the incorrect assumption(s). This will result in the choice of a different interpreting plan.

Whilst taking a more formal approach to the choice of parent actions, POISE, like NOAH, does not incorporate the recognition of incorrect plans, or utilize the information in a student model. It is possible that these attributes will be added to POISE at a later stage.

The FITS-1 program, the predecessor of FITS-2, as reported in Woodroffe (1985), has a number of similarities with the POISE program; however, it does not have the reason maintenance system.

13.2.3 BUGGY

The concept of a procedural network was adopted and modified in the BUGGY system (Brown and Burton, 1978). BUGGY is a program for diagnosing elementary arithmetic errors. It has been incorporated into a teaching game for training student teachers.

In BUGGY an arithmetic algorithm, such as subtraction, is written into a procedural network. Each node in the network (procedure), contains a statement of the intent of the node, for example 'add a column', plus details about how the other procedures can be combined to achieve this intent. These two parts are similar to the effects and expansion of an action.

BUGGY diagnoses student errors by analysing the student's answers to a series of questions. The system attempts to replicate these answers by replacing procedures within the network with 'buggy' or incorrect procedures, and then generating the answers to each of the questions. The buggy procedures represent student misunderstandings, such as not borrowing from the column to the left in a multi-column subtraction problem.

This approach to planning is different from those previously described because it is not possible to observe the individual actions as they are executed. Unlike NOAH and POISE, a student model is generated, in the form of a deviant procedural network, called a diagnostic model. Also unlike many student models, the knowledge within the diagnostic model is not restricted to a subset of the complete knowledge, being augmented by buggy procedures. However, the existence of explicit buggy procedures risks a search explosion when searching through the space of possible student's misconceptions.

13.2.4 The Advisor

The Advisor (Genesereth, 1982) is a program written to act as a consultant for MACSYMA, a computer system designed as a tool for the symbolic manipulation of mathematical expressions. The Advisor reconstructs a representation of the deviant student plan after the student has detected an error and requested help. The reconstruction involves combining information from a number of sources including the heuristic problem solving algorithm, MUSER, a library of frequently recurring errors and a number of domain-independent plan construction procedures. The deviant plan which is generated contains implicit knowledge about the nature of the student's error. This plan is then analysed to locate the error.

Unlike BUGGY, the Advisor is not restricted by a pre-defined procedural network, enabling it to reconstruct any plan. It also extends the error detection process by including domain-independent procedures for completing the deviant plan in addition to the library of frequently recurring errors. This enables the recognition of previously unknown errors.

None of the systems described so far contain an explicit representation of the knowledge, beliefs and intentions of the student. This means that the programs may be able to recognize the errors which have been made, but they only have a shallow understanding of why the errors were made, restricting the program's tutoring abilities.

13.2.5 Allen's work

This limitation is tackled by Allen and Perrault (1980). Allen's program takes the role of a porter in a railway station, being asked by a passenger for help. The program tries to recognize the plan of the passenger, in order to assist him in achieving the inferred goal. The program derives the necessary assistance by recognizing omissions in the plan, such as not knowing the platform from which the train is leaving.

The observed action from which the plan is to be constructed is a speech act. The effects of speech acts take the form of modifications to the beliefs and intentions of the listener. For this reason, the beliefs of both the listener and speaker need to be explicitly represented in order to be able to perform plan recognition and obstacle detection. Allen's program contains a knowledge base which includes representations of the program's beliefs about the world, and the program's beliefs about the passenger's beliefs about the world. This information is used by the plan recognition algorithm which involves generating the passenger's plan using explicit plan inference and plan construction rules, which refer to the inferred *beliefs, knowledge and intentions* of the passenger, as represented in the knowledge base. These rules are applied, and the plan is generated backwards from the goal, and forwards from the speech act. The plan is then checked for goals that the speaker cannot achieve without assistance.

The program is only able to consider a single interaction, and so the information derived from the process of plan generation and assistance is not stored in a student model, for future use.

13.2.6   BELIEVER

The BELIEVER system (Schmidt, Sridharan and Goodson, 1979) attempts to recognize the plan of a single actor pursuing a single plan which involves making and eating something. Like the Allen program, BELIEVER is not a tutoring system; however it utilizes an interesting approach to plan recognition. This approach is referred to as the *hypothesize-and-revise* paradigm and involves generating a plan to interpret the actions already observed (making a hypothesis), and modifying it, as necessary, to match against subsequent observed actions (revising the plan). The hypothesize procedure has two stages: initially it employs a plan generator similar to NOAH, and then the plan is customized so that it is consistent with BELIEVER's representation of the world, and of the actor's beliefs and intentions. BELIEVER also employs revision rules which modify the plan. As in POISE, this approach enables the use of the hypothesized plan to reduce the search space for subsequent inputs. Unlike POISE, BELIEVER's ability to modify the hypothesized plan provides the potential for generating deviant plans, given the appropriate revision rules. If the model of the actor could also be modified accordingly, we would have the potential for a very powerful tutoring system. It is hoped that the existing FITS-2 program will form the basis of such a system. The following section will describe what FITS-2 is currently able to do.

13.3   A DETAILED DESCRIPTION OF FITS-2

13.3.1   Introduction

A plan recognition program called FITS-2 has been developed to form the basis of an intelligent tutoring system (ITS) shell. FITS-2 is written in Prolog and implemented on a GEC 63 computer. FITS-2 attempts to generate a representation of the student's plan by combining pre-defined plan knowledge with knowledge of the student. The hypothesized student plan is used to interpret the student input and to detect errors in the student model. For the sake of brevity, the hypothesized student plan will be referred to in this chapter as 'the student plan'.

FITS-2 attempts to combine some of the ideas from the systems mentioned in the literature review. The major ideas are as follows.

• The knowledge structure at the centre of the system is a *plan hierarchy* of a very similar form to Sacerdoti's *procedural network*. However, like POISE the hierarchy is explicitly represented rather than generated. This facilitates both the coding of domain information and a mixed top-down, bottom-up recognition strategy which helps reduce the search space.

• As in BELIEVER, the student's inferred knowledge, beliefs and intentions are explicitly utilized in the generation of the student plan. This information is stored in a *student model*. Because the plan generated is consistent with the knowledge within the student model, the program shares with the Advisor the potential for generating deviant student plans. Currently, FITS-2 is only able to generate incomplete plans, where an incomplete plan is a plan with actions or constraints missing. Unlike the Advisor, FITS-2 also has the ability to monitor the plan execution, detecting errors in the student model.

• FITS-2 monitors the execution of the generated plan by matching the student inputs against the inputs predicted from the generated plan. If a discrepancy is detected, this means that the student model, which is referred to in the plan generation, is incorrect.

In the current implementation it is assumed that the student will only execute plans consistent with the knowledge in the student model. Future versions of the program will be able to modify the student model, employing the hypothesize-and-revise approach, as in the BELIEVER program. This will enable FITS-2 to check for errors in the student model, at any time during the interaction, allowing for a flexible tutoring strategy.

13.3.2   A typical session

The initial program domain chosen for FITS-2 was the file handling operators of the UNIX operating system.

When the student runs FITS-2 he is presented with information about the UNIX domain. This provides him with the knowledge necessary to solve a problem provided by the program, which involves modifying the UNIX file hierarchy. The student then attempts to solve the problem by entering a sequence of UNIX operators. As the operators are entered, the program generates plans combining knowledge from the student model and from the plan hierarchy. These plans, referred to as student plans, act as interpretations of the input sequence enabling FITS-2 to detect unexpected inputs and the non-satisfaction of constraints and prerequisites.

13.3.3   Student modelling

It has been argued in a number of places, including Self (1974) and Goldstein (1982), that a student model is of great importance for the tutoring process. Usually the model provides assistance in recognizing and analysing student errors, and information for tutoring. Student modelling is very complex, because it is never possible to be certain of the knowledge of the student. In Burton and Brown (1982) some of the problems involved are considered, such as:

- The student may be using skills unknown to the program.
- The student may have forgotten to use a skill he understands.
- The student may have learnt a skill, and this has not been detected by the program.

There are a number of different methods for generating a student model. One method, as used in BUGGY, is to construct the model from what is directly observable in the student's behaviour, this being limited by some form of best-fit technique which avoids the model being corrupted by careless errors.

BUGGY is able to employ this technique because it is provided with a series of examples of the student's behaviour to analyse. Conversely, FITS-2 attempts to understand the student inputs and detect errors as they are being entered. To enable this process to occur assumptions need to be made about the student's knowledge.

For the purposes of FITS-2, I have specified three types of knowledge as being necessary for the generation of plans. These knowledge types relate to: the *effects* of the plan, the *concepts* involved in the domain, and the *ordering* of the actions within the plan.

At the start of the program run, the student model is empty because it is assumed that the student is unfamiliar with the problem domain. FITS-2 then gives the student information about the domain, dividing the information into these three categories. This results in Prolog clauses being added to the student model of the form: told(.., ..).

Examples of this process are given below:

- The student is told the syntax and effects of the UNIX cp operator. A clause of the form: told(effects,cp) is added to the student model.
- The concept of directory files is explained to the student. A clause of the form: told(concept,dir_type) is added to the student model.
- The student is told that a necessary prerequisite to deleting a file is to have write permission on the file. A clause of the form: told(ordering,chmod u + w,rm) is added to the student model.

The student model can be modified by actions called 'model actions'. These alter the representation of the student's beliefs. Currently there exists a single model action:

IF a clause told(Fact) exists in the student model
THEN add clause understands(Fact) to the student model

This means that FITS-2 makes the assumption that the student will remember and understand everything that he is told. It is hoped that future versions of FITS-2 will contain a number of model actions, which will be able to simulate the acquiring of both correct and incorrect knowledge. In UNIX an example of such incorrect knowledge would be the assumption that any file can be deleted using the 'rm' operator. The deviant model would then act as the basis for the generation of deviant student plans.

13.3.4   The plan hierarchy

In FITS-2 the plan knowledge is represented in an explicit hierarchy of increasingly abstract possible plans, which represents all the allowable sequences of inputs. The higher level plans in the hierarchy are general concepts such as 'moving a file', whereas the lower level plans are more specific. The lowest level of plan corresponds to the UNIX operators, such as 'cp' and 'rm'. The reasons for the choice of an explicit hierarchy were:

- Sections of the hierarchy would probably be needed repeatedly and an explicit representation avoids repeated generation.
- It may be unclear which section of the hierarchy to generate.
- Plans in an explicit hierarchy can be coded more easily, because there is no need to define the prerequisites.

The plan hierarchy is made up of plans containing the following slots:

- *Operation*: This is an English description of the operation of the plan. It is used in the user interface.
- *Structure*: This contains information about the child plans in the hierarchy. The child plans, which specify a more detailed description of the plan, form what is known as the plan expansion, with each child being an expansion element. The structure slot also specifies any necessary ordering between the expansion elements and any relevant constraints on their variables. This approach is similar to that taken in the hierarchical planning program NONLIN (Tate, 1976).
- *Effects*: This contains a list of the effects of the plan. In FITS-2 the effects concern adding and removing files from the UNIX file hierarchy.
- *Unary constraints*: This contains a list of the constraints upon individual variables within the plan.

A plan can be represented diagrammatically as shown in Fig. 13.1. In this diagram a plan called copy_ord is represented. This plan, with the arguments: F and Des, represents the copying of file, F to the position in the UNIX file hierarchy denoted by Des. It has five expansion elements, contained within the dotted rectangle; find_prot Des 1, find_prot F, chmod u + rF, chmod u + w Des 1 and cpF Des. The plan find_prot represents the determining of the protection of a file. Each

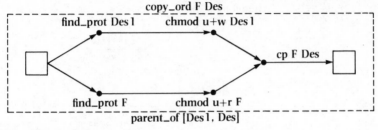

Fig. 13.1. Copy_ord plan.

expansion element is represented by ●. The expansion elements are linked by arrows which specify the partial ordering. The □ are null nodes which represent the beginning and end of the expansion. There is one constraint on the variables: parent_of (Des1,Des). This is listed below the dotted rectangle.

The FITS-2 control mechanism allows for the inclusion of repeated, recursive and optional plans. A repeated plan is a plan which may need to be performed a number of times, such as deleting a number of child files before deleting a directory file. An optional plan is a plan which is not necessary for the satisfaction of the parent plan, but may be considered by the student to be useful. For example, it is not necessary to move the working directory to the parent directory before deleting a file, but it is a correct plan and may be considered useful. A recursive plan is a plan which has a copy of itself within its descendants in the plan hierarchy. An example of this occurs in UNIX when deleting a directory file. In this case it may be necessary to first delete a directory file within the directory being deleted.

13.3.5 Student plans

A student plan is a hypothesized representation of the current student plan. Each student plan which is generated corresponds to a plan in the plan hierarchy. However, the student plan will only contain the parts of the plan which, according to the student model, the student understands. This means, for example, that if the student does not understand the effects of one of the expansion elements, then it will be omitted from the student plan. In the above example, if the student does not understand the effects of the find_prot plan, the diagrammatic representation will be as shown in Fig. 13.2.

If either the chmod u + r or chmod u + w plans are not understood then the find-prot plan before it in the ordering will not be included either because it is assumed that the ordering between the plans is not understood.

As mentioned previously, the author intends to develop a number of model actions. These actions will modify the student model enabling the representation of deviant knowledge. The effect of this will be to facilitate the generation of deviant student plans which will contain incorrect constraints and expansion elements.

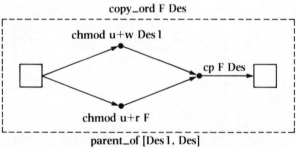

Fig. 13.2. Modified copy_ord plan.

13.3.6 The central control mechanism

There are many types of control mechanism for plan recognition systems. FITS-2 uses a control cycle which moves the focus of attention up the plan hierarchy, locating the plan which is the most likely interpretation of the input sequence, at each level. It then generates a student representation of this plan. The control mechanism then moves the focus down the hierarchy from this plan, generating predictions of subsequent inputs.

In order to understand the following more detailed description of the control mechanism, a definition is required: a plan whose effects were not already achieved in the original FITS-2 representation of the UNIX domain, and have not been achieved by the UNIX operators in the input string, is referred to as being *necessary*.

The description is divided into three informal algorithms, which form the basis of the control mechanism, plus some additional details. For clarity the algorithms have been simplified in certain inessential respects.

a. *Initialization*

This occurs at the start of the program run.

ACCEPT 2 UNIX operators: Op1 and Op2
MATCH Op1 againt P1 a primitive plan (leaf node) in the plan hierarchy
GENERATE the student plan SP1 corresponding to P1, by combining P1 with
    the relevant information in the student model
CHOOSE P2 a parent plan of P1 within the plan hierarchy
GENERATE SP2 the student plan corresponding to P2

b. *The predict algorithm*

This moves the focus of attention down the hierarchy, attempting to match the hypothesized student plans against the received input.

REPEAT
    BEGIN
    1. CHOOSE P3, one of SP2's expansion elements
        P3 is referred to as being a child of SP2
        P3 must be necessary and an ancestor, within the plan hierarchy, of the
        primitive plan which matches Op2
    2. GENERATE SP3 the student plan corresponding to P3
    IF P3 is a primitive plan
    THEN execute 'match algorithm'
    ELSE rename SP3 as SP2: this means that the focus moves down one level in
        the hierarchy in the next iteration of the loop
    END

c.   *Match algorithm*

MATCH SP3 against Op2
IF SP3 and Op2 do not match
THEN Backtrack up the plan hierarchy, through the hypothesized parent plans, choosing alternative child plans
ELSE Accept another input, Op3, and match against further choices of children from the hypothesized parent plans

d.   *Causes of match failure*

SP3 can fail to match Op2 for three reasons:

- The arguments in SP3 may be instantiated to different values to those in the Op2. Example: rm /a will not match with rm /b
- SP3 and Op2 may unify, but the relevant constraints may not be satisfied. Example: rm /a will fail if /a is a directory file.
- SP3 and Op2 may unify, but the preceding expansion elements in the plan from which P3 was chosen may still be necessary. Example: chmod u + x /a may be matched. However if the preceding expansion element, find_prot /a is still necessary, there exists an unsatisfied prerequisite.

e.   *Failure of the match algorithm*

If an input is entered and it is not possible to match it by backtracking up the hierarchy, there are two possible approaches:

- If none of the child plans are necessary, this means that the plan being considered is not necessary either and a parent plan is chosen and generated, and the prediction algorithm applied to this plan.
- If some of the child plans are necessary, the plan being considered does not represent the plan which the student is executing. In this situation the hierarchy is searched for another plan which can match the previous inputs and the currently unmatched input. If this search fails, a parent of the original plan is chosen and the prediction algorithm applied.

13.3.7   An example of the operation of the central control mechanism

A simple example of how this process operates will now be shown. This example only demonstrates part of the program operation. Figure 13.3 shows the relevant section of the plan hierarchy.

- The student enters two inputs; l s-l/ and chmod u + x/a.
- ls-l/matched against the plan ls-lF. The constraints dir_type(/) and know(/) are checked.
- The parent plan find_prot Des of ls-l / is chosen and the student plan

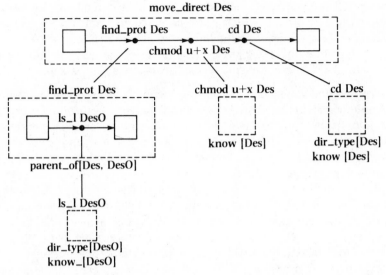

Fig. 13.3. Section of plan hierarchy.

generated. In this example the student plans are identical to the plans in Fig. 13.2, because it is assumed that the student has all the required knowledge.

- The expansion of find_prot Des is fully satisfied, and therefore find_prot Des is unnecessary.
- The parent plan move_direct Des of find_prot Des is found and the student plan generated.
- There are two necessary expansion elements in move_direct Des. The one chosen is the plan which matches the second input; chmod u+x Des.
- The student plan corresponding to chmod u+x Des is generated.
- chmod u+x /a is matched against the plan chmod u+x Des.
- The checks are performed:
  The arguments: /a and Des unify.
  The constraints: know(/a) and parent_of(/,/a) are checked.
  The previous child plans in the parent action: move_direct /a are checked. The only previous plan is find_prot /a which is not necessary.
- Another input is accepted: cd /a
- A further child of move_direct /a is chosen. This time cd /a is chosen.
- When move_direct /a is unnecessary, the focus will move up a level in the hierarchy, and so the process will continue.

13.3.8 Search problems

The above description of the control procedure is incomplete because it does not consider the problems encountered when the input cannot be matched against a descendant of the generated plan, A1. Consider the example in the previous section. If the student had entered as the second input: chmod u + w /a, none of the children of move_direct would have been able to match it.

If FITS-2 assumes that the input sequence is consistent with the knowledge in the student model, there are two different responses to this situation.

1. Assume that the plan A1 is not the correct interpreting plan, and there exists another plan in the hierarchy which will match all of the input string. This will require the program to move the focus down the hierarchy, generating the other parent plans at each level. In the above example this would involve generating the alternative parent plans for find_prot Des, and, if these fail to match the input string, for l s-l /a.

2. Assume that the plan A1 is the correct interpreting plan. A1 will probably have a number of parents each containing a partially ordered expansion. This means that a parent plan may contain an expansion element, parallel to the element matching A1, which is an ancestor of the primitive plan which will match the unmatched input. To investigate this possibility it is necessary to move the focus up the hierarchy, generating the various parent plans until the correct one is found.

This choice could be avoided by trying the first option, moving the focus down the hierarchy, and if this fails, trying the second option, moving the focus up the hierarchy. The problem with this solution is that it involves discarding information which has been generated. Subsequent versions of FITS-2 will contain a knowledge structure, similar to the chart used in chart parsing. This chart will contain copies of the student plans which have been generated, and details about which expansion elements are unnecessary. This information will avoid the repeated generation of plans and provide knowledge for error detection and tutoring. A similar approach is taken in POISE where an *instantiation blackboard* is used.

13.3.9   Constraint handling

Constraint handling which was mentioned briefly in the previous example, is an important feature of the operation of FITS-2. As the focus of attention moves up and down the plan hierarchy, a list of constraints is maintained and amended. These constraints are checked to ensure that they are satisfiable when a student plan is generated and when an input is accepted. This check helps avoid unnecessary plan generation and assists in the detection of erroneous inputs.

As the student enters each UNIX operator, the variables within these constraints become instantiated. When all the variables within a constraint are instantiated and the constraint is found to be satisfied, it is removed from the constraint list.

13.3.10 Conclusions

The FITS-2 program as currently implemented has a number of powerful features. These include the following:

- The ability to represent incomplete knowledge and plans.
- The explicit inclusion of information from the student model in the plan generation process.
- A reasonably sophisticated representation formalism, which, in addition to the partially ordered hierarchical plan network, is able to represent recursive, repetitive and optional plans.
- A high degree of domain independence. The major domain-dependent sections of the program are the plan hierarchy, the representation of the UNIX hierarchy, predicates checking this representation, and the constraints. The central control mechanism has been made as general as possible.

It is anticipated that the FITS-2 program will form the basis of a plan recognition system which will be able to maintain a deviant student model, to be used for deviant plan generation. The inclusion of this system in an intelligent tutoring system will result in the addition of a number of useful features. Two of the most important of these are as follows. Firstly, the tutoring strategy will have the choice over when to give advice – there will be no necessity to advise immediately an error is detected. Secondly, the errors will be represented explicitly, which will facilitate error analysis and tutoring.

ACKNOWLEDGEMENTS

This project is financed by the Science and Engineering Research Council (SERC). I am grateful for the guidance provided by Dr Sam Steel, Jim Doran, and many others in the Department of Computer Science at the University of Essex.

14

Understanding user behaviour in command-driven systems

JOHN JONES, MARK MILLINGTON AND PETER ROSS
University of Edinburgh, Scotland

Users of command-driven systems, such as computer operating systems, are not simply indulging in a planning exercise. They also monitor the execution of their plan, so that errors may be observed as they occur and goals generated to correct them. Users are also distracted while achieving one goal into achieving another. Understanding a user's actions thus requires more than plan recognition. In this chapter we shall describe an approach to behaviour understanding which takes account of these other aspects. We begin, however, with a review of some recent work on straightforward plan recognition.

14.1 INTRODUCTION

Many applications of artificial intelligence include an element intended to manage the 'dialogue' between the 'intelligent' system and its user. Such elements arise in expert systems, intelligent computer-aided instruction and natural language understanding systems, for example. Their task is to make the 'dialogue' individual to the user. The motivation for considering this is that humans seem to do it in the situations being modelled.

For example, consider a teacher observing a student problem-solving. The teacher will typically be able to interpret the actions of the student as implementing some particular strategy for solving the problem and can assign roles in the strategy to individual actions and clusters of actions, as well as infer steps that the student must have performed in his head. From this information the teacher is perhaps able to infer that the student has some difficulty with a concept involved and can then use that hypothesis as the basis for an intervention which is more natural and productive than one based on just the information that the student got the wrong answer. The teacher is able to indicate to the student where his difficulty lies in terms he should recognize as relating to his attempt at the question. A particularly strong benefit of recognizing the intentions behind the student's actions is obtained in cases where the student himself is unable to articulate his difficulties.

In order to construct 'intelligent' systems that are able to replicate the above behaviour, one problem to be tackled is the recognition of the goals and plans of an actor. This is still an open problem. It is the aim of this chapter to describe some previous attempts at this task and to describe our current research on this topic.

14.2 EXISTING TECHNIQUES FOR PLAN RECOGNITION

We shall describe three existing techniques for plan recognition.

14.2.1 The Advisor system __

The Advisor system (Genesereth, 1982) is designed to play the role of a consultant for users of MACSYMA, an interactive system for manipulating and evaluating symbolic mathematical expressions. MACSYMA is intended to be used by mathematicians who are experienced in the domain of application. Typically, however, they will not be expert at the use of MACSYMA and hence may encounter difficulties. Advisor's principal task is to identify misconceptions the user may have, given the complete sequence of actions performed and a specification of the goal he was trying to achieve.

Advisor assumes that the user can correctly plan to achieve the stated aim and that he has no problems with the mathematical concepts underlying the solution of the problem. Thus the difficulty is constrained to lie in the user's conception of the preconditions and effects of particular MACSYMA commands. It is further assumed that the user has only one known goal in mind and that every action performed is intended to be relevant to achieving that goal. Most of these assumptions seem plausible in this domain.

The plan recognition process has two strands, top-down and bottom-up. Given the goal, Advisor employs a plausible model of the novice MACSYMA user's planning process to begin to expand the goal into a number of sub-goals. Given the complete set of actions employed. Advisor begins to identify the actual sub-goals the user attempted as subsequences of the actions. These two strands of the analysis eventually have to be reconciled, and it is here that Advisor detects misconceptions about commands that the user may have. For example, in solving a particular quadratic equation the user may apply operators to extract the coefficients of the expression and then use the standard closed form for solutions. Given the goal, Advisor knows that the closed form is one method of solution and that it requires the coefficients of the expression to be known. However, Advisor also knows that the standard operators for extracting coefficients require the expression to have been previously expanded. The fact that an action to do this is missing from the sequence of user's actions may be interpreted as a misconception on the user's part that there is no such precondition. Advisor can then offer canned advice on the problem.

14.2.2   POISE

POISE (Carver, Lesser and McCue, 1984) is an 'intelligent' interface for an office automation system. The long-term aim is to detect users' errors and misconceptions and to offer task management and completion.

Unlike Advisor, POISE is an on-line monitoring system. Thus, some of the simplifying assumptions of Advisor which would be inappropriate in this domain are not made. Actions in the office domain (such as receiving and checking incoming goods and arranging for invoicing) are observed one at a time, as they are performed, rather than being available all at the same time and after the event. Plan recognition in this context forces the recognizer to maintain a number of plausible plan fragments and goals as being potentially active because it is unable to immediately confirm or discount any particular one of these hypotheses. Only on seeing further actions is it possible that some hypotheses will prove to be well-founded and others unfounded.

A further difference from Advisor is that POISE does not require the user to give a specification of the goals he is trying to achieve. POISE has a record of a small number of typical goals in the domain and plans for achieving them, and reasons about which of these best fits the actions observed so far. Further, POISE attempts to account for other typical planning activity of users in such domains. For example, users can interleave actions from plans for two or more goals. Actions can be shared between plans and goals may be temporarily suspended. Such considerations as these were unnecessary in Advisor because of the nature of its intended use, although there seems to be no inherent limit in the Advisor model of plan recognition with respect to these issues.

POISE uses the so-called 'blackboard' architecture (Hayes-Roth, 1983) for expert systems which allows a number of diverse and independent sources of knowledge to be applied to the solution of the plan recognition problem in an 'intelligent' manner. POISE uses domain-specific heuristic knowledge to focus the search through a space of possible plans for the most likely explanation of the user's activities.

14.2.3   PAM: Plan Applier Mechanism

PAM (Wilensky, 1983) is a plan recognition system designed to understand simple natural language stories such as 'John was hungry. He picked up the Egon Ronay Guide and got into his car'. That is, given a description of the behaviour of the participants it has to infer one or more goals and to relate these to the described actions. In contrast to Advisor and POISE, PAM uses a generative mechanism for constructing the goals of the actors in the story from stored knowledge relating acts and typical goals associated with them. In some sense, this is similar to the bottom-up element of Advisor but without the explicit top-down element to constrain the search process.

The domain of the simple stories is everyday activities. PAM has knowledge about the kind of actions that people perform and how these relate to typical goals. Further, it has some general knowledge relating goals to situations. For example, PAM understands that 'John was hungry' suggests he has the goal of eating, that going to a restaurant is a way of satisfying such a goal, and that the Egon Ronay Guide is a list of recommended restaurants. This is similar to the BELIEVER approach (Schmidt, Sridharan and Goodson, 1978) where goals are hypothesized based on suggestive actions or objects involved in those actions.

The plan recognition process of PAM works as follows. Successive sentences in the story are processed until one which suggests a goal is encountered. All possible goals associated with this statement or described action are hypothesized as active. Later actions are treated similarly, except that first it is attempted to 'fit' the action into what is currently thought to be the explanation of the story. If this is the case, the statement is considered explained. If this is not the case, PAM's general knowledge is tapped to see what goal is a typical explanation of the statement and the same understanding process is re-applied to this new goal. PAM does not attempt to understand every sentence in the story, but rather to link those statements it can.

In this way, a number of goals and plans are constructed to explain the behaviour of the actors in the stories. Unlike POISE and Advisor, PAM has no explicit high-level goals to guide the understanding process. The recognition process of POISE seems to be syntactic in nature and the only way to build in knowledge of the structure of appropriate sequences of actions is to specify them beforehand. PAM uses some knowledge about the semantics of the actions to dynamically recognize and construct valid sequences of actions.

14.3 WHY RECOGNIZE PLANS AND GOALS?

We have indicated in Section 14.1 why recognizing plans and goals will be useful. We shall make explicit here several applications, noting that, of the systems described in Section 14.2, only Advisor goes some way to tackling any of the following.

14.3.1 Knowledge

Many AI systems would benefit from the ability to be able to infer user's knowledge both about itself and the domain of application. In trivial applications it might be adequate to simply observe the use of a concept or command. However, what is really needed is the observation that a concept or command has been used in appropriate circumstances and as part of a rational plan. Further, to hypothesize a lack of knowledge on some issue requires recognizing situations when the issue was not used but could have been, to advantage. This requires a considerable grasp of the aims of the user and how these are being put into effect.

14.3.2　Misconceptions

In many 'dialogues', participants often realise that the behaviour of the other person is being influenced by some misconception. Such hypothesising of misconceptions requires, at the least, an understanding of the plans and goals of the other participant.

14.3.3　Ambiguities

It is often the case that the utterances and actions of participants in a 'dialogue' are ambiguous when considered in isolation. However, in the wider context of the participants' goals and plans, a single interpretation may be seen to be appropriate.

14.4　USER MODELLING IN COMMAND-DRIVEN SYSTEMS

Our long term aim is to investigate techniques for modelling users of interactive devices simply from the commands that they issue. To investigate the issues in a concrete form, we have chosen the UNIX operating system (TM Bell Laboratories) as an example domain. As with most operating systems, users often experience difficulties and part of our overall aim is to develop an on-line advisor for UNIX. We have chosen to concentrate on a subset of UNIX, relating to the file store, which all users have to utilize and which creates sufficient difficulties that there is a need for such an advice system.

Due to the nature of the errors users can make in UNIX, the system we envisage will observe the user's actions as they are performed. This will enable it to prevent the user from making 'destructive' errors. As indicated in Section 14.2.2, this mode of monitoring requires a fundamentally different scheme for plan recognition than the Advisor approach. Goals can only be hypothesized on the evidence currently available and the system may need to maintain a number of competitors and reason between them as further actions are observed.

Unlike POISE and Advisor, we shall not assume that the user's actions are directed towards a known goal or towards one or more of a repertoire of known specific goals. Typically, a UNIX session may involve a number of goals, with all the problems anticipated in POISE of interleaving actions from several plans, actions shared between plans and goals being suspended and possibly resumed later. For this reason, and others, we have selected the blackboard architecture as suitable for our purposes (Ross, 1985) and have constructed a blackboard shell in Prolog as an experimental tool (Jones, 1986). Further, consistency of the blackboard entries will be handled by an assumption-based truth maintenance scheme (de Kleer, 1984).

A further difficulty, not confronted in POISE, is that because the goals the UNIX users have are unspecified, we shall not know when goals have been achieved, or whether they are achieved at all. For this reason, we take the approach to goals described in Section 14.2.3. People's behaviour in UNIX will be explained in terms of concepts natural to the domain and goals will be built up as actions are observed, much as stories are understood as they unfold line by line.

14.4.1 Aspects of user behaviour

Much as in Advisor, we have in mind a general model of the (correct) planning UNIX users undertake. This influences our plan recognition scheme, and will form the basis of the modelling we perform, but we cannot employ it immediately in a top-down fashion as Advisor does because we do not have a specification of the goal(s). Moreover, as will be described later in this section, the behaviour of users we wish to observe is not simply a matter of planning.

Suppose the user has identified a number of (conceptual) goals. As in typical planning systems, a range of (mental) operators are available to the user to identify plans for these goals. These plans may themselves consist of domain actions, further sub-goals requiring planning or a mixture. For the introduced sub-goals, further operators introduce plans to achieve them until the user has a sequence of actions he considers he can begin to implement and which will eventually lead to achieving the goal. The plan need not be complete because initial actions may obtain data which further instantiates later parts of the plan, such as determining the correct location of some file.

For our purposes, an important consideration is that the user is typically faced with a choice to make between (his) applicable operators while planning. For our modelling purposes we are fundamentally interested in *why* the user chose one operator over another. This is contrary to the usual consideration in planning of simply wanting a plan to solve the problem.

First, the actual range of choice open to an individual user is of interest. For example, lack of knowledge of a particular command or of a command option or of a particular feature of UNIX, such as pattern matching, may mean that different users in the same situations have different options open to them (we shall ignore consulting the documentation for the system).

Bearing in mind the range of choice the user has, we may then consider why the user chose one way open to him of expanding his current partial plan over another. For instance:

- One choice may involve a higher cognitive load than another. Thus users occasionally do things the easy way even though they appear to know the smart way.
- One choice may be more 'efficient' than another, in terms of number of keystrokes, CPU time or real time.
- One choice may be seen as more 'risky' than another, perhaps based on previous experience of UNIX or other operating systems. For example, some users employ 'copy then remove' as a *safe* 'rename'.
- Some choices reflect misconceptions that the user has about UNIX commands or system features (Lewis, 1986).

- Some choices reflect misconceptions about the current environment, such as exact location in the file store. This may be explained as correct planning operators being evaluated on incorrect world models, as in the BELIEVER system (Schmidt *et al.*, 1978).

The above model of the planning process goes some way towards a classification of user behaviour in terms of the causes for each aspect.

As indicated at the beginning of the section, planning is but one aspect of user behaviour we need to consider. Several other aspects are interesting because they account for a proportion of users' goals generated while using UNIX. One is that achieving goals with interactive devices means that users can monitor and correct plans as they are being implemented. Incorrect actions are often (but not always) quickly detected because the device cannot perform them. The user can then replan to achieve the goal or plan to extricate himself from the error state before (or after, as appropriate) proceeding with the original plan. In the case of errors which go undetected initially, considerable confusion can ensue when their effects are eventually detected.

Another aspect is that of users being distracted while pursuing one plan into achieving an independent goal, temporarily suspending the current goal. This appears to be a data-driven process and from our observations typical of a significant proportion of users' use of UNIX.

14.4.2 Monitoring behaviour in UNIX

In this section we describe a plan recognition process which can be used to understand the activities of the user, including those aspects of behaviour discussed in Section 14.4.1. The scheme is similar to that employed in PAM. We shall describe the use and generation of a user model in this process in Section 14.4.3.

The previous discussion of the planning process has assumed one or more goals were known to the planner. In plan recognition we need to infer the user's goal(s). We shall adopt the approach of Section 14.2.3 and extract goals from the user's actions rather than exhaustively list goals, the approach of POISE and Advisor. In the following discussion we shall not dwell on the control aspects of implementing the plan recognition process using a blackboard system, although these are by no means insubstantial (Hayes-Roth, 1985).

We have a number of prototype conceptual goals which seem plausible, such as to 'move' files or directories, to 'copy' or 'remove', most of which cause changes in the state of the machine. Associated with these will be the cumulative effect, in terms of change of state of the UNIX file store, which suggest these goals, but no plans. These goals will be quite general. For example, the 'move' goal will just record that objects of various types can be relocated in the file store from one location to another. Such a representation allows us to determine that 'cp a b' and 'cat a > b' achieve the same goal (provided 'b' is not a directory). This representation also allows us to determine relevant relationships between goals, for example 'move' can be implemented as 'copy' and 'remove'. Further, we shall record planning operators relevant to UNIX, such as that applying a command to a number of different items can often be achieved by specifying multiple arguments to a single instance of the command.

The general plan recognition process proceeds as follows. User actions are observed as they are performed. Until an action is observed which is seen to contribute towards one of the conceptual goals, actions are labelled as 'to be explained'. This is because initial actions in achieving a goal, such as 'ls' which displays information, often provide little constraint for the interpretation of the user's actions. On encountering the first 'informative' action, all appropriate goals are hypothesized as potentially active.

The previously 'unexplained' actions are now reconsidered to see if they can be explained as contributing towards an hypothesized goal by utilizing bottom-up information. For example, in the experimental system we have so far implemented, the command 'ls' is represented as a STRIPS-like operator (Fikes and Nilsson, 1971), recording the information it outputs. Thus we can determine whether in a particular context it provides the user with knowledge which is a pre-condition for a particular command or which confirms a post-condition, and so determine whether the 'ls' plausibly belongs in a plan for the corresponding goal which has been hypothesized. This evidence in some way corresponds to PAM's world knowledge. However, because the UNIX world is easily formalizable, we can determine such relationships dynamically. Further, the plan recognition system we have currently implemented can perform a primitive 'chunking' of actions in a sequence based on such evidence and we are currently investigating the utility of this in the general scheme described here.

Thus, rather than pre-specify all possible plans in some form of plan grammar for the goals we expect, we have only pre-specified general goals and use bottom-up information to determine the relationship of other actions to these goals.

Given the relationship between the hypothesized goals and the 'unexplained' actions and information concerning the individual user, to be described in Section 14.4.3, we may be able to order the various hypotheses we have. POISE is able to hypothesize the most likely goal associated with a sequence of actions, but only on the grounds of knowledge about the domain, not of the performer of the actions. For our purposes, this latter aspect is more important because there is no 'right' way of doing anything in UNIX.

The plan recognition process is then ready to consider the next action of the user. Both top-down and bottom-up information will be useful here. For example, STRIPS-like analysis may indicate the action belongs to a currently active plan. If this is not the case, the prototype goals are considered to see if the action suggests another goal. If this is the case, the system will try to explain this new goal in terms of the currently active plans, and the process is repeated as necessary. For example, an action to remove a file may now be seen as completing a plan to move a file, begun by copying it to the desired location. Finally, if all else fails, the new action may again be labelled 'to be explained'. The action will then be reconsidered in the future once other goals have been hypothesized.

The outcome is that the new action is 'explained' as part of the current understanding of the user's current activities, or in terms of a new goal. This new goal may subsume a previously hypothesized goal, which is now explained as contributing towards the new goal. Alternatively, the new goal may indicate that previous goals have been completed or suspended. In fact, whenever a new goal hypothesis is made, it may correspond to the reactivation of a previous goal and this needs to be considered, evidence for reactivation being a bottom-up connection like those described above or top-down relationships expected between goals.

One general consideration in this process is that the 'goals' we determine may not correspond to the goals the user had in mind. For example, as a simple precaution the user may do 'mv file ~ /junk', perhaps using an alias, rather than removing a file. Thus this action really satisfies the goal of removing a file. However, in the above scheme this will not be recognized as such, only being interpreted as moving a file. To determine that the former situation is the case would require arbitrary amounts of real-world knowledge. What we must hope is that recognizing goals and plans in the above manner will be adequate for our purposes. This seems plausible in that users may have abstract goals in mind when planning, but the very nature of the device forces the user to relate these goals to more concrete goals such as states of the machine. This distinction is that between the task level and the semantic level in the Command Language Grammar (Moran, 1981).

With regard to the features of user behaviour described in Section 14.4.1, distraction and parallelism are handled because the recognition scheme is based on the semantics of actions rather than mere syntactic proximity, as is the case with POISE, for example. Error recovery to allow the original plan to be continued may be detected by noting that the goal undoes the effect of a previous goal. Devising a new plan to achieve the goal from an error state may result simply in a complex overall plan being inferred.

14.4.3   The user model: its use and generation

In this section we shall describe how a user model is used to delimit and control the plan recognition process and how such a model can be influenced by the process itself. While this might suggest a conflict, one consideration is that previously studied, non-novice users will change fairly slowly. Thus, we should probably not change the model. With new users and novices, the situation may be reversed.

a.   Employing the user model

The collection of planning operators needed to interpret the user's actions and their respective rankings constitutes part of the user model. The operators will be annotated with the reasons for their presence, for example 'caution', although the exact form of these and their utilization is still a research issue. In general they may resemble endorsements (Cohen and Grinberg, 1983). Further, some record of the user's employment of the system over some time will also be present, such as goals attempted.

b. Generating and updating the user model

The issue of knowledge and lack of knowledge may be handled as follows. The use of a command in a coherent plan to achieve a goal is strong evidence that the user understands that command. Lack of knowledge is inferred from the non-use of a command when it could be used to advantage and requires that the system has the ability to replan the task it hypothesizes the user is trying to achieve. A simple method of determining users' preferences may be to maintain a cumulative record of how often various alternatives were used and in what circumstances.

Persistent misconceptions of the user are hypothesized by supposing that the corresponding operator is among the choices the user has. They may be observed by supplying the system with a repertoire of 'buggy' variants of commands (Brown and Burton, 1978). However, more substantial misconceptions, influenced by the user's mental model of UNIX, will be beyond the scope of such a simple system.

So far, those aspects of the user model discussed have been relatively long term. In the short term, more dynamic information will be of interest. For example, the goals that the user attempts during the sessions. Further, the cumulated annotations of the planning operators which must be invoked to 'understand' the user's actions are also of interest. These can be used as the basis of the advice to be given to the user. For example, should it be concluded that some particular actions are present because they are a cautious way of proceeding then it may not be appropriate to suggest to the user a less cautious sequence of commands simply because it is shorter. Transient misconceptions are proposed by hypothesizing incorrect models of the file store and the user's location in it.

14.5 CONCLUSION

We have seen that understanding the behaviour of UNIX users requires more than plan recognition. We have presented a plan recognition scheme which can accommodate other features of the interaction, such as errors and error recovery. Further, we have begun to exploit bottom-up information in the recognition process, so introducing greater flexibility than is permitted by previous top-down parsing techniques.

ACKNOWLEDGEMENT

The research described here is supported by the SERC under grant GR/C/35967.

15

SCALD – towards an intelligent authoring system

ROD NICOLSON
University of Sheffield, England

An intelligent authoring system (IAS) is defined as a knowledge-based authoring system, that is, a computer-based system which allows a non-programmer (typically a teacher) to create interactively a working CAL program from an initial sketchy idea. This chapter describes the architecture and workings of SCALD – a Scriptal CAL Designer – which is a prototype IAS.

15.1 INTRODUCTION

The objective of this chapter is to outline the research programme – the development of an intelligent authoring system (IAS) – the author has initiated in Sheffield in collaboration with Peter J. Scott. Educationalists (e.g. Ruthven, 1985; Ridgway, 1986, Chapter 2) have expressed misgivings about the potential contributions of ICAI within the school curriculum, and so one major motivation for the programme was the desire to make a useful *applied* contribution of AI within education. Our aim was to find an acknowledged 'real world' educational problem which was ripe for the introduction of AI techniques. Furthermore, we were particularly keen to be able to lay down achievable milestones, both short-term and long-term, which would lead to useful cumulative progress towards a cost-effective solution to the original problem. The problem we chose was that of producing good quality educational software in reasonably high quantity.

Computer hardware continues to double in power and value every two years, but the costs of software remain obstinately constant. Indeed Self (1985c, p. 162) estimates that 90% of computer costs are now associated with software. Space precludes any analysis of the problem here, but in a recent review of current methods for software production (Nicolson and Scott, 1986), we concluded that:

"Neither of the major current approaches to the production of computer-aided learning (CAL) programs is adequate to provide the quantity of pedagogically sound material necessary to support the 'computer revolution' within education. Despite substantial progress in the provision of facilities for content creation and course management, current computer-based authoring systems suffer from the crucial defects of lack of scope and lack of pedagogical support in their role of allowing a teacher to create a working program from an initial educational idea. Team development, on the other hand, promises provision of high quality software, but in practice it is too slow and too dependent upon scarce human resources to permit quantity software solution. It is argued that one of the most fruitful applications of artificial intelligence techniques within education would be the development of an intelligent authoring system (IAS) which provides the solution to the problem of CAL authoring by teachers. The IAS proposed is a knowledge-based system which simulates the expertise of the 'CAL designer' in team production while providing within an integrated authoring environment the rapid prototyping and content creation facilities of authoring systems."

It is important to make clear from the start that the project has no direct bearing on the design or analysis of ICAI programs. We define an IAS as a knowledge-based authoring system, that is, a computer-based system which allows a non-programmer (typically a teacher) to create interactively a working CAL program from an initial sketchy idea. Whether the software produced is 'intelligent' or 'dumb' is not our primary concern – for us, the intelligence of the IAS lies in the simulation of the skills of the human *CAL designer* who normally plays a pivotal role in interfacing between teacher and programmer in team development of educational software. So we're not directly involved in ICAI at all at this stage. Nonetheless, one longer term aim would be the development of an IAS for authoring ICAI, and indeed the complexity of the ICAI authoring process – the interfacing of the teaching model, student model and domain knowledge with the normal 'dumb' CAL requirements – may preclude any less sophisticated development methodology.

15.2   THE DESIGN FOR AN IAS

15.2.1   The role of the human CAL designer

The closest everyday analogy to the CAL designer is that of the architect of a new house. The architect discusses the clients' requirements, eliciting information about the style of house, number of bedrooms, price constraints, exact location etc. He then adds to these 'overt requirements' a great deal of the 'covert requirements' information such as plumbing, cable conduiting, insulation and so on which are necessary to implement the requirements, finally building up a completely specified blueprint or 'design' sufficient to allow a builder to construct the dwelling. In much the same way the CAL designer must first elicit the overt requirements information from the teacher and add the covert requirements information necessary to create a completely specified program design for a programmer to implement.

Clearly, in order to be able to simulate the expertise of the human CAL designer a great deal of knowledge engineering is needed. Of course one vital undertaking is to discover how the designer achieves the task of eliciting the overt requirements from the teacher and then combining the overt and covert requirements to create a rigorous program design. However, the first and crucial decision is how to represent this design knowledge – the choice of the knowledge representation formalism.

15.2.2   Script-based knowledge representation

Frames or schemas (Minsky, 1975) provide an appropriate and efficient method for representing both human and machine knowledge about a domain, and can be used either to 'comprehend' information or to help retrieve information. This dual role is particularly useful for CAL design since it allows the system first to incorporate into the script any information volunteered by the teacher, and

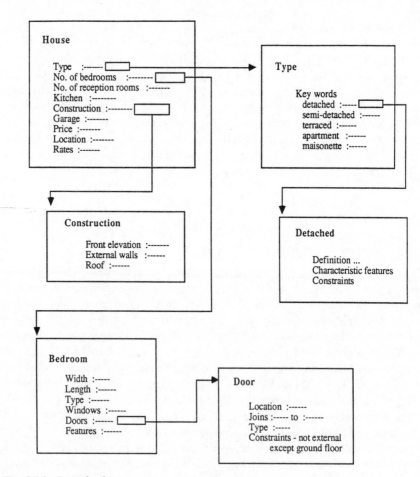

Fig. 15.1. Partial schema representation for a house.

second to 'prompt' the teacher for information that he or she had overlooked. Part of a 'schema' for (British) houses is shown in Fig. 15.1.

One major use of the above schema is to help drive the user interaction. Starting from an 'empty schema' in which none of the empty 'slots' has been 'filled' the architect can ask the client the necessary questions – what type of house do you want, how many bedrooms, and so on, gradually filling in all the slots with values such as 'type = detached', 'no. bedrooms = 4' and so on. Note that the values for the slots may also be hierarchically nested schemas, and the specification may proceed to greater and greater depths of detail. Normally a client would not be expected to specify 'trivial' details such as the exact size of door and would rely on the architect to fill in such details. Much of the power of schema-based representations lies in their ability to fill in such missing details using inheritance, defaults or constraints already built up from the information already specified. It is worth stressing that the information obtained in this manner may be much fuller than the client/user could have created unaided, especially in the case of CAL design where the teacher is unsure of which details are the important ones.

Schank (1975) introduced the word *script* to refer to a schema which had a temporal axis, that is, for a sequence of events in which the ordering is important. By means of a series of 'eating out' scripts Schank demonstrated the power of the formalism not merely for eliciting information but also for 'comprehending' it by identifying the relevant script from the details given (for instance, a 'fast food' script might be distinguished from a 'restaurant' script by such details as 'pay at checkout' versus 'pay hostess'). Obviously order is important in a CAL program and so we have borrowed the term script to refer to our knowledge representation for CAL design.

A further use of a script is as an advisor. It is easy to build into the system a series of constraints and suggestions. Within CAL design, constraints might be 'the Apple Macintosh does not support colour', whereas advice might be 'if you are interested in discovery learning it is important not to introduce many tests' or 'the advantage of having a user trace is that the whole session can be rapidly replayed'. This sort of advice function is one of the most powerful features of computer-aided design programs – checking that all the rooms within a hospital have a door, adequate lighting, heating, cable conduiting etc. Within CAL design the advice is one method of ensuring that pedagogical principles contribute to the finished product.

15.2.3   The need for a hybrid IAS

It has become clear that an IAS must be a complex system combining features of several disparate AI systems. Use of complex knowledge representations would suggest the adoption of one of the purpose-designed 'knowledge representation languages'. Simulation of the human CAL designer indicates adoption of the methodology of rule-based expert systems shells. The need to 'configure' a satisfactory solution seems to suggest the need for a powerful problem solver. It is possible that all these facilities may be offered in due course within one of the purpose-built 'knowledge engineering environments', for example the LOOPS environment developed at Xerox PARC. However, funding deficiencies (both for us and for the educational establishment in general) forced us to attempt to develop a script-based problem-solving expert system without any such support. Fortunately the Prolog language provides an excellent formalism for the representation and utilization of declarative knowledge, and we were able to combine the use of scripts, rules and problem solving within a single system. We named the resulting prototype SCALD – Scriptal CAL Designer – and the rest of the chapter attempts to explain its architecture, knowledge representation, and mode of operation.

15.3   THE SCALD-1 PROTOTYPE IAS

15.3.1   Overview of SCALD-1

Much of the analysis outlined here derives from our experience in developing SCALD-1 which was a simulation of the CAL designer for just one CAL domain – instructional presentation. SCALD-1 was the creation of Peter J. Scott in his doctoral research (1986). Rather than require the author to be familiar with all the aspects of instructional CAL our aim was to create a complex 'script' which represented the full range of possibilities, constraints and educational considerations implicit in the choice of an instructional CAL design. SCALD-1 then used this script to guide its interaction with the author.

The system was designed to produce machine-independent 'program designs' which could then be automatically implemented on any suitable target machine through the use of standardized 'software toolbox' libraries which translate the design language primitives into routines in the appropriate code. The initial target machine selected was the Acorn BBC micro, a limited 8-bit machine which is widely available throughout British schools. Through interaction with the teacher SCALD creates a design for the required program and then automatically creates a working BBC Basic 'program shell' which implements the design on the Acorn BBC micro. This program shell may then be 'tuned' via a selection of 'content creation' programs in BBC Basic.

SCALD-1 is written in Prolog and for expository purposes may be conceived of as three inter-dependent sub-systems: a rule-based specification system to establish the user's requirements by reference to the instructional CAL script; a design system which tries to construct an adequate design from the specification; and an implementation system which automatically implements the design in BBC Basic.

15.3.2   Stages in interaction with SCALD-1

a. *Front end.* This allows the user to select an 'empty script' from a selection of available instructional scripts. In due course we would expect the system to be able to identify a plausible candidate script from an initial 'natural language' requirements definition, but for the time being this is done via a menu of alternatives.

b. *Specification stage.* Through interaction with the user plus use of inference or defaults as necessary, the 'script applier' fills the slots in the empty script. See below for a more detailed explanation of how this is achieved. At any stage in the interaction the user may elect to 'Pass' (that is, decline to answer a question) or to 'View' (that is, terminate the specification stage by forcing SCALD-1 to use inference plus default values to fill in all the remaining slots).

c. *Design stage.* A 'design shell' is created from the specified script by organizing all the script components into the appropriate order and by collecting together all the utilities involved. This design is available as a 'pseudocode' description based on an *ad hoc* design language, but it is normally implemented automatically in BBC Basic. It should perhaps be stressed that the distinction between specification and design is artificial – both the specification and the design may be considered as different descriptions of the underlying script.

d. *Implementation stage.* A 'program shell' – that is, fully implemented code but lacking any of the intended 'content' (questions and answers etc.) – is created using a 'software toolbox' which automatically converts all the design pseudo-code into the corresponding BBC Basic code. If the target language was, say, Microsoft Basic the appropriate code would be produced using a Microsoft Basic toolbox.

e. *Tuning and content creation.* Questions and answers may be input to the program through the creation of a 'content file' under control of further BBC Basic programs. There are programs for graphics creation, text input, windowing, and program compacting. This content may then be accessed by the program shell to provide a fully working complete program.

15.3.3 SCALD-1 Scripts

It is impossible to explain how SCALD-1 functions without first giving a brief outline of the nature of the script-based knowledge representation formalism. There are essentially three data types within the formalism – *scripts, packets,* and *primitives.* A primitive corresponds to a single CAL concept such as 'input-integer-from-keyboard', or 'wait-for-0.5s' and so on. The software toolbox for a given language is essentially the set of code routines necessary to implement each of the library of CAL primitives in the appropriate code. The library of primitives is independent of the particular application. A packet is a more complex entity built up of packets and primitives which will form a single module in the design. The crucial difference between a script and a packet is that the contents of the packet are entirely fixed – and thus will have exactly the same implementation code regardless of the application – whereas the instantiation of a script depends upon how its variable slots are filled. A packet has two descriptors: an 'identifier' which is its unique name, and a generic 'type' which indicates its possible role within a

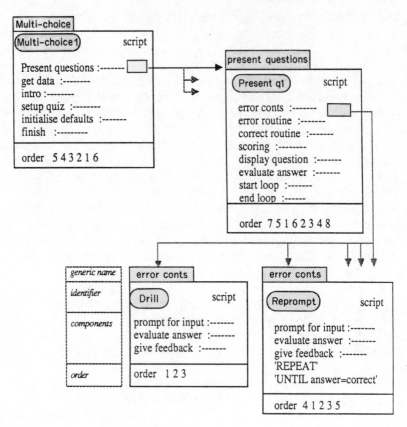

Fig. 15.2. Partial script for multiple choice.

script. In general, packets of the same generic type will be alternatives for a particular slot within a script. A script has four descriptors: the identifier, the generic type, a list of components (each of which may be a script or a packet), and an order list, which indicates the order the components must be arranged in the completed design. The explicit representation of order information allows us to try to arrange the components in descending order of teaching importance, so that the teacher is asked the most pertinent questions first and may then ask to View the design/program when his or her patience is exhausted.

A small part of the script for multiple choice questions is shown in Fig. 15.2. One top-level script for multiple choice questions (which is one possible type of instructional CAL) has identifier Multi-choice1. It has six components (or slots) of which the most important (i.e. the first in asking order) is 'Present questions'. In the complete design 'Present questions' would be the fifth component in temporal order. There are three options for filling the 'Present questions' slot, of which just one is shown, having unique identifier 'Present q1'. This is also a script, and has 'error conts' as its most important component. Actually 'error conts' stands for

general form

script (type, identifier, [components],   [temporal order])
packet   (type,   identifier)

example of script

script (multi-choice,   multi_1,
                [
                                script (present-qn, P1, Elts, Order),
                                packet (get-data, P2),
                                packet (into, P3),
                                packet (setup-quiz, P4),
                                packet (init defaults, P5),
                                packet (finish, P6)
                ],
                [P5, P4, P3, P2, P1, P6]

example packets for type 'intro'

packet (intro, intro_name).
         constraint (intro_name, NOT user(special ed)).
         uses (intro_name, utility8).   /* PROC_title */
         uses (intro_name, utility5).   /* PROC_wait */
         uses (intro_name, utility1).   /* FN_input */

packet (intro,   intro_simple).
         uses (intro_simple, utility8).   /* PROC_title */
         uses (intro_simple, utility5).   /* PROC_wait */

Fig. 15.3. Prolog examples of scripts and packets.

'error contingencies' and determines the course of action after a user has made an error on the multiple choice. Two alternatives are shown – 'Drill' and 'Reprompt'. 'Drill' merely gives the appropriate feedback and then passes on to the next question, whereas 'Reprompt' presents the question again (and again) until the correct answer is given. Other alternatives, such as a remedial loop contingent upon the answer given, may be fairly easily incorporated within this framework.

Figure 15.3 demonstrates how these structures are represented in Prolog, using the Edinburgh style syntax. Note that this represents an empty script. If satisfactory values for the variables P1, P2, P3, P4, P5, P6, Elts and Order can be found then the script will be fully filled. Two examples of packets of the same type are given – alternatives for the introduction. Note that there will be a pseudocode description of each routine in the pseudocode dictionary, plus the associated code in a software toolbox, but that it is not necessary to access this information while filling the script. The only information necessary is that about which other

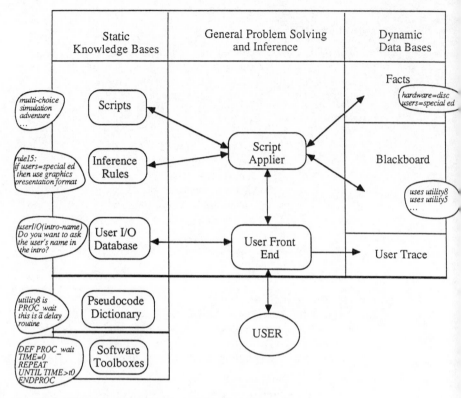

Fig. 15.4. SCALD architecture – script-based expert system.

packets and primitives are involved, and the 'constraints' or pre-conditions which govern the suitability of each packet. Note that one constraint for 'intro-name' is that the users are not children with special educational needs (since they would find it difficult to type in their names).

15.3.4   SCALD-1 architecture

Figure 15.4 presents a schematic form of the SCALD-1 architecture. Note that most of the diagram is devoted to the specification stage (Section 15.3.2b. above), and indeed it is this stage that takes up the bulk of the processing. Once an adequate specification has been derived it is relatively straightforward to turn this specification into a readable pseudocode design (Section 15.3.2c. above) by means of the pseudocode library. Furthermore the specification may also be translated automatically into runnable code (Section 15.3.2d. above) assuming that an appropriate software toolbox library has been created.

It is clear from Fig. 15.4 that the script applier is the crucial component of the system. Starting from an empty script provided by the front end (Section 15.3.2a) it attempts to find a set of values for all the 'slots' which satisfies all the existing constraints and inference rules. The method of operation is sketched out in

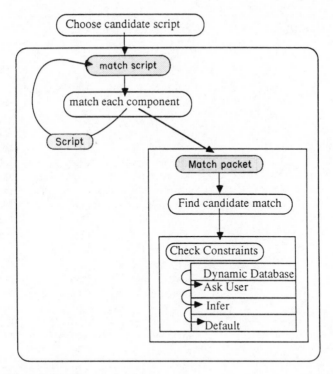

Fig. 15.5. The script applier mechanism.

Fig. 15.5. The script applier takes the first component of the empty script and attempts to match it with one of the existing scripts or packets. Normally there will be several potential matches (that is, scripts or packets of the appropriate generic type). If the first potential match is a script, the script applier will attempt to match that script, and so on, recursively, until the potential match is a packet. It will then ascertain the constraints (pre-conditions) involved and try to check whether they are satisfied, first by checking whether any pertinent facts have been recorded in the dynamic database, then (if necessary) by asking the user – the user I/O database provides a set of appropriate questions. If this fails to yield a result (for instance if the user Passes or asks to View) recourse is made to inference rules, and if all else fails the default value is taken. The matching attempt either succeeds or fails. If the match succeeds the appropriate facts will be inserted into the dynamic database, the blackboard will be updated with information about which packets and primitives will be used and the match process moves onto the next component of the current script to be matched. If the match fails, the next candidate is taken and so on, until there are no further potential matches. In this case, the script has failed to match, and the script applier backtracks, retracting any facts asserted etc. to the next candidate script. If all the matches succeed we are left with a fully filled script and the specification

a. The user trace		b. The facts database		
Questions asked	*Response*	*Fact*		*Method*
CAL type	multiple choice	CAL type	(multi-choice)	told
hardware	disc [1]	hardware	(disc)	told
users	special ed	users	(special ed)	told
rewards	yes	rewards	(yes)	told
reward options	both	reward option	(both)	told
positive rewards	tick	positive reward	(tick)	told
negative rewards	Pass [2]	negative reward	(cross)	Rule 12[4]
error contingency	Pass	error contingency	(reprompt)	default [5]
scoring option	View [3]	present'n script	(1)	Rule 5
		error routine	(1)	default
		correct routine	(1)	default
		question type	(pictures)	Rule 15
		screen windows	(2)	Rule 18
		user prompt	(arrow)	default
		text size	(big)	Rule 23
		BBC mode	(5)	Rule 24
		scoring	(no)	Rule 40
		introduction	(simple)	Rule 36
		breakstate	(2)	Rule 29

Fig. 15.6. Output from SCALD specification stage.

process is complete, otherwise the applier will not be able to produce a design and will fail.

15.3.5   A sample demonstration run of SCALD-1

It is difficult to obtain any idea of how the system really works from an abstract description provided above, and so to give a flavour of the process I shall provide a sample of the information received and displayed during a typical interaction. The user trace (Fig. 15.6a) reveals that the user made only six decisions during the specification, first deciding on a multiple choice format, then deciding on the hardware (see [1] in Fig. 15.6) and the users (these first three questions are actually included within the front-end (see Section 15.3.2a) in order to ensure that the script applier has some information to work on in the case of an early decision to View. Following three decisions about rewards the user elects to Pass on negative rewards (see [2]). The script applier is able to infer that a cross should be used as negative reward through use of one of the inference rules – Rule 12 – which states that if the positive reward is a tick and a negative reward is required then use a cross as a negative reward (see [4]). Incidentally, rule 13 makes an equivalent link for 'Right' and 'Wrong'. Note that inference is used *after* asking the user, and so the user could have selected some other negative reward. The user than Passes on the error contingency option. The script applier is unable

a. Design	b. Code
INITIALIZE the program	PROC_init
SET UP QUIZ (variables, arrays)	PROC_setup_quiz
INTRODUCTION (simple)	PROC_intro_simple
GET DATA (from disc)	PROC_get_data1
FOR question 1 TO all questions	FOR question = 1 TO max_questions
PRESENT question (pictorial)	PROC_display_q2
REPEAT	REPEAT
PROMPT user for response	ans% = FN_get_resp3
EVALUATE response	correct% = FN_eval(ans%)
IF CORRECT give tick	IF correct% THEN PROC_tick
IF ERROR give cross	IF NOT correct% THEN PROC_cross
UNTIL CORRECT	UNTIL correct%
WAIT 1 second	PROC_wait(100)
CLEAR windows	PROC_clear_windows
NEXT question	NEXT question
FINISH without giving final score	PROC_finish_no_score
	END
-------------------------------------	-------------------------------------
then list of modules used	*then the BBC Basic for the*
plus English description	*modules used*

Fig. 15.7. Output from the design stage and the implementation stage.

to find any relevant inferences rules and chooses the default action which happens to be 'Reprompt until correct' (see [5]). Next the user asks to View the program design so far (see [3]) and so the script applier fills in the remainder of the script slots through use of dynamic database, inference and default values (note that asking to View bars the script applier from asking the user any further questions). The decisions made are noted in Fig. 15.6b.

Figure 15.7a shows the top-level design produced via the pseudocode dictionary for the filled script. Note how everything is now in the correct temporal order and that a helpful machine-independent 'structured English' pseudocode notation is adopted. Following this top-level design there is a list of all the modules (packets) and primitives used, together with a pseudocode description of their function. Figure 15.7b shows how this design may be coded automatically in BBC Basic using a software toolbox which maps each packet onto a fixed BBC Basic procedure. Of course, once the appropriate software toolbox has been written it is possible to automate the production of code in any procedural programming language. It can probably be seen that these latter two stages are relatively straightforward once a suitable specification has been derived. The final stage of the program creation, the interactive content creation and tuning (see Section 15.3.2e), is not shown here since it involves little of AI interest (but is of course crucial for the applied success of the project).

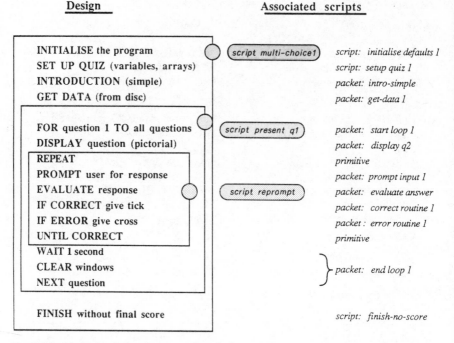

Fig. 15.8. Multiple choice design and underlying scripts.

Figure 15.8 represents a final attempt to explain how the system works in the specific example chosen. The design (on the left) is much the same as Fig. 15.7a but has been broken down to demonstrate the scripts and packets from which it has been composed. The scripts involved are detailed in Figs 15.2 and 15.3. It can be seen that for the script 'multi-choice1' of Fig. 15.3 variables P1, P2, P3, P4, P5 and P6 have been instantiated to 'display-q2', 'get-data 1', 'intro-simple', 'setup-quiz1', 'init-defaults1' and 'finish-no-score' respectively.

15.4 CURRENT STATUS AND PROJECTED DEVELOPMENTS OF THE SCALD PROJECT

15.4.1 Current status

SCALD-1 was intended as a limited prototype IAS which would yield useful cues for the feasibility of the full IAS project. It has certainly justified our initial hopes. At present (August 1986) SCALD-1 has almost reached its full development and we are trying to incorporate the lessons learned within its successor SCALD-2. A series of informal trials of SCALD-1 with teachers and CAL designers suggested that the Prolog script format provides a flexible, efficient knowledge represent-ation which could fairly easily be modified to provide an enhanced range of options. Furthermore, the implementation system seemed to work well in that the implementation system successfully collected the appropriate routines from the 'software toolbox library' and transferred the resulting file to a BBC micro, where it was run immediately.

The two major criticisms of SCALD-1 were actually rather unfair. First that we could only produce instructional programs (we have had to explain endlessly that we selected instructional CAL primarily for its tractability rather than through any belief in its educational superiority!). Second that the content creation facilities were not as powerful as the users would have liked. While perfectly valid, this criticism has little bearing on the AI content of the system and could easily be remedied in a production version of the system.

Probably the two main intrinsic weaknesses of SCALD-1 are, first, the rather *ad hoc* nature of the design language used, and, second, the sequential specify–design–implement development cycle induced by an over-reliance on the formal model of software development. Our experience was that non-programmer authors were not in a position to undertake a full requirements analysis 'cold' – it was necessary to implement the design in order to demonstrate the results of design decisions before they were able to make decisions with any confidence. Consequently it seems vital to allow the author to amend the *design* while interacting with its *implementation*. In order to achieve this it would be necessary to have much more powerful facilities for interactively editing the specified script.

15.4.2   Planned developments

a.   Translation to a portable 16-bit micro

If the system is to be used widely in education it is important that it is available on low-cost educational workstations. We are at present porting SCALD-1 from the SUN workstation (with target language BBC Basic) to a 16-bit micro (with target language Microsoft Basic). This process has entailed the systematization of our design language and of the software toolbox methodology. We have also taken the opportunity to improve the content creation through use of the WIMP interface facilities provided by the 16-bit micro.

b.   Development of more scripts

Reliance on only one major script is a clear weakness of SCALD-1, and use of the instructional script in particular can give rise to the mistaken impression that its scope is no greater than some of the current authoring systems, which also allow a non-expert programmer to create instructional programs. We are at present developing a simulations script in collaboration with Peter H. Gardner, which will then provide the exciting possibility of creating a simulation script which has an instructional component 'grafted on' – a common educational requirement which is almost impossible to achieve by conventional means.

1. Find several exemplars of the intended type.

2. Reduce them to standardized design-based formats.

3. Make each as general/abstract as possible.
   Replace constants with variables.
   Replace specific instances with generalities
       eg. use 'driving file' to specify the necessary parameters and content.

4. Locate the major scripts and sub-scripts.

5. For each script
   What are the potential components?
   What is the relative importance of the components?
   What is the temporal order of the components?

6. For each component
   What are the alternatives?
   What are the constraints?
   What is the pseudocode?
   What is the Basic code?

7. What are the inference rules?
   Which configurations are inconsistent?
   What are the pedagogic issues?
   What advice can be offered?

Fig. 15.9. Creating a new script.

Figure 15.9 sketches out the method we have adopted for the creation of a new script. One of the main problems in creating a new script is that of finding sufficient exemplars of their design, but in general it appears likely that if a design is available for a program then a script can be produced which could produce a range of similar applications.

c.   Systematization of the 'knowledge engineering'

The ability to modify a script is one of the most attractive features of the IAS, but indiscriminate modifications can lead to a tangled mess of data structures and resulting inefficiency and incomprehensibility. Introduction of a feature such as a new primitive will probably require modification of the scripts, the packets, the pseudocode dictionary and the software toolboxes. The need to do each of these by hand is unforgivably tedious and prone to error. One elegant solution is to create a database program in Prolog which systematizes this process by allowing the user to search through all the existing databases for the occurrence of the units involved, which should ensure the production of clean and efficient code. The need for efficiency will become increasingly important as the number and complexity of the scripts increases.

15.5   COMPARISON OF THE IAS CYCLE WITH THE 'STANDARD' PROGRAM DEVELOPMENT CYCLE

Figure 15.10 represents a composite description of the 'standard' computer science model for the production of software (see e.g. Howden, 1982). The model insists that the full specification must be derived initially (by specification experts); then this must be turned into a complete design (by design experts); this design must then be implemented (by implementation experts). At this stage the user is finally allowed to view his or her creation. Any suggested modifications may necessitate a complete reworking, involving a review of all the stages. Note the sequential mode of operation in which each stage must be completed before the next one is started, and the need for unambiguous communication between stages since different personnel are involved at each stage. It is probably fair to say that as much effort must be spent on communication as on the primary objective of creating a program which meets the user's requirements. The larger the software development team involved, the more resources must be spent on inter-team communication. There is, of course, widespread dissatisfaction with the above model, not just because of the resources and timescale involved, but also in terms of the theoretical validity of dissociating the specification stage from the implementation stage (see e.g. Swartout and Balzer, 1982 or Partridge, 1986).

Figure 15.11 (adapted from Nicolson and Scott, 1986) indicates our current belief about the optimal stages of interaction with an IAS. Note in particular how

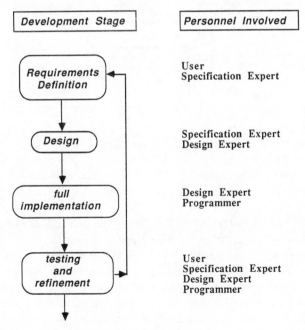

Fig. 15.10. The standard software development model.

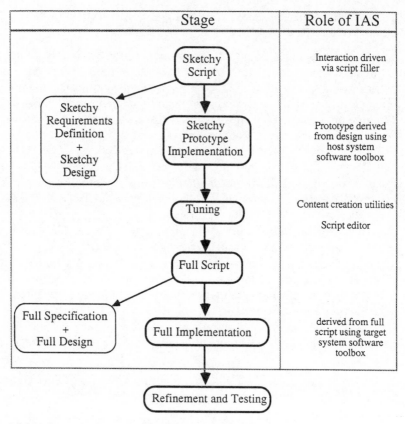

Fig. 15.11. Stages in interaction with an IAS.

the ability to implement a program automatically from the specification allows us finally to escape from the straitjacket of sequential independent stages. The timescale involved for the creation of a working prototype is collapsed to just several hours. This rapid prototyping leaves open the option of further polishing or of translation to other machines, but it does ensure that the final stages of production will be performed on the basis of an accurate and adequate initial specification.

Of course, it must be admitted that the IAS approach can, at present, only be used for relatively straightforward applications involving the creation of a single program. Nonetheless, the greater the complexity of the application, the greater the scope for the assistance provided by an IAS. Indeed, one might expect the contribution of an IAS to be invaluable in situations where the authoring process is particularly complex (such as ICAI), or in situations where a suite of related programs must be developed (such as the creation of integrated software to cover a whole unit of curriculum).

15.6 SUMMARY

The SCALD-1 prototype IAS was motivated by a pressing real world problem – that of allowing teachers to produce educational software of good quality. The applied nature of the problem has influenced the overall design of the project since the completed IAS must be able to run on the relatively low-powered 16-bit micros which will be routinely available within the educational environment. Furthermore, since the intended users are computer-naive teachers, it is very important that the style of interaction must be as 'natural' as possible, and that the IAS should be able to provide a great deal of support especially in the program specification stage.

Consequently we decided to model the skills of the human 'CAL designer' who plays a pivotal role of interfacing between teacher and programmer in CAL development teams. This modelling was based on interview studies, analysis of existing programs and analysis of current author language facilities. Some of this analysis is available in Nicolson and Scott (1986). The usual rule-based knowledge representation formalism of expert systems seemed inadequate for the task of representing the knowledge of the CAL designer, and we adopted 'scripts' instead. Scripts have several useful features for our purposes: they provide a powerful, flexible and efficient formalism capable of representing knowledge about CAL design, about pedagogy and about teaching domains; they may be used either to comprehend or to elicit information from the user; and they are fairly easy to model in Prolog, thus obviating the need for an expensive knowledge engineering environment. The system we produced is a hybrid one incorporating many of the features of expert systems but based upon the scriptal knowledge representation, and we named it SCALD – the Scriptal CAL Designer.

The SCALD-1 prototype has been developed to test the power of the system in the instructional domain of CAL and uses scripts relating to the design and implementation of instructional programs, together with fairly limited rules embodying pedagogic principles. Once the teacher has selected one of the available CAL types, SCALD-1 selects an appropriate 'empty script' and a Prolog 'script applier' drives the interaction with the user to build up an adequate specification which may then be turned automatically into a machine-independent design and/or a 'program shell' which will run on the target machine. The program shell initially uses dummy questions and answers and may next be enhanced using a suite of Basic programs for creating the content and for modifying the screen layout.

Empirical evaluation of the system using teachers and CAL experts indicated that it was easy and pleasant to use, resulting in the creation of the program shell within minutes and adequate working programs within an hour (assuming, that is, that the intended application fell within the limited scope of the SCALD-1 scripts!). Suggestions for improvements and enhancements to the instructional script could be fairly easily accommodated owing to the flexible nature of the script formalism, but a more sophisticated knowledge engineering environment would certainly have eased this process. The major limitation of SCALD-1 (other than the obvious lack of scope of the scripts for non-instructional applications) was probably the difficulty of integrating the 'tuning' of the program shell (using Basic programs) with the original design specification process. We are at present working on SCALD-2, a more complete prototype which incorporates simulation scripts and has a modified architecture which is intended to allow the user to 'edit' the original design *after* interacting with and tuning the program shell.

It is probably fair to say that the creation of SCALD-1 was by adapting and combining existing AI techniques rather than pioneering new ones. The power of the IAS will reside in the harnessing of AI, educational theory and cognitive science in the solution of an applied problem. It is no exaggeration to claim that the widespread introduction of intelligent authoring systems would revolutionize the provision of educational software.

Part three

ICAI applications

16

Design choices for an intelligent arithmetic tutor

TIM O'SHEA, RICK EVERTSZ, SARA HENNESSY, ANN FLOYD, MIKE FOX
AND MARK ELSOM-COOK
The Open University, England

This chapter discusses the design choices facing a project to build an intelligent tutoring system for arithmetic skills. The aims of the project are not only to assist the child in constructing a large, flexible repertoire of efficient written and mental methods of calculation and to develop the child's ability to use alternative methods intelligently, but also to foster the mathematical understanding that necessarily underlies their use.

16.1 INTRODUCTION

This chapter discusses the design choices confronting our project to build an intelligent tutoring system for arithmetic skills. There are five principal dimensions of choice. The most important relates to the types of student model to be constructed. The standard argument for applying artificial intelligence to education depends on the quality of the individualized instruction that could in principle be provided by employing accurate models of individual student competence. The key issues that relate to student model construction include the degree of fit to actual behaviour necessary and the degree to which it is possible to model student learning processes and teaching events that change the student's competence. A closely related dimension of choice is the representation technique(s) to be used for the implementation of the student models. Some techniques, such as production systems are more suited to modelling learning, while other approaches, such as semantic networks seem more suitable for the expression of interrelated concepts.

Teaching style, the third dimension of choice, is independent of the first two. Artificial intelligence techniques have been applied by enthusiasts for complete learner autonomy such as Papert (1980) and by psychologists like Anderson (1984) who advocate keeping the learner on a very tight leash indeed. Other possibilities include varying the degree of learner control, providing motivating games, generating individualized drill and practice problems and allowing the student to explore microworlds (for a review of a variety of approaches see O'Shea and Self, 1983). The fourth dimension of choice is content and this has been an educational debating forum for centuries. What arithmetic skills do we require a person to master before we consider him fully educated? The issues here include the value of the long division algorithm, the need for understanding rather than rote efficiency and the utility of using standard rather than personal methods. The last dimension is the media to be used by the student. Possibilities include paper and pencil, physical objects (such as Dienes blocks or Cuisenaire rods), the mind, abaci, pocket calculators and, more recently, computer keyboards, light-pens, mice and other input devices. In summary, our five dimensions of choice then are: student model fit, model representation technique, teaching style, arithmetic skills and student media.

The project is being undertaken jointly by the Centre for Information Technology in Education, and the School of Education at the Open University. The project team contains people with backgrounds in maths education, and people from an artificial intelligence background. The system is being developed on a Xerox 1109, but the final version will be available on an Apple Macintosh to facilitate evaluation in schools.

Eventually we hope to develop much more precise accounts of individual arithmetic learning and to be able to make strong arguments for the ways in which the new technologies can be used to enhance arithmetic instruction. In the course of this three-year project we are obliged to adopt a less ambitious objective because of the constraints associated with the hardware, software and person-power available to us. However, the immediate objective is to carry out, in conjunction with a commercial software house (SYSTEM Ltd.), research and development work on an adaptive computer tutor for basic arithmetic. The research activities will include: a. identification of the informal calculation methods employed and the difficulties encountered by 7–12 year-olds who are learning arithmetic, b. the formulation of models that accurately represent the informal algorithms and their component skills, c. the construction of a diagnostic consultant for a range of numerical understandings and misconceptions, and ultimately, d. the development of an intelligent arithmetic 'workbook' for use in schools. This will comprise a series of mathematical games and activities involving manipulation of numbers in ways which will help the child to construct a large, flexible repertoire of efficient written and mental methods of calculation, based on a solid foundation of mathematical understanding.

16.2 BACKGROUND TO PROJECT

The arithmetic learnt by children and the associated errors have received significant attention over the last thirty years from various investigators (Downes and Paling, 1958; Williams, 1971). During the last ten years a production-rule-based cognitive model of one of the algorithms has been proposed (Young and O'Shea, 1981), a taxonomy of errors for this and other algorithms has been produced (Brown and Burton, 1978; Attisha, 1983), and finally a theory of error generation (as yet incomplete) has been proposed (Brown and VanLehn, 1980). It has always been clear that, with some additional research, the results noted above could be used to develop diagnostic consultants for these algorithms. For example further work like that of Attisha (1983) is needed on the representation of the algorithms, together with work on error taxonomies. However the programs currently available for arithmetic only possess limited knowledge of errors together with very general remediation messages. They have no representation of the task the child is working on, so they cannot execute the algorithm on the task as part of an explanation, nor can they give detailed remediation specific to that task. In addition the causes of errors may be ambiguous and so suitable disambiguating examples have to be presented as exercises.

While the teaching programs for arithmetic are obviously inadequate there have been various useful developments with diagnostic consultants. A particular piece of work that provided the initial motivation for this project was the diagnostic consultant constructed by Fox (Fox, 1983) for subtraction which was based directly on a family of models for some of the more common errors (Young and O'Shea, 1981). One important deficiency of this past work is that it does not address the source of the arithmetic methods used by children in primary or elementary schools.

16.3 CHILDREN'S CONCEPTIONS OF ARITHMETIC

The work of many researchers shows that children of this age are inclined to invent their own methods of calculation – both correct and faulty ones. In simulating these methods, our approach departs from previous models of conventional written algorithms and the errors associated with them; our specific focus is on mental arithmetic with whole numbers. Firstly, this emphasis on informal methods reflects the fact that current curriculum-based research in Britain and elsewhere is undergoing a significant swing away from standard algorithms towards such methods. This is because the latter provide children with an easier and more natural way of operating, which has been shown to foster greater understanding; ability to use informal methods displays a deep grasp of number concepts and operations and the awareness of a tremendous variety of interconnections, so that the most appropriate and shortest paths come naturally. Secondly, isolating and building upon children's *own* successful invented methods provides a necessary and powerful link between children's numerical understandings and complex written calculation. These methods allow a much more direct access to the child's representation of the domain. In sum, the overall goal of the project with respect to teaching is to develop children's ability to manipulate whole numbers. This involves fostering both proficiency in procedural methods of written calculation and of mental arithmetic, and an understanding of underlying mathematical concepts. Other aspects of the teaching domain represent necessary component concepts of this overall proficiency.

In contrast, previous research has concentrated on children's 'bugs', traditionally described as systematic deviations from taught procedures (Brown and VanLehn, 1982). This approach has several shortcomings. For instance, the nature of the supposed systematicity is difficult to pinpoint and it has never been adequately defined. Moreover, although children do sometimes show patterns of 'buggy' behaviour across a range of problems, they are not nearly as systematic in applying their bugs as has previously been suggested. Children can even be observed to employ two different buggy procedures in solving almost identical problems within a single session (VanLehn, 1982). Consequently, the common practice of broadly classifying children's behaviour on an isolated occasion into various types of buggy and non-buggy procedures is misleading. Another drawback of current techniques for bug diagnosis is that they result in a very high percentage of unexplained errors (~ 30–40%). This unsatisfactory position results in much uncaptured variability in children's performance.

The most important ways in which our investigation departs from traditional research into buggy behaviour are a. that it looks beyond the surface level of bug representation and b. that it focuses on initial teaching of skills, rather than on remediation of bugs. We hope to pre-empt the development of buggy procedures by helping children to construct correct concepts in the first place. Thus, our diagnostic program will not merely be concerned with errors; the idea is to chart children's progress in terms of the numerical concepts and skills that they already possess. Of course, a certain amount of remediation will prove necessary, but in building a student model, our program will specify only common errors in detail; we expect the model to generate the rest. In sum, partial, rather than complete, user modelling will be undertaken. With respect to errors, the major concern of the model will initially be with the more general misconceptions that underlie children's procedures.

The present approach can be seen to endorse the basic philosophy behind the French 'didactic approach' to research on mathematics learning; that is, errors are not merely considered as failures but rather as symptoms of specific misconceptions which influence children's mathematical activity (Balacheff, 1984). The initial success of a misconception – a faulty piece of knowledge – in solving some types of problems means that the child resists modifying or rejecting that misconception, and it becomes an obstacle for further learning. It is probable that children's numerous procedural difficulties are based on a small number of conceptual misunderstandings. This implies that we can avoid having to identify and to remediate an exhaustive set of specific bugs by considering children's difficulties at a deeper level than is customary, and by focusing on more general misconceptions.

Isolating and formally characterizing conceptions is certainly no easy task; the attempt by Johnson, Draper and Soloway (1982) to build a computer tutor for programming in Pascal has illustrated how quickly the specification of a learner's presumed intentions becomes murky, and how additional information outside an area of difficulty needs to be brought to bear. It seems that rather than simply inferring the roots of mathematical behaviour, we will have to begin at the other end by considering what is known about common informal calculation procedures and sources of difficulty for primary school children. Aspects of their conceptual knowledge and potential deficiencies (e.g. the misconception of zero) will have to be specified carefully – through decomposing the children's invented algorithms and non-algorithmic numeracy tasks into their sub-procedures and conceptual components. From this basis, our intention is to build a diagnostic consultant which assesses children's ability by using small arithmetic tasks to examine their understanding of a variety of basic mathematical concepts, in a variety of problem solving contexts. This allows a diagnostic model to be constructed which can then be used as a guide for both teaching and remediation.

Characterization of conceptual understanding requires an understanding of the types of experiential knowledge that children bring to bear on comprehending new problems, and also an understanding of the ways in which this knowledge can be applied. Children use different arithmetic procedures on different occasions, and this causes difficulty for most existing modelling methods.

Stevens and Collins (1980) have advocated multiple models that can be used generatively to test out novel hypotheses and to make predictions about new situations. Specifically, multiple arithmetic skills can be characterized by employing strategies that determine how to map back and forth between models; checking results found in one model against another permits many misconceptions to be counteracted. This has the advantage of permitting more accurate modelling of the individual differences that arise in choosing a procedure for solving a particular problem.

From building static models of the arithmetic knowledge of pupils, it is necessary to move towards developmental models of the arithmetic learning process. We must explore ways in which a computer-based model of problem solving can account for arithmetic learning and face the task of determining what qualitative developmental changes take place in the nature of children's inventions. Research that has examined the stability of children's mathematical behaviour over time is remarkably limited in scope, although the few studies that have been carried out have demonstrated that a developmental shift can occur in the use of procedures over several weeks (Cox, 1974; Hennessy, in preparation; Osburn and Foltz, 1931; VanLehn, 1982). According to VanLehn, the progress observed was not superficial; rather, the children concerned had learned something about subtraction.

A computationally explicit account of such progress entails consideration of both how children manipulate information to meet task demands (processes), and the inter-relations and structures of appropriate knowledge domains (representations). Success of the account clearly depends on characterizing and explicitly representing the conceptual arithmetic knowledge underlying children's procedures, and the ways in which that knowledge is reorganized during the course of development. The term conceptual knowledge refers to children's mental models of the numerical relationships represented by the formal, symbolic code, and the principles which govern the number system. We need to examine the interaction between the procedural knowledge of arithmetic, and the deeper conceptual knowledge about the number system; ideally, conceptual knowledge imposes constraints on the creation and modification of those procedural skills.

Existing simulation models ignore the issue of conceptual constraints on acquisition of procedural skill. They do not portray arithmetic procedures as means for manipulating representations of conceptual knowledge, but deal with underlying misconceptions purely in terms of missing or incorrect rules (e.g. VanLehn, 1983c). In fact, computer representations of mathematical behaviour generally treat written subtraction, for example, as a system of operations on symbols rather than as a system of operations on quantities (Resnick, 1984). The computer program that formalizes repair theory has no representation at all of the total quantity or of the sub-quantities being transferred in the course of a borrow operation. The system does not 'know' that it is adding ten when it places an increment mark in the units column. In order to represent accurately what children do when they invent their own procedures, a program needs to incorporate critics that refer to the principles of quantity.

In conclusion, a general bias in the information-processing approach to cognitive science has to be overcome. Learning is not the consequence of a steady stream of increments in mental functioning, and descriptions which characterize developmental progression purely in terms of increased numbers of production rules are insufficient. In this project, mathematics is viewed not as a set of independent, teachable procedures, but as a collection of ideas and methods that a child builds up in his or her own head. Since learning involves the construction of new knowledge upon the foundation of old knowledge, a system modelling mathematical behaviour cannot ignore, but must attempt to build on, previously acquired knowledge. This begins with those spontaneous concepts which the child constructs before any kind of formal teaching. The strength of the child's knowledge foundation is in fact thought to limit the level of mathematical experiences that can be offered. For example, a firm basis of arithmetic understanding is necessary for learning elementary algebra, and such an understanding prevents the transfer of errors to the new domain (Booth, 1983; Resnick, Cauzinille and Mathieu, 1985).

Two implications for empirical consideration have by now become clear: firstly, that it is essential to analyse arithmetic abilities into their conceptual components, and secondly, that investigation of the components will require characterization at the level of individual children. Thus, our tutor will track the development of individuals and attempt to explain their acquisition of mathematical skills over time. Several questions arise, however, when we try to model arithmetic problem solving in view of those two considerations. For instance:

1. How can children's acquisition of numerical concepts actually be formalized?
2. Are concepts and skills always acquired in the same order?

Work recently completed by Hennessy (in preparation) indicates that although marked individual variation is evident, children do portray some systematicity as a group in their development of more sophisticated problem-solving procedures. A few guidelines for modelling developmental changes in the use of certain procedures can be divined from previous investigations of children's conceptual development and also from those of 'bug' stability, but further theoretical work is certainly necessary. On the whole, researchers have not even acknowledged, let alone adequately measured, the extent of individual variability over time. Nor have they taken into account how the teaching process may alter a child's cognitive state with respect to the mathematical concepts under mastery. We anticipate that close observation of classroom teaching patterns and extensive longitudinal work – examining variation both within and between individuals – will prove to be most helpful in filling in some of the holes in our current knowledge.

16.4   MODELLING THE STUDENT

A number of facets of a tutoring system can be designed to be sensitive to the requirements of the individual student. One of these is the *student model*. The rationale for incorporating a student model is that in order to help a student who is having difficulties with the subject being learned, a teacher needs to have an understanding of what the student's problem is. In other words, the teacher must have an adequate 'model' of the current state of the student's domain knowledge, problem-solving abilities etc. Only then can the teacher provide relevant advice, and set problems which help the student to debug the aberrant parts of her knowledge.

The tutor must possess something capable of using the information present in the interaction with the pupil in order to build a student model. One important requirement of this student-model generator is that it should be able to represent all student models which correspond to empirically observed behaviour. If the tutor cannot do this, then there will be students which the system is unable to help because it cannot adequately represent what they are doing. This is a major problem for traditional approaches to student modelling; not only do the builders of the tutoring system have to collect empirical data on which to base the student model (a time-consuming process in itself), but they can never be sure that a model generator which operates by selection within this data will cover all cases. Indeed, without exception, model generators of this type do not cope with all students; there will always be the student with the inscrutably idiosyncratic algorithm. What enviable quality does the 'master teacher' possess which enables him/her to cope with completely novel bugs? It is this: the skilled teacher can infer how the student went wrong, both by examining the student's written solution, and also by interrogating them: 'What did you do here? Why did you do that?'. It is hoped that the teacher will memorize the bug, and so will be suitably equipped to spot the bug in any future misguided students. For the teacher, and consequently the aspiring intelligent tutoring system, the problem is essentially a learning problem. S/he must inductively infer the nature of the student's misconception.

The student modelling approach mentioned above is typified by the BUGGY subtraction diagnosis system (Brown and VanLehn, 1982). A vast empirical database of student errors was hand-analysed to generate a general model of student bugs from which the system selected subsets to model individuals. We wish to propose an alternative approach to student modelling which bypasses the need for this scale of empirical bug collecting, and improves the ability of the system to handle idiosyncratic models. The proposed solution is to have the program build its own library of student models for the arithmetic skills being taught. In trying to automatically generate simulation models from empirical data, we immediately run into the problems which plague science in general. For example:

1. Which of two models provides the 'best' account of the data?
2. Is it permissible to account for the discrepancy between model and data by hypothesizing that a confounding variable is at work here?

The student model generation process must be a cycle of hypothesis and experimentation, actively testing possible diagnoses of the student. In the domain of arithmetic, many students apply their knowledge inconsistently (Young and O'Shea, 1981; Evertsz, 1982; VanLehn, 1982) or make accidental slips in performance; even the most competent students are not immune – all sorts of external factors can conspire to distract them. The tutoring program will have to cope with this problem. The problem of separating noise from data is one which plagues all learning programs which must deal with 'real-world' data. Accidental slips apart, students are known to migrate between various erroneous algorithms during the course of solving a set of problems. This makes justifying the modelling hypotheses using all the observations of a student very difficult because what we are attempting to model is changing during the course of the data collection. This problem is not unique to arithmetic domains. To a certain extent, one confronts this issue when trying to understand the behaviour of any adaptive system – the more simple the nature of its adaptation, the easier it is to account for the 'algorithm migration'.

We intend to constrain our student models by ensuring that the vocabulary in which they are expressed makes educational or psychological sense. For example, a 'confounding variable' introduced to account for a discrepancy in an individual's performance could be related to past arithmetic teaching that employed different analogies from those the student currently uses or associated with some 'invented method' that students of this age and background are known to employ or even some resource limit on cognitive functioning. We are optimistic that while there is clearly great variation in strategy (Seigler and Shrager, 1984) there is very little real 'noise' in children's arithmetic behaviour and believe that provided we can find a unified framework for expressing the various psychological and educational processes that condition the performance and learning of arithmetic, then we will be able to provide models which make much more accurate predictions of arithmetic competence than those specified by ourselves and others in the past.

16.5 REPRESENTATION TECHNIQUES FOR MODELLING

Our initial choice of representation for modelling procedural skill in arithmetic is the *production system* (PS). From a student modelling perspective, the advantages of PSs stem from their modularity. Because rules do not explicitly invoke each other, but instead must communicate via *working memory*, PSs can withstand small perturbations of their rule set. Researchers have found this attribute useful in modelling those errors which can be characterized as deletions to the correct model of some procedural skill (e.g. Young and O'Shea, 1981). To model such errors, one simply deletes the appropriate production rule from the rule set. Provided that there is sufficient redundancy in the rule set, such a PS will still come up with an answer, albeit the wrong one. Modularity also eases the problems of modelling learning, because it is relatively easy to extend the system by adding discrete components of the skill to the model. From a production rule perspective, learning a procedural skill entails adding new productions to production memory.

Existing PS-based models have limited success in modelling arithmetic skills. They build single-level representations, with no support for modelling multiple algorithms, repair selection, deep knowledge about arithmetic etc. To what extent this formalism is the most appropriate for the task requires further exploration.

In order to generate new rules to account for unrecognized problem solving behaviour, we propose to apply standard machine-learning techniques for building production rules from a library of operators as employed in systems such as LEX (Mitchell, Utgoff and Banerji, 1983) and SAGE (Langley, 1985). In accounting for a given child's problem solving, where the program does not have the appropriate production rules, it applies its general operators to the problem statement, and subsequent problem states, and through a process of search attempts to find a route to the child's answer. The program is then in a position to build rules which can reproduce the path without search. Unfortunately, there are many routes to the goal state. Studies of errors in arithmetic (e.g. Evertsz, 1982) have shown that some children manifest particular combinations of bugs, which lead to the right answer on some problems, but not others. This occurs where a problem has particular characteristics which require the child to use two or more buggy pieces of knowledge, and the bugs' effects cancel each other out (i.e. there is an ambiguous surface manifestation of an impasse). The example below illustrates this:

$$\frac{1}{4} - \frac{1}{6} \rightarrow \quad \text{calculate LCM (but don't factor numerators)} \quad \rightarrow \frac{1-1}{12} \text{(bug)}$$

$$\text{subtract} \quad \rightarrow \frac{0}{12}$$

$$\text{convert zero to one} \quad \rightarrow \frac{1}{12} \text{(bug)}$$

(R. Evertsz, 1982, p. 28)

In order to stand a chance of discovering such algorithms, it would appear that the program must generate all paths to the child's answer, using many permutations of its operators. We do not need to calculate the size of this search space (which would vary for different domains anyway) because the program is not guaranteed to have available all of the operators which the student may use, and hence cannot carry out a complete search. Consider the second bug in the example above. One explanation for this anomalous final step is that the child believes that zero is not a valid numerator in an answer. A program which only relies on its library of operators for finding a path to the solution will not discover this algorithm. Therefore, we are compelled to find some way of enabling the program to inductively infer the required operator. But if all the program has to work from is the start state and goal state, how will it discover an operator as obscure as 'change-zero-to-one-iff-it-is-the-final-numerator'? If we allow the system to invent new operators at will, then it will come up with all sorts of unlikely accounts for the pupil's answer. For example, to a 'liberal' inventor of operators, the rule below is a perfectly valid account of the above answer:

IF the problem is '1/4 – 1/6',
THEN the answer is '1/12'.

Apart from the fact that the above rule is over-specific, it appears ludicrous to us for one very simple reason: we can see the child's intermediate computations. Because of the problem of multiple paths to a solution, we consider good protocols to be vital to the construction of accurate models. In addition, the availability of the child's protocol in real time, enables the program to expand the search tree while the child is solving the problem.

Provided that intermediate working is available, simple sets of production rules are a very effective way of modelling the various correct and non-standard procedures (including the 'faulty' ones) and some of the simpler forms of learning and problem solving (Sleeman and Smith, 1981). Our position on mathematics learning is similar to Pinker's (1984) on language acquisition. In order to learn new concepts it is necessary to carry out some form of 'semantic bootstrapping' with the existing set of concepts. Also by expressing directed graphs in production rules (Heines and O'Shea, 1985) we can express more complex procedures involving sub-procedures such as the use of arithmetic in solving algebra word problems. It is also possible (following Langley and Ohlsson, 1984) to use production rules for the automatic generation of student models. However there are some very hard representation problems which we do not know how to solve. In particular, we would wish to represent a pupil's *understanding* of arithmetic skills and concepts. This understanding includes what the skill or concept is useful for and why and how a skill 'works' or what a concept is relevant or related to. Accordingly we require representational techniques in which we can express familiarity, analogies and metaphors. For example, a child may apply a particular arithmetic skill in the context of a card game or computing the change from purchasing comics and may describe the skill using a standard school analogy (based, for example, on dividing a circular 'pie') or understand the skill via a personal metaphor (based, for example, on how their family share household tasks). Representing understanding is a key problem area in contemporary artificial intelligence research and there is no well developed set of techniques available to apply to this problem. In particular, if you wish to represent the way that the pupils' repertoire of analogies and metaphors condition their learning processes then you are faced with some very acute unsolved problems and there is no consensus on whether any past work in machine learning has had even limited success (see, for example, Ritchie and Hanna, 1984; Lenat and Brown, 1984).

Our attack on the problem of representing understanding will be based on augmenting our production rule representation schemes with object-based indexing systems in the style of those used by Burstein in his work on learning using multiple analogies (Burstein, 1986). One technical advantage of this approach is that it would be possible to construct a two-tiered modelling system (one tier for concepts and the other for procedures) as an extension of one of the object-oriented programming environments (for example, Smalltalk-80 or LOOPS). Burstein's work is already in this style and the standard production rule interpreters useful for educational applications (see O'Shea *et al.*, 1985) can easily and usefully be expressed in this formalism. This extended work on representation may turn out to be too speculative to incorporate in the tutors we build during the course of this three-year project and it may very well turn out that we have to restrict ourselves to representing the most common procedures and rely on a combination of appropriate initial teaching and the 'reflective' properties of the computer-based instructional materials we produce to help the students extend their understanding and debug their more subtle misconceptions.

16.6 METHODOLOGY

The project has two initial main aims. The first is to research the feasibility of constructing an intelligent computer tutor for the usual algorithms taught in the English-speaking world for the arithmetic operators. The second main aim is to construct diagnostic consultants which would be used by children after initial instruction by teachers. This is a conservative aim because a diagnostic consultant that could not comprehensively teach a topic might be able to offer assistance with routine practising by identifying and remediating errors. They could provide appropriate examples. Records of the problems and progress of individual children would be maintained. These would serve as high quality data sources to be used in the development of student models for the tutor.

There are a number of activities associated with the above aims:

a. The collection and analysis of protocol data of paper and pencil work.
b. The construction of student models which should be capable of generating the standard errors exhibited by learners. An attempt would also be made to model the discontinuities due to learning gains.
c. An investigation into how different types of remedial example, explanation or computer screen image affect the performance of learners.

d. The characterization of student models based on b, and c.
e. The characterization of teaching strategies which map from student models to the various types of example, explanation or screen image.
f. An investigation of the utility of written input (via graphics tablets) and speech output (using synthesizer chips) particularly for younger children.

As the project develops we expect to refine our aims and to focus on particular areas of the design space described in this chapter. However the basic style of the investigation is that it is learner and classroom driven and that it involves testing the software we develop in realistic settings. Our starting point is the ways in which pupils are taught and teach themselves arithmetic. We then characterize these learning processes with as much computational explicitness as possible. Subsequent to this we develop and test a range of computer programs which may be remedial, diagnostic or expository and which vary in the degree of freedom for exploration and experiment that is offered to the learner. Following these tests we expect to refine both our models of arithmetic learning and our educational software. This iterative process will continue until this project is completed and at any stage we would expect to have specified more sophisticated models of arithmetic learning than those embodied in the educational software currently being tested.

The data collected will be longitudinal, so that we can attempt to characterize the arithmetic learning of individuals over time. We expect to employ written tests administered to groups, Cyclops equipment for recording synchronized voice and paper and pencil working (see O'Shea and Floyd, 1981; Scanlon *et al.*, 1985) and graphics pads interfaced to Apple Macintoshes. Student models, screen designs and other educational software will be prototyped using Interlisp and LOOPS on a Xerox 1109. Diagnostic consultant and other educational software will be developed on enhanced versions of the Macintosh using, if practicable, one of the object-oriented languages now available such as Object LOGO (Schmucker, 1986). This should minimize the recoding from LOOPS. After refinement the various types of educational software will be delivered for more extensive classroom evaluation on less powerful versions of the Macintosh. Some of the outcomes that we hope to achieve include:

a. A set of diagnostic consultants incorporating simple student models for the four arithmetic functions running on Macintosh computers.
b. An extensive taxonomy of errors for the four arithmetic functions.
c. A set of design guidelines for computer tutors in arithmetic.
d. A set of production-rule models for the four arithmetic functions.

16.7   DIAGNOSTIC CONSULTANTS

A major aim of this project is to design a diagnostic consultant for each of the four arithmetic operations. Minimally, this achievement will necessitate identifying the standard errors exhibited by 7–12 year-olds who are learning arithmetic and constructing models that are capable of generating those errors.

Some progress towards this goal has already been made by other researchers – predominantly in the domain of subtraction. Fox (1983) has developed a prototype diagnostic consultant which provides a starting point for building consultants for the other three arithmetic operations. The work of Brown and Burton (1978) and of Young and O'Shea (1981) shows that children of this age are inclined to invent complex faulty algorithms or 'bugs', and that these bugs can be simulated.

The existence of the prototype and the existing error taxonomies strongly suggest that the successful design of a diagnostic consultant is not an issue. The problem here is whether it can be made acceptable in the classroom and when evaluated is shown to benefit the learning of arithmetic. An obvious approach would be to decompose the final algorithmic tasks into subtasks and operators. Some of the operators correspond to the conventional marks made by the pupils on paper. A straightforward and immediate extension of this would be to apply the same decomposition to the intermediate forms of the algorithms used in teaching. This approach is adequate for dealing with the issues related to knowledge of what to teach and how to teach in a way appropriate for use in a diagnostic consultant.

The existing prototype is always able to say something useful about what has gone wrong. If it proves straightforward to provide all the intermediate working (i.e. the decrement, increment and carry figures) using the graphics tablet then it will be easy to give diagnoses in more detail. Beyond that *ad hoc* rules could be added to deal with why something has gone wrong in as many cases as possible. Three examples of how a diagnostic consultant would work in the realm of paper and pencil arithmetic are given below.

Example 1. Suggesting the sources of errors.

In subtraction by decomposition, borrowing from the bottom line indicates a mix-up with the alternative algorithm, equal addition. This could be suggested if the algorithm was known to have been previously learnt by that student. e.g.

$$\begin{array}{r} \overset{5}{\cancel{6}}\,\overset{\mathsf{I}}{0}\,\overset{\mathsf{I}}{\cancel{8}} \\ -\,2\,\overset{}{\cancel{4}}\,9 \\ \hline 3\,7\,9 \end{array}$$

Example 2. Again, in subtraction by decomposition, borrowing from the leftmost column when a column nearer to the borrowing column should be used indicates that the student is using an over-generalized version of the rule, 'borrow from the column to the left', which may be used in two column subtraction. e.g.

$$\begin{array}{r} \overset{7}{\cancel{8}}\,1\,\overset{\mathsf{I}}{3} \\ -\,5\,1\,5 \\ \hline 2\,0\,8 \end{array}$$

Example 3. However, in a case where borrowing had occurred but the borrow into column had been incremented to 10 and not to 10 + the number at the top of the column, a reliable hypothesis would be harder to suggest so error diagnosis would not proceed beyond noting what had gone wrong without a reasonably detailed student model.

e.g.

$$\begin{array}{r} \overset{5}{\cancel{6}}\;\overset{10}{2} \\ -1\;8 \\ \hline 4\;2 \end{array}$$

The implementation of diagnostic consultants is a modest step on the road to constructing intelligent tutors for arithmetic and a useful way of testing hypotheses about the form and nature of student error patterns. Our past work (Fox, 1983) convinces us that such consultants could in principle be created for all four arithmetic functions. Fully implemented diagnostic consultants will have the following desirable properties:

1. They will accept input from a keyboard and from the use of a mouse or a touch screen. They will also accept input via conventional paper and pencil work using a graphics tablet.
2. They will work with input either from a problem completed on paper or executed by direct interaction with the computer.
3. They will be able to step through the usual algorithms and a variety of informal algorithms for the arithmetic operators.
4. They will be able to diagnose an error in a child's work, usually in substantial detail.
5. Where multiple errors are concerned, only the most likely one will be dealt with in that session.
6. Explanations and/or remediations will be made available at suitable points in the session.
7. When an error is found the consultants will never fail to make some comment no matter how unusual the mistake.
8. They will maintain a record of progress for individual children.
9. They will generate examples for practice.

16.8   MATHEMATICAL MICROWORLDS

We eventually hope to develop a set of mathematical microworlds in which children can develop their understanding of mathematical concepts. Behind these microworlds will be a diagnostic system (based on the diagnostic consultants) which will use information from the activities of the pupil to build a model of the pupil's procedural skills, and from this model it will attempt a deeper model of the underlying misconceptions of the pupil. The deep model will form a base for individualizing the learning experience of the child. We hope to achieve the mapping from activities in the microworld to a procedural model (expressed in production rules) by using student models of the type discussed above. The mapping from this model to the deeper conceptual model involves a mixture of techniques. In particular, this is a point at which the expertise of human teachers can be incorporated into the system. Further empirical work will be carried out on identifying common sources of difficulty for primary school children and on analysing the concepts required in executing informal arithmetic algorithms and some non-algorithmic numeracy tasks. This information will be used to develop a model of the inter-relationships between various concepts and skills.

At the time of writing this chapter we have prototyped the two microworlds described below but have not associated a diagnostic component with either of them.

The purpose of the Dienes block microworld is to aid the child in developing a mapping between concrete arithmetic and formal manipulation of symbols. Clearly there is no point in simply imitating Dienes blocks on a computer – the real thing is cheaper and more effective. It has been observed (Davis and McKnight, 1980) that children experience difficulty in transferring skills learnt with Dienes blocks to pencil and paper arithmetic, and research on assisting this transfer is in progress (e.g. Resnick, 1982). The arithmetic tutor provides a Dienes block world in which a concrete mapping between these representations is provided, so that direct manipulation of one representation has an immediately visible effect upon the other.

For example, if the child borrows from the hundreds column while performing the sum on the right-hand side, a 100 Dienes block is picked up and broken into

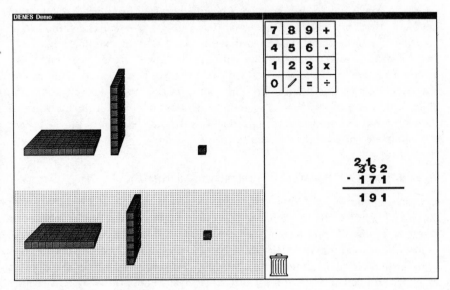

Fig. 16.1. The Dienes block microworld.

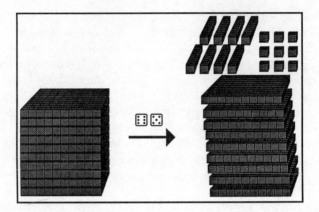

Fig. 16.2. Shrink-a-Cube.

ten 10 blocks (by a little person with an axe). Similarly, moving the 100s block would result in the cancelling and borrowing appearing in the formal representation. Figure 16.1 shows the state of the system after the child has completed the sum. The upper set of Dienes blocks represents the answer, while those in the lower area represent the amount taken away.

The purpose of Shrink-a-Cube is to aid the child in developing an understanding of the principles of exchange and place value. In this game, the child gets the computer to 'throw' its dice, and must then remove from the cube the number of blocks indicated by the sum of the dice. The machine then has its turn – the winner is the one who manages to shrink the cube to nothing. In order to shrink a cube, the child must exchange it for an equivalent set of smaller denomination blocks, so that the requisite number of units can be removed. The game can be played in any base, and is illustrated above in base 10. In this example (Fig. 16.2), the child has thrown a six and a five with the dice and proceeds to exchange the $10 \times 10 \times 10$ cube for ten 10×10 flats; one of these flats is then exchanged for ten 10×1 longs, and finally one of the longs is exchanged for ten units. The child is then in a position to remove the equivalent of eleven units from the set (one long and one unit). The diagram shows the start state and the state after removing the equivalent of eleven units.

16.9 SUPPORTING FORMAL AND INFORMAL ARITHMETIC

In order to support the formal arithmetic taught in schools and practised with paper and pencil work on exercises taken from textbooks we intend to examine whether it is feasible to develop an 'intelligent arithmetic workbook'.

Two key components of arithmetic are the intermediate working and visualization of the meaning of such working. Currently the former is supported by paper and pencil work and the latter by physical apparatus such as Dienes' blocks and Cuisenaire rods. Using this package the student would carry out arithmetic via a computer keyboard, possibly augmented by a pointing device such as a mouse or light pen. The system would provide one or more graphic illustrations of the intermediate workings with the user being able to choose from a menu of illustrative models.

The system would have the full capability of the diagnostic consultant and would comment on and illustrate any errors in working as they occurred. This interactive workbook would help pupils both practice and *understand* arithmetic. The workbook would maintain a record of progress on the four functions and would be able to generate examples for practice. The precise degree of adaptivity to individuals will depend on the quality of the student model produced during the research.

This package would replace both the exercise book and the textbook normally used by pupils. It would provide immediate feedback and an innovative set of mathematical visualization aids. At the end of the project we would expect it to represent the most sophisticated medium available for carrying out and understanding arithmetic.

Another crucial domain which will underlie our games and activities involves providing support for pupils carrying out mental arithmetic using informal methods (Jones, 1975). There are a large number of commonly observed 'alternative frameworks' which are thought to arise from pupils' observations and their reflections upon them. Such methods will thus be closely related to the pupil's personal perceptions of arithmetic (Denvir and Brown, 1986), and they may often conflict with the correct procedures and concepts involved in acquiring mathematical knowledge. (Few attempts have been made to model informal methods; a coherent example is Resnick's (1983) Part-Whole schema, which can cope with preschool arithmetic right up to written multi-digit computation. We will examine the appropriateness of this schema for our needs.) In working within a domain such as mental arithmetic on the computer, we intend to get the pupil to describe explicitly the steps in the informal methods which s/he uses. Hence, we can provide both a support for the pupil in constructing such methods and for the tutor, a valuable key to the *pupil's* representation of the domain.

The rules used in the domain of informal arithmetic can be represented in the form of a production system in which different paths to the solution correspond to different collections of rules. By way of illustration, we present the following two solution paths for the same addition problem:

Problem: $67 + 38$
Solution 1:

Decompose number to tens and units	60, 7
Decompose number to tens and units	30, 8
Add tens	90
Add units	15
Add tens to units	105

Solution 2:

Decompose number to tens and units	60, 7
Decompose number to tens and units	30, 8
Add tens	90
Add tens and one set of units	97
Add on remaining units	105

Our aim is to make rules of this kind the basis of a computer activity in which a child performs informal arithmetic at the computer interface, while the program discovers what is in fact meaningfully understood by him or her and what is not. This achievement requires involving the child in a relatively unconstrained activity and simultaneously constructing a model of understanding at the conceptual level.

16.10   CONCLUSIONS

The space of design choices described above is large and we are now in the process of identifying more precise goals for the project and an overall framework for the intelligent tutor.

Our work on the tutor is constrained by our educational goals and we now find ourselves putting greater emphasis on children's informal invented methods and mental arithmetic and putting less emphasis on some of the more cumbersome formal procedures such as the long division algorithm. We are becoming increasing interested in the potential of mathematical games and microworlds to act as motivating media in which children can work and play whilst reflecting on their own processes and understanding as mirrored in their use of the instructional software. We remain committed to a three-pronged empirical approach which involves firstly the rapid prototyping of all software using high performance AI hardware and software, secondly the incorporation of student models expressed with AI representation techniques as a key component of our arithmetic tutor and finally and crucially the testing of all components of the tutor in classrooms and homes with teachers, parents and pupils.

The general goal of the project is to provide the incentive and the tools which a child needs to construct powerful, concrete ways of thinking about mathematical problems. The tutor should foster the development of conceptual knowledge by replacing the traditional focus on practice and memorization in mathematics education with an emphasis on understanding and creative problem solving, that is, on the constructive aspects of thinking (cf. Papert, 1980). To be more specific, some areas of children's arithmetic competence with which we are concerned are the following:

a. Ability to estimate and hence detect unreasonable answers derived as a result of any means of calculation. The tutor will aim to encourange skills such as answer checking.
b. Understanding of a wide range of numerical concepts and quantity relation-

ships underlying arithmetic operations. Construction of the tutor will entail a detailed exploration of this area.

c. The ability to select an appropriate calculation method in a given situation. This includes knowledge of which calculation procedures and which operation is applicable to a problem, and why. (Note that although the use of calculators is becoming increasingly widespread, their prominence in our teaching package is as yet uncertain. Calculators could well play a major role in computing large numbers if supported by estimation ability.)

The overall framework will be to construct a series of mathematical games and activities involving manipulation of numbers in ways which will foster development in the areas discussed above. Recent research has shown that number games are a much more effective medium than conventional teaching methods (Hughes, 1986; Kamii, 1985). Our games will allow children immense flexibility in creating their own problems to solve and their own ways of manipulating numerical representations. They form the basic link between the pupil and the diagnostic and teaching packages (each of which might use the games in a different way). The games will be based both on abstract representations such as the number line, and on a variety of concrete ones, in order to set problems in context. Representations for concrete mapping instruction need to be familiar, yet stimulating to children. These might include blocks in various bases, money, sweets, etc., and possibly stories with a mathematical framework.

Remediation will consist primarily of choosing an appropriate activity from those available and offering it to the pupil or group of pupils. This, like the proposed large degree of adaptation *within* the activities, is a manifestation of the tutor's 'intelligence'. It provides a valuable level of teaching which is not currently available in the classroom, but it does so without becoming entangled in some of the major tutoring problems which confront less open-ended tutoring systems.

In sum, our ultimate aims are not only to assist the child in constructing a large, flexible repertoire of efficient written and mental methods of calculation, and to develop the child's ability to use alternative methods intelligently, but also to foster the mathematical understanding that necessarily underlies their use.

ACKNOWLEDGEMENTS

The project described in this chapter is being carried out in collaboration with SYSTEM Ltd of Sheffield and is funded by a grant from SERC/Alvey. We are grateful to Olwyn Wilson for administrative support and Dave Perry for practical help. The chapter is a reworking and expansion of the proposal submitted for funding by Tim O'Shea and Ann Floyd. The ideas on diagnostic consultants which provided the initial impetus for the project are due to Mike Fox. Some of the ideas on children's arithmetic were developed by Sara Hennessy in her doctoral research and the work on microworlds was mostly carried out by Rick Evertsz. Mark Elsom-Cook provided helpful motivation and critiques of drafts.

17

A framework for the design of a writer's assistant

MIKE SHARPLES AND CLAIRE O'MALLEY
University of Sussex, England

This chapter sets out a framework for a Writer's Assistant, designed to support writers who already possess basic writing skills, but who need help in developing more mature reflective writing and in managing the multiple constraints involved in creating a complex text.

The student writer (as opposed to the complete novice) is potentially capable of performing all the tasks involved in creating a complex document, but has not yet developed the control skills and reflective processes necessary for managing those tasks in parallel. The purpose of the Writer's Assistant is to reduce cognitive load by providing support tools for 'externalizing cognition' (i.e. providing *aides memoires*, representing the structure of the problem space), and to take care of low-level tasks and constraints which would otherwise compete for processing and other cognitive resources with the higher-level aspects of writing. The system is designed to help the writer to develop the meta-cognitive, reflective aspects of composition, by showing the writer the structure of a text and its underlying ideas; allowing the writer to create and manipulate ideas, text and layout, moving amongst different writing strategies; allowing the writer to specify constraints on the material and assisting in managing and satisfying these constraints.

17.1 INTRODUCTION

Writers need support. Writing is a difficult task involving the management of many simultaneous activities and constraints. It makes severe demands on the human memory and processing ability, and the task can overwhelm even experienced writers, leading to the familiar symptoms of 'writer's block'. To the inexperienced, the problems are compounded by the need to attend to low-level activities like spelling and word selection at the same time as grappling with higher-level aspects such as new modes of expression. The result is what Collins and Gentner call *downsliding* (Collins and Gentner, 1980), where a writer loses track of the overall conceptual structure, plan or style, in an effort to put words down on paper. This might be acceptable if the writer were easily able to revise the text later to bring it back in line with the original plan and style, but often these are either ill-conceived, or so far from the current text that repair is impossible.

For all these reasons, an inexperienced writer (someone who has mastered the basic skills but is still learning to write for a variety of functions and audiences) needs support in making the transition to more mature reflective writing and in designing complex texts. In other areas of education, support tools, such as pocket calculators and dictionaries, already play an important role. The contribution of the computer is to offer 'knowledgeable support', by aiding the student during a cognitively demanding task. A computer-based support tool could act as a *student's assistant*, with the following characteristics:

1. The system has a limited teaching strategy: the student directs the activity and the system acts as a 'co-driver'.
2. There is no specific student model: student and assistant cooperate in building a common representation of the task. The assistant provides support for 'externalizing cognition', showing the student the structure of the problem space, and the steps already taken towards the solution.
3. The assistant reduces cognitive load by taking over some of the demanding but low-level activities (e.g. in arithmetic, performing calculations), leaving the learner free to concentrate on higher-level aspects, such as formulating the problem and planning a solution.
4. The assistant is an adjunct to a familiar activity, such as writing, or arithmetic, or music, performed in a familiar way. (Thus LOGO Turtle geometry does not fall into this category, because it embodies a *novel* way of approaching geometry.)
5. In order not to increase cognitive load by adding new representations and operations, the assistant must be based on the student's perception of the task and must be suited to a range of learners, with different problem solving strategies.

One type of computer-based assistant, already in regular use, is Interlisp-D, a set of tools which aid the planning, development and debugging of complex LISP programs:

> Some tools are simply effective viewers into the user's program and its state. Such tools permit one to find information quickly, display it effectively, and modify it easily ... The other type of programming tool is knowledge-based ... A wide variety of tools have been constructed to ... answer complex queries ... to make systematic changes under program control (such as making some transformation whenever a specified set of properties hold), or to check for a variety of inconsistent usage errors. (Shiel, 1983).

There are many similarities between developing a computer program and composing a piece of prose and in this chapter we set out a framework for a Writer's Assistant, based on a model derived from current research on the writing process. The system is designed to support writers who already possess basic writing skills, but who need help in setting down and managing the multiple constraints involved in the process of text creation.

17.2 WRITING SKILLS

A number of researchers have investigated the writing processes of both children and adults, for a variety of tasks, ranging from structured expository writing to creative fiction. (Humes, 1983, provides a good summary of recent research.) Their aim has been to move from an understanding of writing based on a final product towards a description of the *process* by which writers produce text. What follows is an attempt to integrate the results of these studies into a composite model from which guidelines may be derived for the design of a Writer's Assistant.

17.2.1 Multiple constraints

The task of writing may be described as the act of juggling a number of simultaneous constraints. This is in contrast to seeing it as a series of steps that add up to a finished product (Flower and Hayes, 1980). The primary constraint on the final text is that it fulfils the writer's aims: i.e., that it communicates the author's ideas and arguments to the intended audience. Generally, the writer draws upon a plan or outline to divide the writing task into nearly independent sub-tasks, chosen so that they can be achieved separately, without constant attention to the possible interactions between them. The plan acts as a structural constraint on the delineation and ordering of sub-tasks. These sub-tasks will not be fully independent, but are subject to contextual constraints: conventions of writing style, for example, dictate that spelling and abbreviations should be consistent. Another set of constraints specify the global properties of a sub-task: for example, readability factors, or visual appearance such as typeface and column width. Yet another set may be characterized as resource constraints: the text may need to include particular references, figures, graphs and avoid certain abbreviations or jargon words.

Some constraints, such as conventions of style and layout, may be set before the writing begins. Others, such as consistency and structure, arise during the task. Constraints may conflict; for example, a title may be too long to fit across a column, or a word may not be in the dictionary. These conflicts will then need to be resolved, for example by shortening the title or correcting the word's spelling.

Constraints perform a number of functions. They ensure uniformity of style and content, they restrict the memory search involved in generating text, and they give a focus to the writing. However, they also impose cognitive demands on the writer:

> It is no wonder many people find writing difficult. It is the very nature of the beast to impose a large set of converging but potentially contradictory constraints on the writer. Furthermore, to be efficient the writer should attend to all of these constraints at once ... Unfortunately, this ideal rarely occurs because of the limited number of items our short term memory or conscious attention can handle. (Flower and Hayes, 1980, p. 40.)

17.2.2   Idea generation and reflection

Writing is more than just presenting words neatly on a page. Much of a writer's time is spent in mustering ideas and forming intentions. As Collins and Gentner point out:

> It is important to separate idea production from text production. The processes involved in producing text, whether they operate on the word level, the sentence level, the paragraph level, or the text level, must produce a linear sequence that satisfies certain grammatical rules. In contrast, the result of the processes of idea production is a set of ideas with many internal connections, only a few of which may fit the linear model desirable for text. (Collins and Gentner, 1980. p. 53.)

Not only do ideas guide the writer in creating text, but the act of writing can also give the author new insight (Smith, 1982). Reflection is a valuable aid to writing, and writing is a valuable aid to processes of reflection, abstraction and problem solving (Scardamalia, Bereiter and Steinbach, 1984; Wason, 1980).

In order to move easily between ideas and text, a writer needs to represent and manipulate different *views* of the material. The first is a *structural view*, in which ideas and fragments of text form a network of interlinked concepts. The writer may form this explicitly, as in a written plan or outline, or implicitly, as a web of ideas. The structure must then be traversed and filled out to produce a linear stream of text. This *linear view* is then transformed into a two-dimensional representation to produce a final formatted document. In this *planar view*, the writer is no longer primarily concerned with content, but with the spatial organization of text and graphics on a screen or page.

The three views are mutually constrained. In a structural plan (view 1) the writer specifies possible orderings of words; the string of words (view 2) provides resources for the page layout (view 3). Within any single view the writer may be focusing on a particular level of detail. Thus, in broad focus, a writer will be working with large conceptual chunks (in the structural view, these may be groups of ideas; in the linear view these will be large textual chunks, such as sections or chapters; in the planar view they will be layout blocks). In a fine focus the units will be small (single ideas; words or letters; characters on the page).

17.2.3   Writing strategies

In general, a writer progresses through the views by beginning with an ideas structure and then using this to form a draft and then a layout. This demands less mental effort than, say, trying to fit a first draft to a tightly constrained layout. (Consider, for example, the problems of a writer of concrete poetry who must fit words to a specified layout.) Within this general progression, writers adopt distinctly differing strategies for creating and revising material. Those given below are not meant to be exhaustive, but illustrate a variety of ways of developing views, ranging from mustering loosely related ideas (*thoughtdumping*) to filling out a well-structured framework (*plan–draft–revise*). A good writer will shift from one to another as the task demands.

Brainstorming or thoughtdumping

The writer jots down ideas or fragments of text without worrying about how to organise or title them. This underconstrained structure can then be reflected upon and manipulated, for example, by sorting ideas into conceptual categories as the basis for a plan.

Following a thread or developing a topic

The writer creates a conceptual structure around a topic, a line of narrative, or a chain of reasoning. This involves the generation of embedded sub-topics, in the form of elaborations, examples, definitions, and also digressions or asides, as in footnotes or parenthetical sub-sections. Often the writer does not have much idea of what the eventual structure will look like, since it only emerges when that particular branch of the network of ideas has been expanded.

Writing as dialectic

Another similar strategy for developing a structural view is to construct an argument or dialectic (what Flower and Hayes call *thinking by conflict*). In this case, ideas are connected to each other by links such as contrast, claims, evidence, warrant, and so on. A more constrained form of this would be to fill in a predefined schema, with slots such as *main argument, counter argument* and *supporting evidence*.

Select and transform

This is the method of collecting together pieces of already written material – quotes, notes, extracts from earlier writings – assembling them into a rational order and then tailoring them to the current task, filling in the missing sections.

Draft–redraft

Here the writer sets down a hurried stream of ideas as words on the page. These form a draft which is then expanded and polished, perhaps through a number of redrafting cycles. The strategy differs from *thoughtdumping* and *following a thread* in that the writer begins with a linear view, putting down ideas as a single stream of words.

Plan–draft–revise

This is the traditional strategy for developing text. The writer begins by generating a plan or outline, then produces a linear draft from the outline. The draft is revised for final presentation. In practice, the strategy is invariably more complex. It may be recursive, in that a revision to one part of the text may lead to another pass through the process, involving further planning and drafting.

17.2.4   Operations

The writing strategies outlined above can all be described by a small set of general operations. The differences between the strategies lie in the type of constraints, the level of focus and the number of loops in the cycle. The operations are:

1. Set constraints.
2. Create material for a particular
3. Identify constraint conflicts as a result of the view created.
4. Resolve constraint conflicts by modifying either the view or the constraints.
5. Shift view or level of focus.

The recursive nature of writing arises from the fact that conflict resolution may itself demand a cycle of operations.

The *thoughtdumping* strategy involves 1. and 2. – setting resource constraints and creating a network view – but postponing the problems of conflict resolution. The *thread* and *dialectic* strategies are a matter of setting topic (purpose) constraints and then creating a structural view, again largely ignoring constraint conflicts. They differ in the type of links used to develop the network. In *select and transform* the writer constructs a structural view out of pre-written text. *Draft–redraft* starts with the writer creating a loosely constrained linear view. This provides contextual constraints where conflicts may be resolved by redrafting. *Plan–draft–revise* is just a cycle of the operations from 1. to 5.

17.3   ASSISTANCE FOR THE WRITER

A writer needs assistance particularly in two circumstances: a. when attempting to make the transition to a new, more demanding form of writing which involves learning new techniques (for example, a student learning the art of essay writing), and b. when creating a text with a complex conceptual structure (for example, constructing a difficult argument).

17.3.1 Managing multiple constraints

Flower and Hayes (1980) suggest a number of strategies for reducing the cognitive burden of managing simultaneous tasks and multiple constraints, such as throwing away some constraints, partitioning the problem, or combining constraints into groups. Two other effective strategies, not mentioned by Flower and Hayes, are to operate an external memory, such as a written plan, and to pass responsibility for some of the constraint management (particularly that concerned with the simple rule-governed aspects of writing, such as spelling and layout) over to an automated system.

Brainstorming or thoughtdumping

Although ideas may be 'dumped' in a haphazard manner, the writer must be able to merge, link, and group together notes, and to refind a particular note so that it can be incorporated into the text.

Following a thread or developing a topic

Support is needed for expanding a particular topic, for getting back up to the top level when that expansion is finished, for digressing temporarily along different paths, and for subsequently manipulating the structure created through this process.

Writing as dialectic

Here the user needs to be able to see and alter the structure of the argument emerging from the notes.

Select and transform

The writer needs to find and incorporate text segments written by herself and others, using a variety of reference strategies; keyword, date of creation, date of last access, library classification, theme, author, text string, topic hierarchy, and so on. Often the writer will only have a vague notion of the requirements and so needs powerful tools for browsing through documents.

Draft–redraft

The writer needs to impose structure on a string of words (perhaps roughly formed into sentences and paragraphs), by viewing a representation of major elements of the text, then naming, grouping and reordering the elements.

Plan–draft–revise

Here the writer needs to be supported in keeping the original plan in step with the emerging text. If the writer alters the plan, the text needs to be transformed accordingly; if the writer revises the text, the plan should also be changed.

Both for writing and for browsing, a writer needs not only to be able to move freely between different views of the material, but also, within a view, should be able to choose the appropriate level of focus. Often, when focusing on fine detail, the writer may lose sight of the more global structure (perhaps leading to downsliding). The writer thus needs support in maintaining a global perspective at the same time as attending to lower level details.

17.4 EXISTING SUPPORT AND TEACHING SYSTEMS

Current support systems for writers do little more than assist with the simplest rule-governed aspects of writing such as spelling and punctuation. This is hardly surprising, given the problems involved in developing more intelligent text understanding systems. Diagnostic aids such as the Writer's Workbench (Frase, 1980) and Pain's Spelling Diagnosis System (Pain, 1985) can give a writer information about the finished text, but offer little dynamic support. They could, however, form sub-systems of a more general writer's assistant.

Recently, researchers have begun to design tools for idea exploration and conceptual development; for example, the Notecards system at Xerox PARC (cf. Brown and Newman, 1985) and the Notepad system at the University of California, San Diego (Cypher, 1986) are intended to support brainstorming or thoughtdumping. However support is also needed for reorganizing and re-structuring these ideas so that they can be developed into a coherent text.

Structure editors such as Etude (Good, 1981) and Lara (Gutknecht, 1985) are useful for representing the embedded structures of text, but they do not explicitly represent the multiple constraints involved in writing, nor the structure of ideas.

With respect to tutoring systems, most of the research effort has been concentrated on teaching basic writing skills (e.g. WANDAH: Friedman, 1984; Writer's Assistant: Levin, Boruta and Vasconcellos, 1982; Levin, 1982) which means that these tutorial systems have little to offer in the way of support for people such as more advanced student writers, who already possess the necessary skills.

17.5 FRAMEWORK FOR A WRITER'S ASSISTANT

The description of the writing process that we have set out above has implications for the design of a Writer's Assistant. A Writer's Assistant should:

1. Reduce cognitive load by providing support tools for externalizing cognition (i.e. providing *aides memoires*, representing the structure of the problem space), and by taking care of the low-level operations of writing.

2. Provide multiple views of the material. It should offer the writer three separate, but mutually consistent views of the emerging text, in the form of an ideas structure (whereby the writer specifies relations between ideas in the form of typed links between notes), a stream of text and a layout. The writer should be able to move between them at will and, in altering one view, know that the others will remain in step. Given one view, the system should be able to generate approximations to the other two: for example, a writer should be able to create a linear stream of words and then view it as a network of structures and references. When working within a view the writer should be offered a variety of support tools, for example:

Structural view (ideas): The writer should be able to jot down unrelated notes and later refine them and organize them into an outline or plan. If the writer is developing a particular topic and needs to make brief asides, the system should provide the means for keeping track of the main topic so the writer does not stray too far down 'garden paths'.

Linear view (text): The system should check that spelling is consistent with respect to the dictionary, and within the whole text. It should monitor the use of technical terms, abbreviations, and style (sentence length, passive/active voice, etc.).

Planar view (layout objects): The system should check that items such as footnotes and titles are consistent and correctly formatted.

3. Allow the writer to specify explicit constraints on each item (idea, text, or layout object), or to inherit default constraints for particular types of document. As a view is created, the system should attempt to satisfy these and, where it is unable to do so, should present the constraint conflict to the writer. Most of the support tools described in 2 above could be implemented by general constraint management techniques; special purpose sub-systems would only be needed for the more complex manipulations such as spelling correction.

4. Allow the writer to switch easily between any of the writing strategies: for example by suspending a revision session to jot down some new thoughts, or by producing a rough draft and then forming a plan to cover it.

Thus, the purpose of the Writer's Assistant is: first, to show the writer the structure of a text and its underlying ideas; second, to allow the writer to create and manipulate ideas, text and layout, moving amongst different writing strategies; and third, to allow the writer to specify constraints on the material. The system manages the satisfaction of some constraints, such as formatting and manipulating word and sentence syntax, so lessening the writer's cognitive load. The remainder of this section offers an outline design for such a system.

17.5.1   Representation

Every item manipulated by the system is an active object. In the structural view the basic object is a note representing an idea, at any level of complexity, from a simple indicative header to a fully formed piece of text. A note can be shown by title, or it can be 'opened up' and its contents edited, just like any other piece of text. Notes can have directed links to other notes, representing relationships between ideas. Examples of such links might be *elaboration, example, definition, meta-comment,* and *comparison.* In addition to links explicitly set by the user, there is a default link created by the system to indicate the chronological order. From this the user can get a historical trace of the notes as they were created.

Notes may be collected together into *bins* that, for example, indicate their common purpose or topic. Since a bin is just another object, with pointers to its members, then one note may appear in several bins. Any note with no outside links is put into a special *pending bin.*

Text and layout objects carry out their own itemization (a sentence object forms words into sentences and passes them up to a paragraph object), constraint manipulation (a word object checks in a dictionary that it is correctly spelt; a footnote layout object fits itself at the foot of a page), and cross linking. Each object must therefore have attributes, procedures and constraints associated with it. These properties may be created in one of four ways:

1. They may be explicitly added by the user, e.g. *left margin: 0.*
2. They may be created by the system, e.g. *page number: 2.*
3. They may be inherited from a higher-level object. The writer may, for example, specify *typeface: elite* as a property of the *section* object. Any lower level elements will inherit that property, unless given a different local value.
4. They may be inherited by default, since each object belongs to a generic class and inherits default properties from the class, e.g. a procedure for displaying itself.

Object-oriented programming languages, such as Smalltalk, provide just such facilities. Objects can have associated values and procedures and these may be inherited through a class/instance hierarchy.

17.5.2 Viewing the material

Figure 17.1 shows the screen display after a user has created a network of notes. As each note is created, it is represented in the network window as a box, showing the title, if given, and the links to other notes. The note on which the writer is currently working is highlighted. To the left of the screen is a set of icons that indicate some of the available operations. On selecting the *history* icon, for example, the user is shown a list of the notes in the order in which they were created. The *layout* icon creates a planar view of the text and *links* allows the user to create and name a link to connect notes in the network. On the right is a *bin* of unconnected notes and the other window shows a planar representation of the current note. A planar view consists of layout objects, such as *block* and *page* containing an array of formatted text.

The linear view in Fig. 17.2 shows the entire text formed from the contents of

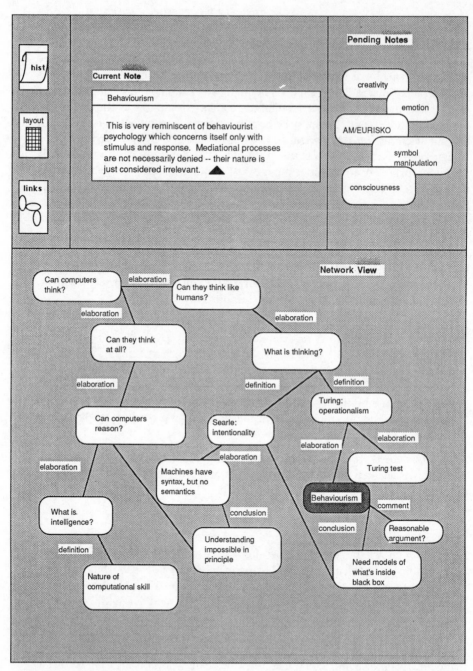

Fig. 17.1. The screen display after a user has created a network of notes. (The example is a fictitious undergraduate essay in the early stages of composition.) Each note is represented in the network window as a box, showing the title, if given, and the links to other notes. The note on which the writer is currently working is highlighted. To the left of the screen is a set of icons that indicate some of the available operations. On the right is a collection of unconnected notes, and the other window shows a planar representation of the current note.

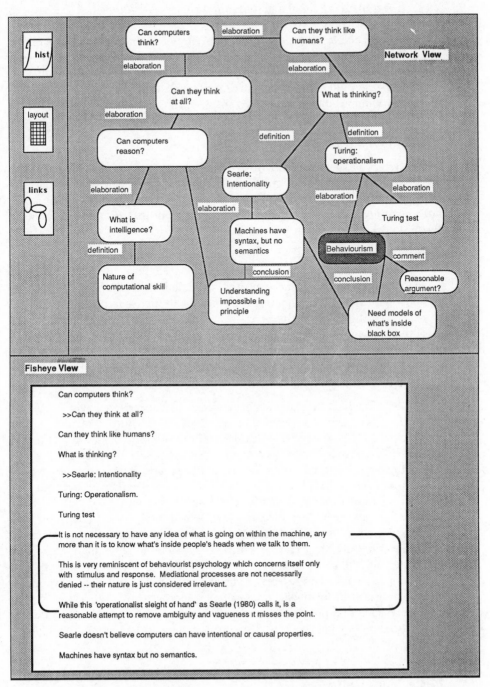

Fig. 17.2. The linear view shows the entire text formed from the contents of the notes. The text is being displayed in a *fish-eye* perspective with text items near the current viewpoint shown in full, and those further away in outline. Moving small window up or down alters the viewpoint as if moving a distorting lens over the text. The other window shows the equivalent network.

the notes (by default, each note is given the status of a paragraph). The text is being displayed in a *fish-eye* perspective with text items near the current viewpoint shown in full, and those further away in outline. Moving the pointer up or down the view alters the viewpoint as if moving a distorting lens over the text. The upper window shows the equivalent network.

17.5.3   Moving between views

If the system is to provide all three views of the text, then it must have a mechanism for automatically creating a linear view from the network. Unless the writer specifies a single thread through the notes, the system will need to make an attempt at linearizing the network. A possible algorithm for creating a linear thread in a useful order, is:

1. Order the link types. The highest value links will be those that form the 'backbone' of the text, e.g. the *follows* link. Ignore those links which indicate structures that will appear explicitly in the final text (e.g. *footnote*).
2. Starting at the current note, carry out a depth-first search of the network, expanding the link with the lowest value first. To avoid loops, keep a record of visited notes and do not revisit a note.
3. If two links of the same value emerge from a note then use a heuristic that picks the 'shallowest' branch first (e.g. if one link points to a large sub-net and the other to a single note then pick the single note).

The order in which the notes are expanded is the linear thread, which will still retain the links, such as *footnote*, that are needed for layout. To move from the linear to planar view the system must satisfy the formatting constraints of the text elements. The general method is for the system to place text objects in order within the bounds of the layout object (page, block, etc.) with annotations, such as footnotes, laid on top of their referencing objects. A second pass sorts out any layout constraint violations, such as overlapping objects.

So far we have been discussing the development of a piece of connected text from ideas created as notes. Another strategy is *draft–redraft*, where the writer begins by generating a stream of words. The system must be able to take this linear view and itemize it to represent the underlying structure. To reconstruct ideas from text would require a text understanding system, and that is beyond the current state of artificial intelligence. A simpler approach is to use surface features such as spacing and punctuation to guide itemization. Each text object has its own procedures for itemizing its elements and passing the item up to a higher-level object.

17.5.4   Editing the views

The user can edit any view. For example, the user can add a new paragraph to a linear view and this is automatically inserted as a new note in the network, with a default link type. A *cut* operation creates a new object containing the cut material which inherits the properties of the object from which it was taken. *Pasting* involves merging two objects and combining their properties. In order to avoid resatisfying all the constraints after each editing operation the system has a 'damage limitation' strategy which serves the same purpose as a *truth mainten-ance system* (Doyle, 1979). This identifies the objects in each view that may be affected by the operation and revises only those elements.

17.5.5 Constraint satisfaction

Associated with each object is a set of constraints. There are four types of constraint: a structural template (specifying, in outline, the organization of the object's contents), boundaries (such as maximum length), resources to be included (such as key phrases or quotations), and context (how the item must relate to others, for example that a particular word must be abbreviated in a consistent way throughout the text). Constraint satisfaction is carried out by comparing the properties of the current object with its constraints, and attempting to resolve any conflicts.

A number of artificial intelligence programs employ constraint satisfaction methods. SOPHIE (Brown, Burton and de Kleer, 1982), for example, propagates constraints in a simulated electronic circuit to diagnose faults set by the user. The constraints of writing bear some similarity to those in the MOLGEN program (Stefik, 1981), which plans genetics experiments, in that they build up gradually, becoming more specific as the text is generated. MOLGEN uses a technique called *constraint posting* to form constraints for each sub-task at an abstract level; they are satisfied only when the plan is instantiated. This method, applied to the Writer's Assistant, sets constraint priorities and delays making decisions about less urgent constraints such as word consistency. The difference is that the plans of MOLGEN are underconstrained and so can generally be satisfied without conflict. The Writer's Assistant must not distract a writer by constantly pointing out constraint clashes; the consequence of this is that conflicts can build up, and if the text strays too far from the constraints the discrepancy may be difficult to repair.

Some constraints, such as those involving formatting, can be satisfied by the system without involving the writer. Others, such as resource conflicts (e.g. a word cannot be found in the spelling dictionary), or boundary violations (e.g. a section contains too many words) pose a difficult problem of whether to resolve the conflicts (e.g. by attempting to correct a misspelt word), or, if not, when to interrupt the writer.

These issues are similar to the ones faced by Burton and Brown (1982) in the design of the WEST coaching program and, as they point out:

> In general, solutions to these problems require techniques for determining what the student knows (procedures for constructing a diagnostic model) as well as explicit tutoring principles about interrupting and advising. These, in turn, require a theory of

how a student forms abstractions, how he learns, and when he is apt to be most receptive to advice. Unfortunately, few, if any existing psychological theories are precise enough to suggest anything more than caution. (Burton and Brown, 1982)

A cautious approach might be to:

1. Automatically resolve conflicts between formatting constraints.
2. If possible, suggest to the user ways of resolving letter, word and sentence level constraint conflicts.
3. Notify the user of other constraint conflicts.
4. Interrupt the user whenever she changes view.

17.6   CONCLUSIONS

In this chapter we have offered a framework for the design of a Writer's Assistant that is informed by a cognitive model of the user, based on empirical research. We have argued that even skilled writers need tools to support the multiple constraints and simultaneous activities that make creative writing a difficult cognitive task. Such support is needed all the more for student writers who have mastered the basics, but are still developing the more sophisticated skills required of an 'expert' writer.

The student writer (as opposed to the complete novice) is potentially capable of performing all the tasks involved in creating a complex document, but has not yet developed the control skills and reflective processes necessary for managing those tasks in parallel, and satisfying the multiple constraints involved. Whereas tutoring systems can offer the more structured support needed in the initial stages of the development of writing skills, the kind of system we have outlined would provide a *scaffold* (cf. Bruner, 1973) in two senses: first, it would help a writer to develop the meta-cognitive, reflective aspects of composition; second, it would take care of the low-level tasks and constraints which would otherwise compete for processing and other cognitive resources with the higher-level aspects of writing (e.g. planning).

Many interesting questions remain to be answered, such as whether the system could support all the usual writing strategies; whether it would be able to maintain the three consistent views throughout the construction of a complex text; when is the most appropriate time to intervene with assistance, and so on. The only way in which such questions can be answered is by building a Writer's Assistant as an environment to test out models of the writing process.

18

Modelling the students' errors in the ELECTRE tutor

MICHEL CAILLOT
LIRESPT*, Paris, France

In the ELECTRE project, the performance of a student solving a set of problems in basic electricity is simulated. To do this, we need a student model which takes errors into account. The student's knowledge is organized in three categories: prototypes related to specific circuits, schemata and heuristics. The most important errors are described at the level of the prototypical knowledge and heuristics of problem solving used by students.

18.1 INTRODUCTION

Since the first years of programmed instruction, teaching with computers has been well developed. All the history of such teaching has been directed towards more and more individualized teaching. The techniques of artificial intelligence (AI) make it possible to think of teaching in which the relationship developed between the machine and the learner is similar to a tutorial one. So the dream of teaching adapted to each student is within the range of possibility. But to do this, some problems must first be solved, such as the representation of knowledge to be taught and also the student's representation.

In an intelligent computer-aided instruction (ICAI) system, the knowledge of a specific domain can be at different levels of sophistication. This can go from the expert's knowledge to a knowledge specially adapted by the teacher for educational purposes. Another issue to be considered is how to build a model of the student's knowledge. Different points of view are possible. First the student's knowledge can be seen as a part, a subset, of the expert's knowledge: that is the overlay model (Carr and Goldstein, 1977). But it can also be considered as knowledge different from the expert's. In this latter case, students can develop misconceptions or alternative frameworks of thinking. They can also produce incomplete or even erroneous reasonings. Some systems are based on such an

*Laboratoire Interuniversitaire de Recherche sur l'Enseignement des Sciences Physiques et de la Technologie (Unité Associée au CNRS).

approach as in the case of learning of addition and subtraction (Brown and Burton, 1978), or of algebraic manipulations (Sleeman, 1982). But in these programs, the knowledge under consideration is composed mainly of procedural skills.

The issue is quite different in semantically rich domains, such as physics, because knowledge in such a domain does not only include procedural skills. Understanding physics is knowing the definition of concepts, how these are organized into the so-called physical principles, and how to use them in order to describe the physical world. The results of research in physics education reveal that the students' difficulties also come from misconceptions developed through everyday life by incorrect reasoning. So the design of a model of the student's knowledge should foresee the representation of the student's errors.

We present here the ELECTRE project which will be a diagnostic system of errors made by students solving problems in basic electricity. Once the errors have been detected, students will be given special training to remedy them. The current state of the project concerns students' knowledge modelling and its implementation.

18.2   OUTLINE OF THE ELECTRE SYSTEM

ELECTRE is a multidisciplinary project on which computer scientists, cognitive psychologists and physics education researchers are working. The chosen physics domain is basic electricity and more specifically DC circuits. The aim of the project is to diagnose the state of the students' knowledge after they have solved a set of problems dealing with computations of currents and/or voltages. A circuit diagram is given with each problem statement. The way students solve these problems and find the requested entities depends on how they have analysed the circuit diagram and decoded the information displayed in graphical form. In order to be able to link the errors made by students to their diagram analysis, ELECTRE proposes three different categories of tasks:

• Description of circuit diagrams,
• Calculations of currents,
• Calculations of voltages.

From the student's answers to the whole series of problems on one of these tasks, the system should infer a student's knowledge base which includes either good understanding or errors. It also describes the student's performance by simulating his/her behaviour. So ELECTRE, when it is completed, will be a system able to test a student's knowledge. Its goal is not primary teaching in which the student discovers a concept and its different possible uses. On the contrary, the ELECTRE system comes after the teaching of basic concepts of electricity; it tests the student's knowledge and diagnoses its deficiencies. After this, it will bring the student into a remedial session in order to change his/her knowledge state and to correct his/her diagnosed errors. However until now, no attempt to design remedial teaching has been developed.

The diagnosis is established on a 'theory' of errors founded on a student's plausible cognitive structure. The different kinds of knowledge in the student's mind have not the same status. Some are directly usable, whereas others need to be processed. Thus the modelling of the student has to take these different knowledge levels into account. This will be presented in the following section. But any student modelling should have certain characteristics to be valid. First a student model should be relevant to the subject matter. So in physics education, if the aim is to focus on concepts then the computation errors can be disregarded. Also it should be relevant to the teacher's goals such as correcting the most frequent errors; in this case the system will not take into account the very rare errors. Another characteristic to be considered is its psychological validity. Any student model, in particular the cognitive models, should be based on the most recent results of cognitive psychology such as those describing, for example, mental models (Gentner and Stevens, 1983). Finally, the model should be general enough to be applied to most students and not only to some, and also to most problems dealing with the same domain. We think that ELECTRE presents these different characteristics. However, as for other ICAI systems, there is still a question left open: is the modelling general enough to be applied to other topics?

Technically, ELECTRE is a knowledge-based system which uses the expert system approach, even if the expertise can be an 'unexpertise' in this case since the model accepts errors. The system uses production rules to describe correct and incorrect knowledge. All the rules are grouped in a rule base. The rule management (firing, control, etc.) is performed by SNARK, an interpreter based on the predicate calculus (Laurière, 1983). As in any expert system, the interpreter (the so-called 'inference engine') is independent of data. The data make up the fact base. Each fact is described by a triplet *object–attribute–value*. The inference engine examines the possible match between the current state of the fact base and the condition part of the production rules. Once a rule is chosen, it is fired. Then the current state of the fact base is modified. SNARK accepts meta-knowledge. Rules are grouped into packages corresponding to different possible strategy levels (Paliès *et al.*, 1986).

18.3 MODELLING STUDENTS' KNOWLEDGE

18.3.1 Cognitive modelling

Preliminary studies (Caillot, 1985) have shown that some high school students describe circuit diagrams and solve problems on DC circuits after having built problem representations based on the surface features present in the problem statement rather than on the principles of electricity. In Fig. 18.1 an example of the different answers given by a skilled student and a novice to the same question is presented. The skilled student answers by applying Kirchhoff's law on currents,

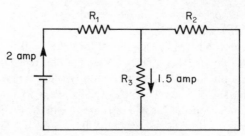

Fig. 18.1. Example of problem statement given to students. The question is: 'What is the current flowing through R_2?'. Skilled student's answer: 0.5 Amp. Novice's answer: 2 Amp.

whereas the novice disregards the junction where three resistors join, considers that the resistors R_1 and R_2 are connected in series, and then concludes that currents in R_1 and R_2 are equal.

Any intelligent tutoring system should be able to detect this kind of error. When an error like this is identified several times on the whole problem set, then the system makes a diagnosis. In this example, the diagnosis for the novice would be the following: the student is considering that any two resistors drawn along a straight line are in series so that the currents flowing through them are equal.

So some configurations of circuits induce erroneous student answers whereas other problems are always solved well. These are problems where the circuits are the canonical ones found in all the physics text-books. In general these circuits are immediately recognized by students. Then the knowledge on currents and voltages associated with them is available. The novice's knowledge base is organized around the notion of prototypes (Reed, 1972) which are very limited and disconnected units of knowledge. They often are associated with canonical circuits, having specific diagrams; so resistors connected in series are drawn aligned whereas those connected in parallel are drawn along geometrical parallel lines. The less proficient students only have this prototypical knowledge, whereas the most skilled students have a very flexible knowledge adapted to different types of circuits. In this latter case, knowledge appears to be structured in schemata as Chi *et al.* (1981) have shown for problems on mechanics. Figure 18.2 shows the differences between the novice's and the skilled student's knowledge.

A prototype can be seen as a very specific instance of a general schema. As very often a schema is structured hierarchically, including sub-schemata, then the prototype will be located at the bottom of the hierarchy.

When the problems deal with circuits different from the canonical ones, the novices reason analogically often using heuristics leading them back to the well known situations of canonical circuits. Now, these heuristics are improper from a physicist's point of view; they can lead to disregarding some problem information considered as crucial by the teacher or to producing incorrect simplifications in considering unjustified sub-problems. So the errors made by students come at

	Types of knowledge		
Student	*Prototypes*	*Schemata*	*Heuristics*
Novice	Many	Few	Over-generalization
Skilled	Few	Many and well organized	Correct and useful

Fig. 18.2. Differences between the novice's and the skilled student's knowledge.

once from knowledge only organized into prototypes and from unfounded heuristics. That is why we propose a knowledge base for each student organized with rules describing the student's knowledge of basic electricity and meta-rules for problem solving strategy.

18.3.2 Rules

a. *Prototypical knowledge*

We have seen that the class of problems on the canonical circuits is well solved by the students. Knowledge about these is going to play a particular role in ELECTRE; the examples of canonical circuits are considered as prototypes and therefore a first series of rules describes prototypical knowledge. An example is given on a prototypical in-series circuit (see Fig. 18.3a).

When students solve a problem on such a circuit, they are able to calculate currents and voltages. The rules given here in natural language are:

P1 – IF a terminal of a resistor R_1 is connected to a terminal of a resistor R_2, AND IF R_1 and R_2 are aligned on the circuit diagram, THEN R_1 and R_2 are in prototypical series.

P2 – IF two resistors are connected in prototypical series, THEN the current is the same along any point of the straight line formed by the wire and both resistors.

These two rules sound correct but they are too specific, too restrictive. The less successful students are only able to solve the class of problems where the in-series resistors are along a straight line. They cannot find the current in a branch where two resistors connected in series are not aligned (see Fig. 18.3b). So the knowledge about prototypes is very limited indeed.

In the rule base there are, of course, other rules describing several other prototypes and associated knowledge. Their number is currently about a hundred.

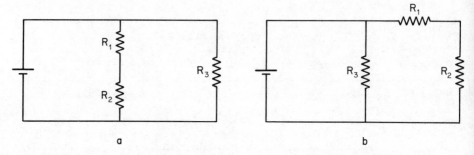

Fig. 18.3. Student's knowledge about two in-series resistors. (a) Example of prototypical pattern. The two resistors R_1 and R_2 are easily recognized as grouped in series because they are in a straight line. (b) The two resistors R_1 and R_2 are not recognized as being in series by the less skilled students.

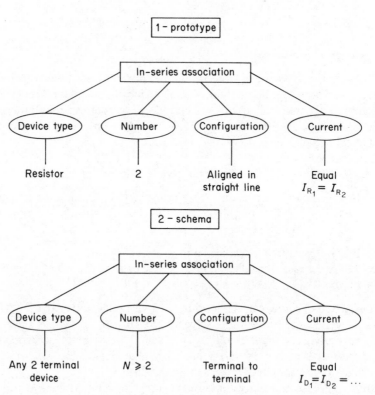

Fig. 18.4. Differences between a prototype and a schema for the concept of 'in-series association'.

b. *Schematic knowledge*

A schema, or frame, represents knowledge less specific than the previous kind. With its slots accepting discrete or continuous values of variables, a schema represents many instances of the same concept fairly well. In addition, procedures can be attached to a schema. So, for example, the schematic student's knowledge about two 2-terminal devices connected in series can be described by the following rule:

S1 – If a terminal of a 2-terminal-device-1 is connected to a terminal of a 2-terminal device-2
AND IF there is no junction between them,
THEN both dipoles are connected in series.

This rule is evidently more general than the rule P1, since all the configurations of two resistors grouped in series are possible, whatever the geometry of the circuit diagram. Figure 18.4 contrasts the prototypical and the schematic knowledge about the concept of the in-series grouping.

c. *Heuristic knowledge*

Schematic knowledge is insufficient when the problems deal with more complex circuits. Then the students utilize heuristic knowledge to find a solution. They try to come back to well-known situations which can be solved easily. In general, to do this students use means–end analysis. They replace the given problem by sub-problems; they simplify the circuit either by replacing resistors by an equivalent resistor whose resistance can be calculated or by removing some component. These heuristics aim to find a prototype or a situation where the schematic knowledge is available. In general, these lead to disregarding one or several elements of the circuit: the battery, a junction or a resistor. Now, most of the students' errors come from these heuristics which are wrong from a physicist's point of view. We give here two examples of improper heuristics.

The first example is relative to the circuit shown in Fig. 18.1. The following rule shows how the student's performance can be simulated:

H1 – IF three resistors are placed along three branches in T,
THEN remove the junction and the vertical branch in the middle of the circuit.

This rule is just the way we describe how the student seems to ignore the resistor on the vertical branch in the middle of the circuit. After having fired this rule, the system states that the circuit is composed with only two aligned resistors. Then the prototype P1 and P2 rules can be fired. So this rule chaining models a plausible student's reasoning which leads him to answer that the currents through R_1 and R_2 are the same, which is of course incorrect.

The second example (Fig. 18.5) is about the heuristic of removing the battery.

H2 – IF on a branch there is a battery between two resistors,
THEN remove the battery.

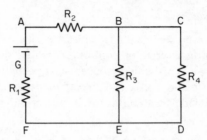

If $V_{AG} = 8V$, $V_{AB} = 2V$ and $V_{CD} = 5V$, what is the voltage V_{FG} between F and G?

Fig. 18.5. Example of an improper heuristic: removing the battery. When a student owns this heuristic, he can answer 5 V (if he considers R_1 and R_3 grouped in parallel) as well as 3 V (if he only considers the set of R_1 and R_2 connected in parallel with R_3).

After the firing of H2, both resistors along the branch are seen in series and the student can use his knowledge about voltages to calculate a requested voltage, omitting the voltage drop at the terminals of the battery.

Of course other heuristics exist. These two examples are just presented here in order to give a flavour of the rule base structure in ELECTRE.

18.3.3 Meta-rules

We have seen that in fact students use heuristic rules when a problem is too complex, that is when they are not able to recognize a well-known situation where prototypical or schematic knowledge is available. So the student's model has to build meta-rules in order to recognize the problem features and to plan a solution. A meta-rule is, for example, a rule which gives an order of priority for looking through the rule base. We hypothesize that the students use sequentially the different types of knowledge (prototypes, schemata and heuristics). First of all they look for prototypical problems; then if they fail they try to instantiate an available schema; and if they fail again, they use some *ad hoc* heuristic. So the strategy developed by the student would be the following:

1. recognition of the prototypical patterns,
2. application of the prototypical knowledge,
3. application of the schematic knowledge,
4. application of the heuristic knowledge.

The order of the rule firing is then fixed by meta-rule. When a type of knowledge cannot be applied to the current state of the problem because the conditions are not fulfilled, then the system tries to use another type of knowledge in considering all the rules corresponding to this knowledge. The meta-knowledge in ELECTRE is presented in more detail in another paper (Paliès *et al.*, 1986).

CONCLUSION

In ELECTRE, we have shown how the student's knowledge has been modelled. Errors in problem solving in basic electricity have been taken into account. They are formalized by production rules. The collection of these incorrect rules describes a sort of 'unexpertise'. They form a rule base from which a diagnosis of the state of the students' knowledge can be built. The differences between students come from different prototypical and heuristic knowledge. The richness of the rule base makes very precise diagnosis possible.

ACKNOWLEDGEMENTS

This research has been supported by CNRS (Centre National de la Recherche Scientifique) under contract No. RCP 080766.

I would like to thank the colleagues working with me on this project: Odile Paliès as computer scientist, responsible for the implementation, and two cognitive psychologists, Evelyne Cauzinille-Marmèche and Jacques Mathieu. All of them have contributed to ideas and results presented in this chapter.

19

Interfaces that adapt to the user

MARTIN COOPER
British Telecom Research Laboratories, England

This chapter discusses user interfaces that adapt themselves to suit the characteristics of the user. The user characteristics that can be used to trigger changes in the interface and the ways in which an interface can change in response are outlined. Several adaptive systems are placed within this framework. The design of an adaptive interface for an electronic mail system is described and some comments on its performance presented. Finally, the lessons learnt from building an example of a self-adaptive interface and plans for further work in this area are discussed.

19.1 INTRODUCTION

The decreasing costs and increasing availability of information processing, storage and communications are increasing the range of people who need to make direct use of computing systems. The text and data manipulation tools provided by an office automation system may have to be usable by, and acceptable to, the managing director, clerical assistants, research engineers, accountants, technicians, and so on. The range of skill, experience, expectation, preferences and needs is very wide and the success of the system depends on these users being able to make good use of the tools provided to help them carry out their diverse tasks. One approach to the problem of matching the heterogeneous user population to a more or less fixed interface is to provide training and support. Although this approach is often necessary, it is also expensive and may not be feasible, in the case of very senior people, for example. Another possible solution is to increase the flexibility of the interface so that it can be tailored to fit individual requirements, although the problem of informing users how to carry out the tailoring may be significant. A third possibility is to design a user interface that adapts itself to each particular user. People infer information about a speaker in a wide range of ways from sources other than the actual meaning of what is said (Giles and Powesland, 1975). A self-adaptive interface would be given some of this ability to assess the limitations and abilities of users and to use this information, together with further clues derived during interaction, to match the style and content of the user-system dialogue to the user.

19.2 SELF-ADAPTIVE USER INTERFACES

In order to adapt to a user, an adaptive interface system must be able to infer relevant user characteristics and to use this information to improve the interface presented to that user.

19.2.1 User characteristics

Relatively stable characteristics, such as knowledge of computers or experience of particular programs, can be estimated by an informed guess and defined by the system manager or based on answers to an initial set of questions from the system. This first assessment is unlikely to be accurate in many cases and so it would probably need to be tuned or even discarded in favour of a better stereotype in the light of evidence gathered during subsequent interaction.

Short-term characteristics relate to the user's immediate goals or particular difficulties experienced during a dialogue. This type of information can be obtained by analysing the recent history of interaction to identify patterns related to particular goals, common misconceptions, etc.

19.2.2 Changes in the interface

The interface between a user and an information processing system can be analysed into a hierarchy of descriptions ranging from the conceptual level, through the communication level, to the physical level (Moran, 1981). Each level of description is largely independent of the others and is a refinement of the previous levels. The conceptual level is a description of what the system can do, how it does it and the conceptual objects and procedures it uses to allow a user to accomplish tasks. The communication level is couched in terms of the language and dialogue structures that support the exchange of information between the system and a user. The physical level is the lowest level description and consists of the controls and displays provided. The changes that an adaptive interface can make in order to improve the match it provides to a user can be located in this hierarchy.

19.2.3 Some adaptive systems

A document retrieval system that adapted the search strategy it used in response to ratings by the user of the relevance of an initial set of retrieved documents has been described (Croft, 1984). The changes in the search strategy varied factors such as the number of documents retrieved and how closely they had to match the target specification. This system is on the borderline between user-tailored and self-adaptive systems. The adaption was driven by explicitly given inform-ation but this was related to the specifics of the search indirectly, by means of a machine-learning algorithm. It was believed that most of the users would not have understood the search methods enough to be able to tailor them directly. The same approach would produce a fully self-adaptive system if the evidence used to produce adaption was derived from user actions such as filing or discarding of particular documents.

The GRUNDY book-recommending system (Rich, 1979) demonstrated the use of stereotypes to guide the selection of books that might suit a reader. Readers were assigned a profile of characteristics related to reading preferences. The extent to which books suited these characteristics had been previously analysed. The system listed the books that were the best fit to a user's profile. The user's reactions to the recommendations were used to 'tune' the profile.

The POISE office system (Croft, 1984) used a plan recognition approach to identifying a user's goal when invoking a series of office tools such as a forms package and a mail system. The identified goal was used to provide support in the form of prompting, notification of unexpected actions that may be errors, and so on. Thus, this system used short-term evidence to trigger changes in its interface.

The SUSI system (Smith, 1985) combined evidence about the expertise and experience of the user of an operating system with knowledge about common errors, such as inefficient command sequences, to provide prompting advice and error correction to users. The CONNECT system (Alty, 1984) is a tool for implementing adaptable dialogues. It was used to provide a user interface to a microcomputer operating system that maintained a user model based on previous dialogue with the system and used this to switch the interface between modes that provided differing amounts of user support (e.g. between menus and a command line). The WIZARD intelligent help system (Finin, 1983) recognized inefficient sequences of operating system commands by means of an array of specialized plan recognizers. Each recognizer monitored the user's input for a particular 'bad plan' and triggered the presentation of an appropriate advice message when the command sequence associated with it occurred. The ACTIVIST system (Fischer *et al.*, 1985) used a similar approach to provide help messages to users of a word processing system.

An interface to a menu-based telephone directory that ordered the items in a menu according to the frequency with which they had previously been selected has been described (Greenberg and Witten, 1985). The frequency profile maintained by this system constituted a model of the behaviour of a particular user and the changes to the menus were designed to improve communication without affecting the conceptual or physical interface. This system, and the intelligent help systems described above, used models of the user that are built up over time to direct or trigger changes in the communication interface to their underlying operating or application systems.

Systems that change their physical interface have been less frequently reported. One example was the use of accumulating evidence to change the performance of a speech-operated control interface (Green *et al.*, 1983). The interface used a word recognizer that operated by matching utterances from the user against pre-stored templates of a set of command words. The adaptive system used utterances that matched its templates particularly well to update the templates. Thus, slow drifts in pronunciation were accommodated while the risk of contamination of the templates by updating with mis-recognized words was minimized. Systems that use short-term information to change the surface characteristics of the interface would include mouse controllers that provide the linkage between mouse and display movement. An adaptive mouse controller could detect large movements and speed up the cursor in relation to the mouse for these. This would allow relatively precise small movements without requiring an excessively large work surface on which to move the mouse for the larger movements.

19.3   AN ADAPTIVE INTERFACE FOR ELECTRONIC MAIL

19.3.1   Background

A collaborative team is investigating adaptive user interfaces as part of the UK Alvey Programme for Advanced Information Technology. The system described in this chapter was designed and implemented as part of the first phase of this investigation. Electronic mail was chosen as the 'back-end' system as it was accessible by the team, of commercial interest to the industrial partners, had a large group of users with varying degrees of experience and background and it seemed to be representative of the types of office systems that would benefit from self-adaptive user interfaces. The system incorporates a user model consisting of an initial stereotype updated by evidence collected during dialogue sessions. Adaption takes place at the communication level and primarily affects the amount of prompting and feedback information presented to the user.

19.3.2   Overview of the system

The system mediates between a user and the distant mail system which it accesses via a public communication network. It contains a set of sub-dialogues, each of which elicits the partial specification of a mail sub-task from the user. The sub-tasks used were identified by means of an analysis of user dialogues with the mail system and a top-down analysis of mail based on Command Language Grammar (Moran, 1981; Browne *et al.*, 1986). The grain size of this analysis can be judged from the following examples of sub-tasks: compose a message, send a message, forward a message. Each sub-dialogue is self-contained, in the sense that it does not need to interact with the back-end system at any intermediate point. When a set of sub-dialogues that completely specify a task has been completed, the system executes the task by generating the appropriate dialogue with the distant system. Any unexpected responses from the distant system, typically caused by inter-ference from line noise, are resolved by further interaction with the mail system. The responses are stored in a database ready for passing to the user as required during subsequent sub-tasks.

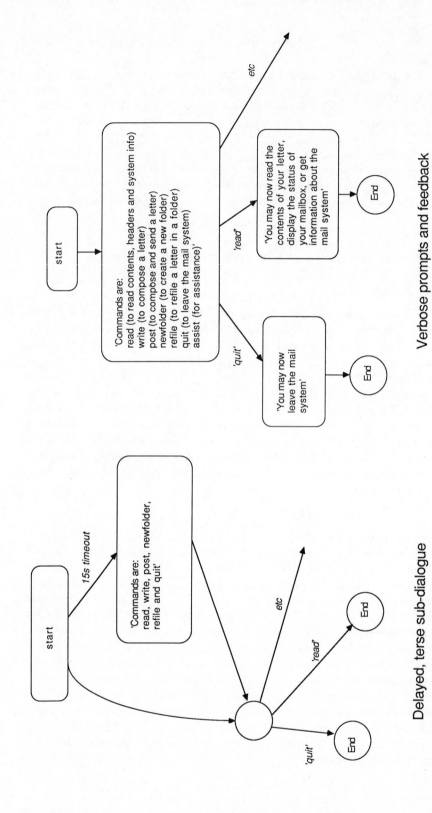

Fig. 19.1. Two examples of sub-dialogues.

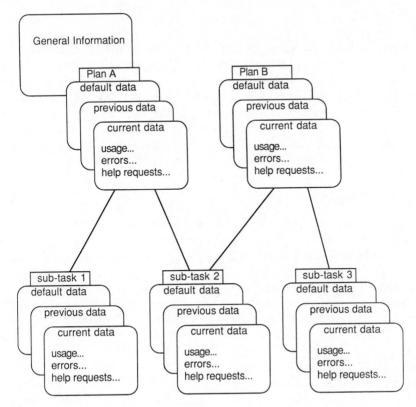

Fig. 19.2. The structure of the user model.

The selection of the next sub-dialogue to be conducted is based on the typical ordering of mail tasks identified during the analysis of mail, but can be overridden by the user typing a command 'out of context'.

Adaption is made possible by the provision of multiple sub-dialogues for each of the sub-tasks. The system has a choice of six sub-dialogues to elicit the specification of each sub-task from a user. These sub-dialogues vary in the amount of guidance information they provide. The networks shown in Fig. 19.1 represent sub-dialogues for the same sub-task with differing amounts of guidance and feedback information.

The process of adaption takes place in two stages. First, dialogue events are used to infer user characteristics which are stored in a user model. Significant events, such as presses of the help key, in each of the sub-dialogues are monitored. Monitored information is passed to a user modelling process which retains it for use in building the user model. When particular combinations of monitored events have occurred an update to the user model is triggered. For example, if a sequence of commands known to achieve a higher-level goal is detected, then the record of the user's usage of that command sequence in the user model is incremented.

Second, at the start of each sub-task, the sub-dialogue to be executed is selected on the basis of the values held in the user model. Data from the current session is used if possible. Data from previous sessions is used if no data has been acquired during the current session. Default data is used if no data based on actual usage is available. Three sub-dialogue selection algorithms have been implemented and can be switched in or out in order to investigate their relative merits. The first algorithm uses error values only, the second uses the average value of errors and help requests, the third uses the maximum value of errors and help requests.

19.3.3   User model

The user model consists of a frame of information about the user's experience with each sub-task and with pre-defined sequences of sub-tasks (plans). For each sub-task and plan, a record of frequency of usage, errors detected and number of presses of the help key, during the current and past dialogues, is maintained. In the absence of evidence from the dialogue, default values are used in the user model. These defaults constitute the initial stereotype model for a user. The structure of the data held in the user model for each user is illustrated in Fig. 19.2.

19.3.4   Implementation

The system has been implemented on Sun workstations. The Rapid/USE dialogue definition and execution tool (Wasserman and Shewmake, 1984) has been used to construct the dialogue control system and the many sub-dialogues. The rest of the system is written in POP11 and Prolog, integrated in the Poplog environment and interfaced to Rapid and the communication network with 'C' processes. The top-level design activity was undertaken by all the partners in the project. The system was then partitioned into the Rapid dialogue description and control module, the 'application expert' module that translates sub-tasks into mail commands and copes with the responses from the mail system and the user modelling module. Each module was implemented, at least in part, on different sites. Then, the whole team was involved in the integration and testing of the system. A simple character-based display terminal is used to 'deliver' the system to users for the purposes of evaluating their performance using it, and its competence at adapting to them.

19.3.5   Evaluation

One of the main objectives of building the system was to conduct a series of evaluation tests on it. Several different types of evaluation have been considered. First, a comparison is planned between the overall performance of people using the adaptive system with control groups using the system with the interface fixed at one of the levels of guidance. The task used in this study will centre on processing the contents of in-trays in a series of role-playing sessions. Performance variables such as time to complete tasks, errors and time spent reading documentation will be monitored. The opinion of users will be assessed by interviews and questionnaires. These studies of users will be complemented by an evaluation of the parts of the system itself. The accuracy of inferences about the user and the value of the adaptions will be assessed by discussing recordings of the dialogues and the underlying changes in the user model, the selection of sub-dialogues, etc. with the user.

In addition to these attempts to gather 'impartial' data about the strengths and weaknesses of the system, the project team will also carry out their own informal evaluations of the system. Initial reactions include the following observations.

- Some of the messages in the dialogues are unclear.
- The system buffers the user from the distant mail system. The system could be used as an interface to a range of alternative mail hosts without imposing any additional learning on the user. On the other hand, a user who is familiar with the back-end system is prevented from making full use of this experience.
- The system response time is variable and can be very long. When the system detects communication problems with the distant mail system it generates a recovery dialogue which increases the time taken to complete a sub-task. The user is unaware of the current state of the interaction with the distant host as the incoming information is stored so that it can be filtered according to the user's requirements later in the dialogue. Hence, the user has to wait passively until the transaction is complete without being able to skim the incoming information, for example.
- The screen has been partitioned into full-width windows to accommodate the prompting, feedback and retrieved mail messages. In some cases, the screen design seems confusing.

19.4   DISCUSSION

The type of system described in this chapter undoubtedly increases the potential for a user interface to be matched to its user. The granularity of the change, and hence the potential 'goodness of fit' with the user is determined by the size of the canned sub-dialogues provided. Ultimately the flexibility of canned dialogues is limited. The generation of the system messages in direct response to a fine-grained model of the user, of the task and of good dialogue style could provide a means of further improving the match between user and system.

One of the key lessons that seems to be emerging from the evaluation of this system is the importance of supporting improvements at higher levels of the user interface with a good quality basic interface. It does not matter how sophisticated the information generated by a system is, if the user has difficulty with the way that information is physically presented, or if the system response time is so great that it interferes with the user's concentration.

The value of recognizing a user's goals and plans when using the system was identified early in the project. Knowledge about what a user is trying to do can allow better guidance and support than would otherwise be possible. However, analysis of dialogue transcripts by human experts suggests that many users tend not to rely on planning to any great extent when interacting with mail, or if they do then the plans are too baroque to be apparent in the dialogue history. The system uses a plan recognition algorithm to guide the selection of the next sub-dialogue and to maintain a record of current unfinished or abandoned plans in the user model. The execution time of the plan recognizer increases the system response time and so some thought is being given to the contribution it makes to the overall performance of the system. An alternative approach is to allow users to specify their goals directly via a menu of possible tasks. The pros and cons of plan recognition will depend on the range and complexity of typical plans, the degree to which users make and use plans during system use and the computational costs of plan recognition.

The design and implementation of the system by a team of partners at different sites posed some significant challenges. Great care was needed to communicate changes that impacted on more than one module, the detailed analysis of mail into sub-tasks for example. The risks of omissions from the specification or in the implementation plans had to be carefully monitored. Most of the evaluation of the system had to await completion and integration of the modules. The next phase of the project, in which it is planned to carry out most of the research, will be organized into a series of parallel streams of relatively fast iterations around the research–design–build–evaluate cycle carried out by smaller groups of people. This change in emphasis reflects the need to encourage exploratory programming (Shiel, 1983), distributed evaluation and the production of a series of demonstration systems rather than the rapid production of a single demonstration system that was a primary aim during the first phase of the project.

19.5 CONCLUSIONS AND FURTHER WORK

The system described in this chapter provides an example of one approach to the implementation of user interfaces that adapt their dialogues according to a model of the user built up from evidence gathered during previous interaction. It has served as a focus for the definition of further research into adaptive systems, to demonstrate the type of system that can be implemented with current technology and as a vehicle for evaluating adaptive systems. The evaluation of the system will continue until a thorough account of its strengths and weaknesses and the reasons behind them have been obtained.

Further work is needed to explore alternative types of user models, methods for deducing user characteristics from ongoing interactions and ways of mapping user model features onto different styles of dialogues. The scope for finer-grained adaption than that provided by the selection of canned sub-dialogues needs to be explored. Further work is also needed to determine the full range of types of adaption that are possible and the circumstances in which the different types improve (or degrade) user performance or opinion.

ACKNOWLEDGEMENTS

I would like to thank the members of the Adaptive Intelligent Dialogues team at Standard Telecommunication Laboratories, Data Logic, Heriot-Watt University, the University of Strathclyde, the University of Essex and British Telecom Research Laboratories for their contributions to the project. The AID project is partly funded by the UK's Alvey Programme for Advanced Information Technology and the Science and Engineering Research Council. Acknowledgement is made to the Director of Research, British Telecom Research Laboratories, for permission to publish this paper.

Rapid/USE was developed jointly by the University of California and the Vrije Universitaet, Amsterdam, Netherlands.

20

Coaching in help systems

JOOST BREUKER
University of Amsterdam, The Netherlands

This chapter focuses on the problem of describing teaching expertise by some generative model. A distinction and some comparisons are made between domain expertise and teaching expertise. This work is being carried out within the context of designing coaching strategies of a help system for UNIX-Mail.

20.1 INTRODUCTION

The EUROHELP project (see also Hartley and Smith, Chapter 21) is aimed at constructing an environment for the development of intelligent help systems. A help system supports the user in a passive and/or active way handling and mastering a particular 'information processing system' (IPS, i.e. a computer system). Heart of this environment will be a shell that contains all domain independent procedures and knowledge. It is assumed that by filling such a shell with an adequate representation of the knowledge required to handle a particular IPS and selecting appropriate instruction strategies specific, add-on help systems can be created effortlessly. In many respects this shell is similar to a shell for intelligent coaching systems, as will become apparent below.

While there is rather an overproduction of shells for 'ordinary' expert systems, there are as yet no shells for intelligent teaching systems (ITS). Originally, expert system shells were constructed by abstracting the domain-independent structures from a particular system (e.g. EMYCIN, CADUCEUS). Such abstraction appears to be much more difficult for ITS than for simple expert systems. One reason is the fact that ITS have in general a more articulate architecture and employ rather heterogeneous formalisms for representing the various types of knowledge required for teaching and coaching, than expert systems do. It is often hard to see in such complex systems what is general and what is domain-specific, particularly because domain and teaching expertise are often some entangled mixture. Aside from the fact that expert systems derived from such flat and uniform shells exhibit a rather narrow sighted view on expertise (Clancey, 1985; Wielinga and Breuker, 1986), an ITS is per definition more complex than an expert system, because it embodies both a domain expert and a teaching expert. Capturing this teaching expertise into some generative model is a major bottleneck in developing an ITS shell, despite decades if not centuries of research into the nature of educational processes (see Ohlsson, 1986).

Although any ITS uses some rudimentary teaching strategy which defines what problems or questions to present to the student, when to interrupt and what to say to the student under what conditions, these strategies are not sufficiently general to be useful within the framework of a shell. In this chapter I will focus on this bottleneck. Of course, I will not be able to present ready-made solutions, but rather discuss a framework for further research, much in line with recent proposals by Ohlsson (1986). Before discussing this framework I will present the context in which this quest for coaching strategies emerged. In Section 20.2, coaching strategies of a help system for UNIX-Mail are described to illustrate the limits of *ad hoc* solutions, in particular when the nature of help systems and the more general characteristics of information processing systems is taken into account (Section 20.3).

20.2   A HELP SYSTEM FOR UNIX-MAIL

In the EUROHELP project a first prototype for a help system was built for the UNIX-Mail system (EUROHELP.P0). UNIX-Mail is an electronic mailing system that allows users to read, send and store messages. There are about 20 different commands available and options can be set to customize this environment. The EUROHELP.P0 system is attached to the normal UNIX (4.2)-Mail system via its normal interface. All communications between user and UNIX-Mail are monitored by the EUROHELP.P0 system. This system is written in LOOPS and Interlisp and runs on a Xerox 1108 (or 1186) connected to a host UNIX system. Only a summary description of the system will be presented here that focuses on coaching strategies; issues related to user modelling, emulation of the actual state of UNIX-Mail during a session, the identification of user plans and performance errors, etc. will not be addressed here (for further details see Breuker, Winkels and Sandberg, 1987).

20.2.1   Performance monitoring and tutor functions

The function of any help system is to provide information about the use of some IPS when needed. The need can be expressed by the user or can be inferred by the help system. The latter is required because many users, in particular novice users, may not be able to express their problems, may not know causes of these, or may not even be aware of their problems. Moreover, the interpretation of questions of the user is supported if not enabled by an interpretation of the performance context. In other words, any adequate help system requires an on-line interpretation of the performance of the user (see also Jones *et al.*, Chapter 14; Zissos and Witten, 1985). In this respect the functionality of help systems that do not 'look over the shoulder of the user' is unacceptably limited for operational use (e.g. UC (Wilensky *et al.*, 1984); AQUA (Quilici *et al.*, 1986)). Of course on-line monitoring and interpreting the performance of the user entails many conceptual and computational problems, but these are not different from those in automated coaching situations in general (e.g. tutoring systems as developed by Anderson and collaborators (Anderson, Boyle and Yost, 1985; Reiser *et al.*, 1985) and by Bonar and Cunningham (Chapter 24)). In EUROHELP.PO the interpretation of questions (or 'user-initiated side') is performed by the Explainer module (see Hartley and Smith, Chapter 21).

The assessment of user needs is accomplished by monitoring her performance. This is called the 'system-initiated side'. A configuration of planning, plan recognition, and diagnostic modules interprets this performance in terms of correctness of actions, adequacy of plans and progress or misconceptions in learning to master UNIX-Mail. This performance interpretation is supported by two data structures. An emulated actual state of UNIX-Mail is updated at every user's action by instantiating its corresponding concept in the domain represent-ation. It registers which message is read, saved, deleted, etc. as can be inferred from the representation of the command that the user has issued. The second instantiated and dynamic data structure is the user model, which reflects the user's progress in skill acquisition, and other user specific data, like preferences for specific forms of help (see below). The user model contains both long term information compiled over sessions, and session specific information. The basic flow of data within this 'performance interpreter' is depicted in Fig. 20.1.

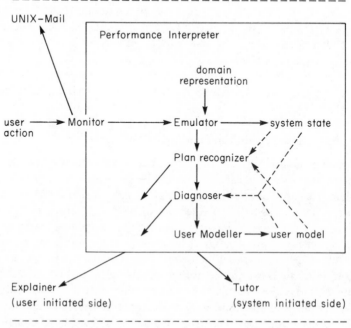

Fig. 20.1. Flow of data in performance interpretation on EUROHELP.PO.

Need	Function
Lack of basic concepts	Initial instruction
Lack of potentially relevant concepts	Expansion
lack of information on correct action	State feedback
Error/misconception	Remedial

Fig. 20.2. User needs and corresponding Tutor functions of EUROHELP.PO.

The result of the performance interpretation is transferred to the Tutor module, if some need or problem has been inferred from the user's performance. Otherwise, only the system state and user model are updated. These needs and the related functions of the Tutor are shown in Fig. 20.2.

The initial instruction consists of an explanation of five UNIX-Mail commands which enable the (novice) user to perform almost all tasks, but often not in the most efficient way. Expansion is aimed at instructing new concepts to enlarge the repertoire of the user when 'genetic precursory' (Goldstein, 1982) skills have been mastered and there is an opportunity for immediate application ('occasion') of the newly acquired concept. The user is interrupted and an expansion is presented by the Tutor. Besides practice – learning by doing – expansions are the driving force towards expertise. Like initial instruction, expansion focuses first on learning by being told. Expansions differ from instruction because they proceed in small steps and the Tutor has a fair understanding of what knowledge and skills have been already acquired, which reduces the likelihood of inducing misconceptions, State feedback describes to the user effects and side-effects of correctly used commands. Many IPS, and UNIX in particular, are not very responsive, which inhibits learning by novice users. As in any coaching system, the identification of errors – and underlying misconceptions – is in principle contingent upon remedial tutorial actions.

20.2.2 Structure of the EUROHELP.PO Tutor

The structure of the Tutor consists of three layers (Woolf and McDonald, 1984). The first layer represents the *didactic goals*. The didactic goals represent what concepts should be taught and in what order. They provide a global control over the tutorial actions. These global goals are by no means a luxury in any help system. Help and advice is offered or requested on the basis of local problems, and apparently simple questions. However, the answers may require long excursions into domains unknown to the user. What will be taught and told to the user is not only dependent on her actual needs and already acquired knowledge and skills, but also on more long term didactic goals. These goals may lead the Tutor to decide whether simple, straightforward advice will be given and/or new concepts will be taught. By giving only advice the Tutor makes no assumptions about learning effects: advices are aimed at immediate task performance. The difference between teaching and advice ('butlering') will be further elaborated in the next section.

The didactic goals for EUROHELP.PO are represented by genetic graphs, as proposed by Goldstein (1982). A genetic graph represents both the order in which concepts are to be learned and the kind of expansion this learning requires with respect to a concept that is already mastered. In the Mail domain and in other command-oriented information-processing systems (i.e. almost all known IPS) there are two types of skills that have to be learned: what commands can do (and when)* and in what way references can be made to objects that are affected by a command. Therefore there are basically two types of genetic graphs. One for learning commands, the other for learning how to refer to objects. Both graphs are associated by specifying what types of objects can be handled by what commands (in which modes).

The next layer of the Tutor is the *strategic* level. At the strategic level decisions are taken as to what to do with information about the performance of the user. In fact, these decisions are for a major part prewired in the structure of EUROHELP.PO. If an error is identified by the Monitor, respectively the Diagnoser, the 'decision' is made to send such data (and control) to the appropriate Remedial strategy. At the strategic level tasks are distributed to various types of strategies, which consist of a sequence of tactics.

At the strategic level there is not only the decision to invoke which strategy, but there is also the previous decision whether to take initiative and to interrupt the user or not. This decision is not only dependent on findings of the performance interpreter, but can also be globally controlled by the user by setting interruption parameters. For instance, the user may state that she only wants to be bothered by EUROHELP.PO in case of a serious error: i.e. the interrupt threshold can be set in accordance with (5) levels of seriousness of error; the highest level being (almost) fatal errors (such as, after delete all, quit without reading any message). Also, the user may always locally suppress actions of EUROHELP.PO because she may say 'no' to the offer of advice that precedes every intervention. The user may have for instance already understood what has gone wrong.

The interrupt functions reflect a style of tutoring. There are two other parameters that set the style of tutoring: the required level of detail and the level of specificity. These are locally controlled by the user: she can opt for more information or more specific tutorial actions, for instance a demonstration of the use of some new concept after it has been described.

---

*This includes the use of such parameters as 'flags' etc. which are used to refer to a special version of a command, i.e. in fact another command.

At the next, *tactical* level the Tutor strategies are specified as sequences of tactics. Tactics are represented by structured text frames, where slots are inserted with the values of objects inferred from the various data structures (emulated state, user model, domain representation). This is similar to the definition of tactics in the Geometry and LISP tutors of Anderson and his collaborators (Anderson, Boyle and Reiser, 1985). The strategies of EUROHELP.PO consist of fixed structures of tactics, which may have some optional branches. Thus, the tactical level of the Tutor is a further refinement of the strategic level, much in the same way as it is proposed. However, the strategic level is not a simple refinement of the didactic level, because it contains a number of additional functions (e.g. the 'style parameters').

20.2.3   A more detailed description of strategy: remedials

Remedials and expansions are the most elaborately structured strategies in EUROHELP.PO. State feedback strategies are relatively simple: the major, and often single, tactic consists of a description that is restricted to the main effect of a command, sometimes followed by a cautionary note that some value (e.g. 'current message') has changed as a side effect. The initial instruction is a traditional CAI program in which tactics are not explicitly represented, but are implicitly similar to those of the expansions. I will discuss here only the remedial strategies.

For each type of error different frames are specified (Breuker and de Greef, 1985a): their common structure can be described as follows:

Announcement signals an interrupt to the user that a (potential) error is made. UNIX-Mail may have done the same in the case of non-executable commands. A side effect is that the user may know that EUROHELP has some more specific information in store, that is applicable to the current situation. If the user has responded 'yes' to the question whether she wants more information, there are two possible continuations.

Explanation. If the error is a non-executable one, an explanation is provided for what reasons the system procedure or the object reference is not executable. The intended effect of this explanation is to have the user focus on the relevant part of the command that provoked the error, and to provide the user with a diagnosis of the actual state (i.e. impasse: cf. Brown and VanLehn, 1980).

Description. If the error is an executable one, the effect of the command typed in is described. The default description is the main effect of the command typed in, but depending on the assumed intentions of the user, one or more of the side effects of the command may be described as well. The intended effect of this tactic is to present the user with explicit feedback on what her actions have accomplished (or might have accomplished: in the case of a potentially fatal error, the help system may have interrupted the execution of the command). A side effect is that EUROHELP has made obvious to the user that it assumes that the effect described may not be the intended one. The user may correct the Tutor and state that the effect was intended.

Correction. Errors are diagnosed with the assumption that the user intended some other action. If this assumption is correct (see above) than a correct command is presented and described to the user. The intended effect is to provide the required information for correct task performance. A side effect is that the user may be reminded of this correct action: i.e. a learning side effect.

Repair. If the command was executable, and not interrupted by help, the Mail system may have gotten into a state that is not intended by the user, and which cannot simply be restored by typing in the correct command. In order to undo the effects of the unintended command, EUROHELP proposes a series of one or more commands to undo this effect. This is also what the intended effect of this tactic is: to present information to restore a previous state. In general, repairs are not intended to provide learning experiences. In many cases the undoing requires actions which are not (yet to be) part of the repertory of the user.

This simple structure of tactics is shown in Fig. 20.3.

The strategies for expansions are structured differently, but some of the tactics overlap. Because the occasion to trigger an expansion is not an error, but the correct use of a command, or a sequence of commands (plan), there is no need for diagnostic explanations or descriptions. The occasions for expansions provide an appropriate context for applying an issue that is introduced by an expansion, but there is no necessity to apply it immediately, because the (series) of command(s) has (have) been executed already when an expansion is started. This rather 'detached' way of providing help may be typical for the UNIX-Mail domain, where the difference between planning efficient and less efficient courses of actions is not so much dependent on the types of tasks that can be performed, but rather on the content of the messages. The Mail domain is 'flat', and does not involve much planning by the user, so that efficient and less efficient courses of action (plans) are difficult to recognize, let alone to foresee. If courses of action can

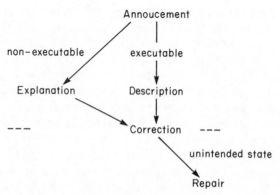

Fig. 20.3. Structure of remedial tactics in EUROHELP.PO

be foreseen, expansions may be triggered, *before* a relatively inefficient course of action is executed. Such will also enhance the learning effect.

Although the Tutor strategies and tactics described above reflect the state of the art with respect to current ITS the solutions appear not to be satisfactory. To be sure, users may benefit from the help provided (Hartley and Smith, Chapter 21), but this is not entirely due to the intelligence of the Tutor. The Tutor is in fact a very shallow sub-system. The major burden of intelligence lies in the performance interpreter. At first sight this may appear correct (see e.g. Woodroffe, Chapter 13), but there are at least two reasons to foresee problems. The first reason is that the Tutor is not sufficiently generative: although the tactics can be described at a more abstract level, there is no 'grounding' theory to justify their adequacy. The second reason is probably more important. The strategies are embodied in some fixed sequences of tactics with some branching, but it is certain that in more complex domains than UNIX-Mail a larger variety is required. Not only a larger variety, but also a more flexible variety that allows for more veridical interactions between user and help system. This issue will be further explored after discussing the functions of help systems in general.

20.3 FUNCTIONS OF HELP SYSTEMS AND THE IPS WORLD

In all respects EUROHELP.PO is a complete coaching system that allows for mixed initiatives from user and system (see also Fischer *et al.*, 1985). Because domain expertise is available in the form of plans related to tasks, EUROHELP.PO is in principle capable of performing the tasks by itself instead of informing the user. Gearing EUROHELP.PO as a butler may simplify the life of the novice user of UNIX-Mail, who can simply type in or select task or goal descriptions to obtain the intended effects. It may also make things easier for the designers of the help system, because to issue a command appears to be easier than to instruct and explain it. In a butler there is no need for teaching expertise. However, there are good reasons to prefer information-providing, and if possible teaching, to butlering.

The first reason is a very practical one. A butler is an interface; a help system is an add-on. Even if it is possible to tamper with an existing target system (IPS), designing a new interface may have very profound effects on the complete system (Moran, 1981). Given the foreseen facilities of the EUROHELP environment, it will often be easier to construct an add-on help system for it, than to redesign the IPS.

There may be other, more fundamental reasons to opt for add-on help systems that look over the shoulder of the user instead of butlering her. A complete butler will hide the underlying IPS. It will prevent the user from acquiring an adequate model of this IPS. The initial overgeneralization of the intelligence of the butler will be replaced by too narrow a view of the functions the IPS may perform; the butler will only perform passively, but will not provide a guided tour through the IPS.

The construction of user friendly and 'intelligent' interfaces for modern software is often thought to make help systems superfluous. In this context, a butler may be viewed as an extreme solution for user friendliness. However, if user friendliness simply means attributing human-like and real-world-like properties to an IPS (e.g. in the form of metaphors or intelligence), such an enterprise is often misguided. A man–machine interface is not intended to hide a machine, but to bridge the user's world and the system's world. The system's world is a world of its own. It may be modelled after a set of tasks and functions that exist in the real world*, but it also has attributes of its own, that create exactly new tasks in an electronic world, in a similar way as television or cars have created new realities. The typewriter has become a bad metaphor for a text editor (Card *et al.*, 1983); a desk top for an operating system; a post office for an electronic mail system (Camstra, 1985).

Although metaphors provide novice users with powerful means to acquire an initial model of a system, such a model should rather be viewed as a 'functional bug' that should be repaired by further experience and insight. Also in EUROHELP.PO a metaphor is available for novice users (ROCONET). Thus help can be provided both in terms of this metaphor, or in terms of UNIX jargon. This metaphor is as artefactual as an IPS, consisting of a world of robots with 'well-defined' attributes. In this way inheritance of irrelevant attributes of a real-world model can be avoided.

Whether real or artefactual, metaphors are advantageous for computer naive users, but they often become a nuisance to more experienced users, who want to have a more direct access to the machinery and be able to transfer their skills to other IPS to which the metaphor may not be applicable. Jargon, i.e. the domain terminology, gives access to new concepts and thus to transfer of skills. Therefore, a more long-term view on initiating users to IPS rather advocates user friendliness in the form of interfaces that do not hide, but that reflect the 'essential' working of an IPS (Moran, 1981; Croft, 1984). A solution which may make help systems obsolete in the future may be metaphor-based systems, in which the metaphor fades away with experience of the user to be replaced by a more direct access, adult interface. However, the process of fading out and supporting the acquisition of the new world is exactly what a complete help system aims at, and this can only be accomplished by monitoring the progress and failures of the user in performing tasks with the IPS. In other words, such IPS would have a help system that is integrated with the user interface. Therefore prospective EUROHELP environment supports the construction of both such integrated interfaces, and of add-on help systems.

20.3.1 The system's world: what's in an IPS?

A description of what should be acquired by the user is a very fundamental issue in a help system, or in any ITS. Which expertise should be the model to be

---

*Of course, the system's world is as real as any other world (see further); this is only a conventional way of speaking.

acquired? The domain expertise in help systems for using IPS should be easier to define than in ITS for 'real-world' domains like medicine, geometry, etc., because an IPS forms a closed world and is, in principle, completely defined in the form of code, machinery etc. However, we do not want to teach the user code or other low-level technical descriptions. The user should understand so much from the IPS that she can perform the tasks the system is designed for, or a subset of these tasks that map onto the goals of the user. This implies a lot of knowledge. It is a fallacy that the user of an IPS can be as ignorant about such objects as files, editing buffers, as a car driver about a carburettor. Moreover, driving a car without having any idea what's under the bonnet does not mean that the driver should not have some functional model that relates clutch, gears, speedo-meter, petrol reserve indicator, steering wheel, etc. which is in many respects not self evident. Therefore, the description of an IPS – i.e. the domain representation – should be at the right, conceptual level (Norman, 1983). But what is this level, and what should be the ingredients of such a conceptual model?

This is partly a design issue, in particular in selecting a formalism, but it is in the first place an empirical question. How do experts view, for instance, UNIX-Mail or the Vi-editor? The answer is not simple (van de Brink *et al.*, 1986). As also pointed out by Ohlsson (1986), expertise may have many adequate forms. The models of expertise may map onto the same problems and solutions, but may have completely different structures. As long as the expertise covers what the user is aiming for (in however long a term) any of these models may do. But the expert's knowledge is also incomplete. For instance, only experts who have worried about the underlying code of the ⟨return⟩ command in UNIX-Mail (i.e. for 'showing the next message') know about its bizarre control structure: at the functional, or conceptual level expert users have a (pseudo) consistent picture of the effects of such commands; only under exceptional conditions this picture appears to be inadequate. Such apparent conflicts are not necessarily resolved by attributing a more complex structure to some command, but may also be put on the list of 'exceptional behaviour'. Sometimes such an exception list is perfectly justified, because it reflects a bug rather than a feature of an IPS, i.e. there is a discrepancy between the 'obvious' functionality and the actual code. This means that expertise in using an IPS may be based to some extent on heuristic instead of precise, deep model knowledge.

This is exactly the dilemma in designing the knowledge base (domain representation) of a help system for some IPS. In its most veridical and accurate form it is the source code of IPS, but that leaves its functionality implicit. It seems that gains in functional comprehensibility quickly diminish (or may even turn into losses) by adding more accurate details to the description of the system. This problem is also known from its other side: in designing and implementing an IPS. Moreover, the same problem occurs in qualitative reasoning, where a qualitative conceptual model may capture *human* understanding of some device better than its quantitative version, but is less accurate and may even be wrong under some extreme conditions (Kuipers, 1985). A solution is to have various levels of detail and abstraction in the model of expertise. At the higher, functional level default reasoning occurs, while the more detailed level may explain conflicts between functional expectations of the user and the actual behaviour of the IPS.

20.3.1.1   *Conceptual model: the task level*

Moran (1981; see also Card *et al.*, 1983) proposes two levels of description of a conceptual model of an IPS: the task and the semantic level. The highest level is the task level, which describes the IPS in functional terms; it mediates between the user world and the system world. The task level is a hierarchy of tasks and subtasks*. The descriptions at the highest layers form the access to understanding what the system can do for the user. For instance, an electronic mail system may be described as: enabling to send, receive, read and store messages. Which tasks are involved in, for instance, sending a message is defined at lower layers. Such task-decomposition should terminate in the unitary operations the IPS can perform (i.e. the commands). This is where the next level starts: the semantic level. Before going into more detail of what is in the semantic level we should have a closer look at what the task level is made of, the more because the domain representation in EUROHELP.PO is similarly structured. The task level is not given: it has to be abstracted from the documentation of an IPS and from expert users. If the commands of an IPS are viewed as the terminal elements of such a task hierarchy, it seems logical that a large variety of structures can be built upon it. This can be illustrated by comparing two different task structures for 'sending messages' (Fig. 20.4).

Aside from terminology, the left-hand structure corresponds to the 'normal' course of action in using, for instance, UNIX-Mail. In fact, it is built in UNIX-Mail as a fixed script (see below). The right-hand structure is not only a possible alternative, but also better reflects naive, or real-world conceptions of sending messages: first, writing the content, then the sending-off procedure. Functionally, creating content in the electronic world is performed by using an editor. Task structures may differ in efficiency, but this may also be dependent on the point of view. The left-hand task structure is efficient from the system's point of view, while the other structure corresponds more with 'cognitive economy'. The main point is not that one is better than the other, or better for different users, but that there may be so many (good ones) that it makes no sense to enumerate all these. This is particularly true, because slight changes in conditions may have strong effects on the efficiency of a task structure. For instance, if one has to write a large number of small messages the left-hand task structure in Fig. 20.4 is certainly

---

*The task level maps onto the semantic level where the actions (commands) of the IPS are defined. It is somewhat surprising that a similar mapping between objects is not considered. For instance, the system definition of the object 'word' is different from what in the 'real world' is considered to be a word: New-York is one word; New York is two words for the machine. Brachman (1978) calls these real world conceptions which do not correspond to system objects pseudo-objects (see also Duursma *et al.*, 1986).

send (message)	send (message)
open (send_mail)	type (message)
type (username)	open (editor; new_file)
type (subject)	insert (text)
type (message)	*correct (text)
*correct (message)	save (new_file)
open (editor), etc.	quit (editor)
*read_in (file)	address (message)
close (message)	open (send_mail), etc.
	read_in (new_file)
	close (message)
close (send_mail)	close (send_mail)

Fig. 20.4. Two task structures for sending electronic mail (between ( ) = goal, or object; * = optional).

more efficient than the right-hand structure. Each task structure is a plan to accomplish a global goal. An experienced user is able to *plan* her course of action in a flexible way by considering on one hand her global goals, and on the other hand the means, i.e. the effects of commands available in an IPS, which is described at the semantic level.

Does this mean that the task level is superfluous? In some sense, it is. It is always possible to achieve a solution by bottom-up planning, but it seems more reasonable that there are semi-fixed structures available for stereotypical or for efficient, expert plans. Therefore, tasks structures can be viewed as 'skeletal plans' (Friedland and Iwasaki, 1985), or 'plan methods' (Genesereth, 1982) that allow for top-down planning (see also Jones *et al.*, this volume). A task level in the representation of an IPS can be replaced by a more flexible planner which uses the commands itself as building stones (i.e. the semantic level), but for computational and didactic reasons the availability of such fixed structures can be quite useful. They represent established skills in handling an IPS*.

20.3.1.2   *Conceptual model: the semantic level*

At the semantic level there is an undeniable need of the user to understand what commands can accomplish. The semantic level is the core of the conceptual model. Several examples of representations of IPS, in particular electronic mail systems and editors, at the semantic level are available (Brachman, 1978 Ch. 7; Moran, 1981; Duursma *et al.*, 1986). The structuring elements of the semantic

*The task level in Moran's (1981) article has been specified to allow for top-down designing of the interface of an IPS ('command language grammar'). Here we are discussing the problem of recognizing the functionality of a system and task planning. Of course, a careful top-down design will facilitate recognition of functionality and constrain the construction of efficient plans. That is exactly what a man–machine interface is for, besides providing feedback on the current state of the system.

level, i.e. the epistemology (Brachman, 1979), of an IPS can be described as follows.

In any IPS there is a distinction between objects and actions that can be applied to these objects. A pivotal type of object is an information 'container'. The most well-known instances of these objects are: files, records, buffers, screens, directories, messages, etc. A generic definition of an action is that it changes the state of an object. A state consists of an object, an attribute and a specific value. A change of state involves an antecedent state and a consequent state. A change of state can be, for instance, the change of the value of an attribute of an object. The consequent state is called: the effect of an action. There can be more to the definition of action, in particular the role of actors, but this is of less importance. In an IPS the actor is the command interpreter. This definition of actions is not new (e.g. Schank, 1975).

Before discussing classes of actions that can be performed with an IPS, I will first define the major objects: the containers of information. In fact, it may be hard to find other objects in an IPS which are not containers of information. These containers of information can be related via 'part_of' hierarchies. For instance:

> directory
> > file
> > > record
> > > > string_of_characters
> > > > > character

This hierarchy is not exhaustive or even generic. Any IPS may have a specific organization of containers. For instance, UNIX-Mail does not know about records, it knows about messages. There may be containers of a temporary nature like 'buffer', 'screen' and 'device'. Within each level of the hierarchy, the containers may be organized in various ways (cf. database systems, where containers may have all sorts of cross references and relations). Such hierarchies should bottom out in primitive objects (e.g. character), where all higher-order objects are in fact compound objects (Duursma *et al.*, 1986).

In the same way as some instance of an information container (e.g. file) is the current (often default) object of actions, a current position in some hierarchy of containers forms the *environment* (see also *marker* below). The higher one is in this hierarchy, the wider the scope of the environment, and the less accessible is specific information.

An environment may consist of many more types of objects. For instance, the environment of an editor may encompass also structures of buffers, a particular screen definition, etc. An environment belongs to an IPS or to a mode (sub-program) in an IPS. Environment and mode are two different, but closely related concepts. Mode refers to the set of actions that can be performed within some subset of an IPS. In general, a mode presupposes, specifies or creates some environment.

Containers have attributes. A class of attributes are *identifiers*. An IPS should be able to identify every instance of an object, e.g. a particular file. In general, such identification is performed either 'by-name' or by referencing to some value of another attribute. Besides reference-by-name, an IPS may have several other object referencing procedures, which have a strong similarity to actions that affect information containing objects. Many commands (system procedures) have object referencing procedures as side effects or defaults. The pragmatic criterion for object reference procedures is that the values of the attributes should be sufficiently distinctive, which may involve the use of attributes which are not identifiers. Besides name-of attributes there is another type of congenial identifier, which is called a *marker*. A marker is a dynamic identifier, referring to a particular, 'current' object. A good example is the cursor position which attributes the 'current' value to some character on the screen.

Other attributes are *parameters**. Parameters indicate states of objects. A file may have a parameter for the number of lines or characters, its version, or its date of last update. Some parameters, like number of lines, characters, etc. can be deduced from or are constrained by the 'part_of' hierarchy of their objects, i.e. their values are the sum totals, or conjunctions of those of the components. A third type of attribute of information-containing-objects is *option*. For instance, read, or write protections for files. These attributes may modify the way an object will be affected by a system action. In general, options have an all or nothing character: either the action applies or not. The wrap-margin attribute (option) of the screen of an editor is an example of a multi-valued option.

As stated above, actions are changes of state of some object, and the new state is called *effect*. Classes of actions can be characterized by the effect they have on an object. Figure 20.5 shows a tentative hierarchical list of such generic actions (and their inverse actions, if relevant) with some typical examples. This list is not meant to be exhaustive. Further research is needed to investigate whether this list is sufficiently distinctive and complete. The objects specified between brackets are abbreviations of state descriptions (effects). A state may have only one object: it asserts then that an object exists, i.e. has been created. The second object in the effect description refers to the type of value (value restriction) of the first object.

Note that the classification of some effect may appear to depend on some point of view. For instance, inserting characters in a file is at the character level an act of creation; at the file level it can be viewed as a compose action, in which characters are added to a file. This apparent conflict can be solved by assuming that inserting a character is in fact a composed action (see below): first a character is created, then it is added to the file (and to the screen)[†].

In an IPS several actions are combined into one *system procedure*, which is syntactically the action part of a command. Inserting a character in an edit file is an example of a system procedure. It is a combination of actions. A system

---

*The use of the word 'parameter' here should not be confounded with the purely syntactic use of parameters in a command expression.
[†]In fact the definition of environment implies that whatever is created is added on to the embedding environment: a character created is added on to the current file-environment; a file created is added on to the current directory.

---

initialize (object)
    open/close (i.c.)
    create/delete (i.c.)
    enter/leave (mode)
    start/kill (process)

transfer (object, location)
    compose/decompose (i.c.1, i.c.2)
    position/return (marking-object, location (list, matrix))
    move (i.c., object)
        store (i.c., device)
        show (i.c., screen, printer)

modify (object1, object2)
    change (object, value)
    restructure (i.c.1, i.c.2)

Fig. 20.5. Generic IPS actions, (between ( ) indicate effects; i.e. = information container).

procedure has a control structure, which is often a straightforward sequence of actions. The control structure is of secondary importance to the effects, as expert descriptions and task performance show. The execution of a system procedure may affect more than one object of various types. For instance, in using the UNIX-Mail command 'delete', a message is deleted and the current message pointer is set to the next one (or EOT). Effects of system procedures can be categorized into *intended* (or: main) and *side* effects (see also Brachman, 1978). This distinction is only of pragmatic relevance. The designer of the IPS often assumes that the user will make such distinctions as well. The names of many commands refer only to the intended effects. For expert users such distinctions may be less relevant, and they may use side effects as intended effect. Often, the expert sees the execution of a system procedure as a parallel process; not as a succession of actions. A system procedure, if well designed, therefore exhibits some coherent behaviour, even if it has multiple effects.

The system procedures (commands') themselves can be structured. In a 'script' the sequence of system procedures is fixed and may involve a fixed interaction scenario with the user. *Mode* differs from a script in that the sequence of system procedures is not fixed. Having entered a mode, the user is free to choose whichever system procedures to perform (if applicable). Modes may be entered from higher level modes. Therefore, modes form embedding hierarchies, rather than part_of hierarchies.

20.3.1.3   *What more is there to an IPS?*

The acquisition of the conceptual model of an IPS is certainly the major problem in learning to handle an IPS. The more extensive and complex an IPS, the longer it may take to learn. There are characteristics of an IPS other than the complexity of the conceptual model that influence this learning process. These are related to the more external aspects of the interface: the syntax, and the interaction (see also Moran, 1981). The learnability is enhanced when the syntax easily maps onto semantic distinctions and is in itself simple. More importantly for speed of learning are the communication aspects. The more visible the effects, i.e. the more feedback is given by the IPS, the faster the learning. Talkative systems may however become a nuisance to more experienced users who do not want their screens cluttered all the time with 'self-evident' information. Therefore, similar to metaphors for IPS, feedback information should fade out with experience (such as is implemented to EUROHELP.PO). Another communication distinction is whether the user specifies a command, or selects it from a menu. Menu selection provides a memory aid and exploration hints, and it minimizes typing/syntax errors. However, menus entail often unnatural mode boundaries because the number of items within one menu is restricted. Trees of menus may impede access. Finally, the content of menus is often very heterogeneous and does not allow for flexible combinations of system procedures and objects. Again, menus are often a good support for the novice user, but may become counter-effective to the experienced user.

This summarizes the know-how that is involved in expertise in handling an IPS. In the next section I will discuss the expertise that is required for teaching these concepts via an intelligent help (teaching) system.

20.4　TEACHING EXPERTISE: STRATEGIES AND TACTICS

The distinction between semantic level and task level in expertise for handling an IPS is quite similar to the distinction between tactics and strategies in expertise for teaching. Wielinga and Breuker (1986) have recently proposed a four-layered, generic model of expertise, in which both these types of expertise (using an IPS; teaching) will easily fit. In both cases it appears that the required flexibility can be obtained by assuming at the highest (meta-)level a strategic reasoning level. Before discussing this strategic level in more detail, and also other similarities at the lower level between system procedures and tactics and their roles, I will first review functions and problems in defining teaching strategies in ITS.

20.4.1　In quest of teaching strategies

Although the EUROHELP.PO Tutor is rather shallow, in particular at the strategic level, it appears that better solutions are not easily available. I will present a short review of what the literature, especially on intelligent coaching systems, has to say about strategies, and discuss some empirical studies that have been recently performed.

There is a general agreement about the major functions that a teaching or coaching strategy should provide (see Miller, 1982, p. 132; Burton and Brown, 1982, p. 80; Brown, Burton and de Kleer, 1982, p. 228; Clancey, 1982, p. 209; Kimball, 1982, p. 296; Goldstein, 1982, p. 66; Stevens and Collins, 1977):

1. When to interrupt? What are good reasons to interrupt the user's task performance or course of reasoning or knowledge acquisition? In EUROHELP.PO this is a function of the outcome of performance interpretation (e.g. diagnosis) and the 'interruption parameters'.

2. What to say? Here authors are more diverse in further specification of this function. A plausible combination is probably the following.

2.1. Topic selection: about what should the system have a dialogue with the user? Topic selection is in the first place guided by the interpretation of actual problems or needs of the user, but for didactic reasons such initial topic selection may have to be extended, or modified.

2.2. Topic ordering: when to say what. If there is more than one topic, the order of introducing/discussing these should be determined. This is called the 'linearization problem' in discourse (Levelt, 1981). The order may be given by the domain representation, teaching goals, and context dependency of tactics (e.g. in a remedial, the error should be explained, before a correction is presented). The selection and ordering of topics may involve careful planning in which the partner's state of mind ('user model') is a very important constraint, as studies about topic selection and expression in normal discourse reveal (e.g. Reichman, 1978; Hobbs and Evans, 1980; Smith, 1982). In EUROHELP.PO this is partly controlled by the user, who may ask for more detailed information ('zooming'), or may change topic by addressing the Explainer with a question.

2.3. How to say it? This is surely the hardest nut to crack. Although almost all the authors referred to above explicitly mention this function as part of coaching strategies, there are hardly any general solutions, and many authors blame this on a paucity of pedagogical theories that are sufficiently detailed (e.g. Miller, 1982, p. 132; Ohlsson, 1986). Often, a number of rules are defined, but a non-*ad hoc* justification is lacking. The 'how to say it' is dependent on 1. what topics are selected and ordered, and on 2. expectancies about how the user will interpret some type of expression (tactic): I will call this the intended effect of a tactic. Topics are selected with an intended effect in mind: e.g. a correction should contain one or more concepts that are correct within the current context (of task performance). In other words, what to say and how to say it are not independent. This interdependency can only be resolved at the strategic level. Probably with the exception of the WHY Tutor (Stevens and Collins, 1977) and the MENO Tutor (Woolf and Donaldson, 1984) no ITS system contains such a framework.

Another source of information on teaching and coaching strategies is educational psychology. Up till now, we have not found much interesting information about teaching and coaching strategies. Reviews confirm the suspicion that the literature talks about global approaches (paradigms) in education (e.g. mastery learning, discovery learning, etc.), rather than supplying information that relates to the questions put forward above (e.g. Kamsteeg, 1984). Ohlsson (1986) comes to a similar conclusion. This may be due to the fact that the paradigms proposed and investigated in educational psychology are not sufficiently detailed for computer implementation, but are easily understood by humans, i.e. teachers, educational researchers, students, etc. They can fill in the self-evident parts. A closer look may reveal puzzles, in the same way as, for instance, the control of human discourse is still a major puzzle.

Such a closer look may be obtained by analysing the interaction and thinking aloud protocols of human coaches and IPS users, who communicate via terminals. For instance, Bison and van der Pal (1985) investigated various types of users of UNIX-Mail, who were monitored and coached by experienced users who acted as tutors. Although this study provided many empirical data about misconceptions and the diagnosis of misconceptions, it appeared to be very difficult to come to grips with the teaching aspects. Tutors varied considerably in their strategies and tactics, and had difficulty in their motivation for choosing a particular course of action. Telling that something had gone wrong and proposing a better solution seemed as natural as normal discourse. However, a follow up study on the use of the UNIX Vi-editor is now being undertaken, and has revealed two things that may account for the disappointing results of the earlier study (Sandberg *et al.*, 1987). First, experienced users are not necessarily good teachers, which shows that teaching is not 'just discourse' but also includes specific expertise. Although the experienced tutors had to improvise often, and had difficulty in 'how to say it', they had less problems in 'what to say', because they had consistent plans, sometimes even very explicit ones. Secondly, it appears that there is such variety of expression that an *a priori* model is required to interpret the data. The role of interpretation models in analysing expertise is explained elsewhere (Breuker and Wielinga, 1987). This article describes the motivations and major ingredients of such an interpretation model. Its empirical validity will be tested as part of the EUROHELP project.

Up till now the concept of strategy itself has hardly been discussed. A strategy is a plan of actions to achieve goals. In the context of a help or coaching system there are in fact two types of goals: there are *learning* (or didactic) goals which are related to knowledge and skill acquisition, and there are *performance* goals which are related to achieving the goals the user has in using some IPS. At first sight these types of goals are not incompatible, because achieving one type may have as a side effect achieving, or facilitating, the other one. The *scope* of these two types of goals is in general different. Learning goals are long-term goals, extending over sessions; task performance goals are short-term ones, often within the scope of one session (the duration of a session is determined by the task performance goals). The strategies to achieve these two types of goals may be different. In the next paragraphs I will not talk about help or coaching systems, but about what it means to support task performance, and what it means to support learning. In a help system both goals should be integrated, but they will be viewed separately first.

20.4.1.1 *Process structures of task performance and teaching*

Task performance can be summarized in a very stylistic way as consisting of the following types of tasks. First, given one or more goals, a plan is conceived. This plan is executed, which leads to behaviour of the IPS, that is interpreted by the user who monitors the state of the system and/or the state of his knowledge with respect to discrepancies with the plan (goals). A discrepancy may consist of an unintended state of the system or lack of immediately available knowledge about how to proceed further. If still on the right track, the user executes the next tasks (system procedures). The result of the monitoring process is essentially a 'go on'/'stop' decision; stop means that a discrepancy has been observed, or that the plan has been successfully executed. If the discrepancy is unacceptable, and needs further interpretation diagnostic activities are started. This may result in the identification of one or more causes or fault classes (wrong command typed in; lack of knowledge about side effects of a system procedure; reference to non existing objects, etc.). Given a cause, there may be some 'therapy' or remedy associated with it: for instance, a correct command. The remedy can then be executed. However, the remedy may not always be executable immediately, because the actual state of the system does not allow for this. Or some values of the actual state may be undesirable. Or no remedy is directly available. Or the fault cannot be identified to such extent that a remedy is available. In summary, there may be so many reasons for failure of the original plan that these outcomes may lead to new planning activities: plans to undo undesired states; plans to ask for help, consult manuals, etc; plans that circumvent the actual problem (e.g. sending mail by moving a file to the main directory of another user), etc. This structure of tasks is illustrated in Fig. 20.6.

Supporting such task performance may consist of supporting or automating one or more of these tasks. The simplest example is providing feedback about the new state of the system after a command has been issued. This facilitates the identification of the state of the system when the execution of a plan is monitored. The other extreme of full automation consists of a butler, who presented with

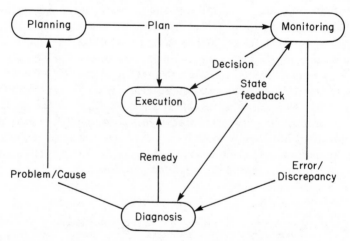

Fig. 20.6. Structure of tasks and objects in IPS task performance.

real-world goals will do the whole job. As stated earlier, an adequate help system should have a full butlering competence, i.e. should contain a full domain expertise, so that user plans can be recognized. This enables, for instance, non-trivial diagnosis. If user plans or goals cannot be inferred, support can only be provided from an 'IPS point of view', and the only problems are non-executable commands. Therefore, it appears that a *perfect* help system must have the competences of a butler. A (perfect) butler may not make errors, therefore monitoring may not be part of its function, but the butler has at least to figure out whether the goals of the user are feasible. This may involve some diagnostic activities, but of a different type to those of a help system.

The process structure of *teaching* is strongly similar to the process structure of task performance (support). The teacher has a structure of goals in mind. In general such goals are fixed, although they may be rather implicit in even most of the formal teaching situations. Therefore, teaching goals can be represented by some fixed structure, like a genetic graph. In coaching, where the system presents problems to a student and monitors her performance, the teaching becomes 'case-driven'. It is dependent on the particular case presented, so that goals are not completely fixed in advance, but have to be generated (e.g. in GUIDON, Clancey, 1982). However, each particular case that is presented to the student is selected as an instance of some subset of teaching goals. In 'occasion-driven' teaching, such as occurs in help systems, the selection of cases is outside the control of the teacher. This does not prevent the existence and use of goal structures, if only to assess what goals can be projected onto a case and to assess progress in learning.

The teaching goals are translated by some planning process into plans of action i.e. into strategies. In a pure teaching situation, where the user is a student and has no other goals than to learn (about an IPS), the strategy is executed by successively applying tactics. The learning 'state' is monitored by observing behaviour that may have been elicited for this purpose. This elicitation of to-be-monitored behaviour is exactly the driving force behind Socratic teaching (Stevens and Collins, 1977). Socratic dialogues are one of the few examples of a fully specified strategy with detailed and rich variations in tactics, but they are little suited for help systems, in which the interaction between user and help system must be kept minimal in order not to interfere too much with the user's performance goals. The major monitoring is via performance interpretation.

If errors occur, the underlying misconceptions may be diagnosed. In the case of simple misconceptions, a standard remedy may be presented, but the deeper the misunderstanding, the more likely that the teaching strategy has to be adapted to cope with this problem situation or, even, problem student. The structure of tasks and objects is shown in Fig. 20.7. Note that the structure is identical to that for task performance, except for the specific names of some of the objects.

We come now to the problem of how to conceive strategies in help systems. As stated earlier, a strategy is a plan. A fully specified plan consists of some hierarchical structure, whose terminal elements form a series of successively executable actions. This view of the construction of a plan is analogous to

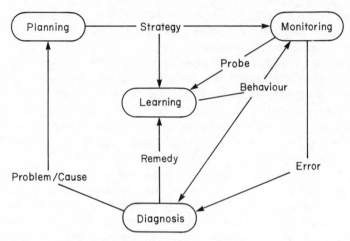

Fig. 20.7. Structure of tasks and objects in teaching.

syntactic sentence generation, where syntactic structures are generated with words as terminal elements. However, many plans are not fully worked out before execution starts. There are various reasons. The first reason is limitations in processing capacities. Once a global structure has been conceived, the detailed sub-plans may be generated, respectively forgotten at the appropriate moments. A second reason for not working out plans in full detail is that the 'execution' is not fully determined by the actions that are specified in the plan. There are uncontrollable or unknown factors. For handling an IPS and with complete knowledge about an IPS the actions – system procedures – are fully determined, except for such uncontrollable and unknown factors as slips and content dependency. The latter refers to the fact that the content of the information of an IPS may determine actions as well (e.g. when a reply to a message is required in using electronic mail). In teaching, a very important additional problem is the fact that the effects of actions are not fully predictable, because the 'interpreter' – the student's mind in general and in particular – is only very partially known. Effects are assumed or hypothesized. In an IPS the effect of each action is fully determined in system terms.

In an occasion-driven domain the uncontrollability of conditions for executing some action is so dominant that even at the macro level hardly any structure can be found. This is what has happened to the strategic level of the EUROHELP.PO Tutor. Its structure consists of a basic instruction, followed by a small list of conditioned classes of (sub-)strategies, which are occasion-dependent. However, in the long run the undeterministic nature of the domain may become more and more constrained. This is what a strategy is about. It differs from plans in general because it is aiming at gaining control by taking opportunities to establish states, which may function as conquered territory. The classical example of strategy is a military strategy. The undeterministic factor is the enemy: its unpredictability is even maximized by the fact that the enemy uses strategies as well, so that the process becomes a complex, probably even never ending, recursive application of planning and counter-planning.

This suggests that occasion-driven strategies as in help systems should not be fixed too much in advance, but developed over time on the basis of the experiences the system has had with a specific user. If strategies develop over time and their development becomes occasion-dependent, help systems (and probably most coaching systems) may need a planning component to generate strategies, rather than have strategies prewired. Because at the global levels, which are ultimately connected to the fixed didactic goals, the strategies may more or less be fixed, it seems likely that some top-down planning method may do the job, e.g. in the form of skeletal plans (Friedland and Iwasaki, 1985). Skeletal plans may contain options, that refer to sub-plans or that bottom out in specific tactics, that can be inserted to adapt the strategy in a generative way.

There is another important reason why the coaching strategy of a help system should be dynamic, rather than static and fixed. As opposed to system procedures, the effects of tactics are context dependent. Therefore, it seems unlikely that full sequences of tactics can be fixed in advance to perform some function at the strategic level: i.e. act as some ready made sub-plan that can be inserted into the macro plan if the circumstances (occasion) requires. The solution in EUROHELP.PO to have the sequence of tactics completely prewired is certainly too *ad hoc* to incorporate into a help systems shell. Therefore, it seems that the strategic level of a help coaching and teaching strategy should rather be a planning component which may assemble at the detailed level the tactics in such a way that the assumed intended effects are the most effective ones in the given context. The building stones, or terminal elements, of such a planner are the teaching tactics. A coaching strategy planner based upon these principles has been constructed, which generates discourse that is surprisingly similar to the advice of human coaches for the same user problems (Breuker *et al.*, 1987; Winkels, 1987).

20.4.2 Tactics in teaching

Tactics form the 'semantic level' of teaching expertise. Similar to system procedures, which can be characterized by their effects, tactics can be classified according to their effects, which may be intended or side effects. The differences between intended and side effects are context-dependent: within some other context, or with other global goals side and intended effects may be reversed. A good example is the use of two tactics which present a description in the remedial strategies of EUROHELP.PO (see Section 20.2). The text frames of both *description* and *correction* tactics are the same: they present the effect(s) of a system procedure. However, their functions (intended effects) differ. The description of the executable, but not intended, system procedure is a diagnosis; the description of the correct command is a remedy or solution. In this respect, tactics differ from system procedures, because the *interpreter of tactics – the user –* is not context-free: after announcing that there is an error, the user will interpret a description of the command typed in differently than after the announcement that there is an opportunity to learn something new. The interpretation of system procedures is not context-dependent, although the user may learn to use side effects as intended effects (or even does not discriminate any more between the various effects, which are so contingent upon one another). Therefore, there is probably no context-free description of tactics: what a tactic will do is dependent on what has happened before, and in particular, what tactics have been employed before. It seems that we are in a vicious circle, because what previous tactics have been employed is to a large extent defined by the strategy. However, strategies appeared to be so difficult to identify.

There are several ways out of this problem. The first solution is to list all possible effects. This means that, for instance, presenting the description of a concept as a tactic does not exist, but that there are at least three different types of tactic with exactly the same expression ('how to say it') and the same content ('what'): presenting 'diagnosis', presenting 'new concept', reminding (or priming) 'old concept'. The disadvantage of such a classification is obvious. The list can become arbitrarily long; there is no articulate structure; the generative power becomes almost zero.

Another way out is to have a partial functional categorization, for instance with respect to the 'what' a tactic refers to. This is similar to categorizing commands in an IPS in terms of the objects that are affected: e.g. commands that affect files, commands that affect characters, etc. Such a type of classification of tactics has been tentatively proposed by Ohlsson (1986). Tactics are classified according to such main effects as 'presenting target', 'presenting precursor', 'presenting purpose', etc. However, such a classification presupposes functional distinctions in the domain representation. Are there such objects to be found in the domain as 'targets', 'purpose', 'precursor', 'justification', 'error', etc.? Domains for teaching can be organized this way, but it appears that this structure reflects some mixture of teaching and domain expertise. Of course, these can be separated out by using some intermediary, or overlay representation, for instance, a genetic graph, in which it makes sense to distinguish between 'target' and 'precursor' concepts. However, this appears to be no satisfactory solution. A second reason for dissatisfaction is that in Ohlsson's classification the 'what' does not constrain the 'how to say it' sufficiently. For instance, if an example is presented, dependent on the context, this may mean the presentation of a target, a justification, or the explanation of a bug. A solution may be some cross-classification, but that is not very elegant either, because it implies two independent functional views: one for 'what to say'; the other for 'how to say it'. In a more elegant, and intuitively more appropriate representation the 'what to say' should constrain the options of 'how to say it'.

A solution proposed by Breuker and de Greef (1985b, see Fig. 20.8) suffers from the same semi-functionality. A difference is that the 'what' categories appear to be

Type of tactic	Knowledge	Object type
description	static (support)	concept static structure (is_a; part_of)
explanation	dynamic (support)	causal structure (model)
direction	operational	effect/goal condition/constraint syntax plan/strategy
concretization	state of system	example case actual state
elicitation	all knowledge	question problem
comment	state of user	evaluation attention

Fig. 20.8. Types of tactics and objects.

more teaching-independent and that at least the names of the types of categories suggest the 'how to say it'. The classification of tactics is focused on the kind of knowledge objects they intend to transfer. A further refinement and empirical support for this classification can be found in Sandberg *et al.* (1987).

Figure 20.8 needs some explanation*. There is a distinction between types of knowledge. There is support – either static or dynamic – and operational knowledge. This distinction is derived from Clancey (1982; 1983). Operational knowledge is the type of knowledge that is used for problem solving, or task performance. It constitutes the *skills*, and may often be not directly 'inspectable', because it is 'compiled out' (Clancey, 1983) or automated (Ericsson and Simon, 1984). Support knowledge gives a 'permanent', context-independent meaning and justification to concepts used. All objects in an IPS are concepts, and are part of the support knowledge. However, some aspects of actions, or system procedures, are also support knowledge – an action is a concept too –, but other aspects are related to its use. For instance, the knowledge that 'type' is a UNIX-Mail command, and that it belongs to the same class of 'show message' commands as ⟨return⟩, 'print' and 'top' is support knowledge. The fact that it shows specified messages on the screen and sets the read-parameter is operational

---

*The terminology does not correspond with that of the EUROHELP.PO specification of the remedial tactic (see Section 20.2). 'Description' tactics of PO are 'directions'. We have chosen the word 'direction', because the probably more appropriate term 'instruction' has already been reserved for (initial) teaching functions (see Fig. 20.3).

knowledge. The correspondence between support and operational knowledge is obvious: there are identity relations (or 'pointers') between these two structures, but the correspondence can be much closer: as the example shows, concepts may be structured in accordance with their use. This is probably not accidental in an IPS, because the concepts are constructed for their use.

Support knowledge may be considered as a kind of luxury, particularly in such practical matters as acquisition of skills in some IPS domain, but it has three (probably correlated) functions. The first one is that it supports skill acquisition: we prefer to know what things are, before we start manipulating them. Support knowledge plays an identificational role, which allows us to interpret operational information in terms of (operational) frameworks we know about already. To a user, familiar with the 'type' command, the description that 'print' is a synonym is sufficient for correct use; and that ⟨return⟩ is also a 'show message' command provides at least heuristics for correct use. The second function of support knowledge is that it allows 'reasoning from first principles' (Davis, 1983). Reasoning from first principles is a very important, often decisive factor in solving non-prototypical, difficult problems and debugging faulty knowledge. The latter is important in mastering an IPS if some intended effect does not occur and the user has to look for reasons why this was not the case. The final function is that support knowledge is often more accessible than operational knowledge, which allows easier communication: combined with the first function it makes support knowledge particularly appropriate for 'learning by being told', i.e. for presenting information.

A concept is instantiated if its attributes have a specific value (Brachman, 1979). An instantiated object is no longer an abstract object; it is concrete. The state of a system is the set (or structure) of all its instantiated objects. The state of an object (which can be system) is its set of attributes and corresponding values. We will not discuss here the fact that this object–system recursion leads to some subtle terminological problems (apparently attributes and values are to objects what (instantiated) objects are to systems). In practice, the term state is often used to refer to a particular combination of an object, an attribute and a value. For instance, it can be said that a message has been read (or at system level, the read-marker has now the value T). This does not express the facts which also apply to that message (e.g. some sender, some date, some number of characters, etc.). The pragmatics of these expressions require us to focus on 'interesting' states; in particular states which have most recently been changed (or, in the case of errors, have incorrectly been assumed). The tactics of the 'concretion' type refer either to presenting information about the actual state of the system (or the most interesting actual 'states') or to fictitious (sequences of) states. An example may consist of an instance of the use of a system procedure (i.e. the 'direction' of instances of conditions and effects; it may include also instances of plans), or an instance of the expression of a system procedure (i.e. the direction of instances of syntax).

This suggests that the tactic 'concretion' may not be a proper type of tactic;

it refers to objects, which were specified under 'direction'. Similarly there can be instances – i.e. concretions – of concepts (e.g. a specific file), of static structures (e.g. specific directories and files), of causal structures (e.g. what happens if '!mail' is typed in UNIX-Mail), etc., i.e. objects listed under 'description' and 'explanation'. The tactic 'concretion' transforms abstract knowledge into concrete situations, or presents information about a specific, concrete situation (situation = state). Therefore, it may not have object types of its own. The object types listed after concretion are rather typical instances of concretizations. The category 'example' may cover a much broader area than Examples in the Expansions of EUROHELP.PO. The difference between a case and an example is that an example refers to a particular state; in a case there is a sequence (or structure) of states, starting with a problem and ending with a solution.

The class of tactics under elicitation may refer to all types of knowledge. In a help system elicitation may not only consist of questions about the user's knowledge, but also about her intentions. The object type 'question' can contain generic knowledge (support or operational) or states. The object type 'problem' is a special case: the user is confronted with some specific state of the system, and some goal. Problem refers to exercises. The user is simply presented with a problem.

A more abstract look at the object types so far (i.e. without the category 'comment') reveals that there are in fact two major types of objects involved: single units, or sets of single units, and structures. However, a complete structure can be treated as a single object. Then, the difference between describing a concept and describing a structure of concepts has disappeared. For pragmatic reasons we will keep to a difference between 'intrinsic meaning' and relations to other concepts, not only because otherwise the scope of description becomes infinite (cf. Quillian's (1969) definition of the meaning of a concept), but also because there is some psychological reality in assuming levels of detail. The meaning of a particular concept is treated as a single unit at the level of the relationships it has with other concepts. Such levels may not be ontological, but pragmatic levels, which depend on the context of discourse or task performance. However, this is what teaching and coaching is about: 'One man's ceiling is another man's floor' (cf. Brachman, 1979). In learning, or in focusing discourse, there are levels or assumptions of what constitute units (acquired structures) and what constitute structures. Assumptions (e.g. in a user model) about these levels may prove to be wrong. In practice, it means that describing a single unit, i.e. a concept, may consist of a single action, while describing a structure may involve a number of steps: it may involve first describing the individual concepts, before describing their relations, i.e. their combined structure. How extensive these descriptions should be is dependent on what is (assumed to be) known about the individual concepts.

Another type of tactic that applies to concrete situations is 'comment'. However, in this type of tactic there is an abstraction process involved. For instance, some action of the user is interpreted in terms of intended or not intended effects (i.e. right or wrong); it takes as an object the result of an evaluation process. Another object type of the comment tactics is the attention of the user. This is not only drawing attention to some interruption, or the presence of a coach but, in particular, drawing attention to a specific problem (e.g. error), or topic (e.g. occasion for expansion). This type of object is well illustrated by the 'announcement' tactics of EUROHELP.PO.

The list of tactics in Fig. 20.8 is relatively context-free; the intended effects are only partially defined, because the (assumed) state of mind of the user certainly influences the interpretation.

Probably the most important user dimension that determines the effect of a tactic – i.e. its actual function – is whether the information that is contained by the tactic is already known to the user. If the information is not known yet, the function of a tactic is *instruction*. If this information is already known, the function is *reminding*. For example, a direction of some system procedure can either be meant as a reminder or as an instruction; in EUROHELP.PO the 'description of an unintended effect' in a remedial strategy has the intention of a reminder; the same frame can be used as instruction in an expansion strategy when a new command is described. Of course, these states of knowledge are assumed by the tutor. Therefore, related to these functions, there is a third one: *inquiry*, which in general will refer to the elicitation tactics of Fig. 20.8.

A second major dimension that affects the functionality of tactics is whether the contents of a tactic refer to actual task performance or to learning processes. This distinction is often rather subtle as we have explained in Section 20.4.1.1. The subtlety is the consequence of the fact that a side effect of task performance is learning, and that task performance can be a good method for learning ('by doing'). This dimension can be viewed as intermediate between the tactics, in particular the object types as presented in Fig. 20.8, and the functions mentioned above. Task performance references are those which refer to actual states of the system, or to one or more previous actions by the user (i.e. the use of system procedures). Learning references are references to (assumed) states of mind of the user. Such states may not be already acquired knowledge, but also lacking knowledge: i.e. in learning, both instruction and reminding functions can play a role.

Although both dimensions of functionality of tactics are conceptually independent, there are certainly some practical correlations. If we assume that coaching covers some set of strategies, then in coaching the emphasis will be on reminding and references to task performance. And if we assume similarly that teaching covers another (maybe partially overlapping) set of strategies, the emphasis will be on instruction and references will be to learning processes. These dimensions will surely not exhaust the ways in which tactics may have their effects: both their direct, intended effects and their side effects.

Although the approach taken thus far seems more promising than the *ad hoc* solutions that have been implemented up till now in ITS, it is not the most fundamental one. In the fundamental approach the effects of tactics should be derived from a model of the interpreter, i.e. of how a generic, and a particular, user performs a task, learns, integrated with a model of communication. This is certainly too much, given the current state of the art. In Section 20.3 I have presented some outlines of a model for IPS task performance, but it is insufficiently hooked up yet with the tactics. This is certainly an area for further investigation. As far as models of learning are concerned, one may think about two, hopefully converging sources: psychology of learning and machine learning. The first may provide hypotheses about (long-term) effects of tactics and strategies; the second may be used to test these assumptions on-line, if incorporated in a user model. Finally, one of the important problems in teaching and coaching strategies is the question of 'how to say it': research in discourse strategies and tactics is an important source of information. Help and teaching tactics can be viewed to a large extent as discourse tactics in general.

ACKNOWLEDGEMENT
The research reported here is partially funded by the Esprit programme of the European Community under contract P280.

21

Question answering and explanation giving in on-line help systems

J. ROGER HARTLEY AND MICHAEL J. SMITH
University of Leeds, England

An important feature of intelligent on-line help programs is their ability to answer questions posed by users as they undertake tasks and seek to learn about the basic system. After reviewing previous work, this chapter considers a methodology for question interpretation and for question answering which takes account of the user's intentions, working contexts, and levels of knowledge. The notion of an inferred anchor task is taken as a focus for identifying the user's knowledge needs when asking questions; maxims of comprehension, convincement and cooperative discourse are used to regulate the question-answering process. These techniques are illustrated from a collaborative European project (EUROHELP) which has taken UNIX-Mail as an application for a first prototype.

21.1 INTRODUCTION: SOME REQUIREMENTS OF AN INTELLIGENT HELP SYSTEM

As computers become more prevalent in the work of industrial, commercial and educational institutions, users from a variety of training backgrounds and experience are required to learn organized systems of knowledge arranged as sets of software tools (e.g. electronic mail systems, on-line editors or spreadsheets), or as software laboratories (e.g. Statlabs, CAD/CAM systems, or Policy Planners). Learners will therefore have a double objective: to employ the software package to successfully complete the task-in-hand, whilst learning about the facilities and the workings of the system itself so that their methods become more wide-ranging and efficient. There are significant difficulties in achieving these learning aims. For example, users have to translate their mental plans into formal command sequences executable by the system. Also, in some instances, it may be hard to pick up direct feedback and work out the current state of the system, or determine why unanticipated 'side effects' have occurred. Further, even if the task is completed satisfactorily, it does not follow that the chosen command sequences are the most efficient or that other system facilities (unknown to the user) would not have proved more effective.

These requirements far exceed those of conventional on-line help systems which typically only permit some browsing of commands and their functions. As O'Malley (1986) has shown, inexperienced users often find these aids of limited value as they do not know what information they require. In other words, they have inadequate access structures to direct their searches of the material. Note, also, that the learners themselves determine the task curriculum and how their attention will be partitioned between completing these tasks and learning about the system. Since many users might have little knowledge of computing, it is clear that providing an intelligent help system contains significant problems to stimulate research.

During the last two years we have been engaged in a collaborative project, funded by the European Commission's ESPRIT Programme, which has tackled these issues. The project itself [participating institutions are the universities of Leeds and Amsterdam, ICL (Knowledge Engineering Division), Courseware Europe (Amsterdam), with the Dansk Datamatik Corporation and Computer Resources International from Copenhagen], has wider aims which embrace the methodologies and software tools needed for building intelligent on-line help systems. As a first working context, it has taken a UNIX utility (UNIX-Mail) and built a prototype help system using Xerox workstations with the Interlisp/LOOPS software environment. The help program, which monitors the users' interactions with the base system (i.e. UNIX-Mail), makes a distinction between passive help, when the user starts a dialogue by asking a question, and active help, when the help system itself takes the initiative and comments on the users' performances. In the former case, questions may concern, for example, plans the user has in mind, particular enquiries about commands, queries on system effects or on errors which seem to have arisen. The replies, managed by an Explainer component, are likely to stimulate further enquiries from the user. The active help facility will interrupt if the feedback from the base system is judged inadequate for the current state of user knowledge, or if the learner is about to make a catastrophic error (when the command will not be passed on to the base system). The Tutoring component can also provide material to correct misconceptions or errors which are detected, and can comment on plans which seem inefficient. Additionally, Tutor might advise that the learner's knowledge should be extended to include other facilities of the base system. (Breuker (Chapter 20) discusses the rationale and techniques of the Tutoring components.)

In order to service these supports of tutoring and question-answering/ explanation, a *user model* must be developed which gives an adequate representation of the learner's knowledge of the domain, and of the goals and plans which the user has in mind in the current working context. These inferences and judgements can only be made by having an organized domain knowledge representation – a domain space – which has to include task goals, system entities and commands, together with a planner and system emulator, to produce and check the help material given to the learner.

It is not our intention, within the confines of this chapter, to review the architecture and potential of help systems but to comment on the passive component of help. This includes the interpretation of users' questions and the generation of replies which can lead to a developing explanatory dialogue. This is prefaced by a review of previous work, and concludes with brief comments on some initial evaluation studies using the prototype demonstrator.

21.2   SOME ISSUES IN EXPLANATION GIVING

Any help system dialogue is translated through linguistic expressions transmitted between the user and the system. This implies a distinction between language *per se* and the use which is made of it (Jackson and Lefrere, 1984). In this sense, meaning is pragmatic since it involves a user's intentions (which may not be directly evident from the message itself) and the interpretation of that message (by the help system, for example) which will be influenced by the context. As Leech (1981) points out, meaning relates to something which is performed and involves action and interaction between the help system and user on the basis of their mutual knowledge. Rather than asking simply what a learner's enquiry means, it is necessary also to ask what sort of act the user was carrying out when the statement or query was made. Jackson and Lefrere (1984) underline this point by arguing that the management of successful dialogue must attend to: 1. the context, i.e. the current action goal; 2. the plan to achieve that goal, leading to 3. the propositional content of the request. Note also that conversation is a cooperative activity, and pragmatic meaning cannot be assigned to the dialogue unless such assumptions are made (Grice, 1975).

Under his Cooperative Principle, Grice sets out maxims which provide useful guiding principles for explanation giving. These cover: 1. quantity of information; 2. quality of information; 3. relevance; and 4. manner of expression. In practice, this points to maintaining coherence under the current focus of attention. For Schank (1984) this is achieved by making sure that a 'smooth chain of causality' exists. A second aspect, that of self-reference, implies relating events to user's experience, particularly failure, since failures represent a mismatch with the user's own expectations and can be a basis for learning. A third criterion (of insight) requires the explainer to have a complete enough model of the user to make predictions; thus explanation can be built from an understanding of the reasons why users have taken particular actions.

In identifying and interpreting users' enquiries, the trend is to point to the inadequacy of keyword and even of natural language (semantic) parsers, and to specialize on particular types of enquiry which can make use of pragmatics. The shortcomings of classifying questions under a keyword WHY/HOW/WHAT system has been well discussed by Lehnert (1978). There are not only problems with near-equivalence (WHY did you do that? HOW did you come to do that?

WHAT made you decide that?), but with ambiguity (e.g. in electronic mail systems the specific answer to the question HOW Send-Message? is' different depending on the context – the mode level within the Mail system). Lehnert's suggestion is to identify classes of question structures. These are built round performance verbs, with the sentence structure and sentence objects identifying that entity of domain knowledge which is being sought (as answer) when the query frame is instantiated. Lipkis (1982) in extending the CONSUL/CUE system uses successive redescription mappings to translate user utterances into formalised system terms. Rich (1982) in designing a help system for the document-formatter Scribe, restricts questions to causal, descriptive and difference questions. Within these classes the input from the user is parsed into anticipated patterns of dialogue structures. Hence, current explainers tend to identify the system objects, and place types of enquiries into formal structures which reference the system/knowledge objects to be used in reply. The importance of context knowledge for identifying these objects and types of enquiries is emphasized but, surprisingly, the role of user models is underplayed in determining what the learner is likely to ask about (or not ask about), or in checking the consistency of the knowledge request to the likely knowledge needs of the user.

In determining the answers to questions, perhaps the best discussed applications are those arising from rule-based expert systems. It is often claimed that, through their provision of explanation and advice, they can enjoy a wider range of application and make the participation of the user in decision making more genuinely interactive. However, it is already clear (Clancey, 1983a) that merely providing pruned traces of rules (which are used to achieve goals) and their outputs is not sufficient to engineer satisfactory explanations. Traces reflect the working of the system but do not adequately reference users' intentions and belief systems. The expert may not need to follow reasoning steps to justify a rule, but the student must do so in order to retain the rule and be able to construct it in the future. For example, Clancey has developed the antibiotic therapy advice system MYCIN into a knowledge based teacher (GUIDON). The program can 'explain' its advice through answering HOW and WHY questions, and it does this by traversing its internal goal structures with successive WHY's moving up the inference stack, and printing the if–then rules which are accessed. WHY means 'How is this information useful?', translated internally as 'In what rule does this goal appear, and what goal does the rule conclude about?'. MYCIN cannot explain why a particular rule is correct, neither can it explain the strategy behind the design of its goal structure.

In order to design help programs which are able to reason about the factors they are explaining, Swartout (1983) in the XPLAIN system uses a refinement structure which is created as the program is generated. It allows the Explainer routine access to the decisions which were made during the creation of the program. The working domain is that of digitalis therapy and the refinement structure is a tree of goals, each one being a refinement (i.e. a breakdown into sub-goals) of the one above it. Thus, a goal is refined into less abstract steps linking top-level policies to bottom-level system primitives.

A useful discussion on natural explanation and its relation to reasoning is provided by Goguen *et al.* (1983) and the BLAH system (Weiner, 1980). As well as setting out a coherent rationale, the authors give prime attention to the ways explanations can be structured so that they do not appear complex to the user. This requires ways of managing the embedding of explanations and deciding how the focus of attention is located and shifted during the interaction sequence. From an examination of discourse transcripts, the authors represent explanatory text as a series of transformations invoked on an underlying tree structure, which represents an abstract form of the argument being developed. Hence, trees are not merely syntactic structures but represent logical links between the parts of an explanation. To be convincing to the user it is necessary to have an adequate model of the learner's knowledge and belief systems (hence questions are often asked by BLAH to obtain such information and the user-model is continually being updated). To make explanations acceptable, learners must feel they have been adequately justified. This can be done by giving reasons, by examples, and by eliminating alternatives. Each of these types of explanation is represented in BLAH by statement/reason couplet trees with the process of explanation expressed as transformations on these trees. The shifting focus of attention is marked by (tree) pointers as the explanation develops. Thus, Goguen *et al.* concentrate on the structure of explanations pointing out that different orderings of statements can be used to indicate time and importance relations, and to place less cognitive load on the enquirer (e.g. by using forward chaining).

Clearly, explanation systems wish to express their comments in terms which are familiar to the user. But the user may know enough to make several explanations possible. Which should be chosen? The system has to have the knowledge to evaluate alternatives and make a choice. On other occasions, it may be necessary during explanation to present the user with new terms or metaphors. In short, explainers have to take up educational as well as direct help objectives.

In summary, research emphasizes the pragmatics of explanatory discourse with users' intentions, goals and task plans being inferred to aid the interpretation of their enquiries. Most help systems specialize in answering particular types of questions and in adapting and developing explanations through continuing dialogue. These explanatory structures can be represented through tree represen-tations at a higher level of abstraction, with pointers trying to indicate and control the focus of attention during user-help system interactions. Difficulties arise because the content of answers has to adapt to users' knowledge levels, be convincing (i.e. able to be justified), and able to develop new knowledge in a coherent fashion. Our experience in trying to overcome some of these problems with the prototype help system is outlined in the next sections of this chapter.

21.3 THE CLASSIFICATION OF USERS' ACTIVITIES AND QUESTIONS

In an attempt to identify users' activities and the particular questions and explanations which are likely to arise as they use and learn about a software package, some initial experimental studies were conducted using UNIX-Mail. A range of subjects (including secretaries and computer scientists) with little or no experience of UNIX-Mail were given a number of tasks to perform individually, with instructions to 'think and talk aloud' as they worked. In cases of difficulty, the users could ask questions and an expert experimenter acted as a reluctant help by providing answers and, where necessary, a comment on errors. Tape recordings were taken of these interactions and a record was also kept of the displays and responses at the terminal.

These data showed that the Mail users undertook a variety of activities in a manner akin to problem solving and, not surprisingly, their requests for help related rather directly to this process. For tasks such as those dealing with incoming mail, users would set goals 'I'll read all the messages' or 'I need to find out how to send a message' or 'How can I find out if that message has gone?'. Not all these goals were specifically concerned with the task in hand – some would identify the facilities or workings of the Mail system and assumed more general learning aims.

Having set a goal, users tended to construct an outline plan with a more detailed first step referencing an implied system command. Typically, the plan was refined after each step was accomplished, resulting in a kind of depth-first planning process. It was observed that such planning could lead to further goal setting in a recursive fashion and often involved 'searching' for information. This plan refinement required the formulation of specific methods to accomplish desired effects. A distinction is being made here between planning and method specification. The latter operates at the system level, as goal plans are mapped onto system command sequences.

When typing these responses, a user might wish to check that each issued command has effects in line with expectations. This is a verification process, and unanticipated effects have to be related to the user's plan in order to assess whether a plan change or some kind of repair action is required. Thus, debugging is undertaken as subjects set about discovering the cause and finding which action is to blame.

There were also a number of situations where a user wished to temporarily suspend or abandon his/her current task and explore the effects of a particular command, test a hypothesis about the system behaviour, or track down the cause of a problem by constructing a test situation. Sometimes users became so embroiled in executing a specific method that, on completion, they temporarily lost the overall plan or task. In such circumstances, they tried to clarify their position and make an assessment of progress against the plan. This was usually followed by re-casting the goal, refreshing the plan, and so forth.

Within this classification of activities, the associated questions asked by subjects as they worked through the UNIX-Mail tasks were assembled, and their verbal structures analysed drawing upon Lehnert's (1978) work on queries and natural language comprehension. The value of this analysis, based on a case-grammar approach, is that it focuses on the purposive nature of dialogue and identifies classes of questions that require a similar type of answer entity despite variety in phrasing. We were able to identify seven general classes of enquiry.

Elaboration questions request a description of an object, a command, or a means of referring to an object. A more complicated form is that of a *comparison*, where users check their (partial) understanding against previous knowledge. (Examples: What is a folder? Tell me about 'type'. What is the difference between 'next' and 'CR'? When do I use 'quit'?)

Enablement questions assist the user in planning and method specification, and an answer should result in the user being 'enabled' to continue with his/her task. (Examples: How do I send a message? How do I deal with my mail?)

Justification questions are usually subsidiary to an enablement question, and request a justification of a decision implicit in the answer to that question. (Example: Why use 'next'?)

Exploration questions often follow an enablement query, and express a wish by users to either modify the assumptions made in an answer, or else simply explore a possibility which is of interest at that particular time. They are an opportunity for users to expand their knowledge, and/or verify their understanding of the system. (Examples: What (would happen) if...? What can I do in Mail?)

Clarification queries occur when users are assessing the system state and/or their progress against some overall plan. (Examples: What is the system status? What messages are left? What mode am I in?)

Interpretation/evaluation questions relate specifically to the understanding of a system response following an action by the user. Typically, the questions seek an explanation of how the system status has come about. (Examples: What happened? Why did that (last command) fail? Has message 2 been deleted? (Why?))

Orientation questions refer to possible moves forward from the current position, usually in relation to an original task plan or in recovery from some error. (Examples: What can I do now? What should come next?)

The dialogue between user and expert often contained sequences of questions-answers as explanations were developed and extended through supplementary enquiries. The way the above question types interlocked to form such sequences under various user activities is summarized in Fig. 21.1. For example, enablement questions are highly relevant to the activity of planning, and justification and elaboration items were often both used in follow-up enquiries.

The experimental data showed that within task activities, the types of questions likely to arise both initially and in follow-up were predictable and could be linked schematically as in Fig. 21.2. The inner loop represents the user giving commands to the system and receiving responses. The top portion depicts a mental model which the user has of the functionality of the system, whether this be complete or partial, correct or misconceived, together with knowledge of the associated system commands. Knowledge of the current working context includes active goals and plans set against a mental model of the current system state. The right-hand loop represents the goal setting, planning, and method specification activities, which collectively we call the *formulation phase*. The left-hand loop represents the interpretation/evaluation and debugging activities (the *evaluation phase*). Any help system must be capable of providing assistance in both these phases, by responding to questions and developing explanations by inviting supplementary and follow-up enquiries.

21.4   THE INTERPRETATION OF USERS' QUESTIONS

Research on question answering underlines the pragmatic aspects of dialogue. Interpretation of users' responses is not merely a semantic parsing of the given words and clauses, but an inference of what acts were engaging the learner, and what purposes were in mind in making the knowledge request. It is hypothesized that the user has some task goals with associated plans, but there is some difficulty, perhaps checking the goal itself or in formulating or executing the method, which points to a knowledge need; hence the user must make a knowledge request so that the (expected) answer will overcome that difficulty.

There are various ways by which the user can ask a question of a help system. The most obvious and flexible method is to use natural language, or some restricted form of it, but understanding such input can encounter such a variety of expressions, misspellings or ambiguity that the computational overheads are disproportionate and result in an unacceptable response time. Further problems arise in conveying any vocabulary and grammatical constraints, and users do not like having to type long strings of characters. Form-filling methods and structured editors which relate to the question types discussed above are other methods which can work more quickly but with some reduction in expressive power. Another approach might be to generate menus of questions which seem to suit the working context and the user's knowledge, so that selections can be made. An obvious disadvantage is that determining and organizing this menu to match the user's intentions could be difficult, and the contents of the menu can divert or unsettle the focus of work. Allowing access to the entire stock of permissible questions through sets of hierarchically arranged menus (a structured browser) can be quick and wide-ranging, but the problem of interpretation is 'solved' by restricting the user to the particular question stereotypes and the fixed organizational schemes determined by the program designer.

The capabilities and weaknesses of such schemes within help systems is a matter for continuing experiment, but our experimental studies showed that inexperienced users find it difficult to identify their specific knowledge needs and ask clear questions. Users have not only to learn the system vocabulary and the effects of commands, but the entities of UNIX-Mail and what facilities are on offer. They have to organize and interrelate this knowledge and so develop a cognitive model of the functioning of the system. With inexperienced users, these frameworks have not been assembled and so their questions are not well-formed. They are unsure of what to ask, and how to express their requirements.

For these reasons it was decided to have the help-system Explainer generate a set of 'best guess' menus which would span the users' requests. In case these guesses did not contain the question in mind, a set of 'browsers' were to provide an alternative and complementary method of access.

Adopting the generated menu approach places heavy emphasis on correctly anticipating the user's requirements from information of the task goals and plans which form the current working context, and the student's knowledge state. The Explainer has to diagnose these knowledge needs and generate a set of associated knowledge requests to form a question menu. In the prototype system dealing with UNIX-Mail, when the help button is pressed by the user, Explainer consults the dialogue record to determine the phase of activity (formulation or evaluation: see Fig. 21.2) and the types of question which are associated with them. In the

Activity	Question type	Subsidiary question types
Goal setting	Exploration	
Planning	Enablement	Justification Elaboration Comparison
Method- Specification	Enablement	Justification Elaboration Comparison
Interpretation/ Evaluation	Interpretation/ Evaluation	Elaboration Comparison
Debugging	Interpretation/ Evaluation Clarification Exploration Orientation	Elaboration Comparison
Exploration	Exploration	Elaboration Comparison
Recapping	Clarification Orientation Elaboration	Elaboration Comparison
Reorganization	Enablement	Elaboration Comparison

Fig. 21.1. Relationship between activities and question types.

formulation phase, a dominant enquiry will be that of enablement – how to do a task – or a knowledge request for information on the commands or system entities which are involved in the task method. Clearly, a key factor is to determine what task the user has in mind, and likely candidates are inferred from an evaluation of the sequence of user responses. A Plan Recognizer, using a pattern matching technique and a stored plan grammar suggests a set of candidate plans which are set against the task hierarchy. This is represented as an AND–OR lattice, arranged under a top goal (in the UNIX-Mail prototype this is 'dealing with mail') expanding down to methods as command sequences. An example of part of the hierarchy is given in Fig. 21.3, where CIT stands for a command issuing task and UT for a user task (like typing the content of a message) which is not under direct system control. Note that for illustrative purposes certain simplifications have been made: no OR node has more than one descendant (or alternative). This permits the collapse of each OR and its single descendant AND node into one, which makes a more readable tree. Indentation is

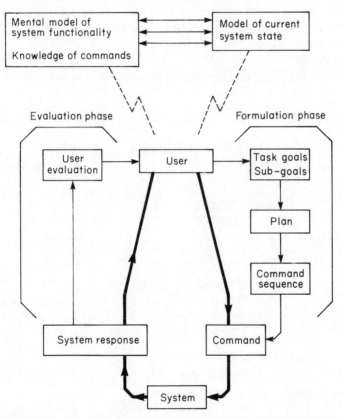

Fig. 21.2. The command issuing cycle, and associated evaluation and formulation phases.

used to indicate the structure of the tree. Each arc or branch of the tree is shown by a labelled dashed line; these labels we call 'imperatives' and have the following meaning:

—Must—— a sub-task is obligatory
—Should— a sub-task is technically optional but usually should be done
—Can—— a sub-task is optional.

Ordering constraints are shown by vertical arrows between the arcs.

Suppose a user has 1. entered MAIL and 2. issued the 'mail ⟨username⟩' command to send a message. Note that the latter action corresponds to mail-CIT in Fig. 21.3, and this action can be labelled as COMPLETE (we will ignore the fact that this command can be issued more than once). Working back up the tree we can label ENTER-MESSAGE-WRITING-MODE as COMPLETE since mail-CIT is its only sub-task. In a similar manner, SEND-MESSAGE can be labelled PARTIALLY-COMPLETE since other tasks have to be taken into account, namely CREATE-NEW-MESSAGE and LEAVE-MESSAGE-WRITING-MODE. This labelling process can continue up to the root of the tree using a kind of mini-maxing technique on the alternative AND and OR nodes; if any descendant of an OR node is COMPLETE then so too is the OR node. Converse reasoning applies to an AND node. However, some account has to be taken of whether a branch is optional or obligatory. Those tasks labelled PARTIALLY-COMPLETE give some information on the 'current

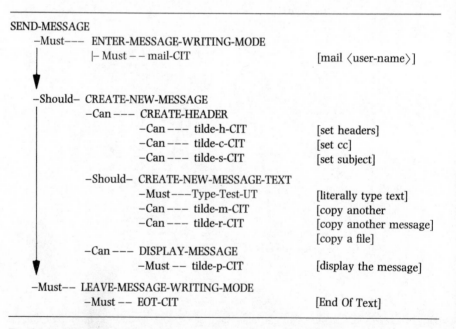

```
SEND-MESSAGE
    –Must——  ENTER-MESSAGE-WRITING-MODE
              |– Must – – mail-CIT                      [mail ⟨user-name⟩]


    –Should–  CREATE-NEW-MESSAGE
              –Can ––– CREATE-HEADER
                       –Can ––– tilde-h-CIT            [set headers]
                       –Can ––– tilde-c-CIT            [set cc]
                       –Can ––– tilde-s-CIT            [set subject]

              –Should–  CREATE-NEW-MESSAGE-TEXT
                       –Must–––Type-Test-UT            [literally type text]
                       –Can ––– tilde-m-CIT            [copy another
                       –Can ––– tilde-r-CIT            [copy another message]
                                                       [copy a file]
              –Can ––– DISPLAY-MESSAGE
                       –Must –– tilde-p-CIT            [display the message]

    –Must–– LEAVE-MESSAGE-WRITING-MODE
            –Must –– EOT-CIT                           [End Of Text]
```

Fig. 21.3. A (sub) task hierarchy for sending a message.

user task' but, for a better focus, we need to find the lowest node whose descendants include all nodes labelled COMPLETE, either directly or indirectly. This node is called the ANCHOR TASK.

To determine the current user task, Explainer uses the Plan Recognizer data to pick out an anchor task which, at least, spans the completed or partially completed tasks so that an ordered selection list of anchor/sub-anchor candidates is prepared (see Fig. 21.4).

To focus more strongly on the current user activity, each partially-complete sub-branch of the ANCHOR TASK is taken and searched for SUB-ANCHOR TASKS (since these are likely sources for users' questions). In the above diagram, T1.1.2 and T1.2.1 are two such foci, and questions would reference components of these sub-tasks. To shorten the candidate list, preference is given to the most recent sub-anchor tasks. Thus, setting the Anchor task tree (Fig. 21.4) against

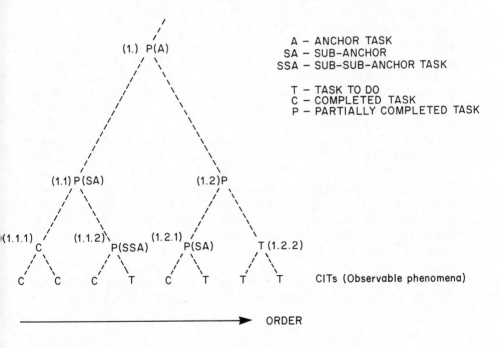

Definitions:

    ANCHOR TASK:
        Lowest task in the hierarchy whose sub-tasks, or
        sub-tasks thereof, span all COMPLETE (observed)
        CITs.

    SUB-ANCHOR TASK:
        Recursive application of the ANCHOR TASK concept.

Fig. 21.4. Anchor tasks and sub-anchor-tasks.

the MAIL example (Fig. 21.3) Explainer would generate these candidate questions. In the actual example of sending a message referred to earlier, these candidates might be:

How do I ⟨CREATE-HEADER⟩?
How do I ⟨tilde-m-CIT⟩?
How do I ⟨tilde-r-CIT⟩?
How do I ⟨DISPLAY-MESSAGE⟩?
How do I ⟨LEAVE-MESSAGE-WRITING-MODE⟩?

together with elaboration (WHAT-IS) questions on the associated commands and system entities.

To concentrate on the learner's knowledge needs, the user model shows which of the sub-tasks and 'objects' referenced in the questions are 'strong', i.e. judged to be understood. These inferences arise from the performance and tutoring history of the user; a strength vector attaches to tasks, plans and issues to give a domain map of user knowledge. Since it is judged unlikely that questions will be about issues which are known, these items are pruned from the candidate list.

The scheme outlined above has general difficulties. For example, the labelling process does not take adequate account of tasks with optional sub-tasks, which will never be marked COMPLETE if any of the optional sub-tasks are not COMPLETE. More fundamentally, although a best-guess technique is necessary to summarize the pragmatics of the working context, the user has not entered a specific question which can be compared with the selection choices, or judged for consistency with the task goal. The current prototype requires a choice from the menu, though it provides a set of question browsers if the user considers the menu does not match requirements. The browsers classify commands and tasks into simple classification hierarchies arranged alphabetically, and on a basic/advanced difficulty scale, and according to task function. These browsers, though coarse in their focusing and only providing access to questions without qualifiers, do give the user an opportunity to explore some of the facilities of the system. No doubt, on occasions this can be an impediment to learning but it does give a wider introduction to some of the system vocabulary. How effective these schemes proved to be during evaluation studies will be discussed in Section 21.6.

21.5 QUESTION ANSWERING

When asking a question of the help system, it is reasonable to suppose that users have certain expectations arising from their beliefs about its knowledge and explanation capabilities. For example, having identified a knowledge need in relation to the current task goal, and made a help request, the user will clearly expect the answer to provide material which will allow further progress towards that goal. But there may be other requirements concerned not only with understanding the answer, but in storing and retaining the information in ways which make it available for transfer to similar contexts in the future. We have identified four guidelines: that the answer should be 1. *comprehensible*, i.e. expressed in terms which are familiar to the user; 2. *convincing*, i.e. can be shown to be consistent with what the user already knows; 3. *cooperative*, helpful and in line with the user's aims for understanding the task and learning about the system – hence cautionary notes can be included and opportunities for extending knowledge can be taken up; and 4. *coherent*, i.e. related in a continuing fashion to the current stream of work. In short, the Explainer has to consider educational as well as direct help objectives. In our prototype help system the user is able to indicate a preferred explanatory style, i.e. whether to receive instructions which simply help with accomplishing the task, or have supporting instruction about the facilities and working of the information processing system (UNIX-Mail).

The Explainer works by generating and assembling an answer 'database' which can be used to give a direct answer to the user's question, but adds supplementary material which explains terms employed in the top-level answer, provides explanations of the answer in terms of the workings of the (Mail) system, and which extends the user's knowledge (where appropriate) by introducing other command facilities related to the current task. These answers are composed using pre-stored templates to receive the generated text, and are displayed in a series of overlapping windows with menus acting as 'continuation' questions to maintain the dialogue.

21.5.1   The answer-base forming the explanation

The Explainer in devising its answer database is dependent upon the knowledge structures which represent the information processing domain. These include information of the system commands (their syntax, properties and effects) which are linked through genetic graphs (Goldstein, 1982) of, for example, specialization and refinement. These relationships are useful in giving direction to learning by suggesting a sequence for the introduction of new commands. The information processing system itself is represented by system entities (e.g. mbox and flags in UNIX-Mail) which are used to provide a parameter description of the current system state. The commands effect changes in these states and an Emulator, conceived as a set of causal rules, can infer the consequences of any sequence of commands. Particular patterns of commands which achieve designated end states are methods for achieving these goals, and can be attached to the task hierarchy. This serves as an organizing structure for the range of tasks which can be carried out with the information processing system. A Planner, given a task goal or a system end state is able to work out plans (i.e. candidate methods) for completing the task, and these are checked and evaluated using the Emulator.

Thus, the domain representation includes static data structures for commands, for system state and state-change descriptions, and for tasks/sub-tasks/methods. (A fuller account of domain representation requirements is given by Breuker in this volume.) When users carry out their tasks, the Emulator can infer and keep a record of system changes and be used dynamically with Planner as it works out, for example, suggested answers to enablement questions put to Explainer.

The domain representation, with Planner and the Emulator, summarize the expert knowledge of the help system, and this is transmitted to the user through the sequence of tasks which determine the working curriculum. Domain knowledge is activated and related to these specific tasks, and users' questions arise from the skills and knowledge required for their accomplishment. Hence the enquiries should be answered in ways which link the specifics of the task to the more general knowledge of domain 'objects' (e.g. commands and information system entities) held by the user. Planner/Explainer, linked to the skills of planning and debugging, are the main mechanisms for achieving this. Thus, enablement (HOW-DO) questions require an answer from Planner, relating the current anchor-task (through sub-task goals and the suggested command sequences for accomplishing them) to knowledge (of commands and their effects) held by the user. Supporting elaboration (WHAT-IS/TELL) material about the domain objects referenced in this reply could be linked perhaps to other commands already familiar to the user, e.g. Quit IS-LIKE Exit . . . . BUT . . . . . (This relational information is held in the genetic graphs of the domain representation.)

Clarification (WHERE-AM-I) enquiries want information on the current task-plan state and/or the system state, interpretation (WHATHAPPENED/WHY DID THAT HAPPEN) questions need a backtracking of the Emulator's records to explain the sequence of typed responses and the resulting system changes. Orientation (WHAT-NOW/NEXT) calls on Planner to provide a suggestion of sub-tasks that can be carried out from the current system-state to move towards the higher level anchor task goal. Follow-up questions can provide more support (WHAT-IS) knowledge for that particular part of the domain, and exploratory questions (e.g. in UNIX-Mail HOW-IF/WHAT-IF I wanted a hard copy . . .) allow variations of methods to be introduced. The recommendations of Planner can be evaluated through justification (WHY) questions which ask Planner to explain its decision points, or through further explanation which uses the Emulator to show how system states are achieved as the plan is executed.

It is clear that answering questions of enablement and orientation, and providing explanations when educational objectives are in mind, can be an extensive exercise. Indeed, Explainer might judge that the question is over-ambitious, outside the user's current range, and should not be answered 'educationally' at this stage – only help instructions may then be given. If the query is within range, the educational focus of the reply will need to be determined and this decision will be based on user model information. For example, if the question is one of enablement, should Tutor be called to provide preparatory support teaching before the answer is given? Should Explainer concentrate on showing how the commands are sequenced to form a procedure? If the method is moderately well-known, should the focus be on introducing extra facilities so that the user has an understanding of a family of related plans, and then should emphasis be given to justification questions in order to comment on

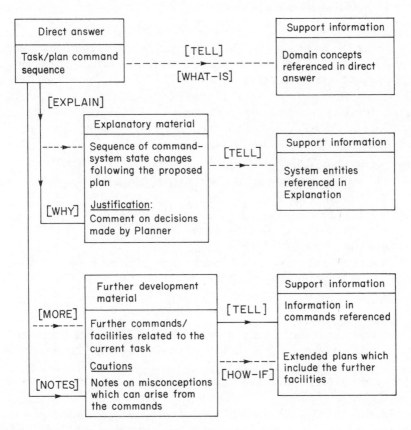

Fig. 21.5. The answer bases for enablement questions.

the process of planning? These tactical decisions depend not only on knowledge held by the user, but also on the principles of teaching/learning which guide Explainer.

In preparation for answering questions, the Explainer prepares an answer base which contains material for direct replies together with supporting explanatory and additional comments to consolidate and develop users' knowledge. For enablement questions, the answer materials and the identifying menus are shown in Fig. 21.5. Which comments are actually selected and made available for a particular user, through a menu-based continuing dialogue, is determined by policy rules, based on the user model, and making the tactical decisions outlined above.

The answer content and associated menus are displayed on overlapping windows (a Xerox Workstation with LOOPS-Interlisp was used in developing the prototype). These allow the user to ask continuation questions and backtrack in order to take up other options which are available in higher level menus.

21.5.2   An example from UNIX-Mail

To illustrate how the system operates in UNIX-Mail, assume we have a novice user who is a secretary, and that he/she has just asked the question, 'How do I ⟨SEND MESSAGE⟩?'. A first consideration is the content of the top-level answer, which should be directly useful to the user even without providing supplementary information. The task hierarchy and Planner provide information for constructing this top-level answer. However, there are several ways of answering the question, and the policy rules regulating the optional material under the sub-anchor task would produce something like:

> To ⟨SEND-MESSAGE⟩
>   you —Must— ⟨ENTER-MESSAGE-WRITING-MODE⟩
>   by using the 'mail' command
>   that is by typing
>   mail ⟨username-spec⟩
>   Then you —Should— ⟨Type-Text-UT⟩
>   Then you —Must— ⟨LEAVE-MESSAGE-WRITING-MODE⟩
>   by using the 'EOT' command
>   that is by typing
>   [a full stop]

Proper English phrases are not substituted for the various task names so as to illustrate how the answer is generated. The immediate descendants of SEND-MESSAGE can be explained in turn. Because the sub-trees for ENTER-MESSAGE-WRITING-MODE and LEAVE-MESSAGE-WRITING-MODE are shallow, it is possible to make a link to what actually has to be typed in terms of commands to the system. For CREATE-NEW-MESSAGE, policy rules decide that, for this user, it is best to omit all the optional branches and concentrate entirely on CREATE-NEW-MESSAGE-TEXT. This simplification makes it possible to collapse part of the tree, and to just present the Type-Text-UT part.

The direct answer is a set of instructions for carrying out the task, and provides no explanatory details; these come through the continuation menus. With this user, the policy rules may decide to show the following continuation menus (the terms in square brackets relate to Fig. 21.5):

Explain what the system does	[EXPLAIN]
Tell me about the 'mail' command	[TELL]
Tell me about the 'EOT' command	[TELL]
What is a ⟨username-spec⟩?	[WHAT-IS]
Give me some notes on other useful facilities (relating to message sending)	[MORE]
Give me any cautionary notes	[NOTES]
Return to the previous help window	
Exit to Mail	

Explain what the system does would concentrate on mode changes and indicate:

that you were in 'Mail mode' (viz & prompt)
that ⟨Mail⟩ puts system in ⟨Message-writing-mode⟩
   and ⟨user-name spec⟩ sets recipient(s) of your message
that 'EOT' command moves system to leave ⟨message writing mode⟩
   and places message in recipient(s) mailbox.

Note that for this information to be helpful and consolidate understanding, rather than make the answer appear more complex, the system entities which are referenced should be held with some strength in the user model.

Selecting *give me some notes on other useful facilities* may display, following policy rule decisions, that:

When you ⟨SEND-MESSAGE⟩
   as well as ⟨Type-Text-UT⟩
      you —Can— ⟨tilde-m-CIT⟩
         to copy a message into your message.

In generating this part of the answer, Explainer examines what has been left out of the top-level answer (in this case all the optional sub-tasks) and assesses which of these are most useful to this type of user and within his/her capabilites. In making such judgements, user model information showing strength of understanding of the commands and their genetic graph links would be used.

And, as a final example, *Give me any cautionary notes* would reply:

There is no prompt from the system in MESSAGE WRITING MODE
You must use the EOT command to ⟨LEAVE-MESSAGE-WRITING MODE⟩
   that is type
[a full stop]

For this response, Explainer would refer to any misconceptions attaching to this task, or any expected lack of feedback which may unsettle the user (cf. Tutor's decisions for providing additional feedback).

The three top menus leading to direct answers within the evaluation phase of user activity, namely *clarification* (WHERE-AM-I), *interpretation* (WHAT-HAPPENED), and *orientation* (WHAT NOW/NEXT) are seen as working in a highly related manner, with the time phase (present, past, and future) being a distinguishing feature. WHAT NOW/NEXT suggestions from Planner cannot be given without some reference to the present system and task state and (usually) to the circumstances which caused it (i.e. the system response to the preceding command). In other words, WHAT-HAPPENED should give an explanation of the WHERE-AM-I top-level answer, and the development of consequent steps or new lines of action are introduced through WHAT NOW/NEXT.

It should be noted that these types of user questions interlink with Tutor comments, for it is through the evaluation of user reponses (and particularly in cases where error remediation is required) that Tutor intervenes. Also, Tutor may provide system feedback and venture some suggestions for 'what next' as it attempts to extend user knowledge in line with user model information held in the genetic graphs. Of course, Tutor might not be called into play, perhaps because of style settings determined by the user (e.g. turning-off tutoring unless serious/difficult errors are made). It is also unwise to assume that Explainer's clarification and orientation (WHERE-AM-I/WHAT-NEXT) help will only be called when overt errors have occurred.

The user might be performing some task plan but be unsure of what can now be done, and what commands are involved. Again, if the user has asked for enablement help under a higher level task, the answer material may be excessive if including all low-level parts of the task. A useful way to proceed would be a sequential walk through each sub-task using the WHAT-NEXT/HOW-DO menu keys at each stage.

21.5.3 Adaptivity and policy rules

In answering questions, the Explainer needs some broad classification of the user in terms of stereotypical classes. This is useful for determining an appropriate form of answer for such user categories as computer scientist or secretary, and for regulating the level of detail which is offered. Also, there should be some measure of the user's experience with the system, both in a global and in a local sense. For example, one might concentrate on the basic facilities of the system when dealing with a novice, and then having some measure of the user's knowledge of individual concepts would enable the help system to be more discriminating in deciding what to explain. Again, the help system requires information of users' preferred styles of working; for example, whether they wish to establish a thorough understanding of the system, or whether their priorities lie in accomplishing tasks. Having a note of the frequency of use of the information processing system (i.e. Is it intermittent, or regular?) will allow Explainer to better regulate the amount of new knowledge which is introduced in a session. However, it should be noted that maintaining a user model requires some rationale of learning (and forgetting) which implies knowledge of the inter-relationships between system concepts, since learning one issue may imply or refresh knowledge of another.

A further consideration is that the help system must maintain an emulation of the information processing system; therefore, heavy reliance is placed upon an adequate representation of the system, particularly for commands and their effects. This can cause difficulties for Explainer. It has to generate answers from these system data at a suitable level of abstraction for explanation whilst, at the same time, capturing sufficient of the system functionality so as not to mislead the user.

Thus, the user model is central to the adaptivity of Explainer. It should contain a detailed knowledge representation through the 'strength of understanding' values attaching to the nodes of genetic graphs, and their links. These local data will permit summary strength measures to be estimated for a sector of the domain. Also, there will be data on type of user (Secretary → Computer Scientist), frequency of use of the base system (Intermittent → Regular/Heavy) and style of use (Doing tasks → Learning the system). For working context information, the user model has a note of the current anchor/sub-anchor tasks with the commands–actions so far completed under that task. In the current version, the user model has no direct representation of how the workings of the systems are understood; this would have to be estimated from strength values which attach to the system entities, and to the effects of commands.

The Explainer has to exercise control over: 1. the actual content (and amount) of will-usually/can-do optional material which forms the initial answer to the question, 2. the amount of supporting explanation which is made available and whether the user should be advised to look at this through continuation-menu highlighting, and 3. the amount and type of 'new' development material which can be introduced through supplementary questions. These comments will link to associated (What-is/How-like) descriptions, to cautionary notes on misconceptions, and extension comments to related but 'new' facilities. Explainer has to employ its policy rules to regulate and organize this information. However, taking account of every setting on the domain strength categories, of type of user, frequency of use, and learning style preference, leads to an over-refined set of policy rules. Currently, Explainer makes its selections only under the two broad themes of *explanation* and *development*, and provides additional support material (for understanding) which the user may or may not take up.

Explainer tries to make these decisions by following *ad hoc* instructional maxims. For example, supplementary explanation (in terms of the working of the base system) is given if the learning style is towards 'learning', if domain knowledge is not strong, if the frequency of use is not intermittent (for here the judgement might be that the user merely wanted to use the system occasionally for a limited range of tasks), and if the user is a computer scientist or has sufficient 'strength' attaching to system entities which are referenced. This takes account of the system-orientated language which Explainer adopts in this part of the material. Whether extension material should be offered within a particular working task will depend upon the user's knowledge of the 'new' entities they would bring into the discourse. The major consideration is if the user would understand the content of the new material. Extensions will be chosen for new commands which are within the learning/explorations area of the genetic graph, but will be given a restrictive category if the preferred style is performing the task, if domain knowledge is weak and if the frequency of use intermittent. If the new commands arising from the current task are judged too 'difficult', e.g. too many steps away from strong issues, either a simple instruction answer should be given, or Tutor should be called to provide some preliminary instruction. Note also that the broad setting for explanation can be decided independently of that for expansions. Usually, the two policies will have complementary weights (i.e. when emphasis is placed on consolidation, extension will have a low setting) but there are exceptions, e.g. for a computer scientist with regular use, who might want a sharp learning (expansions) gradient and to understand also the workings of the information processing system.

21.6 CONCLUDING COMMENTS

The prototype help system implemented on a Xerox Workstation, and interfacing to UNIX-Mail running on a VAX computer, was first tested with seven subjects carrying out a series of inter-related tasks. All the subjects were novice users with UNIX-Mail, though all had some experience with computers and some with other mail systems. The group included secretaries and computer science graduates. As these users worked with the system, they were invited to talk aloud about their intentions, method requirements, and difficulties. These protocols were recorded and copies taken of response and display data together with system state and user model changes. An experimenter was on hand to deal with these arrangements and to serve as a help if there were unforeseen difficulties. Detailed analyses have been reported (Hartley *et al.*, 1985), but several broad conclusions relating to the Explainer became obvious.

Matching the protocols against the 'best guess' menus generated by Explainer, showed that on almost all occasions the answer material required by users was available through the menus, but several times the relevant entry was not recognized. The number of menu selections, e.g. in the HOW TO ⟨X⟩ WHAT-IS ⟨Y⟩ combinations, served to confuse or to mask. Users frequently employ 'skimming' techniques when reading the screens, and (novice) users had to guess whether new concepts were relevant from the short menu descriptions. They could prove misleading; for example, the menu item 'How to create a message' seems to imply that the message should first be created and then sent. If 'What-is folder' is shown as a menu-entry before the term is familiar (and sometimes it might have to be), then the user will be unsure and have to work from some metaphorical interpretation. Menus conceal but do not overcome the difficulties of communication.

Another tendency of Explainer was to present too much material to users. The answering system was seen as an interactive database with menu access. By taking up detailed material, the task goals could become defocused, especially as the language was system orientated, and the pre-stored templates displaying the content were simplistic in style. In short, the system functioned according to its specification, but the policy rules were not finely tuned.

The experience underlined the importance of having adequate educational tactics to control explanation giving, i.e. the content and quantity of material given in reply, its sequencing and its expression. A possible way forward is to relate the type of content of the answer base to its expected effects on the knowledge strengths of the user model if the material were to be accessed (and used) by the learner. The issues which form structures in the user model, i.e. commands related through genetic graphs, system entities and the command based rules which cause system state changes, and task issues forming the task hierarchy, can be labelled to show 1. *strength* of understanding (new, introduced, moderate, strong), and 2. *quality* of understanding (Are there misconceptions? Are the arc links secured to other issues which are strongly known? Are the arc-links of issues differentiated through use in a variety of task–method contexts?).

The material in the answer base is designed to alter the strength and/or quality of understanding, and the selection/decisions form the tactics of the interaction. These include: 1. INITIATE – introducing a new issue; 2. REPAIR – removing misconceptions about an issue; 3. CONSOLIDATE – increasing the strength of a concept already introduced without extending its content by introducing new related issues; 4. EXPLAIN – relating the concept to the workings of the information processing system; 5. EXTEND – linking a concept to one which is already known, e.g. one may be a specialization or refinement of the other; 6. ELABORATE – by introducing additional variations, or features; 7. DIFFERENTIATE issues by comparisons in different contexts through the WHAT-IF and HOW-IF exploratory questions; and 8. EVALUATE – through justification queries to Explainer.

By issue is meant the student's mental model of the command, entity or task-method, and each of these tactics can supply a particular type of material from the answer database which will have an anticipated effect on the strength and quality of understanding represented by the node-based structures in the user model. Note, however, that there are dependencies between the tactics since issues cannot be consolidated before they are introduced, and are unlikely to be differentiated successfully unless they are securely held. Hence the tactical rules have prerequisites (on node/arc strengths) before they can be effective. These tactics are, in effect, hypotheses of learning since they are stored as transform-ation rules which cause changes to arc/node strengths. In order to regulate their sequence of application, Explainer must first determine its objectives for the interaction. This is to say that Explainer should set the end goal strengths, and the dominant (last) tactic to achieve it. The prerequisites for that tactic can then be cleared in a backward-chaining manner, through an educational planner. For example, if a How question relates to a task of weak strength in the user model, then the objective of the explanation instructions might be to CONSOLIDATE and increase that strength by one level without bringing in extra related features/commands, or to introduce HOW-IF, WHAT-IF questions. The answer to the How question shows which component commands and system entities are involved and the strength of these components; whether misconceptions are present, and if they are linked to strong issues, can be ascertained from the user model. Hence the preparatory teaching can be determined (to clear prerequisites) so that Explainer, when giving the answer to consolidate the task, does not need to digress or leave the user having to ask many supplementary questions in an effort to fully grasp the answer. The tactic rules, which point to their particular types of materials in the answer base, can then fire to accomplish expected objectives.

This release of material will determine the course of the dialogue. With more experienced users – and there was a marked difference in our experiments, favouring subjects with greater computing expertise – the controls could be loosened and the continuation menus allowed to be wider-ranging.

Question answering, therefore, is a microcosm of the teaching–learning process. It is an educational act guided not only by the working context and what is known of the user, but by judgements which reflect a theory of learning. On-line help systems will have to address this last issue before they can be fully effective.

ACKNOWLEDGEMENTS

The authors acknowledge the contributions of all the teams participating in the EUROHELP Project, particularly Ian Carr and Andrew Cole at the University of Leeds. The work was financed by the CEC under its ESPRIT Programme.

22

*A Pascal program checker**

MARK ELSOM-COOK AND BENEDICT DU BOULAY
The Open University and University of Sussex, England

This chapter describes the syntactic checking component of a prototype system for commenting on Pascal programs produced by novices. It is based on chart-parsing techniques. The system chooses the error for which there is the most circumstantial evidence and reports it. Some problems associated with the application of chart parsing to this task are discussed.

22.1 INTRODUCTION

This chapter describes a stand-alone system for checking syntactic bugs in Pascal programs written by novices. The term 'novice' is taken to mean someone who is learning Pascal as their first programming language. This will typically be a student in either the secondary or tertiary level of education. The system described here is the first stage of a more general program checking system being developed at Sussex. The body of this chapter will outline the overall goals of the program checker and provide a more detailed discussion of the syntax checker which has been implemented.

It is clear that novices face a variety of difficulties with learning to program. Many of these difficulties are not strictly concerned with the programing language itself, but derive from a misunderstanding of what the program is for or how one sets about making and running a program, e.g. using an editor. This suggests that improvements in the overall programming environment, for example via incremental compilers and interactive debugging aids, will be needed in addition to the kind of program checking described here.

It should be pointed out that, while the syntax checker described here has been implemented, the implementation is not in a suitable state for use with students. In particular, the time taken to parse a program is prohibitively long for what is intended to be an interactive system. Discussion of improvements to the implementation is undertaken in Section 22.4. The syntax checker is capable of dealing with all legal Pascal statements.

---

*This is an extended version of a paper that appeared under the same title in the Proceedings of the 7th European Conference on Artificial Intelligence, 1986.

22.2   OVERALL GOALS OF THE PROGRAM CHECKER

AI-based tools to help novice programmers fall into four broad classes: coaches, tutors, bug finders and environments. Coaches comment on the programming of the novice and offer advice or constrain programmer behaviour as they see fit, e.g. the SPADE system (Miller, 1982). Tutors embody either a curriculum or a mechanism for generating a graded sequence of examples and problems which they present to the student, acting as coaches while the student attempts to solve these problems. Anderson's LISP tutor (Anderson and Reiser, 1985) is an impressive current example. The third class of system is concerned solely with the (hard) issue of identifying and possibly fixing errors in students' programs. The system described in this chapter falls into this class. The final category covers AI programming environments. These are distinguished from other programming environments by the degree of control available over the programs being created and tested, and by the range and flexibility of the representations they support, e.g. Interlisp (Teitelman and Masinter, 1984), Poplog (Hardy, 1984).

Coaches, tutors and bug finders all have the problem of deciding whether or not a student has correctly answered a question or solved a problem. In some domains, such as arithmetic where a numeric answer is required, this is a straightforward problem, but in the case of programming a system will not in general be easily able to decide whether a student's program fulfils the requirements of the problem as set. Some of the approaches which have been taken to deal with this problem in the past will be discussed in the next few paragraphs.

MYCROFT (Goldstein, 1975) is intended to detect and repair errors in LOGO programs which produce line drawings. It makes the program conform to a set of assertions about the geometric properties of the drawing that is supposed to be produced. It is able to relate inconsistencies between the program and the assertions via a theory of program planning and of errors in plans. Establishing these relationships permits repairs to be made to the program. Using related methods Lukey (1980) has shown how certain errors can be eliminated from Pascal programs by sub-dividing the program into smaller logical chunks. His system, PUDSY, can deal with various logical errors which are detected without reference to a specification of the program. It is also able to derive assertions about a program and match these against a specification (which is also represented as assertions). By detecting mismatches and then changing the program to eliminate them, it is able to remove further logical errors.

It is possible to compare a student's program with a specimen answer in the attempt to pinpoint discrepancies. This was the technique adopted in the LAURA system (Adam and Laurent, 1980). This system transforms both programs (the student's program and the 'correct' program) into a graph, performing certain normalizations in the process. These graphs are then compared, using meaning-preserving transformations to try to reduce differences. Irreconcilable differences are reported to students as sites of possible errors. One problem with this is that the system cannot reason about differences, and has no knowledge of novices, and hence no expectations about the kind of error that it might be likely to encounter.

PROUST (Johnson, Chapter 23) is an impressive recent system that can detect a wide variety of algorithmic errors in students' Pascal programs. It makes use of an extensive empirical analysis (Spohrer *et al.*, 1985) of many students' answers to two problems set as part of an introductory Pascal course. The system is primed with what the teacher thinks the 'goals' of a particular programming exercise are (i.e. what the program is intended to do). The system has available a repertoire of 'plans' for achieving each of these goals. It systematically attempts to match the various plans onto the code it is presented with. It tries to understand discrepancies by deforming its plans in accordance with bugs taken from a database built up from empirical studies of novice programmers. Impressive though the system is, it can deal only with a subset of Pascal, with only a limited range of problems, and can easily be fooled by pieces of code that are equivalent to, but not identical with, those expected.

Our program checker (of which this syntax checker is part) is intended to provide feedback on a variety of different classes of error. As with PROUST, the feedback is designed to be helpful to the novice and to focus on errors viewed from the novice's perspective rather than that of the compiler. At the simplest level, basic lexical and syntactic errors should be localized and identified. The next level deals with simple semantic errors which result from inconsistent combinations of program statements (such as functions called with inappropriate arguments or undeclared variables). A higher level will attempt to identify algorithms which the program is intended to implement, and to search for bugs in the implementation of the algorithms which will prevent them from achieving their intended purpose. At the highest level, the program checker can be provided with a specification of the goals which a program should satisfy. It should check whether the program actually satisfies those goals. It is feasible to provide goal specifications, because the anticipated users of the system would be students tackling assigned problems for which the system would be primed.

The program checker is being built as a hierarchy of effectively independent checkers looking for particular classes of error. However, it is not clear at present whether this sequential approach will be the best, or whether a heterarchical system would be more effective (e.g. using knowledge of the goals of the program to guide the syntactic checking phase). This will be discussed further in the summary. The remainder of this chapter describes the existing checker for syntactic bugs.

22.3   A STAND-ALONE SYNTAX ERROR CHECKER

The syntax-error checker is intended to operate as a stand-alone, interactive tool on a UNIX VAX. A novice can invoke the tool with the name of a file containing a Pascal program. It doesn't matter how the program was written (unlike, for example, the Cornell Program Synthesizer (Teitelbaum and Reps, 1981) which requires all programs to be written within the special editor). The syntax-checker attempts to parse the program. If it finds a bug, it tells the user about it in one window, while displaying the relevant code in another window. The user has the option of fixing the bug using the syntax-directed editor which is provided as a front end to the system.

22.3.1   Syntax errors

Handling syntactic errors is normally regarded as an uninteresting problem, and is left to a handful of traditional computer science techniques. In fact, accurately identifying such errors in terms of the user's underlying misunderstanding or slip is a difficult problem for which no completely correct solution can be found. Even if the system could be provided with a formal description of the intentions of the programmer, there would still be the problem of proving the equivalence between the program and that specification. Most compilers produce error messages in the form of descriptions of the internal state of the parser at the time when an impossible input was detected. As an expert, one learns to model the parsing process of a particular compiler, and to rely heavily on this information when interpreting error messages, which are regarded as clues to finding an error rather than as definitive statements identifying the error. For novices, the situation is extremely difficult because the novice has no model of the parser, and (not unreasonably) expects error messages to offer accurate information about the source of error (especially since compilers are so authoritative in the tone of their messages). This often leads to novices looking in the wrong part of the program for their errors.

The term 'syntax error' is used to describe a variety of phenomena of differing degrees of complexity. At the simplest, there are primitive lexical errors such as some typing mistakes, which only affect a single terminal symbol of the grammar. At the other extreme are errors which can drastically alter the structure of the program (such as inserting a semi-colon in an inappropriate place or omitting to terminate a comment).

22.3.2   A parsing strategy

Compilers and other parsers used in computer science normally employ a left-to-right parsing strategy. They detect an error when there is no legal 'next state' of the parser corresponding to the next symbol in the input program. This approach is often misleading, because the position at which this form of detection occurs can be far from the actual point of error (for example, an omitted closing comment symbol normally results in an 'unexpected end-of-file' message). Such compiler messages can be useful to experts who have a good model of the internal workings of the compiler, but are of no help to novices.

The use of LR and LL parsing strategies (see e.g. Aho and Ullman, 1977) has greatly improved the ability of such systems to accurately localize an error, but it is still the case that only information to the left of that error is used in describing the error (though there is often skip-ahead for recovery). Automatic error correction, where it is attempted, is often based upon a least-errors method. This involves finding the smallest number of transformations required to make the program legal. This often results in complete deletion of the section of code around the error, and rarely corresponds to the intentions of the programmer.

To avoid these problems, our syntax checker uses a bi-directional island-driven parsing strategy. An initial (flexible) lexical stage of analysis identifies everything in the program which may be a keyword of the language. The parser works outwards to left and right from these keywords, attempting to build 'islands of reliability' in the input, and to link such islands together. The actual parsing algorithm is an opportunistic one, which combines left-to-right, right-to-left, top-down and bottom-up parsing to produce a best-first effect overall. This strategy has much in common with the approach taken in speech understanding systems (e.g. Bates, 1975; Bolc, 1978; Walker, 1978).

A common difficulty with parsing is that alternative parses may duplicate effort by reparsing the same part of the program into the same structure. This can be avoided by making use of a well-formed sub-string table which allows previous parses of sub-structures to be retained. This saves parsing time at the expense of memory usage within the machine. If the program contains bugs then it is important to retain information about alternative possible parses in order to make the best guess about the appropriate repair. Since the syntax checker operates only on the source code of the program (at present) it can never be certain about a proposed solution.

Recent work on processing malformed natural language input (Carbonell and Hayes, 1984) has identified the importance of being able to 'step back and reason' about the current state of the parser as part of the bug detection process. This involves making the state of the parser both explicit and manipulable. This can be contrasted with the implicit state information embodied in parsers based around Augmented Transition Network formalisms, about which reasoning is difficult.

The approach chosen for the syntax checker uses a chart as the basic representation. This saves re-parsing by preserving well-formed sub-strings for later use, and provides a single data structure containing all the information required to reason about the current state of the parsing process.

Chart parsing

Chart parsing is a technique developed for parsing natural language utterances in ways that avoid re-parsing, by preserving partial parses (called 'edges') in a data structure called a *chart*. This technique does not imply any particular parsing strategy. To illustrate chart parsing consider attempting to parse a sentence top-down, left-to-right from the English noun phrase 'the paper bag'. Initially, lexical edges are assigned to the individual words (Fig. 22.1). These edges are 'complete'

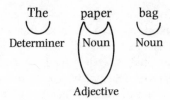

Fig. 22.1. Initial assignment of lexical edges.

because they have found every component which they need to be legal. In this case there are two edges for 'paper' because it is ambiguous, being either an adjective or a noun.

The top-down parsing process is now begun by introducing an 'empty' edge at the LHS (i.e. one which is looking for things to fill itself up). In this case we have added a 'sentence edge', which is looking for a 'noun phrase' followed by a verb phrase. There are no complete edges on the chart with either of these names, so we now add an empty edge called 'noun phrase', which is looking for a determiner, 0 or more adjectives, and a noun, and mark the sentence edge as 'pending' (i.e. we won't think about it again until the 'noun phrase' edge is complete).

Because the noun phrase incorporates 0 or more adjectives, there will be edges corresponding to a noun phrase with 0 adjectives, a noun phrase with 1 adjective, etc. In Fig. 22.2 noun_phrase1 is a complete noun phrase without an adjective, while noun_phrase2 is complete and includes 1 adjective. Noun_phrase3 is actually a difficult edge (i.e. it cannot be completed), which has found a determiner and adjective, and is looking for a second adjective.

Both noun_phrase1 and noun_phrase2 correspond to possible syntactically

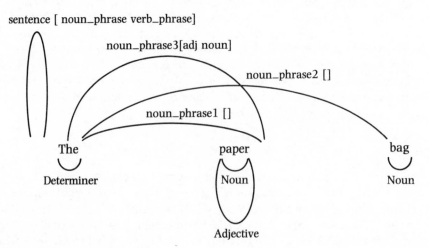

Fig. 22.2. Final state of chart.

correct noun phrases, and imply possible syntactically correct sentences. In the former case we would have a sentence looking for a verb where 'bag' is, which would make that edge difficult, while in the latter we have a possible continuation of the sentence.

This description should illustrate how complex the parsing task can become, even for simple problems, if we are uncertain of the validity of the input. Deciding which noun phrase is the 'correct' one in this context, and whether there was really an error such that the third noun phrase edge should have been legal, is not an easily soluble task.

When a chart is used for processing a sentence in natural language, it is dealing with approximately ten lexical items and generates approximately 100 edges in its search for a complete parse. The Pascal programs being considered here typically contain 200 lexical items and hence result in something of the order of 10 000 possible edges.

22.3.3 Identifying bugs

If a program has no syntactic bugs, then the final chart will contain a set of edges which will include a tree structure spanning the whole program. If bugs exist then there will be no such tree structure. Instead, the chart will contain a number of tree structures and 'difficult edges' which must be coerced into a parse tree. Suppose, for example, we are trying to make a noun phrase from the sentence 'The tried girl', using our bi-directional parsing method. The final chart will include the edges shown in Fig. 22.3.

Each difficult edge is a candidate for a bug in the program. Most of these edges are side-effects of the parsing algorithm and will correspond to places where the parser is searching for things which are simply not present in the program, but some will require very careful consideration in order to decide whether they constitute bugs.

The syntax checker divides the process of identifying bugs into two stages: the first involves collecting evidence about the importance of each bug, and the second involves assessing that evidence (a more sophisticated implementation would combine these phases). In fact the system is performing a more complex task than simply identifying the source of an error – it is collecting information

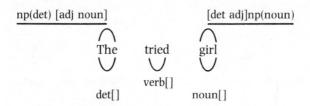

Difficult edges underlined

Fig. 22.3. Parsing a syntactically incorrect sentence.

which allows it to interact with the user about the consequences of various changes to the program, and which permits (at least in theory – it is unlikely to be appropriate for use with novices in practice) a certain amount of automatic error correction.

Evidence for bugs is divided into two classes: local evidence, which is easily found with little processing, and global evidence, which requires more examination of the context in which the error occurs. The task of finding global evidence is not necessarily bounded. The syntax checker looks at three sorts of information in each class. A brief description of each sort of evidence will be given, including an example with a partial representation of the chart and a (slightly simplified) segment of debugger output. In use, the novice will receive several of these output statements for each bug, corresponding to the different forms of evidence. In the diagrams of the chart, edge names are associated with bracketed expressions identifying the next requirement. A bracketed expression on the left indicates a requirement to the left and similarly to the right.

Local information

1. *Alternative possible parses.* As the parser progresses it notes, for each character in the program, how many different hypotheses involve that character. If there is only one such hypothesis, and that hypothesis has become difficult, then it is likely that this difficulty corresponds to a real bug.

In Fig. 22.4, there is only one possible edge explaining the 'while' keyword; it is therefore likely that this is a correct edge which cannot be extended to the right because of a real bug. This diagram also illustrates that 'do write (z)' could be part of either a for_statement or a while_statement. Both these extensions to the left will become 'difficult', but only one (the 'while' statement) corresponds to a bug. The output from the system in this case is not particularly appropriate for novices (see below).

Output: "while _statement at character... No alternative hypothesis."

2. *Mal-rules.* The program checker has a database of mal-rules intended to embody information about the likely errors made by novice programmers. In the current implementation of the system, these rules are common to all pupils. It is anticipated that future implementations will embody three categories of rule:

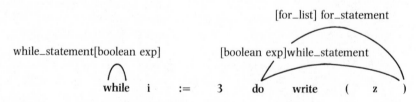

Fig. 22.4. No alternative possibilities for WHILE.

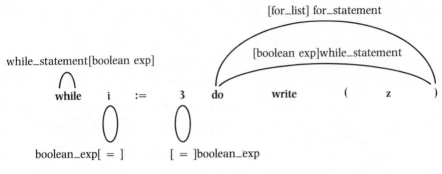

Fig. 22.5. Mal-rule for :=.

errors observed in a particular individual, errors observed on a particular programming course, and errors observed in more general situations. These mal-rules are in the form of common insertions, deletions and substitutions which a novice may make for terminal and non-terminal symbols in the grammar. A program considers a difficult hypothesis to be more likely if it can find a mal-rule which matches both the expectation and the next item actually found in the program. An example of such a rule is ' = replaces := ', which indicates that it is common for a student to use an equality test when an assignment was intended. In the example (Fig. 22.5), this mal-rule could be applied to both the 'boolean_exp' edges. Note that, associated with both the 'i' and the '3' there are several other 'boolean_exp' edges which make other predictions and are not shown.

Output: "The word ' = ' was expected at character ... but ': = ' was found. This is a common error."

3. Spelling correction. A spelling correction mechanism is included in the syntax checker. If a literal item (such as a keyword) or an item defined by a regular expression (such as an identifier) is the cause of difficulty for an edge, then the spelling checker looks for the simplest change in spelling which will relate the expected item with the item actually found in the program (using a minimum Hamming distance as a measure of simplicity (Aho and Ullman, 1977)). In Fig. 22.6 the while_statement is expecting the keyword 'do', and the spelling corrector must attempt to relate this to the lexical item 'di'. The spelling checker has knowledge about the keyboard layout so, in addition to a Hamming distance, it can provide an assessment of the likelihood of a particular error being a typing slip.

Output: "The word 'do' was expected at ... and the word 'di' was found. It is likely that this is a typing error."

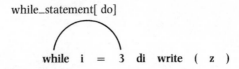

while_statement[do]

while i = 3 di write (z)

Fig. 22.6. Correction of spelling error.

if_then_else_statement[then]

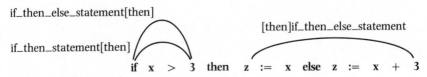

[then]if_then_else_statement

if_then_statement[then]

if x > 3 then z := x else z := x + 3

Fig. 22.7. Multiple predictions of keyword.

Global information

1. *Multiple predictions of bugs.* Certain bugs (for example the misspelling of 'then' in an if_then_else loop) cause difficulty for more than one hypotheses. In cases such as that given above, the net effect is that two edges which could otherwise be linked together are kept separate, yet both are predicting the same problem. By explicitly looking for this type of information in the chart, the syntax checker is very accurate at detecting this class of bug. In Fig. 22.7 the possibility of this combination supports the hypothesis of an 'if_then_else' statement, rather than a simple 'if_then' statement.

Output: "Multiple predictions of the keyword 'then' at character . . . permitting completion of an 'if_then_else' statement."

2. *Linear contextual evidence.* Another possible case is when an edge is stopped by some difficulty but, if that difficulty could be overcome, the other components of the edge (beyond the difficulty) could be found. The syntax checker examines the chart near each difficulty in order to assess the possibility of such a continuation. In Fig. 22.8 an opening round bracket is expected, with a var_name beyond that. Although the opening bracket cannot be found (a square bracket has been typed instead), looking ahead and finding a var_name provides some evidence that this may be a bug.

read_statement[(var_name]

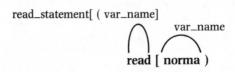

var_name

read [norma)

Fig. 22.8. Looking ahead of the error.

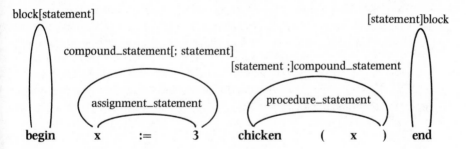

Fig. 22.9. Using the partial program structure.

Output: " '(' was expected at character . . . but '[' was found. Ignoring this, the next expectation for a read_statement can be found."

3. Structured contextual evidence. A major consideration in deciding which edge corresponds to a bug is in deciding how the repaired edge would relate to the rest of the program. Clearly a simple repair which turns the program into a legal one is more valuable than a simple fix which leaves an illegal program as its result. Because the chart maintains information about all the unsuccessful attempts to parse parts of the program (in terms of difficult edges), and a set of dependency relationships between edges (which explain which edges are affected by changes in other edges), this sort of reasoning can be carried out efficiently. The syntax-checker follows these dependencies to locate possible 'parents' of a difficult edge. These parents are then examined to see if they can be linked to other segments of the program to produce a complete legal parse – this ensures that the checker repairs the program using the minimal number of 'powerful fixes'. Such an approach is distinct from the least-errors method discussed above in that not all 'fixes' are of equal importance, since the amount of 'correct' program 'explained' by a fix is being used to determine is value. This contextual evidence provides an assessment of the appropriateness of a particular modification.

In Fig. 22.9 both compound_statement edges predict a semi-colon. If this insertion is made, then the overall structural effect will be to allow a block statement (which spans a large section of the program) to be completed.

Output: "Inserting a ';' at character . . . allows completion of a block."

Assessing the evidence

Having collected these forms of evidence about a bug, the syntax checker then attempts to select those hypotheses which definitely correspond to bugs. This is not, in general, a soluble problem, so the selection is done with heuristic guidance. The guidance indicates likely combinations of evidence. For example, multiple predictions of a bug are taken as a very strong indication that the bug is genuine. In general, the system only reports bugs for which at least three types of evidence have been found.

For our English example, 'The tried girl', this approach would result in the hypothesis that the bug was a spelling error of 'tried' when 'tired' was expected. Supporting evidence for this is the lack of alternative possible parses for the word 'tried' (local 1.), the fact that the spelling checker will report the transposition of 'ir' to 'ri' as a very likely typing error (local 3.), the fact that there are 2 edges predicting an adjective where 'tried' was found (global 1.), the fact that both those edges could be connected together if the change was made (global 2.), and the fact that such a change would provide a complete noun phrase parse (global 3.).

22.3.4   The user interface

At present the user interface is primitive. When the system has analysed the program it initiates an interaction with the user. Rather than telling the novice what is wrong with the program, it offers the bugs which it believes are present, together with a description of the evidence for those bugs, in the form of a hypothesis. It describes the bug about which it is most certain first. Unlike conventional compilers this is unlikely to be the first bug encountered on a left-to-right parse. The evidence is presented as a concatenation of output messages of the forms illustrated above, i.e. there will be several messages about a single bug.

If the user does not regard the hypothesis as corresponding to a genuine bug, then an alternative hypothesis can be requested. The system will retrieve the next most plausible bug, together with the accumulated evidence. If the hypothesis is accepted, then the user is offered the option of carrying out the appropriate modification using a built-in syntax directed editor.

22.3.5   An example

Let us examine the action of the debugger on a simple problem (taken from Brown (1983)).

```
program sillypascal (input, output);
   var mychar:char;
begin
   read mychar;
end.
```

Brown found that this simple program was sufficient to completely confuse the error checking mechanisms of most compilers to which he submitted it. In the case of the program checker, this program causes the generation of about 200 initial hypotheses which, by the evidence selection processes given above are reduced to one, *viz:* the procedure brackets around the variable name 'mychar' have been omitted. This hypothesis is supported by a mal-rule, by linear contextual evidence, and by the lack of evidence for alternative parses incorporating the 'read' procedure name.

22.4 FUTURE DEVELOPMENT

The syntax checker as currently implemented is capable of performing reasonable syntactic debugging but is very expensive in time and space. Two strategies for resolving this difficulty are currently being investigated. The first is to apply a uniform left-to-right parsing algorithm until the first difficult edge is encountered, and at that point change to island-driven parsing as described here. One likely drawback of this approach is that the system will report the first error encountered rather than the one about which it is most certain. This may focus the novice's attention on what is likely to be a relatively unimportant error.

A second possibility is to use higher level information about the goals of the program to provide a further source of evidence which can be used more directly to guide the parsing process. This leads to a more heterarchical system architecture. For example, assigning variables to roles in high-level plans (as in PROUST) during the parsing process would provide guidance for partial parses involving other occurrences of the same variable name.

A planned extension is to provide incremental compilation linked to the syntax editor and program checker. This will allow segments of source code smaller than a complete program to be submitted to the system, thus providing a speedier and more interactive system.

23

Modelling programmers' intentions

W. LEWIS JOHNSON
USC/Information Sciences Institute, California, USA

Accurate identification and explication of program bugs requires an understanding of the programmer's intentions. Without such an understanding, it is impossible to determine accurately what bugs are present and where they are located. This chapter describes a program called PROUST which debugs programs by inferring the intentions of the programmer, and identifying bugs either as faulty intentions or failed attempts to implement intentions. It then describes current research aimed at enriching PROUST's model of intentions, and implementing a system which allows designers to formulate their intentions explicitly. We expect that this work will provide the basis for a new generation of explanation and training tools for programming and for individual programs.

23.1 INTRODUCTION

Learning to program is a time-consuming and frustrating process for most novice programmers. One reason for this is that they have to expend so much effort in debugging their programs. Bugs slow students down when they are trying to write programs, leading to frustration. Furthermore, novices frequently have misconceptions about programming language syntax and semantics, which lead to confusions when their programs behave differently from what they expect. It is extremely difficult for novices to discover on their own the misconceptions which account for the unexpected behaviour.

Bugs need not be a hindrance to novice programmers, however. If a tutor were to supervise a student's work and provide assistance when the student makes mistakes, then errors could signal to the tutor what misconceptions the student has (Brown and Burton, 1978). Given such an understanding, the teacher can then focus on remedying the student's problems, clearing the way for further progress through the curriculum.

This chapter describes a system called PROUST which analyses programs written by novice programmers, looks for non-syntactic bugs, and describes them to the programmers. It identifies misconceptions which might be responsible for the bugs, and uses them as a basis for describing the bugs to the novices. PROUST focuses on non-syntactic bugs because methods for recognizing syntactic errors are fairly well understood at this point (e.g. Elsom-Cook and du Boulay, Chapter 22; Barnard, 1976; Graham and Rhodes, 1975). Semantic and logical error detectors, on the other hand, tend to be very limited in power, focusing only on narrow ranges of bugs, such as uninitialized variables (Fosdick and Osterweil, 1976) or spelling errors (Teitelman, 1978).

The key to diagnosing the non-syntactic bugs in a program is understanding the intentions underlying the program. Furthermore, to some extent these intentions can be inferred from the buggy program. This makes intention-based analysis an effective method for diagnosing bugs in programs. In this chapter we will describe what it means to identify the intentions underlying a program, why knowledge of intentions is needed in order to find bugs, and what process is used in PROUST in finding the bugs. The discussion here is fairly brief; more detailed discussion can be found in Johnson (1986a, 1986b).

Once the overview of how PROUST performs intention-based analysis has been completed, we will conclude by discussing our current work to extend the notion of intentions used in PROUST. In particular, we are interested in modelling the intentions underlying larger programs, ones where a significant amount of specification and design work is required. Such modelling is essential if we are to provide assistance to more advanced programming students. We have developed a framework for describing explicitly the knowledge that goes into specifying programs. This framework will be used to allow software designers to make explicit their intentions, making it unnecessary to infer intentions from the resulting program code. We are in the process of building an intelligent system which implements many of the reasoning processes on specifications that programmers perform mentally when they write programs*. We initially intend our system to be used by software professionals, so that we can test our theories of software specification and design. We then plan to employ our model in various ways for tutorial purposes. First, once the intentions underlying a given software system have been modelled, these intentions can be explained to someone else. We plan to make use of these intention models in a system which explains to maintainers how a system was constructed and why. Next, once the intention model is fully developed and tested, we are considering using it to develop a training system to help intermediate programmers learn the techniques of software specification and design.

23.2 AN OVERVIEW OF PROUST'S INTENTION-BASED ANALYSIS

In what follows, an example buggy novice program will be presented and analysed for bugs. The analysis will illustrate how knowledge of the

---

*This work is being conducted as part of the Knowledge-Based Specification Assistant Project, whose members are Robert Balzer, William Swartout, Don Cohen, Martin Feather, Neil Goldman, Ed Ipser, David Wile, and Kai Yue, and the author.

Noah needs to keep track of rainfall in the New Haven area in order to determine when to launch his ark. Write a Pascal program that will help him do this. The program should prompt the user to input numbers from the terminal; each input stands for the amount of rainfall in New Haven for a day. Note: since rainfall cannot be negative, the program should reject negative input. Your program should compute the following statistics from this data:

1. the average rainfall per day;
2. the number of rainy days;
3. the number of valid inputs (excluding any invalid data that might have been read in);
4. the maximum amount of rain that fell on any one day.

The program should read data until the user types 99 999; this is a sentinel value signalling the end of input. Do not include the 99 999 in the calculations. Assume that if the input value is non-negative, and not equal to 99 999, then it is valid input data.

Fig. 23.1. The Rainfall Problem.

programmer's intentions is the key to the process of diagnosing bugs. PROUST's analysis of the same example will then be described. The discussion will point out some of the issues that intention-based error diagnosis systems must address, and will show how PROUST addresses them.

23.2.1   Intention-based analysis of an example buggy program

The example which we will examine is a solution to a problem that was assigned in an introductory Pascal course. The problem is called the Rainfall Problem; the statement of the problem appears in Fig. 23.1. The Rainfall Problem requires that the students write a program which reads in a series of numbers, each of which represents the amount of rainfall on a particular day. Input termination is signalled when the user types the value 99 999. The program is supposed to check the input for validity, compute the average and the maximum of the input, and count the total number of valid inputs and the number of positive inputs. The program must prevent the final 99 999 from being included in the computations. This problem thus tests the students' ability to combine a variety of computations into a single working program.

Figure 23.2 shows a solution to the Rainfall Problem written by a novice programmer. This program has a number of different bugs; however, there is one set of bugs that is of particular interest. Instead of there being a single loop which reads the data, processes it, and checks for 99 999, there are two. One is a 'repeat' loop, starting at line 8 and ending at line 28. The other is a 'while' loop contained within the repeat loop. The inner while loop is an infinite loop; it tests the variable 'Rain' against 99 999, but never modifies Rain.

Well-known analysis techniques such as data-flow analysis (Fosdick and Osterweil, 1976) are capable of detecting the infinite loop in the program in Fig. 23.2. However, if an infinite loop is a manifestation of a more significant programming error, then simply pointing out the infinite loop may distract the

```
 1 program Rainfall (input, output);
 2
 3 var
 4     Rain, Days, Totalrain, Raindays, Highrain, Averain: real;
 5
 6 begin
 7    Rain : = 0;
 8    repeat
 9        writeln ('Enter rainfall');
10        readln;
11        read (Rain);
12        while Rain < 0 do
13          begin
14              writeln (Rain : 0 : 2, 'is not possible, try again');
15              readln;
16              read (Rain)
17          end;
18
19        while Rain < > 99 999 do
20          begin
21              Days : = Days + 1;
22              Totalrain : = Totalrain + Rain;
23              if Rain > 0 then
24                  Raindays : = Raindays + 1;
25              if Highrain < Rain then
26                  Highrain : = Rain
27          end;
28      until Rain = 99 999;
29
30      Averain : = Totalrain/Days;
31
32      writeln (Days : 0 : 0, 'valid rainfalls were entered');
33      writeln ('The average rainfall was', Averain : 0 : 2, 'inches');
34      writeln ('The highest rainfall was', Highrain : 0 : 2);
35      writeln ('There were', Raindays : 0 : 0, 'in this period');
36 end.
```

Fig. 23.2 A buggy solution to the Rainfall Problem.

student away from correcting the true error. In particular, if a loop does not belong in the program at all, then the question of whether or not the loop is infinite is moot. Our empirical studies of how students debug programs indicate that novice programmers tend to correct the surface manifestations of bugs rather than the bugs themselves; thus proper descriptions of bugs are crucial.

We believe that the proper analysis of the bug in this program is as follows. The student probably did not intend the 'while' statement at line 19 to loop at all. Instead, the effect of an 'if' statement was intended. Since the input statements are at the top of the 'repeat' loop, and the loop exit test is at the bottom of the 'repeat' loop, there has to be a way for control to skip from the input statements to the end of the loop when 99 999 is read. Otherwise the 99 999 would be processed as if it were a rainfall amount. An 'if' statement would serve this purpose, but the student has written a 'while' statement instead. Empirical analyses of novice programming errors (Johnson *et al.*, 1983) have shown that novice programmers commonly confuse the meanings of 'if' and 'while', particularly when they are embedded within other loops. If this bug were to be described to the novice programmer, the description should focus on the probable misconception about the meanings of 'if' and 'while', rather than just on the fact that the while statement is an infinite loop.

Two kinds of knowledge about the programmer's intentions are required in order to come up with the above diagnosis:

- knowledge about the intended function of the program, and
- knowledge about how the programmer intended this function to be achieved.

Knowledge of intended function is required to determine what the input/output behaviour of the program should be. Knowledge of how the function was to be achieved is needed in order to figure out what the while statement is really intended to do.

The key difference between the above analysis and the analysis that a data-flow analyser would produce is the following. A data-flow analyser analyses the behaviour of the program itself, independent of the intentions underlying it. In the above analysis, the focus was on understanding the intentions underlying the program, and then on referring to those intentions in diagnosing bugs. Thus the bug analysis presented above is an *intention-based* analysis; a data-flow analyser, in contrast, performs non-intention-based analysis.

Note furthermore that analysing the intentions underlying a program inevitably implies understanding something of the cognitive process which the programmer went through in forming and acting on those intentions. That is, we must follow the reasoning of the programmer to see what the buggy 'while' statement was supposed to do, and why it is buggy. Thus intention-based error diagnosis can be defined as follows:

> A system for diagnosing errors in artefacts is *intention-based* if it finds errors based on an interpretation of the cognitive process which generated the artefact, rather than on an interpretation of the structure or behaviour of the artefact itself.

23.2.2   PROUST's analysis

PROUST is an intention-based system for diagnosing bugs in Pascal programs written by novices. It is integrated into the Pascal compiler that novices use as part of an introductory programming course. Whenever a student compiles a program, and the program is syntactically correct, the program is passed on to PROUST. PROUST analyses the program for bugs, and prints a report of these bugs on the student's terminal. Fig. 23.3 shows PROUST's output when analysing the program in Fig. 23.2. PROUST finds all of the bugs in the program, including the 'while-for-if' bug. Note that although PROUST's output indicates the possibility that the program will enter an infinite loop, it does not analyse the program by looking for infinite loops. Rather, it tries to understand the intentions underlying the program, and in the process discovers that a while statement was used where an if statement should have been used.

23.2.2.1 Problem descriptions

One of the things which an intention-based analysis system must do, as indicated above, is to determine what the intended function of the program is. It is difficult to infer the intended function of a program just by inspecting the program; there is no way of knowing whether the program's behaviour is really what the programmer had in mind. Some sort of additional information is required. In PROUST this additional information is provided in the form of a description of the

---

NOW BEGINNING BUG REPORT:

$\rangle\rangle\rangle$ Now Reporting CRITICAL Bugs in the SETUP part of your program:

You left out the initializations for the variables HIGHRAIN, DRYDAYS, RAINDAYS, and TOTALRAIN. Programs should not fetch values from uninitialized variables! If you don't initialize these variables to the values that you want, you will have no way of knowing what values they will be initialized to.

(TO CONTINUE, PLEASE PRESS CARRIAGE RETURN)

$\rangle\rangle$ Now Reporting MINOR Bugs in the SETUP part of your program:

The initialization at line 7 appears to be unnecessary.
The statement in question is:
    RAIN := 0

(TO CONTINUE, PLEASE PRESS CARRIAGE RETURN)

$\rangle\rangle$ Now Reporting CRITICAL Bugs in the CONTROL part of your program:

You used a WHILE statement at line 19 where you should have used an IF. WHILE and IF are NOT equivalent in this context; using WHILE in place of IF can result in infinite loops. The statement in question is:
    WHILE RAIN $\langle \ \rangle$ 99999 DO...

(TO CONTINUE, PLEASE PRESS CARRIAGE RETURN)

$\rangle\rangle$ Now Reporting CRITICAL Bugs in the OUTPUT part of your program:

The maximum and the average are undefined if there is no valid input. But lines 34 and 33 output them anyway. You should always check whether your code will work when there is no input! This is a common cause of bugs.

You need a test to check that at least one valid data point has been input before line 30 is executed. The average will bomb when there is no input.

BUG REPORT NOW COMPLETE.

Fig. 23.3. PROUST's output for the program in Fig. 23.2.

?DailyRain isa ScalarMeasurement.

Achieve the following goals:

    Sentinel-Controlled Input Sequence (?DailyRain, 99 999);
    Input Validation (?DailyRain, ?DailyRain < 0);
    Output (*Average* (?DailyRain));
    Output (*Count* (?DailyRain));
    Output (*Guarded Count* (?DailyRain, ?DailyRain > 0));
    Output (*Maximum* (?DailyRain));

Fig. 23.4. The Rainfall Problem in PROUST's problem description notation.

problem that was assigned to the students. Since the students are attempting to complete the assigned problems, the problem description can be expected to match the intended function of the students' programs fairly closely.

Problem descriptions, for PROUST, are sets of goals to be satisfied, and sets of descriptions of the data objects that these goals apply to. Figure 23.4 shows one of the problem descriptions that PROUST uses, the description of the Rainfall Problem*. It defines a data object, '?DailyRain', which is a parameter of many of the goals in the problem description. Then the goals are listed. One of these, *Sentinel-Controlled Input Sequence*, is the goal that a series of values be read, stopping when a specific sentinel value is reached. '*Output* (*Average* (?DailyRain))' specifies that the average of the rainfall inputs should be computed and output. '*Input Validation* (?DailyRain, ?DailyRain < 0)' is the goal of checking the input values read into '?DailyRain' to make sure that the input is never negative. Note that goals implied by the listed goals, such as checking for division by zero when the average is computed, are omitted. Explicitly mentioned goals are more likely to match the student's intentions than implied goals, which the students often overlook or get wrong.

23.2.2.2 *Relating problem descriptions to actual intentions*

Given a problem description, the task of identifying the intentions underlying a program amounts to answering the following questions:

- How do the goals in the problem description relate to the goals that are actually implemented in the program?
- How did the programmer intend to implement these goals?

PROUST starts by assuming that the student's goals match the problem descriptions's goals, or are a variant on the problem description's goals. If no plausible attempt to implement a particular goal can be found in the program, PROUST retracts its initial assumption and concludes that the student omitted the goal. In this way PROUST determines the relationship between the problem goals and the student's goals.

---

*The syntax of the description has been altered to make it more readable.

Although the problem description helps determine what the intended function of the program is, it says nothing about how that function is to be implemented. In fact there is nothing it could say, because each student is likely to implement the problem goals in a different way. In small programs it may be possible to enumerate the different ways of solving the problem, but in more complex problems such as the Rainfall Problem the number of possible solutions is too great. When an intention-based diagnosis system works in a complex domain such as PROUST's, it cannot rely solely on a canned description of possible solutions. Instead, it must be able to construct a description of the intentions underlying each individual student solution.

In order to construct descriptions of novice intentions, PROUST relies upon a knowledge base of programming plans. Programming plans, as defined by Soloway, are stereotypic methods for satisfying programming goals (Soloway and Ehrlich, 1984). PROUST combines these plans into possible implementations for each goal, and then matches the plans against the program. If the student's code matches one of the predicted plans, then PROUST concludes that the students' intended implementation matches fairly closely to the plan that matched. PROUST thus uses an *analysis-by-synthesis* approach to identify the intentions underlying programs.

Figure 23.5 shows, in simplified form, one of PROUST's plans. The plan is called the *Sentinel Read-Process Repeat Plan*; it is a method for implementing the goal Sentinel-Controlled Input Sequence. As this example shows, plans are represented in PROUST as combinations of subgoals to be satisfied and patterns which match statements in the program. The repeat statement in this plan appears as a pattern to match against the program. The body of the repeat statement, on the other hand, consists entirely of sub-goals: an *Input* sub-goal and a *Sentinel Guard* sub-goal. The Input sub-goal requires that data be input from the terminal. The Sentinel Guard sub-goal requires that the exit condition of the loop, namely reading the sentinel value, be checked for immediately after the data is input.

When PROUST combines plans into predictions of how the student implemented the problem goals, it is said to be generating possible *goal decompositions* for the problem. A goal decomposition relates the goals that a program is supposed to achieve to the plans that achieve it. In the process of going from goals to plans, it may be necessary to break goals into sets of sub-goals, combine related goals into

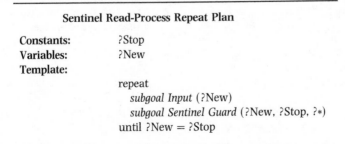

Sentinel Read-Process Repeat Plan

Constants: ?Stop
Variables: ?New
Template:

```
repeat
    subgoal Input (?New)
    subgoal Sentinel Guard (?New, ?Stop, ?*)
until ?New = ?Stop
```

Fig. 23.5. A plan for implementing *Sentinel-Controlled Input Sequence*.

```
write ('Enter rainfall value:');
read (Rain);
while Rain < > 99 999 do
   begin
      if Rain < 0 then
         writeln ('Invalid input, try again');
      if Rain > 0 then
         Raindays: = Raindays + 1;
      if Highrain < Rain then
         Highrain: = Rain;
      if Rain > = 0 then
         begin
            Totalrain: = Totalrain + Rain;
            Days: = Days + 1;
         end;
      write ('Enter rainfall value:');
      read (Rain);
   end
```

Fig. 23.6. An alternative way of combining input and input validation.

a larger goal, and add goals that are not explicitly stated in the problem. For non-trivial problems, there is often a large number of possible goal decompositions.

An example of where goals can be combined in different ways in the Rainfall Problem is in deciding whether the goal of inputting the rainfall data and the goal of checking it for validity should be combined. If the two goals are combined into a single plan, then a program such as the one in Fig. 23.2 results. There the continuous block of code from line 10 to line 17 reads, tests, and then re-reads the data. If the Input goals and the Input Validation goal are not combined, then they may wind up in separate parts of the program, as in the example in Fig. 23.6.

It should be emphasized that the goal decomposition that PROUST hypothesizes for a program need not *correctly* implement the goals in the problem description. The student may have decomposed goals improperly, or have used an inappropriate plan. In such cases PROUST's goal decomposition should still reflect what the student did. PROUST's programming knowledge base is therefore extended so that it can generate incorrect goal decompositions. PROUST is thus able to predict some kinds of bugs as it constructs goal decompositions. Not all bugs are recognized in this fashion, but a significant number are.

23.2.2.3 *When predicted intentions fail to match*

Even though PROUST generates a number of goal decompositions for each goal, there is no guarantee that any of them will match the student's program exactly. In fact, the reverse is more often the case; usually the predicted plans match only partially. PROUST must then try to account for the differences between the plans and the code. One such plan mismatch arises when PROUST tries to match the Sentinel Read-Process Repeat Plan in Fig. 23.5 against the example program in

IF a while statement is found in place of an if statement,
AND the while statement appears inside of another loop,
THEN the bug is a while-for-if bug, probably caused by a confusion about the control
flow of embedded loops.

Fig. 23.7. Paraphrase of a plan-difference rule for explaining while-for-if bugs.

Fig. 23.2. PROUST first matches the repeat statement pattern in the plan against the repeat statement at line 8 in the program. It then selects plans to implement the sub-goals in the plan, Input and Sentinel Guard. No plan for implementing the Sentinel Guard sub-goal matches the program. All of PROUST's plans for implementing Sentinel Guard require that there be an if statement to test for the sentinel value; no such if statement appears in the program.

A knowledge base of production rules, called *plan-difference rules*, is used in PROUST to account for mismatches between the expected plans and the actual code. These plan-difference rules are responsible for suggesting bugs and misconceptions which account for the mismatches. One such rule, a rule for recognizing when while statements were used in place of if statements, is paraphrased in Fig. 23.7. Plan-difference rules either account for the differences between the plan and the code by means of bugs and misconceptions, or suggest a way to transform the plan to make it fit the programmer's apparent intentions better.

Since PROUST generates a number of goal decompositions for each goal, and plan-difference rules can recognize many variations on each goal decomposition, the number of possible programs that PROUST can analyse is immense. Unfortunately, PROUST can sometimes interpret a program in more than one way. In the case of the program in Fig. 23.2, different interpretations result depending upon whether the repeat loop at line 8 or the while loop at line 19 is taken to be the main loop. PROUST must therefore heuristically choose among alternative program interpretations, according to the number and the nature of the bugs which are presupposed in each interpretation.

23.3 EMPIRICAL EVALUATION OF PROUST

Some results from empirically evaluating PROUST will now be presented. These results will give the reader a sense of what has been achieved using PROUST's approach, and where the weaknesses are in the approach. Further results appear in Johnson (1986a) and Sack *et al.* (1985).

23.3.1 Results on the Rainfall Problem

Figure 23.8 shows the results of running PROUST on a corpus of 206 different solutions of the Rainfall Problem. PROUST analysed 81% of the program completely, i.e. it was able to come up with a consistent model of the intentions

Total number of programs:	206	
Number of programs receiving full analyses:	167	(81%)
Total number of bugs:	598	(75%)
Bugs recognized correctly:	562	(94%)
Bugs not recognized:	36	(6%)
False alarms:	66	
Number of programs receiving partial analyses:	31	(15%)
Total number of bugs:	167	(21%)
Bugs recognized correctly:	61	(37%)
Bugs not reported:	106	(63%)
False alarms:	20	
Number of programs PROUST did not analyse:	9	(4%)
Total number of bugs:	32	(4%)

Fig. 23.8. Results of running PROUST on the Rainfall Problem.

underlying the entire program. In these cases, PROUST found 94% of the bugs that we identified in these programs. This is a far higher recognition rate than people are able to achieve in code walkthroughs (Myers, 1978); in fact, PROUST was more likely to spot bugs that we had overlooked than *vice versa*. In the remaining 19% of the programs, PROUST was only able to interpret part of the students' code. PROUST's accuracy was much less in these cases, so it warns the programmer that the analysis is fragmentary and likely to have flaws.

23.3.2   Results on a different problem

In a further test, PROUST was tested on a different programming problem, called the Bank Problem. The text of this problem appears in Fig. 23.9. In this problem,

Write a Pascal program that processes three types of bank transactions: withdrawals, deposits, and a special transaction that says: no more transactions are to follow. Your program should start by asking the user to input his/her account id and his/her initial balance. Then your program should prompt the user to input

1. the transaction type, and
2. if it is an END-PROCESSING transaction the program should print out the (a) final balance of the user's account, (b) the total number of transactions, and (c) total number of each type of transaction, and (d) the total amount of the service charges, and stop;
3. if it is a DEPOSIT or a WITHDRAWAL, the program should ask for the amount of the transaction and then post it appropriately.

Use a variable of type CHAR to encode the transaction types. To encourage saving, charge the user 20 cents per withdrawal, but nothing for a deposit.

Fig. 23.9. The Bank Problem.

Total number of programs analysed:	64	
Number of programs receiving full analyses:	32	(50%)
Total number of bugs:	211	(50%)
Bugs recognized correctly:	191	(91%)
Bugs not reported:	20	(9%)
False alarms:	41	
Number of programs receiving partial analyses:	26	(41%)
Total number of bugs:	168	(40%)
Bugs recognized correctly:	56	(33%)
Bugs not reported:	112	(67%)
False alarms:	24	
Number of programs PROUST did not analyse:	6	(9%)
Total number of bugs:	41	(10%)

Fig. 23.10. Results of running PROUST on the Bank Problem.

the students are required to write a program which behaves similarly to an automatic bank teller machine. The program is supposed to input a series of deposit and withdrawal commands, followed by an end-processing command. The user's account balance is updated according to the amount of each deposit and withdrawal. At the end of the program a summary of the transactions is printed.

Figure 23.10 shows PROUST's current performance on the Bank Problem. The frequency of completed analyses is much lower than in the case of the Rainfall Problem; it analysed 50% of the programs, as opposed to 81% on the Rainfall Problem. PROUST's performance on the completely-analysed programs is almost as good as it is on completely-analysed solutions of the Rainfall Problem. 91% of the bugs in the Bank Problem solutions were correctly identified, compared with 94% of the bugs in the Rainfall Problem solutions. The incidence of false alarms, however, is relatively high; there were 41 false alarms in the completely-analysed Bank Problem solutions, compared with 211 total bugs in the same group of programs.

There appear to be several reasons why PROUST's performance on the Bank Problem is less than that on the Rainfall Problem. First, the problem requires that more goals be satisfied than the Rainfall Problem requires; this was an intended feature of the problem. Second, there were no explicit cues in the problem statement which could guide plan matching. For example, the Rainfall Problem states explicitly that the sentinel value is 99 999; the plans for matching Sentinel-Controlled Input Sequence therefore usually match unambiguously, since there is only one loop in a given solution which tests for 99 999. The Bank Problem, on the other hand, does not state specifically which commands are to be used to indicate deposit, withdrawal, or end-processing transactions. There is therefore a much greater risk of ambiguous matches, and consequently of misinterpretations of the program.

A third source of errors in PROUST came from the fact that many more of the goals of the Bank Problem were left implicit. For example, the problem statement says nothing about what to do if the balance becomes less than zero. Some solutions had no checks for negative balance, some checked the balance only after the last transaction was complete, and some checked the balance after each transaction. As a result, there was a wider degree of variability in the goal decompositions of novice solutions than PROUST was prepared to handle. PROUST was able to follow the student's goal reasoning in some cases, but not in others. These results suggest that as programming problems become harder, and more design decisions are required on the part of the programmer, goal reasoning becomes an increasingly dominant part of the programming process. PROUST's ability to analyse programs is thus limited by its ability to infer goal decompositions from code.

23.4   CURRENT AND FUTURE DIRECTIONS

The experience with PROUST has shown that the intention-based program analysis can do a very good job of identifying bugs, provided that the programmer's intentions are properly understood. Furthermore, these intentions can usually be inferred from the program, given a description of the programming problem. Work is currently under way to build a simplified implementation of PROUST, called Micro-PROUST (Johnson and Soloway, 1985); Micro-PROUST is being extended to cover a range of programming problems, so that it can be more fully tested in a programming curriculum.

At the same time, we see problems lurking on the horizon. PROUST has to predict the intentions underlying programs, but it has to infer the intentions from the product program. The student's intentions become harder to infer as the student has to do more reasoning about the problem requirements. This in turn limits the amount of assistance that PROUST can provide, since if the student makes mistakes in the design process PROUST is less able to identify the error properly. It may be unable to determine whether a particular error is a design error or an implementation error. Even worse, it may be unable to determine what requirements the student is trying to achieve, and consequently misinterpret the code.

What is needed is a way to allow programmers to describe their intentions directly, and to manipulate those intention descriptions in a machine-understandable way. Bonar and Cunningham's Bridge tutor achieves this for small problems, such as computing the average of a set of numbers (Bonar and Cunningham, Chapter 24). Our current work is aimed at modelling the intentions underlying more complex problems, the kind which PROUST has trouble debugging. Such a framework would not only be useful to students who are learning software design; it would also be useful to software designers and maintainers. By making explicit the knowledge underlying a design, and the process of applying this knowledge, the design becomes easier to understand and to maintain (Swartout, 1983; Pavilin and Johnson, 1986). Because the computer could then help the designer in reasoning about the design, the design errors would be more likely to be caught early in the design process.

Accordingly, we are developing a framework for incrementally building program specifications. A specification, in our view, states precisely what a program should do, but says as little as possible about how the program should do it. It differs from a problem description as in PROUST in that implicit goals have been made explicit, and interactions between goals have been identified and resolved. For example, PROUST's problem description for the Rainfall Problem states that the average of '?DailyRain' should be computed. A completed specification of the same program would state that the average of '?DailyRain' be computed after the user is done inputting '?DailyRain', except if no valid values of '?Daily Rain' were input, and excluding 99 999, as well as any invalid inputs that might have been read. We assume that a major part of the program design process is taking informal descriptions of goals and turning them into a precise set of requirements that could be implemented in a program. This reasoning about specifications is precisely the information that PROUST has difficulty inferring from programs, since it is the furthest removed from the actual code.

Our current framework is based upon the GIST specification language, developed at USC/Information Sciences Institute (Goldman, 1983; Goldman and Wile, 1986). GIST was developed in order to formalize the contents of English-language specifications of software. It attempts to model users' views of *what* a system should do, as opposed to *how* it should do it. GIST was designed to be used to write complete specifications, in which every significant system requirement has been identified. It can describe a wider range of specification constructs than PROUST's goal language can describe. On the other hand, there is little provision in GIST for modelling how specifications are developed. Nevertheless, we find that we can use GIST as a starting point for describing specifications and their development. We have added constructs to GIST for describing incomplete specifications, and we have developed a way of describing how specifications develop in terms of changes to GIST descriptions.

23.4.1   Specification from fragments and scenarios

What distinguishes the current view from previous work on GIST is that specifications are now viewed as being built up stepwise out of fragments. We accept the notion that specifications can arise through stepwise refinement (DeMarco, 1978); however, when the process is viewed in greater detail, a somewhat different picture emerges. In order to decide how to refine a specification, specifiers go through a process of collecting local views of what they want and expect, and relevant examples of behaviour. We call these local views *specification fragments*, and the examples *scenarios*. The specifier's task is to identify the right fragments and scenarios and integrate them into a coherent specific-ation. The resulting specification looks as if it was generated via top-down refinement, even though the process of identifying the scenarios and fragments is not itself top-down.

To see the need for scenarios and fragments, consider the problem of specifying a patient-monitoring system, as described by Stevens *et al.* (1974). The system to be specified monitors the vital signs of a number of patients, and notifies the nurse station when these signs fall out of the safe range specified by the nurse station. Such a system must be able to respond to a variety of situations. Monitoring devices may fail; they may be connected and disconnected to patients; the nurse may change the safety ranges for vital signs while the monitoring is in progress. The goals of the system may have to be compromised; e.g. it may turn out that it is impossible to monitor all of the patients continually, so some sort of polling procedure will be required instead.

Fragments arise in the specification process when specifiers first describe the system's desired behaviour locally, ignoring interactions and conflicts. For example, the specifier may consider the process of connecting and disconnecting patients' monitoring devices separately from the process of recognizing unsafe vital signs. Although disconnecting monitoring devices will most certainly affect the system's ability to monitor patients' vital signs, the effects are not analysed until the requirements for each process are understood separately.

Figure 23.11 shows two fragments that might arise during the process of specifying the patient-monitoring problem. The first fragment, 'notify_unsafe', describes a goal of the monitoring device, namely to notify the nurse whenever one of the patient's vital signs is outside of the safe range. This fragment makes a number of simplifying assumptions; for one thing, it is written as if there were only one patient. If there is more than one patient, then 'safe_range (patient), is indeterminate, since there is nothing to indicate which patient's safe range is being considered. 'notify_unsafe' will therefore have to be refined later on to deal with multiple patients. Our observations indicate that this technique, of describing a desired behaviour first in terms of individual agents and then generalizing, is commonly employed by specifiers in their mental analysis of problem requirements.

The second fragment in Fig. 23.11, 'discharge', is the nurse's procedure for

```
notify_unsafe isa goal of monitor: = {
    forevery v of_type vital_sign do {
        event outside((vital_sign_value(v), safe_range(patient));
        action notify (nurse) by monitor;
        }
    }
discharge isa plan of nurse (patient): = {
    action notify (monitor, disconnecting, patient);
    action disconnect (patient:associated   device)
    }
```

Fig. 23.11. Two specification fragments.

discharging patients. Even though the nurse is not part of the monitoring system, his or her behaviour is still specified, so that the specifier can evaluate whether the monitoring system interacts properly with the nurse. 'discharge' consists of two actions, to notify the monitor that the patient is being disconnected, and then to disconnect the monitoring device assigned to that patient. Each patient is assumed to have a different monitoring device, that is in turn connected to the monitoring system; these associations are defined in separate fragments, not shown here.

Scenarios are employed in order to describe how a system is supposed to behave in a particular case, or to explore how different fragments should interact. For example, in order to see how discharging a patient affects reading the vital signs, the specifier imagines a particular scenario in which the two fragments might interact. Suppose that the nurse notifies the monitor that the patient is being disconnected from the monitoring device, as is indicated by 'discharge'. The monitor then ought to stop monitoring the patient's vital signs. 'notify_unsafe', on the other hand, monitors a patient's signs regardless. This indicates that 'notify_unsafe' needs to be refined: it should only apply to patients that are connected to a monitoring device. The specifier therefore refines 'notify_unsafe' by adding the restriction on 'patient'. This example illustrates how scenario analysis can motivate stepwise refinement of specifications.

This discussion gives just a taste of the model of the specification process that we are developing. It is strongly influenced by Adelson and Soloway's empirical studies of software designers' behaviour (Adelson and Soloway, 1985), as well as Kant's model of algorithm design (Kant, 1985; Kant and Steier, 1985). It also is consistent with PROUST's view of the specification process. In PROUST's analysis, a problem starts out as a set of fragmentary goals; these are progressively expanded and reformulated. PROUST's model does not account for how and why those expansions and reformulations occur; our new model is an improvement in this regard. More empirical studies are required in order to test out the hypotheses presented here. Initial protocol studies have been performed, and so far are encouraging.

23.4.2 Utilizing the specification model

The above model of specification is currently being implemented in an automated aid for professional software specifiers. This system will keep track of fragments and how they are identified and integrated, and will allow specifiers to execute the partial specification using scenarios. It will automatically recognize and point out inconsistencies between fragments. We are currently targeting professional programmers for practical reasons, since professionals are likely to benefit directly from such a system. At the same time, building and testing such an automated tool is a good way of evaluating our theory of specification. Our theory is still speculative, and interaction with a concrete reification of the theory will make its flaws easier to see.

Our next task will be to employ the specification model in explanation and instruction. First, we wish to make the specification aid keep a record of the steps that the specifiers went through. Maintainers have difficulty inferring the expectations and rationales underlying code. Earlier work on ODETTE was aimed at making such expectations and rationales explicit (Pavlin and Johnson, 1986). By observing the process of creating a specification, these expectations and rationales become apparent: scenarios describe expectations, and goal fragments describe rationales. We plan to build an intelligent explanation facility to aid maintainers, by extracting from the specification history the information they need to understand an unfamiliar program.

It should be possible to use our specifications as a basis for developing training systems for users. In the patient-monitoring example described above, the behaviour of the user, i.e. the nurse, is modelled explicitly. The nurse's goals and plans, and their relationship to the monitor's goals and plans, are identified. Such information is important for describing to a novice user what the system expects him to do, and what the system will in turn do for him.

Finally, we wish to employ our specification model in teaching intermediate and advanced students how to specify programs. Our specification model would have to be combined with a domain model which can generate fragments and scenarios for a given set of problems, and a coach describing how best to refine the fragments into a specification. By working with such a system, students could learn how to specify and design software systematically. The methodology of software specification and design would then no longer be a collection of vague maxims. It would be a well-defined method for turning desires into programs, one which students could readily assimilate.

ACKNOWLEDGEMENTS

I would like to thank Elliot Soloway, my adviser, for insightful suggestions regarding this research, and for comments on an earlier draft of this paper. William Clancey, William Swartout, and Robert Neches all made helpful suggestions as well. I would also like to thank my co-workers in the Knowledge-Based Specification Assistant Project at ISI: Robert Balzer, William Swartout, Don Cohen, Neil Goldman, David Wile, Kai Yue. Edward Ipser collaborated with me in developing the model of software design presented here.

The work on PROUST was co-sponsored by the Personnel and Training Research Groups, Psychological Sciences Division, Office of Naval Research and the Army Research Institute for the Behavioral and Social Sciences, under Contract No. N00014-82-K-0714, Contract Authority Identification Number, Nr 154-492. The work on incremental specification was sponsored by the Rome Air Development Center, Contract No. F30602-85-C-0221. Approved for public release; distribution unlimited. Reproduction in whole or part is permitted for any purpose of the United States Government.

24

Bridge: an intelligent tutor for thinking about programming

JEFFREY BONAR AND ROBERT CUNNINGHAM
University of Pittsburgh, Pennsylvania, USA

This chapter introduces Bridge, a prototype tutorial environment for novice programmers. Bridge is intended to allow a student to talk about his or her designs and partial work. The chapter gives an overview of the current Bridge implementation, summarizes some experience with students using Bridge, and discusses future plans.

24.1 INTRODUCTION

Our goal is a complete tutorial environment for novice programmers. Not only should the tutor find and report student errors, but it should also understand student designs and partially complete programs. This implies that the tutor must provide and teach a language (or languages) that allows a student to talk about his or her designs and partial work. In addition, we intend that the tutor must take into account the cognitive processes of novice programmers. In particular, the tutor must deal with errors stemming from confounds with step-by-step natural language procedures (Bonar and Soloway, 1985), incorrectly merged goals and plans (Spohrer, Soloway and Pope, 1985), and losses in student working memory (Anderson and Jeffries, 1985).

Current programming tutors fall short of such a complete tutorial environment. The PROUST system (Johnson, Chapter 23) acts as a consultant for the novice programmer, examining potentially buggy novice code and reconstructing the reasoning that might have led to the novice's errors. Although a diagnostic *tour de force*, PROUST is limited in that it cannot have a rich interaction with the student. The LISP tutor developed by Anderson's group (Reiser, Anderson and Farrell, 1985) is highly directive, forcing a student to proceed in a more or less top-down manner. There is no provision for informal ideas and intermediate components in the problem-solving process.

In this chapter we introduce Bridge, a prototype tutorial environment for novice programmers. In Section 24.2 we discuss the principles upon which Bridge is built. In Section 24.3 we give an overview of the current Bridge implementation. Section 24.4 outlines our experience with students using Bridge. In Section 24.5 we discuss open questions and future plans.

24.2 DESIGN ISSUES FOR AN INTELLIGENT PROGRAMMING TUTOR

We begin with a discussion of the design principles used in Bridge. While these principles do not constitute a theory of teaching programming, they are a step in that direction. In particular, these principles contrast with the approach seen in most textbooks.

24.2.1 Start with informal (natural) specifications

A programming tutor should allow novice programmers to initially formulate their programming ideas in an informal, English-like way. The tutor should be able to understand these informal specifications and provide initial tutorial advice based on them. Our proposal for these informal specifications are based on the pre-programming experience of novice programmers and the errors that arise from this experience.

Beginning programming students have extensive experience with step-by-step informal (natural) language procedures (SSNLP). These are simple written procedures for accomplishing day-to-day procedural tasks like getting to a friend's house, lighting an oil furnace, or assembling lawn furniture. Studies suggest that there are many regularities in the way non-programmers write SSNLP (Miller, 1981; Bonar 1985). For example, different non-programmers will use the same phrases to indicate looping structures and other standard programming tasks.

SSNLP has been shown to play a key role in novice programmer errors (Bonar and Soloway, 1985). Students confuse phrases in SSNLP with the English keywords of a language like Pascal, writing the Pascal as if it had the semantics of the corresponding SSNLP. So, for example, students write a Pascal while loop expecting the semantics of 'while' in English, e.g. 'while the road is two lanes, keep heading north'.

As the most relevant knowledge a novice brings into programming, we feel that SSNLP can be an important bridge between a novice's ideas and a final Pascal program. Also, since many novice errors are rooted in their experience with SSNLP, allowing a student to use SSNLP gives an intelligent tutor more direct access to the misconceptions and naive models used by the novice.

24.2.2 Teach about programming plans

Most programming texts teach students almost nothing about standard programming practice above the statement level. That there are standard techniques for implementing common tasks like running totals and array traversals is usually only covered implicitly through examples. We call these standard techniques *programming plans*. Studies of novice programmers have shown an understanding of plans to be crucial for their success (Soloway and Ehrlich, 1984). We propose to include programming plans as the second building block for our programming tutor.

Most programming texts introduce a programming language by discussing the syntax and semantics of each statement type. Unfortunately, this approach exacerbates a common novice tendency to adopt a syntactic matching strategy to problem solving. For example, physics students will often attempt to solve elementary mechanics problems by matching knowns and unknowns against standard formulae (Chi *et al.*, 1981). Their problem solving degenerates into a syntax directed search with no understanding of the quantities being manipulated. Experts, in constrast, analyse a problem in terms of standard intermediate concepts and techniques. These include component vectors, free body diagrams, and conservation of energy.

Programming novices exhibit syntactic strategies similar to those of the physics novices. In our video protocols of novice programmers (Bonar, 1985) we see novices working linearly through a program, choosing each statement based on syntactic features of the previous statements. Programming plans are exactly the concepts students need to step above the syntactic approach. Students can work on programming problems using standard approaches as encoded in plans.

A tutor that allows students to use programming plans has other advantages. Because the plans are high level, they allow the student to address issues of plan merging. Plan merge errors are a critical area of novice errors (Spohrer, Soloway and Pope, 1985). With an explicit plan representation, students can talk about plans and plan interactions, without concern for how the merged plans will be turned into code. That is, by introducing programming plans as an intermediate representation between informal language and programming code, we can break the programming process into three steps:

1. informal language specification of the solution,
2. translation from the informal language to a plan specification, and
3. translation from the plan specification to a programming language code solution.

This is the approach taken in Bridge.

24.2.3   Students can request feedback as programming proceeds

A programming tutor should allow students to request feedback as they work. One of the main features of intelligent tutoring is the possibility of supervising student work when a human teacher is not available. A programming tutor like PROUST, which runs in 'batch mode' on a finished program, is very limited in the support it can provide to a student.

24.2.4   Coaching should be provided as problems arise

Without intermediate feedback from a tutor, programming students can get very far off-track. A tutor must be able to recognize common error patterns and address them before a student's solution has become hopelessly muddled. On the other hand, the feedback must not be so quick and draconian that students never have an opportunity to discover their own solution to a new problem (a problem in the LISP tutor described in Reiser *et al.*, 1985). In Bridge, students are interrupted based on a series of novice models of programming operations. A student is only interrupted if there is an error relative to the model the tutor decides the student is using. Students with an error that is unimportant at their current level of understanding will not be interrupted. The mechanism for this approach is explained below.

24.2.5   Students can approach a solution by successive approximation

The 'final answer' to a programming problem is *very* rich: there are many correct answers and many answers that are close to correct but still contain several errors. A programming tutor ought to recognize a solution that is close to correct. Also, it ought to recognize the correct components in a program that is only partially complete. Most work in Bridge involves translating from one represent-ation to a more formal representation. Bridge knows what the student is working on because the student is translating a component from one representation into the equivalent component in another representation. This makes it relatively easy for Bridge to understand student partial solutions.

24.2.6   Students should be able to see a problem-solving trace

It is useful for a programming tutor to support a student with effective visual representations of the problem solving. There are two advantages to such an approach. First, there is less load on a student's working memory because more of the solution steps are available on the screen explicitly. Anderson and Jeffries (1985) have documented the relationship between working memory failures and novice programming errors. The second advantage to a visual representation is that it provides students with a visual model for the abstract operations and relationships represented in the text.

Our use of visual representations in Bridge is best understood by reading the system overview in Section 24.3.

24.3   AN OVERVIEW OF THE BRIDGE SYSTEM

In Bridge, the student user is presented with a problem which is of a level of difficulty such that it could be presented in the first ten weeks of an introductory programming course. The student passes through three phases while solving the problem.

In the first phase, the student constructs a set of step-by-step instructions using English phrases. In the next phase, the student matches these phrases to programming plans and builds a program using a representation of these plans. In the final phase, the student matches the plans to programming language constructs and uses these to build a programming language solution to the original problem. Currently the only language implemented in Bridge is Pascal, although many other programming languages could be used with the same approach.

We will use an example problem to demonstrate the three phases of Bridge. This problem is the Ending Value Averaging Problem (EVAP). The problem is:

> Write a program which repeatedly reads in integers until it reads in the integer 99 999. After seeing 99 999, it should print out the CORRECT AVERAGE without counting the final 99 999.

In the following description, several things should be kept in mind. First, Bridge is highly interactive. The figures will only give some sense of the display in action. Remember, most of the objects of concern to the student are created, manipulated and edited by moving objects on the screen with a mouse.

Bridge has been designed for students who have some familiarity with programming plans. Since they are not covered in most texts, we have developed a programming plan workbook for our students. We assume that users of Bridge are familiar with the plans in the workbook, up to the exercise they are attempting. Of course, students do not need to be skilled at using the plans, only familiar with the idea and basic purpose of plans.

Finally, the terminology and complex screen display of Bridge may seem overwhelming. The EVAP is probably two-thirds of the way through the programming curriculum we have designed. The problems students will see initially are much simpler than EVAP, initially involving only one or two plans at a time.

24.3.1   Phase 1: building the natural language 'Program'

Figure 24.1 shows the screen from Phase 1 with EVAP as the current problem. The problem specification from above is in the lower left corner of the screen.

The user is to build his English language solution to the problem by making choices from the 'Natural language selections menu'. The menu selections are the beginnings of phrases. Some of these selections are redundant, e.g. 'Print...' and 'Output ...'. This is done because people use different phrases to refer to the same task.

After the student chooses the beginning of a phrase, a smaller menu appears to the right of the selection. This menu contains choices which complete the phrase (see Fig. 24.2). This second choice may or may not effect the meaning of the phrase. The student is to construct the phrase that most precisely states his intentions.

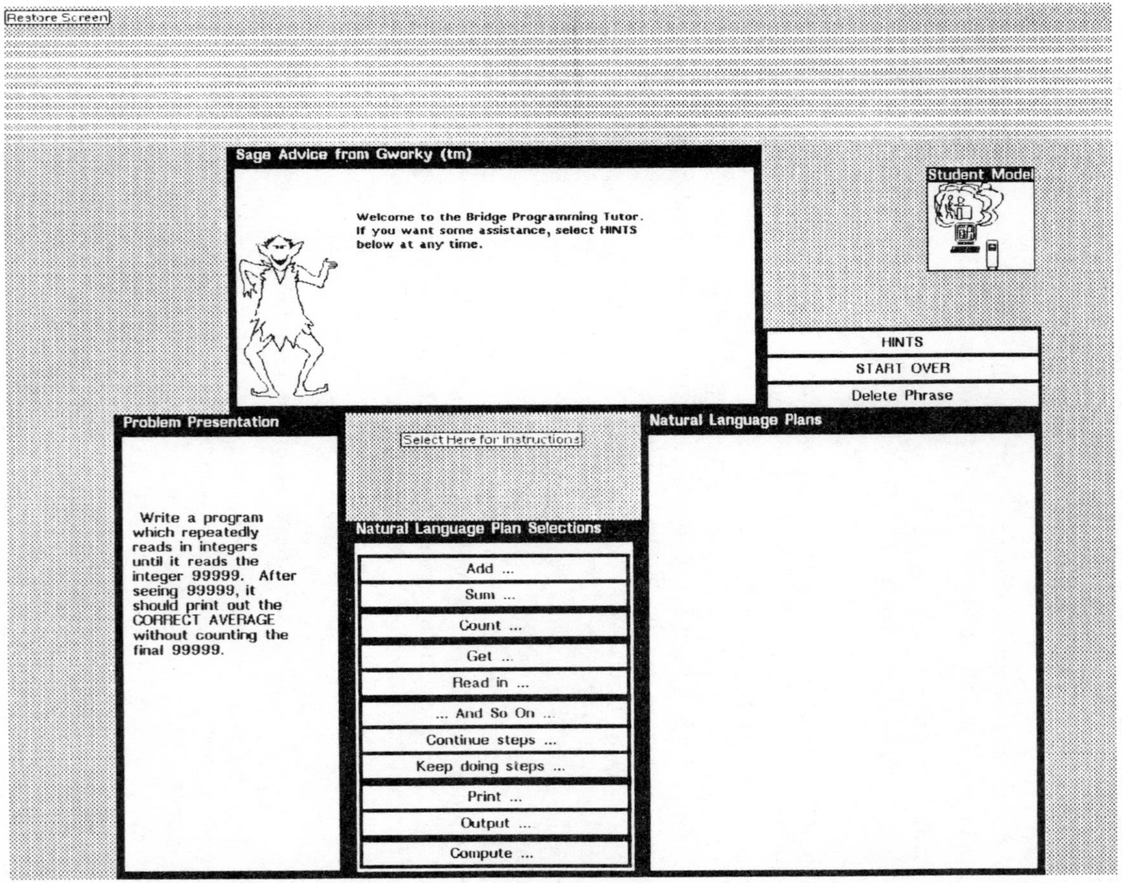

Fig. 24.1. Phase 1 of Bridge.

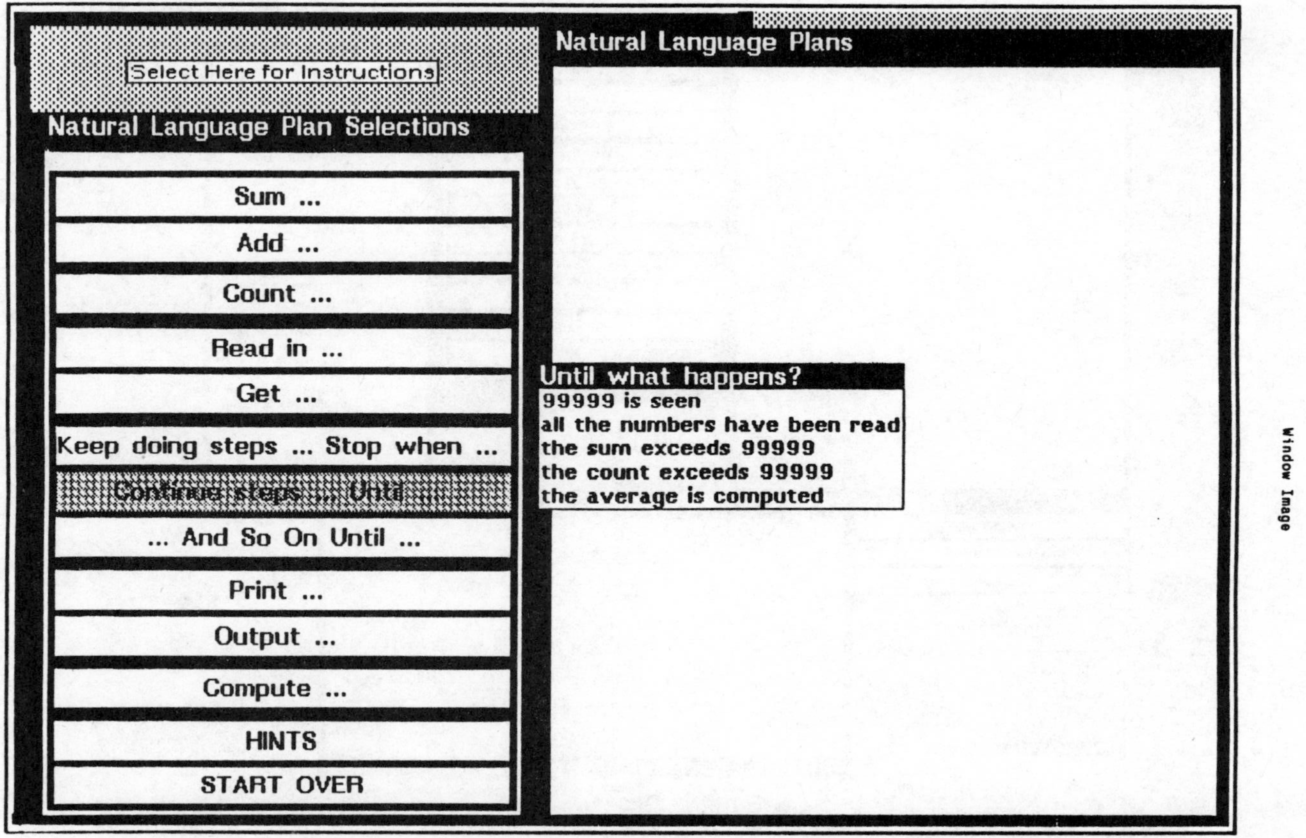

Window Image

Fig. 24.2. Menu showing the construction of a Natural Language Plan in phase 1.

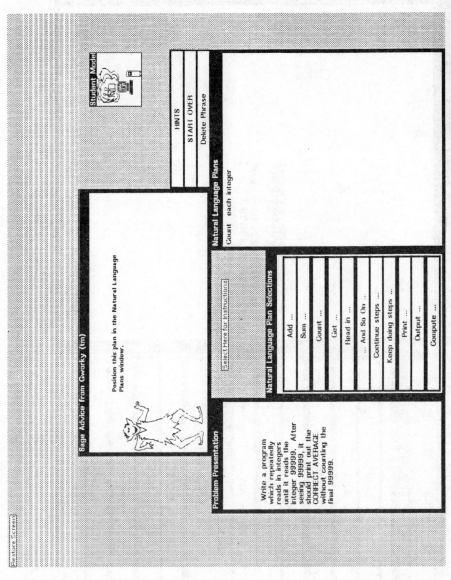

Fig. 24.3. A partially complete natural language solution to the Ending Value Averaging Problem with advice from Gworky, the friendly troll.

Once a phrase is completed, it appears in the 'Natural language plans' window (see Fig. 24.3). The student then moves the phrase to where he wants it placed. The student builds the 'natural language program' by combining these phrases in an order that correctly specifies a solution to the problem. At any time during Phase 1 the phrases may be repositioned or deleted from the program entirely.

24.3.1.1 *Solving the problem*

If the student needs help or thinks that the program is correct, he can select 'Hints' from the main menu. The program responds to the student in the guise of 'Gworky' the friendly troll (see Fig. 24.3). When 'Hints' is selected, Gworky checks the program and coaches the student if there are any errors. To do this checking, the tutor builds a formal representation of the natural language program where each English phrase corresponds to a Programming Language Plan. The tutor notes the order and detailed contents of each plan. The student's natural language program is compared with requirements for a correct solution to the problem. If any of these requirements are unfulfilled, the program is incorrect. (See below for details on the diagnosis and coaching process.) The requirements are supplied by the instructors as part of a problem description.

The natural language programming problem may be solved on any one of four levels. Figure 24.4 shows the student model with which the tutor diagnoses the student's solution. The four levels are indicated by the four columns in the model. Each level shows the plans that must be present in the solution to satisfy that level. In EVAP, the only requirement for level one is that the Result Value Plan must be part of the program. The phrase that starts out 'Compute ...' corresponds to this plan. So, in a sense, the phrase 'Compute the average' is a natural language solution to the problem.

Clearly, this solution is not specific enough to use as a guide to solving the problem in a programming language, so if the student uses this solution the tutor will ask for more information.

A level-two solution specifies that it is necessary to keep track of the sum and count but does not explicitly mention that there are a number of individual steps that must be done repeatedly. Rather, the student uses phrases that imply that the sum and count are calculated all at once. An example of such a phrase is 'Add ... all the integers'. A level-three solution mentions getting the numbers as well as keeping track of the sum and count. It also explicitly uses some phrase that

Student Model Chart			
Level1	**Level2**	**Level3**	**Level4**
EVAPResultValuePlan	EVAPResultValuePlan	EVAPResultValuePlan	EVAPResultValuePlan
	EVAPArithmeticSumVariablePlan	EVAPInputNewValueVariablePlan	EVAPResultOutputPlan
	EVAPCounterVariablePlan	EVAPArithmeticSumVariablePlan	EVAPNewValueControlledLoopPlan
		EVAPCounterVariablePlan	EVAPInputNewValueVariablePlan
		EVAPNewValueControlledLoopPlan	EVAPArithmeticSumVariablePlan
			EVAPCounterVariablePlan
Sage Advice from Gworky (tm)			**Level being worked on:** Level1

Fig. 24.4. The student model chart from phase 1 of the Ending Value Averaging Problem.

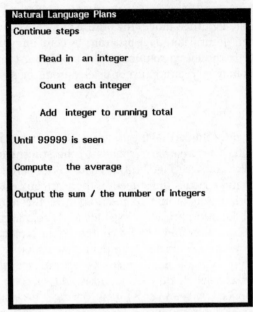

Fig. 24.5. A correct solution to phase 1 of the Ending Value Averaging Problem.

indicates a looping construct, such as 'Continue Until 99 999 is seen'.

To complete Phase 1 it is necessary to satisfy all four levels of the problem. To satisfy the fourth level, the student must mention the individual steps of getting an integer, adding it to the running total, and updating the count. The student must also use the loop construct effectively, indicating both the beginning and end of the loop. Finally, the user must explicitly use a phrase that prints the average. A level-four solution to the problem is shown in the 'Natural language plans' window of Fig. 24.5.

24.3.1.2 *Representation of requirements*

The *requirements* for a correct solution to the problem are associated with a problem specific part of each plan specification. These requirements include information about what phrases should appear in the program and the correct order of those phrases. We have defined a special language to specify the requirements. This language defines a group of operators which specify plan components, ordering information for those components, and the relationship between various components. Some of the operators we have found useful are:

Sequence: this describes the order that the plans should appear in the program. Figure 24.6 shows three such sequence requirements. The '...' that separates some plans indicates that zero or more plans can come between them in the student's solution.

```
DEdit of expression
(PushToHighest (EVAPCounterVariablePlan
                Exists?
                (Hints (In order to compute the average,
                        you will need to divide the sum
                        of the integers by the number of
                        integers read in. Include a plan
                        to read in the number of
                        integers.)
                    (To compute the average, you must
                        divide the sum of all the
                        integers read in by the count of
                        the number of integers. Include
                        the %"Keep count of ... %" plan
                        now.)))
        (EVAPCounterVariablePlan Sequence ...
            EVAPInputNewValueVariablePlan ...
            EVAPCounterVariablePlan ...
            (Hints (You have to acquire the numbers
                        BEFORE you can count them.)
                (Put the step you use to acquire the
                        numbers above the step you use to
                        count them.)
                    (Put %"Keep count of ...%" plan below
                        the %"Read in ...%"
                        or %"Get ....%" plan.)))
        (AnyOf (EVAPCounterVariablePlan Sequence ...
                EVAPCounterVariablePlan ...
                EVAPResultOutputPlan ...)
            (EVAPCounterVariablePlan Sequence ...
                EVAPCounterVariablePlan ...
                EVAPResultValuePlan ...)
            (Hints (You must count the numbers BEFORE you
                        can compute the average.)
                (Put the statement you use to count
                        the numbers higher than the one
                        you use to compute the average.)))
        ))
```

Fig. 24.6. An example of the requirements language used in the diagnosis of the student's program.

Exists?: This operator indicates that the plan mentioned must appear in the program. In Fig. 24.6, the Counter Variable Plan is required to be in the program.

AnyOf: this is the equivalent of an OR operator. It is satisfied if any of its arguments are satisfied.

All: this is the equivalent of an AND operator. It is satisfied only if all of its arguments are satisfied.

Not: this is the usual NOT operator. It is satisfied only if its argument is not satisfied.

PushToHighest: This manages several requirements at once and selects a hint dealing with the first unsatisfied plan.

When the student requests help by selecting 'Hints', a representation of the student's solution is given to the tutor. This representation contains information about what phrases are present in the problem, their order of appearance, and the wording of the phrases that make up the program. The tutor then iterates through the required plans, level by level, and matches the requirements from the plan at that level against the student model. When a requirement is unsatisfied, the tutor uses the first hint that is associated with that requirement. If the student selects 'Hints' a second time, he receives a more detailed hint. Requirements usually have three hints: the first hint is fairly vague, the second more specific, and the third usually gives the answer away.

24.3.2   Phase 2: building a 'Plan Program'

A student begins this phase by matching his English phrases from Phase 1 with a menu selection of programming plan names. The plan names are intended as a more formal description of the program steps described with English in phase 1. The student is checked for the correct match after each match is made. After the matching is complete, the student begins building the Programming Language Plans (PL Plans) version of their program. Figure 24.7 shows the screen during Phase 2. The natural language version of the program constructed in Phase 1 is now shown in the lower left corner of the screen.

24.3.2.1   *Matching*

The first thing that the student must do is match each English phrase with a selection from the 'Plans menu' that describes the purpose of the phrase. For instance, the phrase 'Add integer to running total' matches the 'Plan to: Keep a Running Total'. Once the correct match is made, the box that will represent this plan in Phase 2 appears on the screen. The student must match all of the phrases to the appropriate plans before he can proceed to building the PL Plans program. As he continues to match the phrases, the PL Plans representations are constructed and stacked in the middle of the screen.

24.3.2.2   *Boxes and tiles*

In Phase 2, we use boxes and tiles to represent the PL Plans. Each plan has its own box and many of the plans have tiles as well. The tiles represent the different roles of the plan. In Fig. 24.7 we see the representations of the 'Plan to: Input a New Value', 'Plan to: Count How Many', and 'Plan to: Keep a Running Total'. The last plan, for example, contains three tiles which represent the *initialize, update,* and *value* roles.

There are two kinds of boxes: those that supply tiles to the program and those that have empty slots into which tiles are placed. An example of the second type is the 'Plan to: Control Loop with Sentinel'. If an action is to be performed inside the loop, its tile should be placed in the bottommost slots inside this box.

24.3.2.3   *Building the PL plans Program*

After the matching is complete, the 'Plans menu' disappears and a new menu appears at the top of the 'Programming language plans' window. This menu has two selections, 'Hints' and 'Start Phase 2 Over'. At this point the student can begin to build the program. The student must select a box or tile from the centre of

Select Here for Instructions

Programming Language Plans

Plans Menu
Plan to: Compute the Result
Plan to: Output the Result
Plan to: Control Loop with Sentinel
Plan to: Input a New Value
Plan to: Count How Many
Plan to: Keep a Running Total

Sage Advice from Gworky (tm)

Hi, welcome back to Bridge. First, please match all the Natural Language Plans with the appropriate selection from the menu.

Natural Language Plans

Continue steps

Read in an integer

Count each integer

Add integer to running total

Until 99999 is seen

Compute the average

Output the sum / the number of integers

Plan to: Input a New Value

Ask the user to type in a value:

Input Plan: GET VALUE

yielding:

Input Plan: USE VALUE

Plan to: Count How Many

First,

Counter Plan: INITIALIZE

then, for each new value,

Counter Plan: INCREMENT

finally yielding:

Counter Plan: VALUE

Plan to: Keep a Running Total

First,

Sum Plan: INITIALIZE

then, for each new value,

Sum Plan: UPDATE

finally yielding:

Sum Plan: VALUE

24.7. Phase 2 of Bridge.

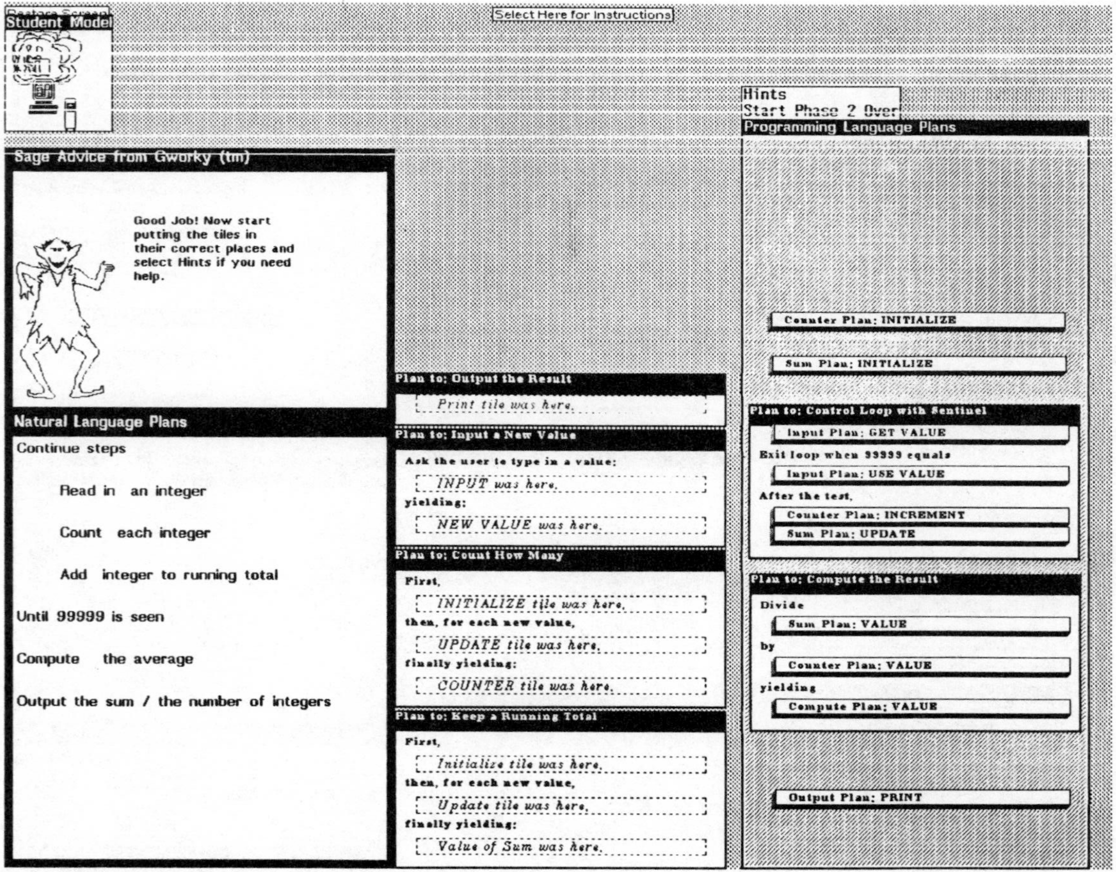

[Select Here for Instructions]

Hints
Start Phase 2 Over
Programming Language Plans

Sage Advice from Gworky (tm)

Good Job! Now start putting the tiles in their correct places and select Hints if you need help.

Natural Language Plans

Continue steps

Read in an integer

Count each integer

Add integer to running total

Until 99999 is seen

Compute the average

Output the sum / the number of integers

Plan to: Output the Result

Print tile was here.

Plan to: Input a New Value

Ask the user to type in a value:

INPUT was here.

yielding:

NEW VALUE was here.

Plan to: Count How Many

First,

INITIALIZE tile was here.

then, for each new value,

UPDATE tile was here.

finally yielding:

COUNTER tile was here.

Plan to: Keep a Running Total

First,

Initialize tile was here.

then, for each new value,

Update tile was here.

finally yielding:

Value of Sum was here.

Counter Plan: INITIALIZE

Sum Plan: INITIALIZE

Plan to: Control Loop with Sentinel

Input Plan: GET VALUE

Exit loop when 99999 equals

Input Plan: USE VALUE

After the test,

Counter Plan: INCREMENT

Sum Plan: UPDATE

Plan to: Compute the Result

Divide

Sum Plan: VALUE

by

Counter Plan: VALUE

yielding

Compute Plan: VALUE

Output Plan: PRINT

Fig. 24.8. A correct solution to phase 2 of the Ending Value Averaging Problem.

the screen and place it in the 'Programming language plans' window. He continues placing the boxes and tiles in the window until he arrives at a correct solution to the problem. The correct solution to EVAP is shown in Fig. 24.8.

24.3.2.4 *Hints in Phase 2*

Hints in Phase 2 are very similar to hints in the Phase 1. The student selects 'Hints' whenever he needs help or thinks he has a correct solution to the problem. The diagnosis is performed similar to Phase 1, comparing the student's solution to the requirements. In this phase however, there is only one level at which the problem can be solved.

24.3.3 Phase 3: building the Pascal program

In Phase 3 the student is to build a programming language solution to the original problem. Bridge currently uses Pascal as its only programming language.

24.3.3.1 *Matching and building the Pascal program*

Figure 24.9 shows the screen from Phase 3. The PL Plans program from Phase 2 is now in the lower left corner of the screen. The student will use this to match each box or tile to the appropriate programming language construct. Once constructs are selected they are inserted and manipulated with a Pascal structure editor provided in the 'Pascal edit window' on the right side of the screen.

The student works by selecting a plan or role, indicated by a box or tile from the PL Plans program, and then selecting the programming language construct that would best implement that plan or role. This usually means selecting a statement type from the 'Pascal statement types' menu in the middle of the screen. If the student makes the correct choice, he will then be asked to indicate the position for the statement in the 'Pascal edit window'. Occasionally, boxes or tiles will match something other than an entire statement. For example, the 'Input Plan: USE VALUE' tile inside the loop box matches the < Expression > non-terminal node in a while loop. Such a counter-intuitive match is an illustration of the non-trivial match between Pascal constructs and the fundamental plans of programming. Not only is it a difficulty for Pascal, it also is a human-interface problem for Bridge. We are currently working on a smoother way of associating plans with programming language constructs.

Bridge provides a structure editor in Phase 3 to help the student build the Pascal program. This editor implements a subset of Pascal which does not include procedure and function definitions. The editor does not allow the student to build a syntactically incorrect program. We decided to use such a structure editor to minimize the syntactic concerns of the novice programmer, thus allowing him to concentrate on semantic and pragmatic aspects of the program. In addition to managing syntactic concerns the editor also manages variable declarations. Figure 24.10 shows a finished Pascal program.

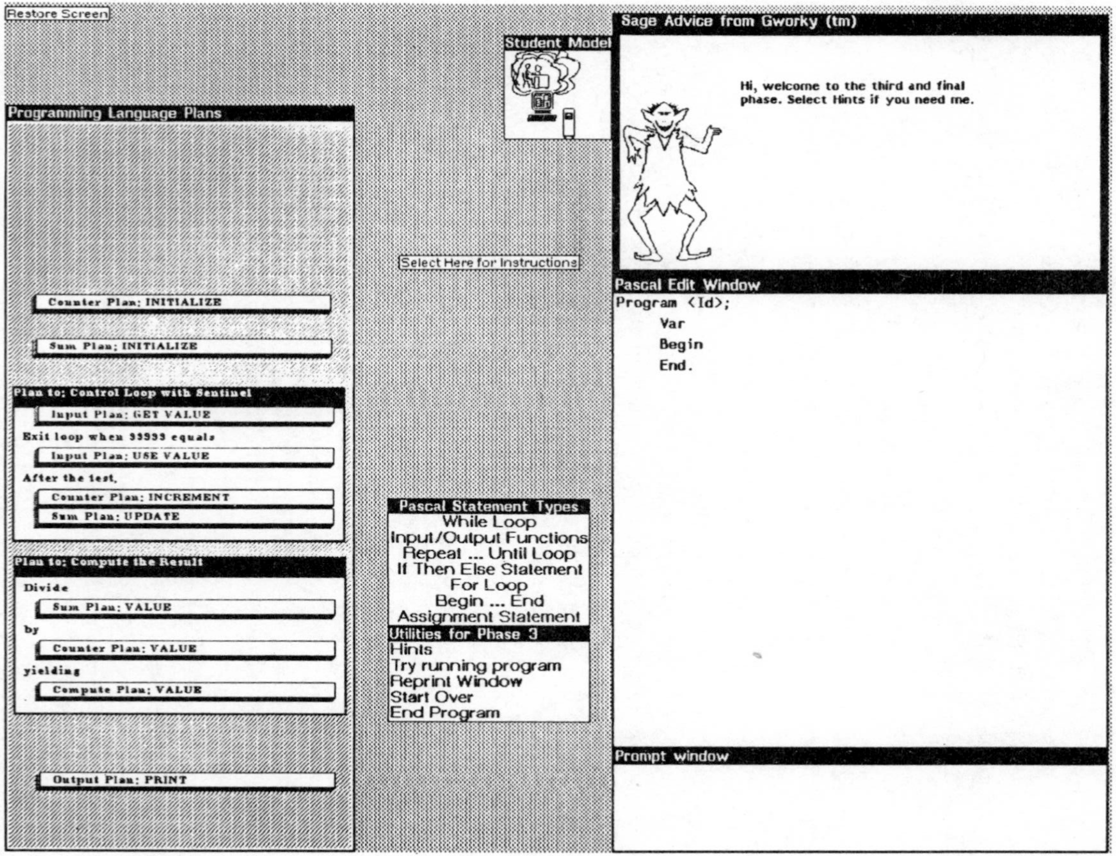

Restore Screen

Sage Advice from Gworky (tm)

Hi, welcome to the third and final phase. Select Hints if you need me.

Student Model

Select Here for Instructions

Pascal Edit Window

Program <Id>;

Var
Begin
End.

Programming Language Plans

Counter Plan: INITIALIZE

Sum Plan: INITIALIZE

Plan to: Control Loop with Sentinel

Input Plan: GET VALUE

Exit loop when 33533 equals

Input Plan: USE VALUE

After the test,

Counter Plan: INCREMENT

Sum Plan: UPDATE

Plan to: Compute the Result

Divide

Sum Plan: VALUE

by

Counter Plan: VALUE

yielding

Compute Plan: VALUE

Output Plan: PRINT

Pascal Statement Types
While Loop
Input/Output Functions
Repeat ... Until Loop
If Then Else Statement
For Loop
Begin ...End
Assignment Statement

Utilities for Phase 3
Hints
Try running program
Reprint Window
Start Over
End Program

Prompt window

Fig. 24.9. Phase 3 of Bridge.

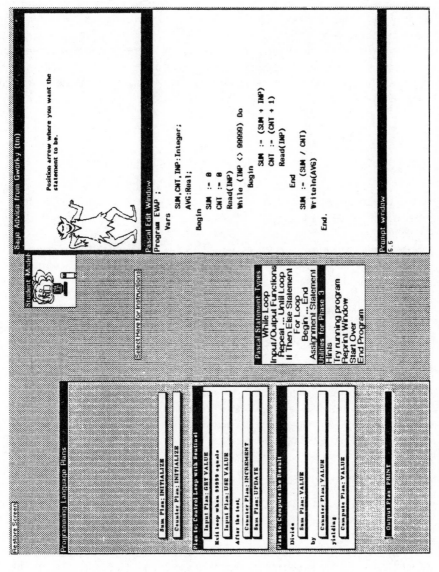

Fig. 24.10. A correct solution to phase 3 of the Ending Value Averaging Problem.

24.3.3.2   *Editing the Pascal program*

Once a statement is added to the Pascal program, there are several things that the student can do with it. First, any non-terminal nodes must be expanded before the program can be run. There are two kinds of non-terminal nodes, expressions and identifiers. To expand them, the student selects the node he wants to expand and then types the identifier or expression he wants to appear at that location. The tutor currently checks the type-in to verify that it is correct for the statement.

There are three things that the student can do with entire statements once they are part of the program. He can move them to another location in the program, delete them from the program, or show the role or plan that the statement represents.

24.3.3.3   *Phase 3 utilities*

There are several utilities at the student's disposal in Phase 3:

Hints: This is very similar to Phases 1 and 2. The student selects 'Hints' whenever he needs help or if he thinks he has a correct program. The diagnosis is done the same way as Phase 2. There is only one level at which the problem can be solved.

Try running program: This selection will attempt to execute the program. As it runs through the program, it will highlight each statement as it is encountered. If some error is discovered during the run, a type mismatch, for example, the program will halt and indicate where the error occurred by flashing the offending line of code. The tutor will also give a message that explains the error.

Reprint window: This reprints the Pascal program. Sometimes part of the program may not look like it is indented properly. This is corrected by selecting this option.

Start over: This starts Phase 3 over again. It deselects whatever boxes or tiles are selected in the 'Programming language plans' window, erases the Pascal program, and initializes a new Pascal program.

End program: This ends Bridge. When this is selected, everything in Phase 3 is destroyed and Bridge is exited.

24.4   USING BRIDGE WITH STUDENTS

We have run Bridge with approximately 10 students. This is by no means a complete evaluation, but does allow an initial report about student reactions. Phase one was quite successful with the students. They were usually able to work through the phase with little or no intervention from our human monitor. Students were pleased to be able to represent their ideas informally. Students liked Gworky and were usually able to follow his instructions successfully.

Phase 2 was not as successful as Phase 1. Students found the display too complex. In particular, they lost track of the relationship between a plan and its associated tiles. Also, the textual material in the plans was not always clear. We are currently improving the comprehensibility of Phase 2 by using shading to make connections between selected plan components and simplifying the texts that label plans and tiles. Our next round of tests with Bridge will have students work many more problems before attempting EVAP.

Phase 3 was moderately difficult for our students. They liked the structured editor and had little trouble using it. Matching between the Phase 2 output and Pascal code was problematic, however. Because there is not always a simple match between a plan component and Pascal code, students will sometimes make a reasonable selection that Bridge doesn't accept. We are currently working on a smoother interface that still maintains all the correct matches.

24.5 FUTURE PLANS

We have a number of plans for Bridge. First we plan to use Bridge with 10 problems in an introductory Pascal class in the Fall of 1987. At that time we will work on a more complete evaluation of Bridge and our overall approach. We are currently updating our plans curriculum for this trial. Also, we are developing a set of indices and protocol tools to assist in characterizing a student's performance with Bridge.

On a longer time scale, we are interested in relaxing some of the rigidities of Bridge. In particular, we would like students to be able to begin in Phase 3. The tutor would only ask the student to work in Phase 1 or 2 if the student's actions in Phase 3 could not be understood by the tutor. This would greatly simplify the use of Bridge for a good student without making large changes for weaker students. It would also require a more sophisticated diagnositic capability in Phase 3.

Finally, we are interested in developing principles for use of intermediate representations like those in Phases 1 and 2. We feel that these representations are an important contribution of Bridge. In particular, we think this idea can be quite effective in providing students with a tool for reasoning about relationships between plan-like knowledge structures.

ACKNOWLEDGEMENTS

An earlier version of the Bridge system was developed by Mary Ann Quayle. John Corbett and Jamie Schultz contributed substantially to the development of Bridge. We are grateful to the Intelligent Tutoring Systems group for their suggestions and encouragement in this project. In particular, we wish to thank Alan Lesgold for his suggestions and support.

This work was supported by the Air Force Human Resources Laboratory under contract number F41689-84-D-0002, Order 0004 and by the Office of Naval Research under contract numbers N00014-83-6-0148 and N00014-83-K0655. Any opinions, findings, conclusions, or recommendations expressed in this report are those of the authors, and do not necessarily reflect the views of the US Government.

References

Achinstein, P. (1983) *The Nature of Explanation*, Oxford University Press, New York.

Adam, A. and Laurent, J.-P. (1980) LAURA, a system to debug student programs. *Artificial Intelligence*, **15**, 75–122.

Adelson, B. and Soloway, E. (1985) The role of domain experience in software design. *IEEE Transactions on Software Engineering*, **11**, 1351–60.

Aho, A.V. and Ullman, J.D. (1977) *Principles of Compiler Design*, Addison-Wesley, Reading, MA.

Allen, J.F. and Perrault, C.R. (1980) Analysing intention in utterances. *Artificial Intelligence*, **15**, 143–78.

Alty, J.L. (1984) The application of path algebras to interactive dialogue design. *Behaviour and Information Technology*, **3**, 119–32.

Anderson, J.R. (1975) *Language, Memory and Thought*, Erlbaum, Hillsdale, NJ.

Anderson, J.R. (1982) Acquisition of cognitive skill, *Psychological Review*, **89**, 369–406.

Anderson, J.R. (1983) *The Architecture of Cognition*, Harvard University Press, Cambridge, MA.

Anderson, J.R. (1984) Cognitive psychology and intelligent tutoring. *Proc. Sixth Annual Conference of the Cognitive Science Society*, Boulder, Colorado.

Anderson, J.R. (1986) Knowledge compilation: the general learning mechanism, in *Machine Learning: an Artificial Intelligence Approach* II (eds R.S. Michalski, J.G. Carbonell and T.M. Mitchell), Kaufmann, Los Altos.

Anderson, J.R. and Jeffries, R. (1985) Novice LISP errors: undetected losses of information from working memory. *Human-Computer Interaction*, **1**, 107–31.

Anderson, J.R. and Reiser, B.J. (1985) The Lisp tutor. *Byte*, **10**, 159–75.

Anderson, J.R., Boyle, C.F. and Reiser, B.J. (1985) Intelligent tutoring systems. *Science*, **228**, 456–62.

Anderson, J.R., Boyle, C.F. and Yost, G. (1985) The geometry tutor. *Proc. Ninth International Joint Conference on Artificial Intelligence*, Los Angeles.

Anderson, J.R., Farrell, R. and Sauers, R. (1984) Learning to program in LISP. *Cognitive Science*, **8**, 87–129.

Anderson, J.R., Boyle, C.F., Farrell, R. and Reiser, B.J. (1986) Cognitive principles in the design of computer tutors, in *Modelling Cognition* (ed. P.E. Morris), Wiley, London.

Anderson, J.R., Greeno, J.G., Kline, P.J. and Neves, D.M. (1981) Acquisition of problem-solving skill, in *Cognitive Skills and their Acquisition* (ed. J.R. Anderson), Erlbaum, Hillsdale, N.J.

Appelt, D.E. (1982) Planning natural language utterances to satisfy multiple goals, Technical Note 259, S.R.I. International.

Attisha, M.G. (1983) A microcomputer based tutoring system for self-improving and teaching techniques in arithmetic skills, unpublished M.Sc. thesis, Exeter University.

Ausubel, D.P. (1968) *Educational Psychology: a Cognitive View*, Holt, Rinehart and Winston, New York.

Balacheff, N. (1984) French research activities in didactics of mathematics. *Proc. Fifth International Congress on Mathematical Education*, Adelaide.

Barnard, D.T. (1976) A survey of syntax error handling techniques, internal report, Computer Science Research Group, University of Toronto.

Barr, A. (1979) Meta-knowledge and cognition. *Proc. 6th International Joint Conference on Artificial Intelligence*, Tokyo.

Barr, A. and Feigenbaum, E. (eds) (1982) *The Handbook of Artificial Intelligence*, Vol. 2, Kaufmann, Los Altos.

Barr, A., Bennett, J. and Clancey, W. (1979) Transfer of expertise: a theme for AI research, Working Paper HPP-79-11. Heuristic Programming Project, Stanford University.

Barrows, H.S. and Tamblyn, R.H. (1980) *Problem-Based Learning: an Approach to Medical Education*, Springer, New York.

Bates, M. (1975) Syntactic analysis in a speech understanding system, BBN Report 3116, Bolt Beranek and Newman, Cambridge, MA.

Becker, H.J. (1984) School uses of microcomputers. *Journal of Computers in Mathematics and Science Teaching*, Summer, 24–33, Fall, 38–42 and Winter, 42–49.

Benoit, C., Caseau, Y. and Pherivong, C. (1986) Knowledge representation and communication mechanisms in LORE. *Proc. 7th European Conference on Artificial Intelligence*, Brighton, U.K.

Bialo, E.R. and Erickson, L.B. (1985) Microcomputer courseware: characteristics and design trends. *Journal of Computers in Mathematics and Science Teaching*, Summer, 27–32.

Bison, P. and van der Pal, F. (1985) Using UNIX-Mail: an experiment in on-line tutoring, internal report, Department of Social Science Informatics, University of Amsterdam.

Bobrow, D.G. (1984) Special issue on qualitative reasoning about physical systems. *Artificial Intelligence*, **24**, 1–5.

Bolc, L. (1978) *Natural Language Communication with Computers*, Springer, New York.

Boden, M. (1977) *Artificial Intelligence and Natural Man*, Harvester, Brighton.

Bonar, J. (1982) Natural problem solving strategies and programming language constructs, *Proc. Fourth Annual Conference of the Cognitive Science Society*.

Bonar, J. (1985) Understanding the bugs of novice programmers, unpublished doctoral dissertation, University of Massachusetts, Amherst.

Bonar, J. and Soloway, E. (1985) Pre-programming knowledge: a major source of misconceptions in novice programmers. *Human–Computer Interaction*, **1**, 133–61.

Booth, L.R. (1983) *Children's Strategies and Errors in Algebra: a Report on the Strategies and Errors in a Secondary Mathematics Project*, NFER-Nelson, Slough.

Brachman, R.J. (1978) A structural paradigm for representing knowledge, BBN Report 3605, Bolt Beranek and Newman, Boston, MA.

Brachman, R.J. (1979) On the epistemological status of semantic networks, in *Associative Networks* (ed. N.V. Findler), Academic Press, New York.

Brachman, R.J. (1983) What ISA is and isn't: an analysis of taxonomic links in semantic networks. *IEEE Computer*, **16**, 30–6.

Breuker, J.A. and de Greef, P.H. (1985a) Functional specification of teaching and coaching strategies for EUROHELP, Deliverable 4.2, ESPRIT Project 280, University of Amsterdam.

Breuker, J.A. and de Greef, P.H. (1985b) Information processing systems and teaching and coaching in HELP systems, Deliverable 12.1, ESPRIT Project 280, University of Amsterdam.

Breuker, J. A. and Wielinga, B.J. (1987) Use of models in the interpretation of verbal data, in *Knowledge Acquisition for Expert Systems: a Practical Handbook* (ed. A. Kidd), Plenum Press, New York.

Breuker, J.A., Winkels, R. and Sandberg, J. (1987) A shell for intelligent help systems. *Proc. 10th International Joint Conference on Artificial Intelligence*, Milan.

Broudy, H. (1969) Socrates and the teaching machine, in *The Human Encounter* (eds S. Stoff and S. Schwartzberg), Harper and Row, New York.

Brown, J.S. (1977) Uses of AI and advanced computer technology in education, in *Computers and Communications: Implications for Education* (ed. R.J. Seidel), Academic Press, New York.

Brown, J.S. and Bell, A. (1974) SOPHIE: a sophisticated instructional environment for teaching electronic troubleshooting (an example of AI in CAI), BBN Report 2790, Bolt Beranek and Newman, Boston, MA.

Brown, J.S. and Burton, R.R. (1978) Diagnostic models for procedural bugs in basic mathematical skills. *Cognitive Science*, **2**, 155–92.

Brown, J.S. and Newman, S.E. (1985) Issues in cognitive and social ergonomics: from our house to Bauhaus. *Human–Computer Interaction*, **1**, 359–91.

Brown, J.S. and VanLehn, K. (1980) Repair theory: a generative theory of bugs in procedural skills. *Cognitive Science*, **4**, 379–426.

Brown, J.S. and VanLehn, K. (1982) Towards a generative theory of bugs, in *Addition and Subtraction: a Cognitive Perspective* (eds T.P. Carpenter, J.M. Moser and T.A. Romberg), Erlbaum, Hillsdale, N.J.

Brown, J.S., Burton, R.R. and deKleer, J. (1982) Pedagogical, natural language and knowledge engineering techniques in SOPHIE I, II and III, in *Intelligent Tutoring Systems* (eds D.H. Sleeman and J.S. Brown), Academic Press, New York.

Brown, J.S., Burton, R.R. and Zdybel, F. (1973) A model-driven question-answering system for mixed-initiative computer-assisted instruction. *IEEE Transactions on Systems, Man and Cybernetics*, **3**, 248–57.

Brown, J.S., Collins, A. and Harris, G. (1977) Artificial intelligence and learning strategies, in *Learning Strategies* (ed. H. O'Neill), Academic Press, New York.

Brown, P.J. (1983) Error messages: the neglected area of the man/machine interface? *Communications of the ACM*, **26**, 246–9.

Browne, D.P., Sharratt, B.D. and Norman, M.A. (1986) The formal specification of adaptive user interfaces: command language grammar. *Proc. Computer–Human Interaction 86*.

Bruner, J.S. (1973) Organisation of early skilled action. *Child Development*, **44**, 1–11.

Bruner, J.S., Goodnow, J.A. and Austin, G.A. (1956) *A Study of Thinking*, Wiley, New York.

Bundy, A., Silver, B. and Plummer, D. (1985) An analytical comparison of some rule-learning programs. *Artificial Intelligence*, **27**, 137–81.

Burstein, M. (1986) Concept formation by incremental analogical reasoning and debugging, in *Machine Learning: an Artificial Intelligence Approach*, Vol. II (eds R.S. Michalski, J.G. Carbonell and T.M. Mitchell), Kaufmann. Los Altos.

Burton, R.R. (1982) Diagnosing bugs in a simple procedural skill, in *Intelligent Tutoring Systems* (eds D.H. Sleeman and J.S. Brown), Academic Press, New York.

Burton, R.R. and J.S. Brown (1982) An investigation of computer coaching for informal learning activities, in *Intelligent Tutoring Systems* (eds D.H. Sleeman and J.S. Brown), Academic Press, New York.

Caillot, M. (1985) Problem representations and problem solving procedures in electricity, in *Aspects of Understanding Electricity* (eds R. Duit, W. Jung and C. von Rhoneck), IPN-Arbeitsberitchte, Kiel.

Camstra, B. (1985) An information system metaphor for EUROHELP, Report COE/EUROHELP/003, Courseware Europe BV, Purmerend, The Netherlands.

Carbonell, J.G. and Hayes, P.J. (1983) Recovery strategies for parsing extragrammatical language. *American Journal of Computational Linguistics*, 9, 123–46.

Carbonell, J.R. (1970) Mixed-initiative man–computer instructional dialogues, BBN Report 1971, Bolt Beranek and Newman, Boston, MA.

Card, S.K., Moran, T.P. and Newell, A. (1983) *The Psychology of Human–Computer Interaction*, Erlbaum, Hillsdale, N.J.

Carr, B. and Goldstein, I. (1977) Overlays: a theory of modelling for computer aided instruction, AI Memo 406, M.I.T.

Carver, N.F., Lesser, V.R. and McCue, D.C. (1984) Focussing in plan recognition. *Proc. Annual National Conference on Artificial Intelligence*, pp. 42–8, Austin, Texas.

Catterall, P. and Lewis, R. (1985) Problem solving with spreadsheets. *Journal of Computer Assisted Learning*, 1, 167–79.

Cerri, S.A. (1983) Teaching a (second) (programming) language, Scientific Report S-83-3, Department of Informatics, University of Pisa, Italy.

Cerri, S.A. (1986a) Conceptual processing for the casual user: perspectives in educational technologies from the artificial intelligence viewpoint, in *Children in an Information Age* (eds P. Sendov and J. Stanchez), Pergamon, Oxford.

Cerri, S.A. (1986b) Ambiguity in knowledge representation. *Proc. 7th European Conference on Artificial Intelligence*, Brighton, U.K.

Cerri, S.A. and Breuker, J. (1980) A rather intelligent language teacher. *Proc. AISB Conference on Artificial Intelligence*, Amsterdam, The Netherlands.

Cerri, S.A. and Landini, P. (1985) Misconceptions in multilingual translations, *Proc. 2nd International Conference on Artificial Intelligence and Education*, Exeter, U.K.

Cerri, S.A., Landini, P. and Leoncini, M. (1986) Cooperative agents for knowledge-based information systems. *Applied Artificial Intelligence Journal*, 1, 1.

Cerri, S.A., Colombini, C., Grillo, M. and Mallozzi, R. (1984) Reasoning on ADA rubbish. *Proc. 6th European Conference on Artificial Intelligence*, Pisa, Italy.

Chang, C. and Lee, R. (1973) *Symbolic Logic and Mechanical Theorem Proving*, Academic Press, New York.

Chi, M., Feltovich, P. and Glaser, R. (1981) Categorization and representation of physics problems by experts and novices. *Cognitive Science*, 5, 121–52.

Chomsky, N. (1965) *Aspects of the Theory of Syntax*, M.I.T. Press, Cambridge, MA.

Clancey, W.J. (1979a) Transfer of rule-based expertise through a tutorial dialogue, Report STAN-CS-79-769, Department of Computer Science, Stanford University.

Clancey, W. J. (1979b) Dialogue management for rule-based tutorials. *Proc. 6th International Joint Conference on Artificial Intelligence*, Tokyo, Japan.

Clancey, W.J. (1982) Tutoring rules for guiding a case method dialogue. in *Intelligent Tutoring Systems* (eds D.H. Sleeman and J.S. Brown), Academic Press, New York.

Clancey, W.J. (1983a) The epistemology of a rule-based expert system – a framework for explanations. *Artificial Intelligence*, 20, 215–51.

Clancey, W.J. (1983b) GUIDON. *Journal of Computer-Based Instruction*, **10**, 8–15.

Clancey, W.J. (1985) Heuristic classification. *Artificial Intelligence*, **27**, 289–350.

Clancey, W.J. (1986) The science and engineering of qualitative models, KSL Report 86-27, Knowledge Systems Laboratory, Stanford University.

Clancey, W.J. and Letsinger, R. (1984) NEOMYCIN: reconfiguring a rule-based expert system for application to teaching, in *Readings in Medical Artificial Intelligence: the First Decade* (eds W.J. Clancey and E.H. Shortliffe), Addison-Wesley, Reading, MA.

Clowes, I., Cole, I., Arshad, F. *et al.* (1985) User modelling techniques for interactive systems, in *People and Computers: Designing the Interface* (eds P. Johnson and S. Cook), Cambridge University Press, Cambridge.

Cockcroft, W.H. (1982) *Mathematics Counts*, Her Majesty's Stationery Office, London.

Cohen, P.R. and Grinberg, M. (1983) A theory of heuristic reasoning about uncertainty. *AI Magazine*, **4**, 17–24.

Collins, A. and Gentner, D. (1980) A framework for a cognitive theory of writing, in *Cognitive Processes in Writing* (eds L.W. Gregg and E. Steinberg), Erlbaum, Hillsdale, N.J.

Costa, E. (1986) Artificial intelligence and education: the role of knowledge in teaching. *Proc. European Working Session on Learning*, Paris.

Cox, L.S. (1974) Analysis, classification and frequency of systematic error computational patterns in the addition, subtraction, multiplication and division of vertical algorithms for grades 2–6 and special education classes, ERIC Document No. ED 092 407.

Craik, K. (1943) *The Nature of Explanation*, Cambridge University Press, Cambridge.

Croft, W.B. (1984) The role of context and adaptation in user interfaces. *International Journal of Man–Machine Studies*, **21**, 283–92.

Cypher, A. (1986) The structure of users' activities, in *User Centered System Design: New Perspectives on Human–Computer Interaction* (eds D.A. Norman and S.W. Draper), Erlbaum, Hillsdale, N.J.

Davies, N.G., Dickens, S.L. and Ford, L. (1985) TUTOR – a prototype ICAI system, in *Research and Development in Expert Systems* (ed. M. Bramer), Cambridge University Press, Cambridge.

Davis, R. (1983) Reasoning from first principles in electronic trouble shooting. *International Journal of Man–Machine Studies*, **19**, 403–23.

Davis, R. (1986) Knowledge-based systems. *Science*, **231**, 957–63.

Davis, R., Buchanan, B. and Shortliffe, E. (1977) Production rules as a representation for a knowledge-based consultation program. *Artificial Intelligence*, **8**, 15–45.

Davis, R., Shrobe, H., Hamscher, W. *et al.* (1982) Diagnosis based on description of structure and function. *Proc. National Conference on Artificial Intelligence*, Pittsburgh, PA.

Davis, R. B. and McKnight, C. (1980) The influence of semantic content on algorithmic behaviour. *Journal of Mathematical Behaviour*, **3**.

Davis, R. B., Dugdale, S., Kibbey, D. and Weaver, C. (1977) Representing knowledge about mathematics for computer-aided teaching, part 2: the diversity of roles that a computer can play in assisting learning, in *Machine Intelligence 8* (eds E.W. Elcock and D. Michie), Horwood, Chichester.

DeJong, G. (1986) An approach to learning from observation, in *Machine Learning: an Artificial Intelligence Approach*, Vol. II (eds R.S. Michalski, J.G. Carbonell and T.M. Mitchell), Kaufmann, Los Altos.

deKleer, J. (1984) Choices without backtracking. *Proc. Annual National Conference on Artificial Intelligence*, 79–85, Austin, Texas.

deKleer, J. and Brown, J.S. (1984) A qualitative physics based on confluences. *Artificial Intelligence*, **24**, 7–83.

deMarco, T. (1978) *Structured Analysis and System Specification*, Yourdon, New York.

Denvir, B. and Brown, M. (1986) Understanding of number concepts in low attaining 7–9 year olds: Part II: the teaching studies. *Educational Studies in Mathematics*, **17**, 143–64.

Downes, L.W. and Paling, D. (1958) *The Teaching of Arithmetic in Primary Schools*, Oxford University Press, Oxford.

Doyle, J. (1979) A truth maintenance system. *Artificial Intelligence*, **12**, 231–72.

Duursma, C., Maas, S. and Romeyn, T. (1986) A next step towards an epistemological description of an IPS, Report COE/EUROHELP/016, Courseware Europe BV, Purmerend, The Netherlands.

Elsom-Cook, M.T. (1984) Design considerations of an intelligent tutoring system for programming languages, Ph.D. thesis, University of Warwick.

Elsom-Cook, M.T. (1985a) Design considerations of an intelligent tutoring system for programming languages. in *Human–Computer Interaction: Interact 84* (ed. B. Shackel). Elsevier, Amsterdam.

Elsom-Cook, M. (1985b) Towards a framework for human–computer discourse, in *People and Computers: Designing the Interface* (eds P. Johnson and S. Cook), Cambridge University Press, Cambridge.

Elsom-Cook, M. (1985c) Machine learning and user modelling, CAL Research Group report, Open University.

Ericsson, K.A. and Simon, H.A. (1984) *Protocol Analysis, Verbal Reports as Data*, M.I.T. Press, Cambridge, MA.

Esterson, D. (1985) The management of computing resources in schools. *Journal of Computer Assisted Learning*, **1**, 134–48.

Evans, J. St. B. T. (1982) *The Psychology of Deductive Reasoning*, Routledge and Kegan Paul, London.

Evertsz, R. (1982) A production system account of children's errors in fraction subtraction, CAL Research Group Technical Report No. 28, Open University.

Evertsz, R. (1986) MIMIC: discovery of simulation models by machine, Ph.D. thesis (in preparation), Open University.

Feltovich, P.J., Johnson, P.E., Moller, J.H. and Swanson, D.B. (1984) The role and development of medical knowledge in diagnostic expertise, in *Readings in Medical Artificial Intelligence: the First Decade* (eds W.J. Clancey and E.H. Shortliffe), Addison-Wesley, Reading, MA.

Fikes, R.E. and Nilsson, N.J. (1971) STRIPS: a new approach to the application of theorem proving to problem solving. *Artificial Intelligence*, **2**, 189–208.

Finin, T.W. (1983) Providing help and advice in task oriented systems, *Proc. International Joint Conference on Artificial Intelligence*, 176–8, Karlsruhe.

Fischer, G., Lemke, G. and Schwab, T. (1985) Knowledge-based help systems. *Proc. Computer-Human Interaction 85*, 161–7.

Flower, L.S. and Hayes, J.R. (1980) The dynamics of composing: making plans and juggling constraints, in *Cognitive Processes in Writing* (eds L.W. Gregg and E. Steinberg), Erlbaum, Hillsdale, N.J.

Forbus, K. and Stevens, A. (1981) Using qualitative simulation to generate explanations, Report No. 4480, Bolt Beranek and Newman, Cambridge, MA.

Forbus, K. (1984) Qualitative process theory. *Artificial Intelligence*, **24**, 85–168.

Ford, L., Rivers, R. and Tang, H. (1986) TUTOR – final technical report, Defence Research Information Centre, St. Mary's Cray, London.

Fosdick, L.D. and Osterweil, L.J. (1976) Data flow analysis in software reliability. *Computing Surveys*, **8**, 305–30.

Foster, D. (1984) Computer simulation in tomorrow's schools. *Computers in the Schools*, **1**, 81–9.

Fox, M. (1983) Studies and programming for an expert consultant for part of junior arithmetic, M.Sc. thesis, University of Essex.

Frase, L.T. (1980) Writer's workbench: computer supports for writing and text design, paper presented at the annual meeting of the American Educational Research Association, Boston, MA.

Fraser, R., Burkhardt, H., Coupland, J. *et al.* (1986) Human–human–machine interactions, *Abacus* (in press).

Friedland, P.E. and Iwasaki. Y. (1985) The concept and implementation of skeletal plans. *Journal of Automated Reasoning*, **1**, 161–208.

Friedman, M.P. (1984) WANDAH: a computerized writer's aid. *Computers and Composition*, **4**, 113–23.

Freud, S. (1965) *The Psychopathology of Everyday Life*, Norton, New York.

Genesereth, M.R. (1982) The role of plans in intelligent teaching systems, in *Intelligent Tutoring Systems* (eds D.H. Sleeman and J.S. Brown), Academic Press, New York.

Genesereth, M.R. (1984) Partial programs, Memo HPP-84-1, Heuristic Programming Project, Stanford University.

Genesereth, M.R., Greiner, R., Grinberg, M.R. and Smith, D.E. (1984) The MRS dictionary, Report No. HPP-80-24, Heuristic Programming Project, Stanford University.

Gentner, D. and Stevens, A. (1983) *Mental Models*, Erlbaum, Hillsdale, N.J.

Giles, H. and Powesland, P.F. (1975) *Speech Style and Social Evaluation*, Academic Press, London.

Gilmore, D.J. (1986) Concept learning: alternative methods of focussing. *Proc. International Meeting on Advances in Learning*, Les Arcs, France.

Goguen, J.A., Weiner, J.L. and Linde, C. (1983) Reasoning and natural explanation. *International Journal of Man–Machine Studies*, **19**, 521–59.

Goldman, N.M. (1983) Three dimensions of design development, Report RS-83-2, Information Sciences Institute, University of Southern California.

Goldman, N.M. and Wile, D. (1986) Gist language description, draft report, Information Sciences Institute, University of Southern California.

Goldstein, I.P. (1975) Summary of MYCROFT: a system for understanding simple picture programs. *Artificial Intelligence*, **6**, 249–88.

Goldstein, I.P. (1982) The genetic graph: a representation for the evolution of procedural knowledge, in *Intelligent Tutoring Systems* (eds D.H. Sleeman and J.S. Brown), Academic Press, London.

Goldstein, I.P. and Papert, S. (1977) Artificial intelligence, language and the study of knowledge. *Cognitive Science*, **1**, 84–123.

Goldstein, M. and Goldstein, I.F. (1980) *How We Know: an Exploration of the Scientific Process*, De Capo, New York.

Good, M. (1981) Etude and the folklore of user interface design. *Proc. ACM SIGPLAN/SIGOA Conference on Text Manipulation*, Oregon.

Graham, S.L. and Rhodes, S.P. (1975) Practical syntactic error recovery in compilers. *Communications of the ACM*, **18**, 639–50.

Green, T.R.G., Payne, S.J., Morrison, D.L. and Shaw, A. (1983) Friendly interfacing to simple speech recognizers. *Behaviour and Information Technology*, **2**, 23–38.

Greenberg, S. and Witten, I.H. (1985) Adaptive personalized interfaces – a question of viability. *Behaviour and Information Technology*, **4**, 31–45.

Greeno, J.G. (1983) Conceptual entities, in *Mental Models* (eds D. Gentner and A.L. Stevens) Erlbaum, Hillsdale, N.J.

Gregory, R. (1979) Personalised task representation, Report TM 79103, Admiralty Marine Technology Establishment.

Gregory, R. (1981) Personalised task representation, Report TM 81104, Admiralty Marine Technology Establishment.

Grice, H.P. (1975) Logic and conversation, in *Syntax and Semantics 3, Speech Acts* (eds P. Cole and J.L. Morgan), Academic Press, New York.

Gutknecht, J. (1985) Concepts of the text editor Lara. *Communications of the ACM*, **28**, 942–60.

Hardy, S. (1984) A new environment for list-processing and logic programming, in *Artificial Intelligence: Tools, Techniques, and Applications* (eds T. O'Shea and M. Eisenstadt), Harper and Row, New York.

Hartley, J.R., Carr, I.G. and Hijne, H. (1985) Human factors experiments with intelligent HELP systems, Deliverable Report WP10-22, Commission of the European Communities (CEC) ESPRIT Programme (P280), Project EUROHELP, University of Leeds.

Hasselbring, T.S. (1984) Computer-based assessment of special-needs students. *Special Services in the Schools*, **5**, 7–19.

Hayes-Roth, B. (1983) The blackboard architecture: a general framework for problem solving?, Report HPP-83-30, Heuristic Programming Project, Stanford University.

Hayes-Roth, F., Waterman, D. and Lenat, D. (eds) (1983) *Building Expert Systems*, Addison-Wesley, New York.

Hayward, S.A., Killin, J.L., Morris, A. and Breuker, J. (1984) Theoretical and empirical issues underlying the emergence of a methodology for the development of knowledge based systems, Esprit P12 Synthesis report, Deliverable 9.1, Commission of the European Communities.

Heines, J.M. and O'Shea, T. (1985) The design of a rule-based CAI tutorial. *International Journal of Man–Machine Studies*, **23**, 1–25.

Hennessy, S.C. (1986) The role of conceptual knowledge in the acquisition of arithmetic algorithms, Ph.D. thesis (in preparation), University College London.

Her Majesty's Inspectors of Schools (1979) *Aspects of Secondary Education in England*, Her Majesty's Stationery Office, London.

Hobbs, J. and Evans, D. (1980) Conversation as planned behaviour. *Cognitive Science*, **4**, 317–45.

Hollan, J., Hutchins, E. and Weitzman, L. (1984) STEAMER: an interactive inspectable simulation-based training system, *AI Magazine*, **5**, 15–27.

Holte, R.C. (1985) Artificial intelligence approaches to concept learning, in *Advanced Digital Information Systems* (ed. I. Aleksander), Prentice-Hall, London.

Howden, W.E. (1982) Contemporary software development environments. *Communications of the ACM*, **25**, 318–29.

Hughes, M. (1986) *Children and Number: Difficulties in Learning Mathematics*, Blackwell, Oxford.

Humes, A. (1983) The composing process: a summary of the research, ERIC Report No. ED-222-925.

Hunt, E.B., Marin, J. and Stone, P.T. (1966) *Experiments in Induction*, Academic Press, New York.

Jackson, P. and Lefrere, P. (1984) On the application of rule-based techniques to the design of advice-giving systems. *International Journal of Man–Machine Studies*, **20**, 63–86.

Jansen, J., Verloop, A. and Blegen, D. (1986) Recovery boiler tutor: an interactive simulation and training aid. *Proc. Technical Association of the Pulp and Paper Industry Engineering Conference*, Seattle, Washington.

Johnson, W.L. (1986a) *Intention-Based Diagnosis of Errors in Novice Programs*, Pitman, Marshfield, MA.

Johnson, W.L. (1986b) Understanding and debugging novice programs, Internal Report, Information Sciences Institute, University of Southern California.

Johnson, W.L. and Soloway, E. (1984a) PROUST: knowledge-based program debugging. *Proc. Eighth International Software Engineering Conference*, Orlando, Florida.

Johnson, W.L. and Soloway, E. (1984b) Intention-based diagnosis of programming errors. *Proc. National Conference on Artificial Intelligence*, Austin, Texas.

Johnson, W.L. and Soloway, E. (1985) PROUST: an automatic debugger for Pascal programs. *Byte*, **10**, 179–90.

Johnson, W.L., Draper, S. and Soloway, E. (1982) Classifying bugs is a tricky business, presented at 7th NASA/Goddard workshop on software engineering.

Johnson, W.L., Soloway, E., Cutler, B. and Draper, S. (1983) Bug collection I, Technical Report No. 296, Department of Computer Science, Yale University.

Johnson-Laird, P.N. (1983) *Mental Models*, Cambridge University Press, Cambridge.

Jones, D.A. (1975) Don't just mark the answer – have a look at the method. *Maths in Schools*, May.

Jones, J. and Millington, M. (1986) An Edinburgh Prolog blackboard shell, Research Paper 281, Department of Artificial Intelligence, University of Edinburgh.

Kamii, C.K. (1985) *Young Children Reinvent Arithmetic: Implications of Piaget's Theory*, Teachers College Press, New York.

Kamsteeg, P. (1985) Kennis van docenten bij individuele coaching. Master thesis, fl.25.6.84.421, University of Amsterdam.

Kant, E. (1985) Understanding and automating algorithm design. *IEEE Transactions of Software Engineering*, **11**, 1361–74.

Kant, E. and Steier, D.M. (1985) The roles of execution and analysis in algorithm design. *IEEE Transactions of Software Engineering*, **11**, 1375–85.

Kelly, G. (1955) *The Psychology of Personal Constructs*, Norton, New York.

Kimball, R. (1982) A self-improving tutor for symbolic integration, in *Intelligent Tutoring Systems* (eds D.H. Sleeman and J.S. Brown), Academic Press, New York.

Kodratoff, Y. (1985) Une théorie et une methodologie de l'apprentissage symbolique. *Proc. Cognitiva 85*, Paris.

Kolodner, J.L. (1982) The role of experience in development of expertise. *Proc. National Conference on Artificial Intelligence*, Pittsburgh, PA.

Kolodner, J.L. (1983) Towards an understanding of the role of experience in the evolution from novice to expert. *International Journal of Man–Machine Studies*, **19**, 497–518.

Kolodner, J.L. and Simpson, R.L. (1984) Experience and problem-solving: a framework. *Proc. Sixth Annual Conference of the Cognitive Science Society*, Boulder.

Kuhn, T.S. (1970) *The Structure of Scientific Revolutions*, International Encyclopedia of Unified Science, University of Chicago Press, Chicago.

Kuipers, B. (1985) The limits of qualitative simulation. *Proc. Ninth International Joint Conference on Artificial Intelligence*, Kaufmann, Los Altos.

Laird, J.E., Rosenbloom, P.S. and Newell, A. (1984) Towards chunking as a general learning mechanism. *Proc. National Conference on Artificial Intelligence*, Austin, Texas.

Laird, J.E., Rosenbloom, P. and Newell, A. (1986) Chunking in SOAR, the anatomy of a general learning mechanism. *Machine Learning*, 1, 11–46.

Langley, P. (1985) Learning to search: from weak methods to domain-specific heuristics. *Cognitive Science*, 9, 217–60.

Langley, P. and Ohlsson, S. (1984) Automated cognitive modelling. *Proc. National Conference on Artificial Intelligence*, Austin, Texas.

Langley, P., Ohlsson, S. and Sage, S. (1984) A machine learning approach to student modelling, Report CMU-RI-TR-84-7, The Robotics Institute, Carnegie-Mellon University.

Larkin, J.H. (1981) Enriching formal knowledge: a model for learning to solve problem in physics, in *Cognitive Skills and their Acquisition* (ed. J.R. Anderson), Erlbaum, Hillsdale, N.J.

Larkin, J.H., McDermott, J., Simon, D.P. and Simon, H. (1980) Expert and novice performance in solving physics problems. *Science*, 208, 1335–42.

Lauriere, J.L. (1983) SNARK: à moteur d'inferences pour systèmes experts en logique du premier ordre, Report 431, Institut de Programmation, Université Paris 6.

Lebowitz, M. (1983) Generalization from natural language text. *Cognitive Science*, 7, 1–40.

Leech, G. (1981) *Semantics*, Penguin Books, Harmondsworth.

Lehnert, W. (1978) *The Process of Question Answering: A Computer Simulation of Cognition*, Erlbaum, Hillsdale, N.J.

Lenat, D.B. and Brown, J.S. (1984) Why AM and EURISKO appear to work. *Artificial Intelligence*, 23, 269–94.

Levelt, W.J.M. (1981) The speaker's linearization problem. *Philosophical Transactions of the Royal Society*, B295, 305–15.

Lewis, J. (1986) Analysing the actions of Unix users, Working Paper 188, Department of Artificial Intelligence, University of Edinburgh.

Lewis, M.W. and Anderson, J.R. (1985) Discrimination of operator schemata in problem solving: learning from examples. *Cognitive Psychology*, 17, 26–65.

Lipkis, T. (1982) Descriptive mapping for explanation production, Information Sciences Institute report, University of Southern California.

Lukey, F.J. (1980) Understanding and debugging programs. *International Journal of Man–Machine Studies*, 12, 189–202.

McDonald, D. (1983) Natural language generation as a computational problem: an introduction, in *Computational Models of Discourse* (eds M. Brady and R. Berwick), M.I.T. Press, Cambridge, MA.

McKendree, J., Reiser, B.J. and Anderson, J.R. (1984) Tutorial goals and strategies in the instruction of programming skills. *Proc. Sixth Annual Conference of the Cognitive Science Society*, Boulder, CO.

McKeown, K. (1980) Generating relevant explanations: natural language responses to questions about data base structure. *Proc. National Conference on Artificial Intelligence*, Stanford, California.

Maes, P. (1986a) Introspection in knowledge representation, *Proc. 7th European Conference on Artificial Intelligence*, Brighton, U.K.

Maes, P. (1986b) Meta-concepts in KRS, Technical report, Artificial Intelligence Laboratory, Vrije Universiteit, Brussels, Belgium.

Mann, W., Moore, J. and Levin, J. (1977) A comprehension model for human dialogue. *Proc. International Joint Conference on Artificial Intelligence*, Cambridge, MA.

Marr, D. (1982) *Vison: a Computational Investigation in Human Representation of Visual Information*, Freeman, San Francisco.

Matz, M. (1982) Towards a generative theory of high school algebra errors, in *Intelligent Tutoring Systems* (eds D.H. Sleeman and J.S. Brown), Academic Press, New York.

Mayer, R.E., Larkin, J.H. and Kadane, J.B. (1984) A cognitive analysis of mathematical problem solving ability, in *Advances in the Psychology of Human Intelligence*, Vol. 2 (ed. R.J. Sternberg), Erlbaum, Hillsdale. N.J.

Medin, D.L. and Smith, E.E. (1984) Concepts and concept formation. *Annual Review of Psychology*, **35**, 113–38.

Michalski, R.S. (1983) A theory and methodology of inductive learning, in *Machine Learning: an Artificial Intelligence Approach* (eds R.S. Michalski, J.G. Carbonell and T.M. Mitchell), Tioga, Palo Alto.

Michalski, R.S. (1986) Understanding the nature of learning: issues and research directions, in *Machine Learning: an Artificial Intelligence Approach* Vol. II (eds R.S. Michalski, J.G. Carbonell and T.M. Mitchell), Kaufmann, Los Altos.

Michalski, R.S., Carbonell, J.G. and Mitchell, T.M. (eds) (1983) *Machine Learning: an Artificial Intelligence Approach*, Tioga, Palo Alto.

Miller, L.A. (1981) Natural language programming: styles, strategies and contrasts. *IBM Systems Journal*, **20**, 184–215.

Miller, M.L. (1982) A structured planning and debugging environment for elementary programming, in *Intelligent Tutoring Systems* (eds D.H. Sleeman and J.S. Brown), Academic Press, New York.

Minsky, M. (1975) A framework for the representation of knowledge, in *The Psychology of Computer Vision* (ed. P. Winston), McGraw-Hill, New York.

Mitchell, T.M. (1981) Generalization as search. *Artificial Intelligence*, **18**, 203–26.

Mitchell, T.M., Keller, R.M. and Kedar-Cabelli, S.T. (1986) Explanation-based generalization. *Machine Learning*, **1**, 47–80.

Mitchell, T.M., Utgoff, P.E. and Banerji, R. (1983) Learning by experimentation: acquiring and refining problem-solving heuristics, in *Machine Learning: an Artificial Intelligence Approach* (eds R.S. Michalski, J.G. Carbonell and T.M. Mitchell), Tioga, Palo Alto.

Moran, T.P. (1981) The command language grammar: a representation for the user interface of interactive computer systems. *International Journal of Man–Machine Studies*, **15**, 3–50.

Moran, T.P. (1983) Getting into a system: external–internal task mapping analysis. *Proc. Computer–Human Interaction 83*.

Myers, G.J. (1978) A controlled experiment in program testing and code walkthroughs/inspections. *Communications of the ACM*, **21**, 760–68.

Neves, D.M. (1978) A computer program that learns algebraic procedures by examining and working problems in a textbook. *Proc. Second National Conference of the Canadian Society for Computational Studies of Intelligence*, Toronto.

Newell, A. (1973) Production systems: models of control structures, in *Visual Information Processing* (ed. W.G. Chase), Academic Press, New York.

Newell, A. (1981) Reasoning, problem solving and decision processes: the problem space as a fundamental category, in *Attention and Performance*, Vol. 8, (ed. R. Nickerson), Erlbaum, Hillsdale, N.J.

Newell, A. (1982) The knowledge level. *Artificial Intelligence*, **18**, 87–127.

Newell, A. and Rosenbloom, P. (1981) Mechanisms of skill acquisition and the law of practice, in *Cognitive Skills and their Acquisition* (ed. J.R. Anderson), Erlbaum, Hillsdale, N.J.

Newell, A. and Simon, H.A. (1972) *Human Problem Solving*, Prentice-Hall, Englewood Cliffs, N.J.

Nicolson, R.I. and Scott, P.J. (1986) Towards an intelligent authoring system, Internal Report, Department of Psychology, University of Sheffield.

Norman, D.A. (1979) Slips of the mind and an outline for a theory of action, Technical Report 7905, Center for Human Information Processing, University of California, San Diego.

Norman, D.A. (1981) Categorisation of action slips. *Psychological Review*, **88**, 1–15.

Norman, D.A. (1983) Some observations on mental models, in *Mental Models* (eds D. Gentner and A. Stevens), Erlbaum, Hillsdale, N.J.

Norman, D.A., Gentner, D.R. and Stevens, A.L. (1976) Comments on learning schemata and memory representation, in *Cognition and Instruction* (ed. D. Klahr), Erlbaum, Hillsdale, N.J.

Ohlsson, S. (1982) Tell me your problems: a psychologist visits AAAI82, *AISB Quarterly*, **46**, 27–31.

Ohlsson, S. (1986) Some principles of intelligent tutoring. *Instructional Science*, **14**, 293–326.

O'Malley, C.E. (1986) Helping users help themselves, in *User Centred Systems Design* (eds D.A. Norman and S.W. Draper), Erlbaum, Hillsdale, N.J.

Osburn, W.J. and Foltz, P.J. (1931) Permanence of improvement in the fundamentals of arithmetic. *Educational Research Bulletin*, **10**, 9.

O'Shea, T. and Floyd, A. (1981) Recording children's mathematical behaviour, in *Microcomputers in Secondary Education* (eds J.A.M. Howe and P.M. Ross), Kogan Page, London.

O'Shea, T. and Self, J. (1983) *Learning and Teaching with Computers: Artificial Intelligence in Education*, Harvester, Brighton.

O'Shea, T., Bornat, R., du Boulay, B. *et al.* (1985) Tools for creating intelligent computer tutors, in *Human and Artificial Intelligence* (ed. A. Elithorn), North-Holland, Amsterdam.

Pain, H. (1985) A computer tool for use by children with learning difficulties, Ph.D. thesis, University of Edinburgh.

Palies, O., Caillot, M., Cauzinille-Marmeche, E. *et al.* (1986) Student modelling by a knowledge-based system. *Computational Intelligence*, **2**, 99–107.

Papert, S. (1980) *Mindstorms: Children, Computers and Powerful Ideas*, Basic Books, New York.

Partridge, D. (1986) *Artificial Intelligence: Applications in the Future of Software Engineering*, Horwood, Chichester.

Pask, G. (1976) Styles and strategies of learning. *British Journal of Educational Psychology*, **46**, 128–48.

Patil, R.S., Szolovits, P. and Schwartz, W.B. (1981) Causal understanding of patient illness in medical diagnosis, *Proc. 7th International Joint Conference on Artificial Intelligence*, Vancouver.

Pavlin, J. and Johnson, W.L. (1986) Enhancing maintainability of object-oriented systems, Internal Report, Information Sciences Institute, University of Southern California.

Payne, S.J. (1986a) Naive theories of computation: metaphor and inference, paper presented at the Annual Conference of the Cognitive Science Section of the British Psychological Society.

Payne, S.J. (1986b) Complex problem spaces: modelling the knowledge required to use an interactive system, Technical Report 27, Centre for Research on Computers and Learning, University of Lancaster.

Payne, S.J. and Green, T.R.G. (1986) Task-action grammar: a model of the mental representation of task languages. *Human–Computer Interaction*, **2**, 93–133.

Peters, R.S. (1966) *Ethics and Education*, Allen and Unwin, London.

Piaget, J. (1971) *Genetic Epistemology*, Norton, New York.

Pinker, S. (1984) *Language Learnability and Language Development*, Harvard University Press, Cambridge, MA.

Polya, G. (1962) *Mathematical Discovery*, Wiley, New York.

Quilici, A.E., Dyer, M.G. and Flowers, M. (1986) AQUA, an intelligent UNIX advisor. *Proc. 7th European Conference on Artificial Intelligence*, Vol. 2, 33–8, Brighton.

Quillian, M.R. (1968) Semantic memory, in *Semantic Information Processing* (ed. M. Minsky), M.I.T. Press, Cambridge, MA.

Quinlan, J.R. (1983) Learning efficient classification procedures and their application to chess end-games, in *Machine Learning: an Artificial Intelligence Approach* (eds R.S. Michalski, J.G. Carbonell and T.M. Mitchell), Tioga, Los Altos.

Quinlan, J.R. (1986) The effect of noise on concept learning, in *Machine Learning: an Artificial Intelligence Approach*, Vol. II (eds R.S. Michalski, J.G. Carbonell and T.M. Mitchell), Kaufmann, Los Altos.

Reason, J.T. (1979) Actions not as planned: the price of automatisation, in *Aspects of Consciousness* (eds G. Underwood and R. Stevens), Academic Press, London.

Reed, S.K. (1972) Pattern recognition and categorization. *Cognitive Psychology*, **3**, 382–407.

Reichman, R. (1978) Conversational coherency. *Cognitive Science*, **2**, 283–327.

Reiser, B.J., Anderson, J.R. and Farrell, R.G. (1985) Dynamic student modelling in an intelligent tutor for Lisp programming. *Proc. Ninth International Joint Conference on Artificial Intelligence*, Los Angeles.

Resnick, L.B. (1982) Syntax and semantics in learning to subtract, in *Addition and Subtraction: a Cognitive Perspective* (eds T.P. Carpenter, J.M. Moser and T.A. Romberg), Erlbaum, Hillsdale, N.J.

Resnick, L.B. (1983) A developmental theory of number understanding, in *The Development of Mathematical Thinking* (ed. H.P. Ginsburg), Academic Press, New York.

Resnick, L.B. (1984) Beyond error analysis: the role of understanding in elementary school arithmetic, unpublished manuscript. Learning and Development Research Center, University of Pittsburgh.

Resnick, L.B. and Neches, R. (1984) Factors affecting individual differences in learning ability, in *Advances in the Psychology of Human Intelligence*, Vol. 2 (ed. R.J. Sternberg), Erlbaum, Hillsdale, N.J.

Resnick, L.B., Cauzinille-Marmeche, E., Mathieu, J. (1985) Understanding algebra, paper presented at the International Seminar on Cognitive Processes in Mathematics and Mathematics Learning, University of Keele.

Rich, E. (1979a) Building and exploiting user models, Ph.D. thesis, Carnegie-Mellon University.

Rich, E. (1979b) User modelling via stereotypes. *Cognitive Science*, **3**, 355–66.

Rich. E. (1982) Programs as data for their help systems, *AFIPS National Computer Conference*, 483–5.

Ridgway, J. (1986) Research needs for educational uses of information technology, I.T.E. Occasional Paper 9, Economic and Social Research Council.

Ridgway, J. and Mansell, K. (1985) Fostering and observing problem solving in mathematics classrooms, Shell Centre for Mathematical Education, University of Nottingham.

Ridgway, J., Benzie, D., Burkhardt, H. *et al.* (1984a) Investigating CAL? *Computers and Education*, **8**, 85–92.

Ridgway, J., Benzie, D., Burkhardt, H. *et al.* (1984b) Conclusions from CALtastrophes. *Computers and Education*, **8**, 93–100.

Ridgway, J., Swan, M., Haworth, A. and Coupland, J. (1984c) Innovation in mathematical education – the TSS approach, in *Proc. Fifth International Congress on Mathematical Education* (ed. M. Carss), Birkhauser, Boston.

Riesbeck, C.K. (1981) Failure-driven reminding for incremental learning. *Proc. 7th International Joint Conference on Artificial Intelligence*, Vancouver.

Ritchie, G.D. and Hanna, F.K. (1984) AM: a case study in AI methodology. *Artificial Intelligence*, **23**, 249–68.

Robinson, J. (1965) A machine-oriented logic based on the resolution principle. *Journal of the ACM*, **12**, 23–41.

Ross, P., Jones, J. and Millington, M. (1985) User modelling in command-driven systems, DAI Research Paper No. 264, Department of Artificial Intelligence, University of Edinburgh.

Ross, P., Jones, J. and Millington, M. (1986) User modelling in intelligent teaching and tutoring, in *Trends in Computer Aided Education* (eds R. Lewis and E.D. Tagg), Blackwell, Oxford.

Rouse, W.B. and Morris, N.M. (1985) On looking into the black box: prospects and limits in the search for mental models, Technical Report 85-2, School of Industrial and Systems Engineering, Georgia Institute of Technology.

Rousseau, J.J. (1762) *Emile*, Everyman edition (1974), Dent, London.

Rumelhart, D. (1975) Notes on a schema for stories, in *Representation and Understanding* (eds D. Bobrow and A. Collins). Academic Press, New York.

Rumelhart, D.E. and Norman, D.A. (1983) Representation in memory, CHIP Report 116, University of California, San Diego.

Ruthven, K. (1985) The AI dimension?, in *Information Technology and Education: Signposts and Research Directions* (ed. D.J. Smith), Economic and Social Research Council, London.

Sacerdoti, E.D. (1977) *A Structure for Plans and Behaviour*, Elsevier, New York.

Sack, W., Littman, D., Spohrer, J.C. *et al.* (1985) Empirical evaluation of PROUST, internal report, Department of Computer Science, Yale University.

Sandberg, J.E., Winkels, R. and Breuker, J.A. (1987) Coaching strategies and tactics of UNIX-Vi editor consultants, Deliverable 2.2.1, Esprit 280, University of Amsterdam.

Scanlon, E., Hawkridge, C., Evertsz, R. and O'Shea, T. (1985) Novice physics problem solving behaviour, in *Advances in Artificial Intelligence* (ed. T. O'Shea), North-Holland, Amsterdam.

Scardamalia, M., Bereiter, C. and Steinbach, R. (1984) Teachability of reflective processes in written composition. *Cognitive Science*, **8**, 173–90.

Schank, R.C. (1975) *Conceptual Information Processing*, North-Holland, Amsterdam.

Schank, R.C. (1981) Failure-driven memory. *Cognition and Brain Memory*, **4**, 41–60.

Schank, R.C. (1982) *Dynamic Memory*, Cambridge University Press, Cambridge.

Schank, R.C. (1984) The explanation game, Report 307, Department of Computer Science, Yale University.

Schank, R.C. and Abelson, R.P. (1975) *Scripts, Plans, Goals and Understanding*, Erlbaum, Hillsdale, N.J.

Schmidt, C.F., Sridharan, N.S. and Goodson, J.C. (1978) The plan recognition problem: an intersection of psychology and artificial intelligence. *Artificial Intelligence*, **11**, 45–83.

Schmucker, K.J. (1986) *Object-oriented programming for the Macintosh*. Hayden Press, London.

Schuster, E. and Finin, T. (1985) VP2: the role of user modelling in correcting errors in second language learning. *Proc. AISB Conference on Artificial Intelligence*, 187–95, Warwick.

Scott, P.J. (1986) The SCALD intelligent authoring system, unpublished Ph.D. thesis, University of Sheffield.

Self, J.A. (1974) Student models in computer-aided instruction. *International Journal of Man–Machine Studies*, **6**, 261–76.

Self, J.A. (1985a) A perspective on intelligent computer-assisted learning. *Journal of Computer Assisted Learning*, **1**, 159–66.

Self, J.A. (1985b) Intelligent computer assisted instruction, paper presented at the ICAI Spring Seminar, Logica Cambridge Ltd, Cambridge.

Self, J.A. (1985c) *Microcomputers in Education: a Critical Appraisal of Educational Software*, Harvester Press, Brighton.

Sharples, M. (1985) *Cognition, Computers and Creative Writing*, Horwood, Chichester.

Shell Centre for Mathematical Education (1984) *Problems with Patterns and Numbers*, Joint Matriculation Board, Manchester.

Shell Centre for Mathematical Education (1986) *Language of Functions and Graphs*, Joint Matriculation Board, Manchester.

Sheppard, C. (1981) The Applied Psychology Unit Man–Computer Studies section: rationale and work programme 1981–83, Report E1/P4.1/198/81, Admiralty Research Establishment.

Shiel, B. (1983) Power tools for programmers. *Datamation*, **29**, 131–44.

Shortliffe, E. (1976) *Computer Based Medical Consultations: MYCIN*, American Elsevier, New York.

Siegler, R.S. and Shrager, J. (1984) Strategy choices in addition and subtraction: how do children know what to do? in *Origins of Cognitive Skill* (ed. S. Sophian) Erlbaum, Hillsdale, N.J.

Skinner, B. (1968) *The Technology of Teaching*, Appleton-Century-Crofts, New York.

Slater, J., Petrossian, R. and Shyam-Sunder, S. (1984) An expert tutor for rigid body mechanics: Athena cats – MACAVITY. *Proc. Expert Systems in Government Symposium*, IEEE and Mitre Corporation.

Sleeman, D.H. (1982) Assessing aspects of competence in basic algebra, in *Intelligent Tutoring Systems* (eds D.H. Sleeman and J.S. Brown), Academic Press, New York.

Sleeman, D.H. (1983a) Inferring (mal) rules from pupil's protocols. *Proc. International Machine Learning Workshop*, Illinois, 221–7.

Sleeman, D.H. (1983b) Basic algebra revisited: a study with 14 year olds, Report HPP-83-9, Heuristic Programming Project, Stanford University.

Sleeman, D.H. (1984a) An attempt to understand students' understanding of basic algebra. *Cognitive Science*, **8**, 387–412.

Sleeman, D.H. (1984b) Mis-generalization: an explanation of observed mal-rules. *Proc. Sixth Annual Conference Cognitive Science Society*, Boulder, Colorado.

Sleeman, D.H. (1984c) UMFE: a user modelling front end subsystem. *International Journal of Man–Machine Studies*, **23**, 71–88.

Sleeman, D.H. and Brown, J.S. (eds) (1982) *Intelligent Tutoring Systems*, Academic Press, New York.

Sleeman, D.H. and Smith, M.J. (1981) Modelling pupil's problem solving. *Artificial Intelligence*, **16**, 171–87.

Smith, F. (1982) *Writing and the Writer*, Heinemann, London.

Smith, J.J. (1985) SUSI – a smart user-system interface. *Proc. Human-Computer Interaction 85*, Cambridge University Press, Cambridge.

Smith, N.V. (ed.) (1982) *Mutual Knowledge*, Academic Press, London.

Soloway, E. (1984) A cognitively-based methodology for designing languages/environments/methodologies. *Proc. ACM SIGPLAN Conference*, 193–196.

Soloway, E. (1985) From problem to programs via plans: the content and structure of knowledge for introductory LISP programming. *Journal of Educational Computing Research*, **1**, 157–72.

Soloway, E. and Ehrlich, K. (1984) Empirical studies of programming knowledge. *IEEE Transactions on Software Engineering*, **10**, 595–609.

Soloway, E., Bonar, J., Woolf, B. *et al.* (1981) Cognition and programming: why your students write those crazy programs. *Proc. National Educational Computing Conference*, North Denton, Texas.

Soloway, E., Rubin, E., Woolf, B. *et al.* (1982) Meno-II: an AI-based programming tutor, Technical Report CSD/RR No. 258, Yale University.

Soloway, E., Woolf, B., Rubin, E. and Barth, P. (1981) Meno-II: an intelligent tutoring system for novice programmers. *Proc. 7th International Joint Conference on Artificial Intelligence*, Vancouver.

Sowa, J.F. (1984) *Conceptual Structures*, Addison-Wesley, Reading, MA.

Spohrer, J.C. *et al.* (1985) Bug catalogue 2, 3, 4, Computer Science Report 386, Yale University.

Spohrer, J.C., Soloway, E. and Pope, E. (1985) A goal/plan analysis of buggy Pascal programs. *Human–Computer Interaction*, **1**, 163–207.

Steels, L. (1984) Object-oriented knowledge representation in KRS. *Proc. 7th European Conference on Artificial Intelligence*, Pisa, Italy, 333–6.

Steels, L. (1985) The KRS concept system, Technical report 85-1, Artificial Intelligence Laboratory, Vrije Universiteit, Brussels, Belgium.

Steels, L. and van der Velde, W. (1985) Learning in second generation expert systems, in *Knowledge Based Problem Solving* (ed. J.S. Kowalik), Prentice-hall, Englewood Cliffs, N.J.

Stefik, M. (1981) Planning with constraints (MOLGEN: Part 1), *Artificial Intelligence*, **16**, 111–40.

Stevens, A.L. and Collins, A. (1977) The goal structure of a Socratic tutor, BBN Report 3518, Bolt Beranek and Newman, Cambridge, MA.

Stevens, A.L. and Collins, A. (1980) Multiple conceptual models of a complex system, in *Aptitude, Learning and Instruction*, Vol. 2 (eds R.E. Snow, P. Federico and W.E. Montague), Erlbaum, Hillsdale, N.J.

Stevens, A.L., Collins, A. and Goldin, S. (1982) Misconceptions in student's understanding, in *Intelligent Tutoring Systems* (eds D.H. Sleeman and J.S. Brown), Academic Press, New York.

Stevens, W.P., Myers, G.J. and Constantine, L.L. (1974) Structured design. *IBM Systems Journal*, **13**, 115–39.

Suchman, L.A. (1985) Plans and situated actions: the problem of human–machine communication, Technical Report ISL-6, Intelligent Systems Laboratory, Xerox Parc.

Swartout, W.R. (1981) Explaining and justifying expert consulting programs. *Proc. 7th International Joint Conference on Artificial Intelligence*, **2**, 815–22.

Swartout, W.R. (1983) XPLAIN: a system for creating and explaining expert consulting programs. *Artificial Intelligence*, **21**, 285–325.

Swartout, W.R. and Balzer, R. (1982) On the inevitable intertwining of specification and implementation. *Communications of the ACM*, **25**, 438–50.

Tate, A. (1976) Project planning using a non-linear planner, DAI Report No. 25, Department of Artificial Intelligence, University of Edinburgh.

Teitelman, T. and Reps, T. (1981) The Cornell program synthesiser: a syntax-directed programming environment. *Communications of the ACM*, **24**, 563–73.

Teitelman, W. (1978) Interlisp reference manual, Xerox Palo Alto Research Center.

Teitelman, W. and Masinter, L. (1984) The Interlisp programming environment, in *Interactive Programming Environments* (eds D. Barstow, H.E. Shrobe and E. Sandewaal), McGraw-Hill, New York.

Thomas, L.F. (1976) Nothing more theoretical than good practice, S.S.R.C. Report, C.S.H.L. publication, Brunel University.

Thomas, L.F. and Harri-Augstein, E.S. (1976) The self-organised learner and the printed word, Final progress report to S.S.R.C., C.S.H.L. publication, Brunel University.

Thomas, L.F. and Harri-Augstein, E.S. (1983a) The personal scientist as self-organised learner: a conversational technology for reflecting on behaviour and experience, in *Applications of Personal Construct Theory* (ed. J. Adams Webber), Academic Press, New York.

Thomas, L.F. and Harri-Augstein, E.S. (1983b) The self-organised learner and computer-aided learning systems, Final Report, ARE/APU contract No. 2066/020, Admiralty Research Establishment.

Thomas, L.F. and Harri-Augstein, E.S. (1985) *Self-Organised Learning*, Routledge and Kegan Paul, London.

Todd, R.R. (1982) Initial report on submarine command tactics training, E1/P2.10/13/82, Admiralty Research Establishment.

van der Brink, H. (1986) Experiments: expert task performance in Vi, Report COE/EUROHELP/017, Courseware Europe BV, Purmerend, The Netherlands.

VanLehn, K. (1982) Bugs are not enough: empirical studies of bugs, impasses and repairs in procedural skills. *Journal of Mathematical Behaviour*, **3**, 3–72.

VanLehn, K. (1983a) Validating a theory of human skill acquisition. *Proc. International Machine Learning Workshop*, Illinois.

VanLehn, K. (1983b) Human procedural skill acquisition: theory, model and psychological validation. *Proc. National Conference on Artificial Intelligence*, Washington, D.C.

VanLehn, K. (1983c) On the representation of procedures in repair theory, in *The Development of Mathematical Theory* (ed. H.P. Ginsburg), Academic Press, New York.

VanLehn, K. and Brown, J.S. (1980) Planning nets: a representation for formalizing analogies and semantic models of procedural skills, in *Aptitude, Learning and Instruction: Cognitive Process and Analyses* (eds R.E. Snow, P.A. Frederico and W.E. Montague), Erlbaum, Hillsdale, N.J.

von Wright, G.H. (1971) *Explanation and Understanding*. Cornell University Press, Ithaca.

Walker, D.E. (1978) *Understanding Spoken Language*, North-Holland, Amsterdam.

Wason, P.C. (1980) Specific thoughts on the writing process, in *Cognitive Processes in Writing* (eds L.W. Gregg and E. Steinberg), Erlbaum, Hillsdale, N.J.

Wasserman, A.I. and Shewmake, D.T. (1984) The role of prototypes in the user software engineering (USE) methodology, in *Advances in Human–Computer Interaction* (ed. H.R. Hartson), Ablex, Norwood, N.J.

Webster, N. (1983) *Webster's Ninth New Collegiate Dictionary*, Merriam-Webster, Springfield.

Weiner, J.L. (1980) BLAH, a system which explains its reasoning. *Artificial Intelligence*, **15**, 19–47.

Wenger, E. (1986) *Artificial Intelligence and Tutoring Systems: Computational Approaches to the Communication of Knowledge*, in press, Kaufmann, Los Altos.

Wertheimer, N. (1945) *Productive Thinking*, Harper and Row, New York.

Whitehead, A.N. (1932) *The Aims of Education*, Benn, London.

Wielemaker, J. and Bundy, A. (1985) Altering the description space for focussing. *Proc. Expert Systems 85*, Warwick.

Wielinga, B.J. and Breuker, J.A. (1984) Interpretation of verbal data for knowledge acquisition. *Proc. 6th European Conference on Artificial Intelligence*, Pisa, Italy, 41–50.

Wielinga, B.J. and Breuker, J.A. (1986) Models of expertise. *Proc. 7th European Conference on Artificial Intelligence*, Vol. 1, pp. 306–18.

Wilensky, R. (1982) Talking to UNIX in English: an overview of UC. *Proc. National Conference on Artificial Intelligence*, Pittsburgh.

Wilensky, R. (1983) *Planning and Understanding: a Computational Approach to Human Reasoning*, Addison-Wesley, New York.

Wilensky, R., Arens, Y. and Chin, D. (1984) Talking to UNIX in English: an overview of UC. *Communications of the ACM*, **27**, 574–93.

Williams, M.D., Hollan, J.D. and Stevens, A.L. (1983) Human reasoning about a simple physical system, in *Mental Models* (eds D. Gentner and A.L. Stevens), Erlbaum, Hillsdale, N.J.

Williams, J.D. (1971) Teaching techniques in primary maths, National Foundation for Educational Research.

Wilkins, D.C., Clancey, W.J. and Buchanan, B.G. (1986) An overview of the Odysseus learning apprentice, in *Machine Learning: a Guide to Current Research* (eds T.M. Mitchell, J.G. Carbonell and R.S. Michalski), Academic Press, New York.

Winkels, R. (1987) PSP: a prototype strategy planner for intelligent help systems. Deliverable 2.2.4, Esprit 280, University of Amsterdam.

Winograd, T. and Flores, C.F. (1985) *Understanding Computers and Cognition: a New Foundation for Design*, Ablex, Norwood, N.J.

Winston, P.H. (1984) *Artificial Intelligence*, Addison-Wesley, Reading, MA.

Woodroffe, M. (1985) FITS: a framework for an intelligent tutoring system. *Proc. 2nd International Conference on Artificial Intelligence and Education*, Exeter.

Woolf, B. (1984) Context-dependent planning in a machine tutor, Ph.D. thesis, Department of Computer and Information Science, University of Massachusetts.

Woolf, B. and McDonald, D.D. (1984a) Design issues in building a computer tutor. *IEEE Computer*, September, 61–73.

Woolf, B. and McDonald, D.D. (1984b) Context dependent transitions in tutoring discourse. *Proc. National Conference on Artificial Intelligence*, Kaufmann, Los Altos.

Young, R.M. (1976) *Seriation by Children: an Artificial Intelligence Analysis of a Piagetian Task*, Birkhauser, Basel.

Young. R.M. (1983) Surrogates and mappings: two kinds of conceptual models for interactive devices, in *Mental Models* (eds D. Gentner and A. Stevens), Erlbaum, Hillsdale, N.J.

Young, R.M. and O'Shea, T. (1981) Errors in children's subtraction. *Cognitive Science*, **5**, 153–77.

Zissos, A.Y. and Witten, I.H. (1985) User modelling for a computer coach: a case study. *International Journal of Man–Machine Studies*, **23**, 729–50.

Index

ABLE 71–2
ACM *see* Automated cognitive modelling
Acquisition of mathematical skills 261–2
ACT 73–4, 142, 146, 184–5
ACTIVIST 302
Adaptive interface 300–9
Advanced computer tutoring project
    184–5
Advisor *see* Macsyma advisor
Algorithmic knowledge 153
Algorithm migration 264
ALICE 99
Ambiguity 104–5
Analysis-by-synthesis 381
Appraisal of ICAI systems 109–23
Attentional processes 146
Authoring 236–7, 252
Automated cognitive modelling 73,
    183–4, 186

Beliefs and intentions 215–16
BELIEVER 216–17, 229, 232
Blackboard 228, 230
BLAH 342
Bounded user modelling 165, 172–8
Bridge 144, 386, 391–409
Browser 350
Bug 61–3, 75–6, 172, 180–1, 259–60,
    265–6
Bug catalogue 180–1
BUGGY 180, 214–15, 218, 264
Butlering 317

CAI 4
CAL designer 237–8, 253
Canned dialogue 307
Chart parsing 365–73

Coaching 167, 310–37
Cockcroft Report 41–2
Cognitive context 74–5
Cognitive diagnosis 63
Cognitive skill acquisition 69–73
Collaborative learning, 192–5
Command language grammar 234, 303,
    321
Computer based consultant 213
Concept learning 186–91
Conceptual knowledge 10, 76–7, 185–6
Conceptual model 319–25
Conceptual modelling system 88–107
CONNECT 302
Constraint handling 224–5
Constraint satisfaction 289–90
Context calculus 106–7
Cooperative dialogue 88
Cooperative principle 340
Core procedure 125
Cornell program synthesiser 363–4
Cumulative hit curve 132–7

Data-flow analysis 378
BEBUGGY 30–2, 64, 66, 180
Decision trees 186–8
Derivation trace 52
Device space 80–7
Diagnosis 30–1, 60–3
Diagnostic consultant 259, 267–70
Diagnostic modelling 60
Didactic goals 313–15
Dienes block microworld 271–2
Differential model 15
Discourse Management Network 21–5
DMN, *see* Discourse Management
    Network

Domain knowledge 4–14
Domain model 50–2
Domain representation 319, 351–2
Downsliding 277

Educational software 236–7
ELECTRE 291–9
Episodic memory 141–55
Error fit measure 129–30, 135
Error taxonomies 258–9
Etude 283
EUROHELP 311–60
Evaluation (of ICAI system) 25–6,
    383–6, 408
Evaluation of micro-theory systems
    128–37
Executable model 55–6
Experiential knowledge 78–9
Expert knowledge 142–3
Expert-less training 199–200
Expert system 46, 57, 96, 157–8, 170,
    293, 310, 341
Expert system shell 310
Explanation 58, 116, 341–2
Explanation-based learning 190–1
Explanation giving 338–60
External–internal task mapping 81
Externalizing cognition 276–7

Failure-driven learning 153–5
Feedback 16
Figurative account 83–7
FITS-2 212–25
Focusing algorithm 173, 188–9
Functional model 59

Generality 122
Generative theory of bugs 62–3
Genetic graph 174, 314, 351
Geometry tutor 16, 57, 184–5
GIST 387
Glass-box expert 57
Goal space 80–7
Goal stack 72–3
Group work 40–2
GRUNDY 302
Guided discovery 165–77
Guided discovery learning 167–71

GUIDON 15, 57, 64–5, 166–7, 341

HC-Tutor 114–20
Help system 310–60
Heuristic knowledge 11–12, 297–8
HUNKS 197–211
Hypothesize and revise paradigm 216

ID3 187
Idea generation and reflection 279
IDEBUGGY 31
Identifying bugs 367–72
IMPART 166–8, 173–8
Impasse 66
Individual differences 74
Inductive learning 186–8
Inference engine 52, 120–1
Informal methods in arithmetic 259,
    272–4
Inheritance mechanism 92–5
Instantiation blackboard 224
Intelligent authoring system 236–54
Intelligent help system 302, 310–60
Intelligent interface 317–18
Intention-based analysis 375–83
Intentions 374–5
Intermediate representations 409
ITSSOL 201–11

Knowledgeable support 277
Knowledge base 119–22
Knowledge compilation 73
Knowledge engineering 88–90
Knowledge of teaching 14–25
Knowledge of the domain, *see* Domain
    knowledge
Knowledge representation 88–9
KRS 90, 108

Lara 283
LAURA 362–3
Learnability 325
Learner as 'personal scientist' 200, 205
Learner model, *see* Student model
Learning by being told 157
Learning by doing 157
Learning manager 201
Learning through interaction 157